EXCESSIVE SUBJECTIVITY

INSURRECTIONS: CRITICAL STUDIES IN RELIGION,
POLITICS, AND CULTURE

INSURRECTIONS: CRITICAL STUDIES IN RELIGION, POLITICS, AND CULTURE

Slavoj Žižek, Clayton Crockett, Creston Davis, Jeffrey W. Robbins, Editors

The intersection of religion, politics, and culture is one of the most discussed areas in theory today. It also has the deepest and most wide-ranging impact on the world. Insurrections: Critical Studies in Religion, Politics, and Culture will bring the tools of philosophy and critical theory to the political implications of the religious turn. The series will address a range of religious traditions and political viewpoints in the United States, Europe, and other parts of the world. Without advocating any specific religious or theological stance, the series aims nonetheless to be faithful to the radical emancipatory potential of religion.

For the list of titles in this series, see page 341.

EXCESSIVE SUBJECTIVITY

KANT, HEGEL, LACAN, AND THE FOUNDATIONS OF ETHICS

DOMINIK FINKELDE

TRANSLATED BY DEVA KEMMIS AND ASTRID WEIGERT

Columbia University Press
New York

Columbia University Press
Publishers Since 1893
New York Chichester, West Sussex
cup.columbia.edu

Library of Congress Cataloging-in-Publication Data

Names: Finkelde, Dominik, author. | Kemmis, Deva, translator. | Weigert, Astrid, translator.
Title: Excessive subjectivity: Kant, Hegel, Lacan, and the foundations of ethics / Dominik Finkelde; translated by Deva Kemmis and Astrid Weigert.
Other titles: Exzessive Subjektivität. English
Description: New York: Columbia University Press, [2017] | Series: Insurrections: critical studies in religion, politics, and culture | Includes bibliographical references and index.
Identifiers: LCCN 2017009185 | ISBN 9780231173186 (cloth: alk. paper) | ISBN 9780231545778 (e-book)
Subjects: LCSH: Ethics. | Subjectivity. | Kant, Immanuel, 1724–1804. | Hegel, Georg Wilhelm Friedrich, 1770–1831. | Lacan, Jacques, 1901–1981.
Classification: LCC BJ1114.F515513 2017 | DDC 170.9—dc23
LC record available at https://lccn.loc.gov/2017009185

Columbia University Press books are printed on permanent and durable acid-free paper.

Printed in the United States of America

Cover design: Chang Jae Lee

IN MEMORIAM RACHEL CORRIE

If one tries to grasp what the statements of our mentally healthy test-persons have in common and what characterizes their worldview as a whole, the most distinctive feature is their tendency to strike a compromise, to mitigate contradictions, and simply to ignore what cannot be mitigated. The ideas of Plato, Augustine, Kant, Hegel, and Nietzsche are, in the worldviews of our healthy persons, much more blurred and indistinct than in the worldviews of our patients.

—Hans and Shulamith Kreitler

The [psychotic] subject . . . is well aware that his reality is uncertain. He even admits their unreality up to a certain point. But, contrary to the normal subject for whom reality is always in the right place, he is certain of something, which is that what is at issue—ranging from hallucination to interpretation—regards him. Reality isn't at issue for him, certainty is.

—Jacques Lacan

I am the Way, the Truth, and the Light.
No one can come to the Father but through me.

—Jim Jones/Jesus of Nazareth

CONTENTS

ABBREVIATIONS

KANT

Anthro. "Anthropology from a Pragmatic Point of View." Translated by Robert B. Louden. In *Anthropology, History and Education*, edited by Günter Zöller and Robert B. Louden. Cambridge: Cambridge University Press, 2007.

CBHH "Conjectural Beginning of Human History." Translated by Allen W. Wood. In *Anthropology, History and Education.*

CF "The Conflict of the Faculties." Translated by Mary J. Gregor and Robert Anchor. In *Religion and Rational Theology*, edited by Allen W. Wood and George di Giovanni. Cambridge: Cambridge University Press, 1996.

CPJ *Critique of the Power of Judgment.* Edited by Paul Guyer. Translated by Paul Guyer and Eric Matthews. Cambridge: Cambridge University Press, 2000.

CPR *Critique of Pure Reason.* Edited and translated by Paul Guyer and Allen W. Wood. Cambridge: Cambridge University Press, 1997.

CPrR *Critique of Practical Reason.* In *Practical Philosophy.* Edited and translated by Mary J. Gregor. Cambridge: Cambridge University Press, 1996.

CS "On the Common Saying: That May Be Correct in Theory, but It Is of No Use in Practice." In *Practical Philosophy.*

En. "An Answer to the Question: What Is Enlightenment?" In *Practical Philosophy.*

GrMM *Groundwork of the Metaphysics of Morals.* In *Practical Philosophy.*

LP "Lectures on Pedagogy." Translated by Robert B. Louden. In *Anthropology, History and Education.*

MM *The Metaphysics of Morals.* In *Practical Philosophy.*

Rel. *Religion Within the Boundaries of Mere Reason.* Translated by George di Giovanni. In *Religion and Rational Theology.*

HEGEL

Aesth. *Hegel's Aesthetics: Lectures on Fine Arts.* 2 vols. Translated by T. M. Knox. Oxford: Clarendon, 1998.

ESL *Encyclopedia of the Philosophical Sciences in Basic Outline.* Part 1, *Science of Logic.* Translated by Klaus Brinkmann and Daniel O. Dahlstrom. Cambridge: Cambridge University Press, 2010.

LHPh *Lectures on the History of Philosophy.* Vol. 1, *Greek Philosophy to Plato.* Translated by E. S. Haldane and Frances H. Simon. Lincoln: University of Nebraska Press, 1995.

NL "On the Scientific Ways of Treating Natural Law, on Its Place in Practical Philosophy, and Its Relation to the Positive Sciences of Right." In *Political Writings,* edited by Laurence Dickey and Hugo Barr Nisbet. Translated by Hugo Barr Nisbet. Cambridge: Cambridge University Press, 1999.

PH *The Philosophy of History.* Translated by J. Sibree. Buffalo: Prometheus, 1991.

PhS *Phenomenology of Spirit.* Translated by A. V. Miller. Oxford: Oxford University Press, 1977.

PM *Philosophy of Mind.* Translated by W. Wallace and A. V. Miller. Oxford: Oxford University Press, 2007.

PR *Elements of the Philosophy of Right*. Edited by Allen W. Wood. Translated by Hugo Barr Nisbet. Cambridge: Cambridge University Press, 1991. An R refers to one of Hegel's Remarks (*Anmerkung*), an A to one of his Additions (*Zusatz*).

SL *The Science of Logic*. Edited and translated by George di Giovanni. Cambridge: Cambridge University Press, 2010.

LACAN

S.I *The Seminar: Book I, Freud's Papers on Technique, 1953–1954*. Edited by Jacques-Alain Miller. Translated by John Forrester. New York: Norton, 1988.

S.II *The Seminar: Book II, The Ego in Freud's Theory and in the Technique of Psychoanalysis, 1954–1955*. Edited by Jacques-Alain Miller. Translated by Silvana Tomaselli, with notes by John Forrester. Cambridge: Cambridge University Press, 1991.

S.III *The Seminar: Book III, The Psychoses, 1955–1956*. Edited by Jacques-Alain Miller. Translated with notes by Russell Grigg. London: Routledge, 1993.

S.VII *The Seminar: Book VII, The Ethics of Psychoanalysis, 1959–1960*. Edited by Jacques-Alain Miller. Translated with notes by Dennis Porter. New York: Norton, 1997.

S.X *The Seminar: Book X, Anxiety*. Edited by Jacques-Alain Miller. Translated by A. R. Price. Cambridge: Polity, 2014.

S.XI *The Seminar: Book XI, The Four Fundamental Concepts of Psychoanalysis*. Edited by Jacques-Alain Miller. Translated by Alan Sheridan. New York: Norton, 1998.

S.XX *The Seminar: Book XX, Encore, on Feminine Sexuality, the Limits of Love and Knowledge, 1972–1973*. Edited by Jacques-Alain Miller. Translated with notes by Bruce Fink. New York: Norton, 1999.

EXCESSIVE SUBJECTIVITY

INTRODUCTION

On the Necessity of the Deed

In the second part of his essay "The Conflict of the Faculties," Immanuel Kant expresses his esteem for the French Revolution. He says it has spread "enthusiasm" in Europe (Rel. 302). In so doing, he says, it has revealed the capacity of human reason to discover in certain events the progress of history toward the improvement of human nature—and that it is this improvement which serves as the narrative-historical organizational principle of history's own self-reassurance.[1] Yet there is some tension here between Kant's tribute to the French Revolution as an occasion for the spread of "enthusiasm" (in spite of the Reign of Terror) and his assertion in the *Metaphysics of Morals* that revolutionaries must be universally condemned (MM 474–75).[2]

How are we to understand these two statements? Is it permissible to be drawn into an enthusiastic, visionary image of historical progress by people whom one must at the same time sentence to death for embracing Realpolitik under the guise of revolutionary action? Johann Georg Hamann pointed out a similar tension when criticizing, in his own polemical style, Kant's concept of "self-incurred minority." In his essay "What Is Enlightenment?" Kant "accuses the minor," Hamann writes, "of cowardice," but fails to recognize that he, Kant, having achieved "maturity," has behind him "a well-disciplined, numerous army to stand for the surety of his infallibility and orthodoxy." The state power at Kant's back in fact relieves him of the burden of true maturity, which distinguishes itself through "bravery," "will," and "resolve."[3] Hamann sees in Kant only a "blind legal guardian" rather than someone who might speak with true moral—that is, political—authority. Thus Kant exemplifies the tension between a thinker's freedom and a subject's duty, or between an observer's *enthusiasm* for a political movement and that same observer's *rejection* of any concrete, courageous act that undermines the political order. And certainly this tension is just as relevant now as it was then, and just as unsatisfactory. In Hamann's treatment, the question of political maturity converges with the question of political-revolutionary resolve or "resolution." Kant should have recognized, Hamann argues, that freedom of the mature presupposes certain conditions of support. He who speaks as a political "grown-up" does so only because of those structures, that is, because of the "army" at his back. He who cannot speak as a "grown-up," in contrast, must first act in order to establish the conditions for his own "grown-up"/mature action—however paradoxical that may sound. Hamann indirectly establishes a retroactive correlation between maturity and action while rejecting Kant's notion that maturity follows simply from a resolution of will to be "grown-up," without the need for concrete and radical action to implement necessary conditions of it.

The status of free action in relation to processes of reformation or revolution—*before* the acknowledged (and rational) conditions of possibility for that freedom have been established—is a question that also interested Hegel in his reception of Kant. Hegel is concerned (indirectly) with reinforcing Hamann's attack on Kant, but also with *defending* Kant from Hamann, since Hamann seems to underestimate the radicality of Kant's moral philosophy when he interprets it as simply reactionary and, moreover, sustained by the Prussian monarchy.

The notion of Hegel defending Kant contradicts the image of Hegel as Kant's antipode, a common notion in many lines of reception, which see Hegel as the representative of a practical-everyday tradition of philosophical ethics dating back to antiquity. In keeping with this image, many branches of contemporary philosophical ethics divide themselves between Hegel and Kant as between dichotomous, mutually exclusive sovereign ethical realms of the particular and the universal. While for Hegel the particular moment of individual "ought" (*das Sollen*) is supposed to remain tied to the individual's life-world (understood as a kind of normative web of living an ethical life [*Sittlichkeit*] under the paradigm of antiquity), for the early critical Kant of the *Groundwork of the Metaphysics of Morals* and the *Critique of Practical Reason*, all dimensions of moral action are supposed to stand or fall by the frequently criticized "formalism" of the categorical imperative. In light of this stereotyped image, the "universality" of Kantian ethics refers to the formal character of objective claims and maxims that renounce the influence of subjective and culturally determined "inclination" (*Neigung*). Ethical stances derived from this view are accused of subscribing to a two-worlds theory and attempting to found the moral ought on a notion of reason with no context.[4] For Elizabeth Anscombe, moral philosophies that proclaim an "emphatic moral ought" pose a risk to our ability to judge actions normatively by limiting our ability to describe them properly.[5] Hegel, at least as defined in opposition to Kant, appears in contrast to legitimize the claims of the particular will, since those claims are always already a fact of reality within practical-everyday traditions of *Sittlichkeit*. Such an ethics of established practices is criticized as relativistic. It provides ethical recommendations for any given cultural domain based on the norms already prevalent within that sphere, always already including the description of the situation itself. Hence it approaches each particular case by way of too much context, resulting in a fundamentally relativistic view—or so the critics say.

Hegel's own criticism of Kant is often cited at this point, since the supposed polarity between the two German idealists is understood as a dichotomy still driving many contemporary debates (formalistic/deontic/realistic vs. pragmatic/"praxeological"). What this polar opposition ignores, however, is that Hegel's criticism of Kant is explicitly directed at the question of moral motivation—and *not* primarily concerned with the status of the universal and the formalistic as such. While Kant asserts that moral actions must be derived from duty alone rather than from inclination, Hegel's *Philosophy of Right* can be seen as an attempt to outline a living system of morality in which individuals realize that their inclinations and socially instilled motivations coax and even coerce them into continuously molding and fulfilling the moral law. Hegel's claim that morality can be actualized only against a background of shared customs and social institutions leads him nevertheless to the question of how such a system of actualized morality, that is, an ethical life, can ever be inaugurated and brought into being in the first place.[6] Here Hegel distances himself from Kant's formalism, while simultaneously introducing the radical dimensions of this same formalism into his own theory of foundation.

How exactly are we to understand Hegel's constructive and destructive reception of Kant and to what extent does Hegel develop his theory of political action *with* Kant, and to what extent *against* him? These questions are at the heart of two principal chapters in this book (chapters 2 and 3). As we will see, Hegel's *Philosophy of Right* does provide a justification for moral evolution, albeit an idiosyncratic one, linked as it is with Hegel's theory of contingent necessity within the context of his own philosophy of Spirit (*Geist*). The result is a multilayered explanation, spread over various places in Hegel's work, as to how the ethical realm, or at least political action of ethical import, can result from a situation of unlegalizable indeterminacy. In such a situation, political agents "will have shown" themselves—the future-perfect conjugation is pivotal here—capable of overextending the established episteme toward a new horizon of meaning, a horizon that can be legitimized only retroactively.

The real rift between Hegel and Kant can be seen, among other areas, in the frequently cited differences between the two thinkers' assessments of revolutionary upheavals during moments of political crisis. Kant saw his own time as standing on the threshold of an era of freedom and as on the path to attaining (at least potentially) the moral perfection of mankind through the expansion of legality. But he did not see any chance for progress by way of illicit revolt, as we have already observed. In his reflections on the "mode of thinking of the spectators" (CF 302), Kant is willing to allow a *fascination* with revolutionary action as a vision of progress, but not any concrete *participation* in the action. For Kant, (nearly) every form of political rebellion is forbidden. This prompts Hegel to reinterpret the question of political revolt *in favor* of a theory of revolutionary action. His theory, which will be unfolded in the course of this analysis, attempts to carve out some space for freedom within an area to which reason, in the sense of a justified and consciousness-saturated behavioral realm, gains access only *too late*. Such a theory of retroactive normativity, as we might call it for the moment, also lays claim to a Kantian inheritance, and this inheritance is often overlooked by scholars of both Kant and Hegel. It can be seen in the way Hegel portrays founding ethical acts, which he does repeatedly in his work, in various experimental constellations of *Realphilosophie*. He portrays these acts namely as a radical "new start" that opens the space for its own realization only by "having occurred," and without (and here we come to the Kantian inheritance) externally conditioned motivation, internal inclination, or social justification.[7] In this study, I call these founding acts of retroactive normativity acts of "excessive subjectivity." I understand them as a structural force, but not in the realization of what ethics, as the philosophical discipline of explicable and justifiable actions, attempts to prescribe. Excessive subjectivity emerges rather as a force of "the ethical" as an ethical surplus-power that breaks with the context of established ethical life and founds and justifies itself through a conflation of universality and exception, that is, the exception of its own particularity.

My analysis of excessive subjectivity, bound up as it is with an "ethics of excess," that is, the notion of an extraethical act of retroactive normativity (which in the following I call an "act-deed"), can be easily assimilated neither into the Kantian/formalistic nor into to the Hegelian/pragmatic tradition of ethics. The goal of my analysis is to uncover a deficiency in both traditions. The retroactive normativity of the "deed" cannot be defined as a duty derived from principle alone and freed from all context, nor should it be read in the light of Aristotelian virtue ethics, in connection with a view of the human being as a thinking and choosing or flourishing, everyday-practical being. Particularly Kant's moral philosophy, which aims at clarifying a formal basis for maxims of action (as in the *Groundwork of the Metaphysics of Morals* and the *Critique of Practical Reason*), cannot do justice to the contingent necessity of this kind of "deed," a deed that "will have recognized," *après coup*, its own legitimacy. Nevertheless it is the early critical Kant, with his emphasis on the unconditional nature of ethical action, who provides us with the crucial motif of an aporetic split within the moral subject. That motif will be taken up in chapter 2, where it forms a central component of the theory of excessive subjectivity.[8]

Hegel adopts this Kantian motif repeatedly. Especially in the second part of his *Philosophy of Right*, he shows how his own thought was challenged and provoked by Kantian moral philosophy. In this book I argue that it was in fact Kant's motif of a split within the moral subject that gave rise to Hegel's notion of a split that acts as a structural force within the political realm. It is because of this split that ethical life, despite its belief in its own universal validity, is again and again shaken to its core by excessive subjects that arise from a previously unacknowledged universality, as if emerging out of the ethical life's own blind spot. Thus the universal realm of the political shows itself structurally dependent on the particular (the exception). Particularity is the inversion point of universality's inherent incompleteness and the gateway to its "as yet" inconceivable future. The task of this book, then, is to demonstrate how the founding act of ethical radicality represents a legacy of both Kantian *and* Hegelian philosophy. I pursue this task in the first principal chapter (2) through an analysis of Kant's ethics, showing how he attempts to formulate a theory of the universal at the level of the subject/the particular. I pursue the task further in the second principal chapter (3), the Hegel chapter, where I analyze the abyss of freedom and individuality in Hegel's so-called *Realphilosophie*. In the closing chapter (4), I discuss the postulate of an ethics of excessive subjectivity in relation to the psychoanalysis of Jacques Lacan. Here we see that Lacan, himself an expert in the philosophy of Kant and Hegel, exposed a deep affinity between psychoanalysis and the "philosophy of the subject" (*Subjektphilosophie*) in German idealism. Lacan's perspective on idealism deepens our understanding of its basic insights, especially as they pertain to the status of the legal subject. That, in turn, helps us put our theory of excessive subjectivity on a more solid footing. Lacan illuminates central theoretical forces of idealism within the framework of individual psychology. The reception of Lacan by representatives of contemporary Left Hegelianism (Ernesto Laclau, Alain Badiou, Slavoj Žižek, et al.)[9] has shown, moreover, that psychoanalysis has not merely a certain overlap with the *Subjektphilosophie* of German idealism, but indeed takes up an analogous object of inquiry when probing the aporias of normativity inherent in the fraught relationship between the individual and society. Such aporias include both the split of the subject into a sensible (*sinnlich*) and a noumenal part and the structures of recognition that expose the human psyche in its eccentricity. Furthermore, Lacan's mining of the intrasubjective antagonism between particularity and universality brings to light how the subject's desire articulates himself both in submission to the Law and in transgression against the Law. The subject penetrates to the level of his own realities and potentialities only through a gesture of excess that remains incommensurable even to him, and yet this dimension of his subjectivity demands continuous exploration. This excess marks both the subject's submission to the Law and his simultaneous need to cancel the Law out. For Lacan, as for the idealists Kant and Hegel, subjectivity always includes a boundary between normativity and transgression as the subject's source of life and enjoyment in one.

My analysis is divided as follows. After this introduction, the first chapter expounds the need for a theory of excessive subjectivity in light of a philosophical problem that emerged during the eighteenth and nineteenth centuries in the effort to define human autonomy. My central concern here is with the so-called paradox of autonomy. Hegel inherited this paradox from Rousseau by way of Kant, and discovered in it the notion of a split that is again and again *constitutive* of community. I take a close look at this issue, as it formed the backdrop against which excessive subjectivity first came into view. My particular focus is on Hegel's own remarks on the paradox of autonomy; these I explain in reference to contemporary contexts.

The second chapter is centered on Kant, offering an analysis of his *ethics of the universal at the level of the subject.* Kant's practical philosophy brings the problem of justification to the foreground of ethical inquiry and does so with a radicality that is probably unmatched in the history of ethics. This has led to the well-known reproach that Kant's ethics are hopelessly formalistic and at the same time out of touch with reality. It is a reproach that has been voiced, in different guises, ever since Kant's time—from Fichte and Hegel, with their talk of the "emptiness" of the moral imperative, to Bernard Williams,[10] to Ernst Tugendhat and his criticism, reminiscent of Pistorius, that Kant has jumbled together distinct senses of the word *good.*[11]

What this criticism—when judged from the perspective of my own reading of Kant—fails to account for adequately is that Kant makes the formalistic thrust of his ethics contingent upon self-legitimation, and this self-legitimation in turn depends on a state of subjectivity for which formalistic criteria alone do not provide sufficient cause. But Kant's ethics also resists complete absorption into an everyday-practical ethics of classical or Aristotelian *phronesis*, which is a perspective that informs many contemporary readings of Kant (Höffe, Korsgaard, Walsh, Esser).[12] It is between these two alternatives (formalistic vs. everyday-practical) that contemporary debates over the legacy of Kant divide themselves. In my own reading of Kant, I wish to subscribe to neither of these traditions directly, but rather to undertake an unveiling of the paradoxical structural forces within Kant's moral philosophy, forces that Kant uses to establish the incommensurability of ethics with another, competing entity that I call "the ethical realm." What interests me here is the noncoincidence between the categorical imperative, which plays such a central role in Kantian ethics, and the self-obligation of the moral agent. This noncoincidence leaves behind an irresolvable tension within the moral realm, a tension I wish to explore in various contexts of Kant's moral philosophy and in opposition to specific Kant interpreters, paying special attention to Kant's theory of "disposition" (*Gesinnung*) and the "revolution of disposition" (*Gesinnungsrevolution*), which he also calls a "revolution in the mode of thought" (*Revolution der Denkungsart*). To put it plainly, for Kant the subject is either premoral or extramoral, but never (just) inferential-moral, as Robert Brandom and John McDowell would have it in their own Kant-based moral philosophies. These two Kantian thinkers, who also have in common their orientation to the philosophy of the late Wittgenstein, are interested in the conditions of justification for moral principles within a reason-based system of mutually attributed obligations. They alter the bent of Kant's thinking, though, by deflecting the central demand of autonomy (which the early critical Kant especially emphasized) into an external, "inferentialistic" space of collective and "praxeological" normativity. Thus Brandom and McDowell join company with other recent American interpreters (Pippin, Munzel, Baron, Wood) who have likewise sought to free Kant from the reproach of formalism. In the works of these thinkers, we encounter a Kant whose position has been stabilized with arguments from value theory and theories of moral motivation. And although such interpretations may find some justification in Kant's writings, I would like to draw attention to how such approaches overlook an essential force in Kant's moral philosophy, specifically because of their emphasis on the ethics of value theory and inferentialism and because of their motivation-specific interpretation of those ethics (by way of the collective, practice-based concept of reason propagated by discourse ethics). In this book, I locate this essential force at the crux of Kant's revolution of disposition, which I take to exemplify aporetic subjectivity in line with the image of a split subject of moral agency. I find the same force in Kant's remarks on education (*Pädagogik*), as well as in that portion of his theory of judgment that deals with the application and the breaking of rules. Ethics do require that our actions conform to the ethical-universal, but—as Alenka Zupančič rightly points out—that condition alone does not exhaust the ethical dimension.[13] The tension that so many interpreters have found in Kant's ethics is a consequence of Kant's attempt to conceive of the moral subject as a singular universal. Such a subject's duty matches one to one neither with the normativity of discourse ethics (Habermas), nor with the normativity of inferentialism (Brandom/McDowell); nor can it be circumscribed by a concept of autonomous, undivided self-identity such as Christine Korsgaard claims to find in her alignment of Kantian and ancient Greek ethics.[14] The Kantian subject is, rather, a subject that must bridge her internal split by construing herself in the light of a future morality—and that must do so not once, but again and again. I end the chapter with an attempt to capture excessive subjectivity at work in the example of a (moral) deed that made history within the context of the US civil rights movement in twentieth-century America, namely, the "provocation" Rosa L. Parks achieved on December 1, 1955, in Montgomery, Alabama by refusing—in disobedience to the established normativity of public transportation rules legitimized by law and practice—to give up her seat within a whites-only section of a public bus. Here I discuss the simultaneous possibility and impossibility of viewing Parks's act of moral courage as an ethical deed demonstrating the Kantian split of the moral subject in the context of a societal crisis. The central point of interest, at least in terms of our line of inquiry, is that it was only the abrupt breach of the practice—the breach effected by Rosa Parks's deed in refusing to give up her seat to a white passenger—that retroactively demonstrated the amorality of that same practice, whereas prior to the breach, many participants in the practice could not perceive the moral misconduct of it as cognitively disturbing. They failed to notice their own misconduct because it was the dominant norm, the proper standard that the law, as mediated through representatives elected by the community of voters, had established as "well posited" and as the universal good of ethical life.

After treating Kant in the second chapter, I devote the third to the issue of the split in Hegel's understanding of ethical life. Opening my discussion with Hegel's own frequently cited criticism of Kantian moral philosophy, I argue that this can easily lead one to overlook how Hegel, aside from being influenced by Fichte, also repeatedly took inspiration from Kant's crucial insights on the autonomy of the moral subject. Kant's influence was important, not only for Hegel's concepts of conscience (*Gewissen*) and morality (*Moralität*), but also for his understanding of antagonism within the political as a necessary condition of politics. In short, in the third chapter I argue that Hegel adapted Kant's theorem of the individual-moral revolution in the disposition into a theory of revolution for the political realm. In a number of his writings on practical philosophy, which is the context that interests us here, Hegel shows how nonconformist political agents acting at crucial moments have forced the symbolic orders that succeed one another from century to century as sociocultural manifestations of human history to take on new shapes. Those agents—who include not only Jesus, Antigone, and Socrates, but also, albeit in a different way, the heroes of the so-called heroic age and charismatic political leaders such as Caesar, Napoleon, and others—each stand for an inner antagonism in the established consciousness of a political order.[15] In some cases, when the antagonism goes beyond merely shuffling the inner parameters of the era's episteme and instead manages to undermine that episteme in its self-relation as the authority over the definitive representation of reality (a self-relation that otherwise "subsists in and for itself"), it does so by necessarily developing into tragedy—a theme I will explore. My overarching thesis is that the founding gestures of a new consciousness can be understood as performative political acts that "will have" verified themselves—that is, retroactively—and that therefore cannot be negotiated, explained, or judged from a neutral, third-person perspective, but must be (for the most part) simply *believed*. This is why *faith* is an important ingredient of excessive subjectivity. Hegel worked out such a theory in the *Phenomenology of Spirit* and in his *Philosophy of History* and *Philosophy of Right*. He was guided in this by the certainty, which went beyond anything he found in Kant, that the universe's space of reasons—in his term "world-spirit" (*Weltgeist*)—was constantly entrapping itself in antinomies through the agency of subjects engaged in scientific research or political action. World-spirit is phylogenetic: It accumulates all the categorical shifts that take place in the processes of self-consciousness constantly unfolding between the world of objects and collective subjects. Both these parties—objects and subjects—are, like two sides of the same coin, necessary forces within one rational process of progress by way of growing complexity.[16]

I take a close look at Hegel's reception of Antigone in order to show why Antigone is mentioned in the *Phenomenology*, at the end of the "Reason" chapter and the beginning of the "Spirit" chapter, not as a law-breaker, but as the embodiment of an ethical substance, a substance that emerges only because through her deeds Antigone incites "Spirit" to disintegrate into its several forces. Antigone unconsciously serves as the "vanishing mediator" of another polis. The change she provokes takes place retrospectively after, and because of, her death.

Antigone's distinction is, in Hegel's interpretation, similar to that of Socrates. In the tragedy of Socrates (my next point of inquiry in this study), Hegel traces the intrusion of a new normativity into the space of "common sense" in ancient Greek culture. By intransigently defending his philosophical thought against the polis, despite the tendency of that thought to dissolve certain accepted universals, Socrates comes to embody an insistence, seemingly solipsistic, though anchored in "conscience," that coming to a head retroactively legitimizes itself as an ethical norm that was always already in place. This paradoxical structure of a retroactive normativity emerging through excessive subjectivity can be assimilated neither to the picture of Hegel as a totalitarian-minded theorist of the modern state (Popper, Tugendhat), nor to the more widespread picture of Hegel as a spokesman for paradox-free recognition structures (Pippin, Taylor, et al.). Central to Hegel's discussion of Socrates are his analysis and theory of "conscience." In this way, Hegel distances himself from an ethics of moral judgment in the tradition of Kant, while at the same time drawing on Kant's split subject of the founding ethical act as an essential source for his theory.[17]

The individual and the spirit of a people (*Volksgeist*) are cogenerative, and Hegel's social theory of freedom emphasizes that a person cannot be a free being by herself. Yet a problem emerges as soon as we attempt to determine precisely how much tension to allow for within this cogenerative relation, the relation of ethical substance and subject. Both Hegel's paradigm of the classical polis (evoked in the "Essay on Natural Law," and to some extent also in the *Phenomenology* and the *Philosophy of Right*) and Hegel's theory of ethical life (particularly in the *Philosophy of Right*) frequently seem to suggest that in a nation-state the cogenerative relation remains, if not free from conflict, then at least free from escalation.[18] My interpretation of Hegel in this book is based on the conviction that Hegel's various "positions," especially between the *Phenomenology* and the *Philosophy of Right*, the latter of which forms the bulk of his theory of ethical life, cannot not be harmonized. Hegel's position on the amount of tension that exists between an individual and the spirit of the people or between the particular and the universal is a perpetual conflict. For that reason, I consider the debate between Tugendhat and Siep[19] some years back, namely, over whether Hegel's legacy qualifies as ethical or antiethical, to be irresolvable. In fact, I consider irresolvability itself to be the only adequate solution. In the breadth of their development, Hegel's writings reveal a tension that would not do justice to Hegel if, arguing exclusively from his theory of ethical life, we interpreted it as a genealogical harmonization process of particularity and universality in which only war (between states) each time draws ethical life out of its complacency (PhR §333–34). The reconciliation of the universal with the individual must be found, as Slavoj Žižek remarks, *in the split*, which the subject/the particular and the universal have in common. The excessive subject and the universal communicate through their noncoincidence because they face each other within the blind spot of the split that affects them both. Their shared split may make them enemies, but it also makes them rely on each other in their conflict, in which they must "recognize in each other a different answer to the same fundamental 'antagonism.'"[20] Political agents who embody a structure of excess, such as Jesus, Antigone, and Socrates (it remains to be shown exactly how this excess structure differs from Hegel's category of "great world-historical individuals"), demonstrate that the establishment of a new form of ethical life remains dependent on an unintelligible, pseudoethical founding act. Outfitted with excessive particularity, these "armies of one" form the complementary counterpart to Hegel's notion of the "flight of the owl of Minerva." They are the conquerors of a future that will have arrived too late, if at all.[21] Excessive subjectivity, being predicated upon a noncoincidence of prevailing norms with the unintelligible certainty of personal morality, cannot be negotiated through any power of judgment—and it is precisely because of this, its impenetrability by reason, that excessive subjectivity is capable of realizing a utopian potentiality that lies outside both reality and possibility.

The fourth and final chapter deepens the conclusions reached in the previous two by revisiting them in the context of the philosophy of Jacques Lacan. My objective here is to provide the insights gleaned from Kant and Hegel with an enriching foundation in psychoanalytic theory, specifically in Lacan's analysis of the subject. Kant and Hegel anticipate certain propositions of psychoanalytically informed political philosophy, without, of course, using the vocabulary of psychoanalysis. I draw out these preemptions, calling attention to the points where the thought of the two German idealists overlaps with that of the French Freudian: for example, on the motivation of moral will, on the trauma-like incommensurabilities inherent in subjectivity, on the psyche's integration into normative semantic webs, or on the psyche's subjugation to the normative space of society, which never fails to confront it with overdeterminations. Lacan traverses all these fields in a philosophy that resists systematization and is available to us, for the most part, only through transcripts of the seminars he held from the 1950s through the 1970s. But in this corpus he addresses the mutual influence of social space and subjective psyche from various angles; he addresses both the excessive influence that society's enigmatic appellations exert on the subject's unconscious and, conversely, the influence of excessive subjectivity on society, an influence stemming from the fact that society can never "be everything" to the individual, can never fully compensate the individual's fundamental insufficiency, and thus stands as a constant rebuke to the subject's self-image and her desires. It is one of Lacan's basic theses, after all, that neither language nor the unconscious can ever be a private affair of "my own" subjective being. Where the ego inhabits its innermost thoughts, where it believes itself alone in the private, inner sanctuary of its being (as, for example, in a dream)—precisely there we discover a trap door to the outside world or, as Lacan says, the "big Other." Thus, continuing to pursue our topic of excessive subjectivity, we see in this final chapter that the subject in Lacan's philosophy is generated as a political being—in a moment approximating a Freudian "choice of neuroses"—via a "distortion" of the phantasmatic framework outlining the space of subjectivity, a distortion that is to be regarded as a performative act of freedom. In this connection I explore the potential of psychoanalysis in political philosophy and demonstrate the link between psychoanalysis and the philosophy of the subject in German idealism. That link has been established, over the past decades, in various publications from contemporary philosophers and cultural theorists (among whom Badiou, Gardner, Laclau, Lear, and Žižek stand out), and it sheds light on, among other things, how we should understand excessive subjectivity in the context of political "deeds."[22] One might assume that such a link entails the mixing of incompatible philosophical categories, since propositions of German idealism are being set in relation to categories of psychoanalysis. But the relation between the two is already manifest. That much is apparent due not only to the affinity, amply discussed in Kantian studies, between the Freudian superego and a moral will, and not only to Hegel's psychology of the soul in his *Anthropology*, but also to Lacan's many references to Kant and Hegel in his seminars, the biographical circumstance of Lacan's having attended Alexandre Kojève's famous Paris lectures, and Lacan's use of the master-slave dialectic as a central source for his own psychoanalytical model of subjectivity, which he bases on antagonistic structures of recognition.

Lacan's metapsychology can provide us with a new understanding of the political philosophy of idealism and its attempts to define human freedom because it shows how techniques of reference and appellation lead to the subject's turning toward the appellative-political instances within the doxa of established normativity—or to his sense of being entirely untouched in its "legitimacy" by those instances. When the subject does assent to the established institutions, this demonstrates her readiness, as Martin Schulte aptly puts it, "to act as an enthralled spectator for the mise-en-scène of the mythic primal formula and the prohibitions."[23] By "Law" Lacan generally does not mean the positivized, normative legislation of a nation; instead, he takes aim at the original psychic mechanism that first makes subjectivity possible through the enigmatic emergence of norm-recognition. This subjectivity also shows, through its pathological, paranoid inability to locate itself, how everyday reality only becomes "normal" to the individual through the mediation of institutionally driven virtualities (or imaginative powers). The ethics of excessive subjectivity emerges in part along the border between normality and virtuality, since in this ethics there is no longer any distinction between potentiality and virtuality, as there is no big Other. As Lacan's meditations on the phenomenon of subjectivity show, the subject's desire—embedded in the same "subject of the unconscious" that, according to Lacan's most famous line, is "structured like a language"—can speak out either for or against legal obligation and the authority of the law. In this way, Lacan offers a whole range of differentiations for our analysis of the legal system. These differentiations are strongly connected to Hegel's philosophy of freedom and Kant's notion of the moral will, and go well beyond any of Freud's pronouncements on culture, law, and society.

One more reflection to conclude this introduction: In entry section 223 of his book *On Certainty*, Ludwig Wittgenstein asks himself whether he might possibly be crazy and, as a result, whether he is *not* doubting aspects of the reality around him that he *should* doubt. Societies heavily influenced by politics often provoke an analogous doubt in their citizens: Can I really tell the difference between what is doubtable and what is not? And a society can have this effect despite signals, even many signals, that the current state of affairs merits a great deal of doubt.[24] If the doubt still fails to be articulated, then that is in part because the modus operandi of an administration can confirm the performative efficacy of the state of affairs through practices. And in this way any political apparatus, no matter whether totalitarian or democratic, can much more easily escape the accusation of paranoia. It can point to its public authorities and to the collective of citizens, who support it in elections or gather in stadiums to hold up colored panels depicting it as a head or a dove of peace.

The administration thus has little reason to worry about its future. Instead, it is the individual opposing the administration—casting doubt on his performative facts, its efficacious legitimacy—whose future appears to be in jeopardy. That individual must also fear for his mental health. Are his objections perhaps only a luxury, only the grumblings of a malcontent who at the same time profits from the status quo? Lacan shows that societal, collective paranoia cannot always be distinguished from the private paranoia of the subject. That follows directly from the noncoincidence of "reality" (which is necessarily experienced within the individual psyche) and the symbolic (that is, the collectively maintained belief in the big Other). Although this noncoincidence generally remains hidden from view, it is always lurking. Hegel likewise explores this ambiguity of paranoia residing on the border of the two central categories of his philosophy, the universal and the particular. "Spirit" and "consciousness" can disappear from a society almost without notice. Then it may be only individuals who detect the lack, while the form itself and all those who rely on it for protection continue to believe in their own fulfillment within the modus operandi of practices that were long ago superseded but nevertheless lumber on. The inversion from full to empty can occur gradually or in a sudden flash (Hegel: "by a sunburst" [PhS §11]), and the event that triggers it may be entirely contingent—a natural catastrophe recognized too late, the collapse of a financial system. But the contingency can also be understood as the emergence of a subjectivity that is not derived monocausally from the established doxa of dominant ethical life, but that rather—analogously to Kant's revolution of disposition—"proves" itself with an act-deed. The difficulty of precisely delineating paranoia along the borderline of the universal and the particular arises from the blurriness of the partition itself, a problem that Kant, Hegel, and Lacan all address in their respective epistemologies. That blurriness in fact represents a challenge for the whole of practical and even theoretical philosophy. I attempt to describe that challenge in this book, but I do not offer any clear solution, nor do I have one. For that reason, I also do not assert any claim to completeness. I do not reproduce every pertinent opinion that has been expressed in the secondary literature on Kant, Hegel, and Lacan, nor do I examine every relevant argument (which, given the wealth of publications on these three authors, would be impossible anyway). My goal is rather to call attention to excessive subjectivity as an important issue, and to outline the boundaries and contours of this question as an aid to future analyses.

1

EXCESSIVE SUBJECTIVITY AND THE PARADOX OF AUTONOMY AS ITS PREREQUISITE

Excessive subjectivity often manifests itself in the form of underrepresented normative claims. When these claims collide with the established political sphere, they necessarily fail to meet with understanding, but in that failure succeed in revealing something about the nature of the political sphere itself: structured by mechanisms of collective hegemony, it can (to put it somewhat simply) accept and process only those cognitions that allow themselves to be subsumed under its established terms. In contrast, normative claims that appear excessive—claims traveling on a frequency outside the bandwidth of the universal—cannot even be advanced within the political community; they remain for all intents and purposes unrepresentable. Hegemonic processes are no doubt often essential for any political community, since every community's notion of the universal (its values, norms, customs, and so on) occupies a position of sovereign authority, a position from which it can and may only absorb cognitions that lie within its limits of tolerance. Only through structures that lead to a cognitive stress reduction—that relieve tension between all-too-divergent claims within the political realm—can a community spring up and build normative judgments. Not infrequently the alignment of those judgments occurs independently of any process of deliberation within the realm of the established political order—and nevertheless therefore in support of the universal, because these are the judgments that provide for the homogeneity of the universal in the first place. Excessive subjectivity, meanwhile, emerges on the far side of such blinders. Thus it calls attention to the close link between the question of the autonomy of the subject and the definition of the universal that nourishes the established doxa. Here, already, we see that the concept of the autonomy of the subject is not free from paradoxical forces. Being autonomous also obligates the subject to be part of the ethical life of his life-world (*Lebenswelt*), even if this ethical life, in turn, often appears to contradict his autonomy. Hegel was well aware of this problem. He inherited it from Rousseau and Kant as the "paradox of autonomy," a term that was understood to refer to the conflicting relationship between the individual and society, that is, between the universal and the particular.

Before going into detail on Kant, Hegel, and Lacan, the three authors that stand at the center of my analysis of excessive subjectivity, I would like to preface the theory of excessive subjectivity by outlining the problem of the paradox of autonomy. This is necessary because the paradox of autonomy forms the matrix from which excessive subjectivity emerges, like a figure emerging from a background. Hegel, in particular, recognized the challenge that the paradox of autonomy represents for political philosophy. For this reason, I will begin with him.

Hegel's well-known thesis from his *Philosophy of Right* that the "spirit of a nation" (*der Geist eines Volkes*) is "the nature and development of its self-consciousness" (PhR §274) has led many commentators to object to his theory of ethical life on the basis that the "spirit of a nation" provides the individual not only with the paradigm of ethical duties, but also with the criteria of application of those duties.[1] This seems to suggest that every spirit of a nation functions as a self-contained, totalitarian whole, and this impression has repeatedly brought Hegel in for strong criticism. In fact, Hegel makes clear that the spirit of a nation is *not* closed off: He points to the individual who in certain "epochs"—times of crises, for instance—is authorized to determine for herself "what is right and good" (PhR §138). Thus, while the impression of totalitarianism proves false, correcting it presents us with some interesting problems. How, for example, are we to know when a time of crisis has arrived? How can an individual be authorized at such a time to determine "what is right and good"? The individual is, after all, a child of her times: the dominant criteria of application for her time period's hegemonically defined good are part of her inner nature (of her own ethical life) and part of the inner nature of her fellow citizens as well. Nor is it immediately clear how the individual who has autonomously determined what is "right and good" should be understood by the majority who hegemonically dominate the spirit of the people—assuming, that is, that the individual's position differs sharply from the majority's own estimation of the "right and good."

Here one can deescalate the situation somewhat by pointing to the overdetermination of societal contexts and the polymorphism of political bodies within the spirit of a people/nation. The spirit of a people is never as autocratically one-dimensional as the talk of "a people" or "a nation" would seem to suggest. Especially in democratic societies, the spirit of the people is a conglomerate of civil society's diverse "discourses." Yet even here there exists the undeniable tendency for one discourse to assume hegemonic dominion over the others and make them dependent on its premises—which will therefore come to seem restrictive. Thus the problem remains: How can a discourse that diametrically contradicts the hegemonic order assert itself, considering that the normative premises of argumentation are always defined by the ruling body politic? Doesn't there exist here the danger that the collision of opposing worldviews will lead to a conflict in which, to quote Wittgenstein, "each man declares the other a fool and heretic"?[2]

Hegel, wishing to distance himself from Kant, considered it important to show how interiority is preceded not simply by an external world, but by an external world that indirectly, through customs and conventions, defines interiority down to its innermost regions. Hegel writes that the good lives when it is "*concrete*" in deeds (PhR §141), and deeds are concrete inasmuch as they give form to the living good. Economic conditions, for example, give subjects (living during one era) behavioral options that other subjects (living centuries earlier) did not have. Thus, by taking up the courses of action it finds at its disposal, an ethical world becomes actual according to a specific, time-dependent autonomy. Today, in 2017, many citizens of Western industrialized countries understand themselves as autonomous by the premises of their societies, which in most cases are organized around capitalist principles. Their autonomy is of course greater than that of the citizens of Chad, for example, one of the poorest countries in the world, or that enjoyed by the people of the Middle Ages, but even in modern industrialized countries, autonomy is only autonomous to a degree. Children of poor families enjoy less potential for self-realization than children of wealthy parents, who have put themselves in a position to give their offspring a wider range of options for self-realization by amassing capital. The poorer families would have to rob the richer ones in order to make the contingency of options allowing for material realization appear less contingent. They of course are held back by the legal system, which protects the right to property as a cornerstone of bourgeois society. Thus, in order to avoid trouble, the poor accept the (limited) autonomy this century offers them and in so doing reaffirm a legal system that, although backed by a so-called justice system, seems to fall somewhat short of justice.

Thus one could say that, in a way, ethical life is inscribed into the subject even before the subject, in his autonomy as *subjectum*, can relate to himself or to the "living good." Robert Pippin speaks in this regard of the "Kantian paradox," while Terry Pinkard points to the importance of "practices,"[3] which provide the conditions for the subject to make himself autonomous, namely, by seizing certain courses of action and forgoing others.[4] As Pippin demonstrates in his book *Hegel's Practical Philosophy*,[5] determining ends about practical matters, choosing means, being able to perform actions, and so on, show that the subject's power of judgment is inscribed with an extrinsic body of rules: rules that determine subjective interiority and that have their origin in the outer world. They are controlled and maintained by collectively avowed processes that nevertheless always remain partially obscured from the viewpoint of the collective. The established practices generate the ability to judge them and vice versa.[6]

If the spirit of a nation is the true source of ethical duties, then this same spirit endorses a complete set of ethical duties and their criteria of application. Then the good exists in established customs of my era inasmuch as I do not question them with extraordinary stubbornness and do not, for example, incite a revolt against established ethical life or loot my rich neighbor's apartment. I accept the autonomy allotted to my family and myself in a bourgeois society, for example, not because I believe it is perfect, but because it is the autonomy to which I am accustomed through cultural imposition. Thus the ethical world is to a certain extent determined by a circular interlacing of conditions between the subject and its historically established form of life. Only political revolts and revolutions show that this interlacing of conditions is not necessarily stable.

My noninsurrection against prevailing customs can thus be understood as a passive act of certification of social practice, even if I judge this practice to be unethical at various levels. Passive sufferance of immoral laws and norms is *a part* of legal culture. This has led Peter Sloterdijk to coin the term *cynical reason* for the exhausting coercion of false consciousness, as it accepts with ridicule what it despises.[7] Slavoj Žižek interprets this concept in his book *The Sublime Object of Ideology* and, inverting Karl Marx's famous definition of ideology in *Das Kapital* ("They do not know it, but they do it"),[8] twists the concept to represent the current zeitgeist: "They know very well what they are doing, but still, they are doing it."[9] The problems and aporias caused by this ideological twist for questions of normativity will be revisited frequently in the course of this analysis.

Hegel emphasizes that a subject must be called autonomous even if she is continuously part of an inferential network of behavioral options. In this way, Hegel believes he has overcome Kant's understanding of autonomy. The subject that acts morally need not be thrown back solipsistically on her pure practical reason in order to prove her abstinence from inclination. The subject constitutes herself as autonomous only due to her participation in practices that, being normative, *are* her autonomy. Any power of judgment is then partly determined by the established good and the established power of judgment.[10] In this regard Hegel writes: "The *right of individuals* to their *subjective determination to freedom* is fulfilled in so far as they belong to ethical actuality; for . . . it is in the ethical realm that they *actually* possess *their own* essence" (PhR §153). The laws of practices are "not something *alien* to the subject. On the contrary, the subject bears *spiritual witness* to them as to its *own essence*" (PhR §147).

Acknowledging a practice means being inferentially bound up in a structure of reasons, that, of course, may also include errors. Reasons are conceptual norms; they have been self-referentially embedded into themselves by the prior enactment of their corresponding normative protocols.[11] Thus with Hegel one might say: a fact or state of affair is part of a judgment inasmuch as it is part of a practice.[12]

Yet even if norms are recognized as binding such that they form a dimension of normativity in the discursive and practical structures of social reality and affect the ethical life of individuals, the whole community may still be in error in terms of its ethical life, as "the features of the new world" (PhS §11) are already illuminated, but the old one, though "gradual[ly] crumbling" (PhS §11), has not passed away yet. One day, though, forms of political life can collapse "in one flash" because the interlacing of truth and justification, each in their own historical objectifications, no longer achieves harmony. Truth does not legitimize itself for Hegel—as it does for Richard Rorty—only inferentially or epistemically; rather, Hegel's inclusive monism makes clear that the priority of truth is necessary as a precondition for the revision of deceptions, and this priority is written into Hegel's philosophy where he describes the progress of knowledge toward truth as the coming-to-itself of the *Begriff*, "the concept."[13] His notion of progress as a cumulative overcoming of deceptions in the development of Spirit contradicts any purely epistemic, inferentialist theory of truth.

Does the interlacing of the "living good" and the practicing subject within this living good rob the subject of his autonomy? If the subject is only autonomous when he is already a participant in practices, how can he then relate *to* those practices (for example, through resistance or questioning)? One could, like Pippin, interpret Hegel as saying that the subject realizes his autonomy within the given established good of dominant ethical life only if he *participates* in that ethical life: making judgments, questioning others' judgments, allowing himself to be judged, relating to himself in a recognition relation with others, and so on. This view of Hegel has led Pippin, Neuhouser, and Honneth to understand Hegel's *Philosophy of Right* as a theory of social recognition. Indeed, participation is a precondition for any "relation to." The dominant practices are not dogmatic *codices*, such that the individual only executes certain behavioral procedures implanted within him like a computer code. Due to the overcomplexity of circumstances, which is a permanent challenge to inferentialism, Hegel knows that within the domain of inferentialist argumentation, norms generated by practices necessarily and repeatedly provoke a redefinition of the given established ethical life. Yet as long as an item of knowledge or a practice is considered justified, there is no cognitive framework with which to question it, or to judge *differently* the judgments passed on in this practice. Arguments in the established cognitive realm may be interchangeable, but what about the premises that prestructure the actual discursive framework?[14]

This question gives rise to a problem, one that has been among the factors behind contemporary political philosophy's shift toward a radical, anti-Kantian, anticommunitarian decisionism (as advanced by Badiou, Žižek, and Laclau). For it is not entirely clear how an inferential web of norms, despite its reciprocal recognition structures, could ever free itself from, for example, a collective error, if that error affected the premises of the web of belief itself. If the practice prestructures the conditions for judgments, and the judgments in turn justify the practice (as legitimate), then a structural or, as Luhmann would say, "systemic" blindness is always already a condition of the inferentialist system itself. Revolutions in world history are examples of how inferentialist edifices of norms and beliefs can sometimes be changed only through political insurgence, for instance, because a dominant class is unable to give up the premises structuring its notion of power and reality. If practice is a condition of judgment, how can it be challenged as practice? Is the influence of cognitive justifications on practice perhaps not as compulsory after all?

Hegel argues that such a challenge to practice is possible, provided that the spirit of the people has ceased to be an adequate representation of the world-spirit. At that point, the spirit of the people has become a mere "shell" concealing a "kernel" (PhH 30). The kernel can then be revealed by individuals who, with "*their* interest, and *their* work" (PhH 30), bring about the historical upheaval. Such an emergence of individual claims—claims that are initially inadmissible to the spirit of the people, but that then manage to assert themselves anyway – proves that, at such historical tipping points, "a general principle of a different order" from that "on which depends the *permanence* of a people or a State" (PhH 29) was *already present* in the form of a more advanced spirit of world history, namely, in the "inmost soul" of those who helped bring about the transition (PhH 30).

An example can perhaps help to clarify this point: Why do we in some cases begin to question the supposed "exploitation of nature" only after it is, or at least appears to be, too late? The reason might be that consciousness at a collective level "will have shown" itself as one that, due to a collective consciousness, recycles plastic bottles and so on only through and posterior to the gradual establishment of the practice. Hegel's talk of a "kernel" present within the world-historical process can be misleading here. When Hegel makes a distinction between the spirit of a people (or a nation) and the world-spirit, as in the lines quoted earlier, he gives the impression that world-spirit is a teleological corrective and as such always present as a concrete potentiality for acts that give Spirit a new shape. To assert, as Hegel does, that the Spirit can be "more advanced" than the "*permanence* of a people" suggests that there is a facet of world-spirit capable of legitimizing the step concealed within the potential "kernel"—and even the step that is to come after it—not merely ex post facto but indeed before those steps are taken. However, for Hegel the world-spirit precedes the advancement of self-consciousness often only in retrospect. In Hegel's understanding, the future of the world-spirit always defines itself too late; so it is not only the future that is undetermined, but the past as well. The past can be rewritten.[15] What Hegel suggestively calls the "kernel" is in constant danger of being recognized or misrecognized because of virtual forces of misrecognition that cause the spirit of the people to appear as a kind of hologram.

Thus it would seem that the matter of *when* a practice will have determined the autonomy of the subjects in a certain habitual political order is influenced—in an essential but nonexclusive way—by contingencies, and so cannot simply be a process of clearly structured, normative consultation between, for instance, rational agents. This is a point that was widely ignored by Hegel critics until the 1980s, especially by the representatives of the first generation of the Frankfurt School.[16] These critics often interpreted Hegel based on a concept of the universal that does not acknowledge contingency as its particular/other. However, it is precisely through Hegel that contingency experiences an ontological elevation.[17] In Hegel's work, contingency is not merely the collateral damage of the deeply passive and ultimately autonomous processes that these critics describe, processes that only "happen to" the subject or befall it. Rather, contingency designates an ontological dimension of universality through which Hegel's cyclical interweaving of subject and practice refers us to an externalization of the subject's interiority, and it is this externalization that universality needs in order to arrive (under the influence of acyclical forces) at a new shape.

Ultimately Hegel shows, particularly in his philosophy of history, that in times of crises, certain contingent historical situations can turn against an established practice (and the epistemic interest connected to that practice) and can thus cause ethical life to tip over into a new form. But these moments can also be missed. Especially in his treatment of Jesus, Antigone, and Socrates, Hegel conceptualizes the breakthrough of normative stages of consciousness through tragedies in ethical life. Such tragedies are produced by a noncoincidence between two different truth claims. That noncoincidence is the subject of the following three chapters of this book.

Walter Benjamin writes in his famous twelve theses on history—citing the Swiss author Gottfried Keller—that "'the truth will not run away from us.'" He continues: "This statement by Gottfried Keller indicates exactly that point in historicism's image of History where the image is pierced by historical materialism."[18] With this famous remark Benjamin criticizes the Hegelian historicism of the nineteenth century. What Benjamin writes here *against* a specific interpretation of Hegel is nonetheless precisely what Hegel himself understood: that a truth can, in a sense, run away from us. It can run away, for instance, when a new potential "kernel" of the world-spirit, despite arising at a historical tipping point like a fata morgana before the empty shell of the spirit of the people, nevertheless fails to break through. In retrospect, this may show that the time was "not yet ripe." However, it may also show, in retrospect, that the world-spirit has endured yet another tragedy it could have been spared. Thus the world-spirit can repeatedly fall short of itself. Or, to put it more radically: world-spirit always necessarily falls short of itself since, from the view of its reflexive observation, the force of contingency, which acts as an important motor of its function and as the necessary condition for any real human freedom, does not appear as a part of itself.

The inversion point at which a new cognitive insight morphs into the practical implementation of itself can be described both by theoreticians of the pragmatics of discourse, for instance, and by theoreticians oriented toward Hegel. Without getting into a deeper discussion of Karl-Otto Apel's transcendental-pragmatic approach and the Habermasian theory of communicative action, we might say that these approaches conceive of such an inversion point as the result of a cognitive deliberation process in which rational justifications for norms achieve new validity after passing through a series of intersubjectively monitored argumentative examinations. Thinkers oriented toward Hegel, in contrast, will understand the inversion point as being strongly influenced by contingencies and unreflected practices that rational deliberation processes cannot overtake, since these practices become a cognitively intelligible explanation only in retrospect. There are numerous cases where the inversion point has arrived in an untimely fashion (sometimes too early, sometimes too late) or where a catastrophe has been needed to trigger it, cases where, for example, the cognitive inversion establishes itself on the level of ethical life by furtively revealing itself to have been *always already present (at least partially) through certain practices.* Thus, what at first glance may appear to us to be an autonomous process of justification taking place among free, responsible, and rational agents within a democratic public is, in truth, not really autonomous. Why? Because *practices* occurring behind the back of any review of norm justifications—that is, behind the back of discursive reason itself—might have already paved the way for certain premises.

I do not want to contend that mind-independent justifications effected through passive practices are exclusively of importance in the political realm. At all levels, civil society forms groups that interact with one another, that shape values and norms, advance arguments, reject and rearticulate them. That is beyond dispute. However, there still exists a "passive" or "retroactive" understanding that is determined in part by contingencies. Why, for example, do we still eat animals, even after a potentially new moral consciousness has, via Peter Singer, suggested to us the immorality of this practice?[19] Do we have difficulty understanding Singer cognitively? On the contrary, we understand perfectly well what this particular individual says—it is rather that our understanding entails little in the way of consequences for our practice. The latter seems to have its own cognitive power and shields itself from objections through its own collective dispersion. Perhaps this practice will be questioned one day, and perhaps then, when quite simply it is no longer carried out—that is, once it truly *can* be questioned, since it (the consumption of animals) no longer exists.[20] Accordingly, the good that "lives" when it is "actual" in deeds is always conditioned in part by a process of competing practices—some of which run parallel to one another, some of which contradict one another, and none of which are primarily negotiable on a cognitive plane—and by the cognitive claims bound up in those practices. When then finally, on the other hand, a practice *is* initiated by individuals, it is not yet part of the "living good." When such a practice *is* part of the living good, it seems that in some cases it is always already part of that which the individual no longer does consciously, but rather does unconsciously, specifically because it is the "living good."[21] One might say that the "symbolic order" (to introduce a Lacanian concept that will play a central role in chapter 4) has relieved the individual of his insight into the situation. When practices thus temporarily break away from cognitive penetration, one might say, in the words of the late Wittgenstein, "This is simply what I do."[22]

Hegel realized that adjustment processes are consistently distorted and untimely. Therefore he also understood the need for individuals to consistently and provokingly stand up for new, normatively superior potentialities, even to the detriment of the communicative structures of everyday practice. The force that interests us here is precisely the unbridgeable chasm between the individual and intersubjective practice. For Hegel, the subject is allotted an *asocial* dimension, an aspect that Pippin, for one, underestimates. It is this dimension that is essentially responsible for the social realm's ability to generate new worlds from within the blind spots of the "space of reasons." The chasm between the individual as individuality and the "living good" as universality is decisive for Hegel's understanding of the political realm.[23] That sounds paradoxical, but the consistent prematurity of excessive subjectivity's arrival in the inferentialist space of reasons—or, conversely, the consistent belatedness of the majority's comprehension of states of affairs that the world-spirit has already uncomprehendingly comprehended (at least potentially/virtually)—points to a permanent distortion of the political realm, which must thus assert its stability through harmonization myths that never advance beyond virtuality. Philosophy, meanwhile, often legitimizes itself by sharing in the upkeep of these myths. Both Hegel's own philosophy of history and his hidden theory of excessive subjectivity demonstrate that he was aware of the ontological dimension of contingency (in the shape of subjectivity) in his analysis of the political realm. It is precisely the irrepressible distortions, contradictions, errors, and crises that turn against an established practice and the epistemic interest connected to that practice that repeatedly call ethical life into question. My own liberation from a custom/habit that is dearer to me than the idea of a political uprising against this custom would have to entail—as Christoph Menke correctly points out—turning even my inner habitual nature (or "second nature") into its opposite by means of a revolution of disposition.[24] The revolution of disposition would have—"in one flash" (PhS §11)—*to break* in "lawlessly."

That brings us to the concept of the "revolution of disposition" that plays a decisive role in Kant's moral philosophy and that will stand at the center of my analysis in the next chapter. This concept will help us understand why Kant sets up his theory of the ethical deed to hinge on the motif of the split subject, and how in doing so he provides us with the first component of our theory of excessive subjectivity.

2

KANT

The Split Subject of Ethical Agency

The madman is the man who has lost everything except his reason.

—G. K. CHESTERTON

KANT AND KANTIANISM

In his *Critique of Pure Reason*, Kant borrows the term *focus imaginarius* from perspectivist visual theory and employs it in an attempt to develop the idea of a regulative illusion. The latter counters the understanding that the world, rather than an organized manifold, is no more than a multiplicity of contingent multiplicities, that is, arbitrary natural processes. As such the concept of "focus" provides the faculty of understanding with an orientation toward an end. It does so by "directing the understanding to a certain goal . . . which, although it [the goal] is only an idea (*focus imaginarius*)—i.e., a point from which the concepts of the understanding do not really proceed, since it lies entirely outside the bounds of possible experience—nonetheless still serves to obtain for these concepts the greatest unity alongside the greatest extension" (CPR 591).

As with an architectonic drawing, the *focus imaginarius* constitutes the vanishing point toward which the vertical and horizontal proportional lines align themselves.[1] When Kant refers to this term, he does so to illustrate that the vanishing point lies outside of the picture, which means "outside the bounds of possible experience." It is the totalization-inflicting turning point from which the faculty of reason brings the partial perspectivity of understanding (and its individual objects) under the sovereignty of its claims. One might say that the focus creates a coordinate from which reason can view itself as (virtual) totality. This necessary illusion results from a transcendental reflection whereby the notion of totality becomes reason's "self-portrait,"[2] as Friedrich Kaulbach writes so fittingly. Transcendental philosophy's emphasis on this vanishing point allows for the realization that even contingent proportions subordinate themselves to the normativity of reasonable perspectives.[3]

If this were translated into Kant's philosophical program, one could then say: The regulative ideas of reason that inhabit Kant's term *focus* as transcendentally deduced concepts constitute the objectivity of objects but are, as Kant explicitly says, merely subjective functions of perceptions (CPR 591–92). Constitutive determinants are intrinsic to the subject (CPrR 247–48) and yet they determine the target horizon of objective knowledge.

Although God, world, freedom, and soul are only "*ideas* of reason, which cannot be given in any experience at all" (CPrR 249), their reality is to be determined via transcendental philosophy because these ideas must not be allowed to be empty, particularly with regard to practical reason (but also according to the teleological judgment in the *Critique of the Power of Judgment*). In the same way, Kant points out in his later philosophy of history ("On the Common Saying," "On Perpetual Peace") that we, as moral agents in light of a history of mankind (which is seemingly on the path to bettering itself), can entertain the hope that there will be past and future allies in the fight for morality, although there is no objective assurance of it. The attainability of the good may—and must—be nevertheless thought of as a never quite "broken off" (CS 306) historical process, in spite of a morality that empirically is never thoroughly verifiable, neither as existing, nor as having actually existed in historical phenomena.

In his text on the *Faculties*, Kant interprets the virtuality of progress as a narrative organizational principle of historical self-assurance employed by each generation that considers itself political.[4] The world may then very well be in and of itself (*an sich*) a grand illusion. However, it cannot be denied that the illusion of the world's coherence is "nevertheless indispensably necessary" (CPR, 591 [A 645/B 673]). As such it is condition for the possibility of knowledge, duty, and progress in the world of phenomena. The illusion of totality, as *noumenon*, presupposes a meaning in the manifold that constitutes the *phenomenon*. This allows the plurality and contingency of the manifold to come into view without in turn being subsumed by a dogmatic precritical metaphysics. For Kant, then, the *focus imaginarius* is a transcendental illusion that is the condition allowing the system-creating mind to achieve synthesis as well as to enable ethical acts (CPR 591).[5] Despite admitting that the world may conceivably be grounded in contingency, Kant sees practical reason as conditionally required to act in the world as if it, the world, were upheld by a "highest good," a "kingdom of ends." With this, his moral philosophy opens up the chasm between *is* and *ought* that is the condition for human freedom.[6] This chasm between the world as it may well exist in reality, however contingent and irrational, and the world that must be presupposed as if it stood in the light of a horizon of an immanent kingdom of final purposes, such that the human being as a rational being is to act in accord with the moral good, is unbridgeable for Kant. This chasm is necessarily unbridgeable, for a holy will would not after all be in need of a categorical imperative. A world in perfect correspondence with reason, in which man would, just like in paradise, live in the direct presence of and with God, would turn man into a "marionette" (CPrR 221), in which case his consciousness of spontaneity, "if taken for freedom, would be mere delusion" (CPrR 221).

Any form of human determination of ends done both out of and within freedom, any ethical-moral act, would in this case be brought to naught. Yet it is only through this type of action with the mentioned chasm in the background that man is called upon to prove himself as a noumenal being (CPrR 258).[7] Only a world permeated by the problem of theodicy can be the place where human freedom can be active, because the human capacity for setting autonomous ends can only show itself in such a world, even if, per Kant's *Critique of Pure Reason*, there is no empirical proof for the existence of such freedom. As Kant conceded, the moral agent can never, even with regard to the surety of progress in which he sees himself in a continuum with like-minded others, past and present, judge the reality of progress with absolute certainty, although he is called upon to construe it as an essential part of the condition of the possibility of his acting morally.

The chasm between *is* and *ought*, closely tied to Kant's early writings on moral philosophy, proceeds from the insight that the criterion for the ethical-moral dimension of an act is not the empirically observable side of things where a fact is to be evaluated by a second or third party; rather, this dimension, in its essence, anchors itself in the agent's free determination of will. In the realm of public law, which Kant calls "external freedom" in his "Doctrine of Right" of the *Metaphysics of Morals*, this realm does not sanction will over action. There, it is the state's authority that determines exact norms and may demand sanctions. That is the authority's right and its meaning. The area of "external freedom" is in this context subject to the free determination of will only in an indirect sense, if at all, which leads to the much-analyzed particularization of Kant's ethics in law, theory of duty, and virtue.[8]

In the realm of morals, however, almost all of Kant's important writings make evident that man is an intelligible, free being who cannot be epistemologically objectivized. Kant sets morals apart from a "system of self-rewarding morality" (CPR 679), which (in turn) makes itself dependent on external ends. In this, he sees the true ground of morality, with which he attempts to differentiate himself from philosophical tradition. Jacques Lacan gets to the heart of the matter when he writes in a side comment to Kant's ethics that Kant had penetrated the unsolvable interplay of Final Judgment, unquenchable desire, and permanent failure. While "traditional morality," as Lacan argues, drawing on Aristotle, requires us "to act insofar as it is possible," Kant unmasks that the dimension of the possible exactly does *not* touch the "topography of [human] desire. The breakthrough is achieved by Kant when he posits that the moral imperative is not concerned with what may or may not be done. To the extent that it imposes the necessity of a practical reason, obligation affirms an unconditional 'Thou shalt.' This field derives its importance from the void that the strict application of the Kantian definition leaves there" (S.VII 315–16).

One problem for Kant, then, is the question of ethical motivation. For if morality, in order to realize itself, needs human agents who by necessity will be shaped by pathological tendencies (freedom is not a topic of relevance for pure rational beings), then, as Hermann Andreas Pistorius already pointed out, it remains unclear how these human beings should act in a morally good manner without ever having experienced the notion of the good via their senses, that is, for instance, as reward, benefit, or simply as a good feeling.[9] For the early Kant, man follows the moral maxims of his will due to an absolute obligation, although he lacks any empirical proof of the guarantee of a moral reality, and only the idea of God can animate man's venturing an ethical will (without, of course, this idea itself being the motivational ground). The *ought's* claim of morality can exactly *not* take recourse to an *is* in nature and her laws.

It is these difficult and complex entanglements of his teachings on morality, virtue, and law that differentiate Kant from the idealism of a Fichte, Schelling, and Hegel. By letting the world as illusion remain in its own contingency and pointing out that man necessarily will have to attempt to overcome this contingency again and again, both in terms of a theoretical philosophy and practically, Kant's actual philosophy still seems to belong to skepticism—at least for the idealists who succeeded him. Similarly to Hegel, Kant also clearly discerns teleological progress in humankind's history. Yet, in contrast to Hegel, he does so based on a "mere" transcendental understanding of the faculty of reason.

Unlike the concept of a determinative power of judgment, the reflective power of judgment as developed in the *Critique of the Power of Judgment* succeeds in discerning something universal, or noncontingent, in a multiplicity of individual phenomena, but this purposiveness remains a necessary transcendental pattern of thought that has to be read into the phenomena,[10] that is, it (the purposiveness) is a function of transcendental philosophy itself and provides no objective proof of its own accord. As an intelligible being, man is called upon by logical necessity to push the rock of reason against the possible infinitude of purely contingent natural processes on the teleologically structured path as it appears in the *focus imaginarius* as an "end" in the kingdom of ends; yet this occurs precisely with the awareness that man can never epistemologically incorporate the world as such or this "end" as an end in and of itself. Therefore, in transcendental philosophical terms, man's knowledge is seen as essentially imaginative, though not irrational.[11] In practical philosophy, then, Kant can assume progress in the realm of phenomena, yet not understand this progress as one that encompasses morality. Even one of Kant's earliest critics, Carl Leonhard Reinhold, expressed regret that Kant did not succeed in subsuming his three critiques into one "common source for the highest principles,"[12] that is, bring them under *one* faculty of reason.

Many idealists agreed with him, which is why Fichte and Hegel enumerated the alleged price to pay for Kant's dichotomy of *is* and *ought*.

For Fichte, the insight into the absoluteness of the moral claim simultaneously constitutes theoretical knowledge of both absoluteness and the unconditioned, such that it no longer allows separating the I-awareness from the thing-in-itself, of thinking and being. Theoretical recognition, for Fichte, already constitutes half of the action by declaring the will to perform an act as absolutely necessary. For Hegel, Kant was, through his theorem of the power of imagination, always closer to the actual monistic idealism than he wanted to admit to himself.

Hegel articulates his much-commented-upon critique of the "void" of the Kantian moral philosophy during the first years of his time in Jena and continues to mention it in his *Encyclopedia* of 1830. What this traditional critique of Kant often does not sufficiently take into account is that Kant ties his formalistic moment to a subjectivity that rests on a self-legitimization, which has been inadequately appreciated by several critics and lacks sufficient causal relationship with the formalistic. At the same time, however, Kant's metaphysics also stands in tension with an ethics of practical life of Aristotelian *phronesis*, as, for instance, represented by Otfried Höffe, Christine Korsgaard, and Drysdale Walsh.[13] These two alternatives—the formalistic one and the one orientated toward practical life—continue to divide contemporary debates on Kant's legacy.[14]

Kant's ethics, according to critics, has a monologic character and provides merely a "thought construct of agreement"[15] to morality in weighing the wills of others. For example, when Kant ties the moral formation of the will to the demand that it refer to a universal principle of human reason, Kant is said not to be cognizant of the fact that this universalizable principle of communication is precisely lacking in real discourse. Critics further claim that Kant does not take the "step from the mere imagined argumentation to the real one."[16] Critics on the other side see Kant as an ethical constructivist,[17] whose formalistic dimension does not exclude an ethics oriented toward practical life and *phronesis*, but rather favors it.[18] In particular, Kant's writings on virtue, his talk of "broad" vs. "narrow" duties, and his repeated emphasis on the mutual referentiality of morals and virtue are understood as a variation of antiquity's teachings on virtue, drawn in part from a concept of practical reason oriented to "common sense"[19] and the "golden rule."[20] In the first case, one wonders, however, (similar to Kant's first critics) whether a purely formalistic morality that tries to protect itself as carefully as possible from contingency was not in the end written for angels, and must appear absurd to fallible beings such as humans. In the second case, one gains the impression that Kant's rule-bound ontological character is being undermined by "common sense." Here, Kant's ethics seems to be almost equated with Hegel's ethics of morality, in which the integration of moral questions into practices of life at least seemingly weakens the intelligible moment of *ought* or ties this moment back to a pure realization that lies praxeologically in the phenomena, that is, in the "impure." One might justifiably ask what demon must have compelled Hegel—by no means an incompetent interpreter of Kant's—to deliver such blows against Kant's moral philosophy over the course of many years, often polemically, in both his early and his late works.

In my reading of Kant in this study, I argue against both of these schools of Kantian scholarship, which have admittedly only been briefly sketched out here. This does not imply that both are simply to be rejected. Kant's system of ethics has proven too complex to declare a clear exegetical victory for dichotomous either-or readings. While this, too, may not be very satisfying, it cannot be ignored in view of the numerous masterful studies on Kant.

Our reading of Kant does not intend to directly ascribe itself to both traditions but rather to dedicate itself to exposing the paradoxical structural moments in Kant's moral philosophy with which he, according to our thesis, positions "the ethical" as incommensurate with ethics.[21] We are interested in the noncoincidence of the central theorem of the categorical imperative in Kant's ethics and the agent's self-imposed duty to act morally—a noncoincidence that leaves behind an unresolvable tension within morality itself. It is this tension that we intend to address in the following sections, with a particular view toward Kant's theory of disposition and the revolution of disposition (also referred to as the revolution of the mode of thinking) in various contexts of Kant's moral philosophy and in differentiation from other Kant scholars.

The concept of disposition is a particularly apt exemplification of that which we wish, in the end, to uncover as Kant's theory of the split moral subject. Our understanding is that Kant, in admitting to the aporetics of the ethical act-deed, points to the ethical as an excessive and supernumerary moment. This moment serves less as the point from which the subject instantiates the universal as a preconstructed ethical rule that needs to be applied from a realm of ideas, made up of premade judgments and instructions to act, corresponding to ethical realism; rather, the subject allows the universal to occur from the level of particularity. This means that the universal results post facto from an empty space that was not even noticeable as such when the event occurred. While this may sound rather enigmatic here, it will become clearer further on. Similarly, the unique aporetics of the moral act in Kant proves itself to be one that proceeds in each case from the assumption of a retrospectively self-discovering subject who escapes herself in each moral act and simultaneously preshadows herself.

This aspect of a *super*numerary ethical whose incommensurability, in contrast to the numerariness of the ethical as a commensurable factor (that is, can be explained by intersubjective reasons), has been little explored in the discussion of a General Ethics.[22] This is understandable because the supernumerary, excessive ethical eludes a normative, inferential area of ethical norms that can be weighed, calculated, and motivated and therefore appears unethical, almost by definition. Twentieth-century experiences in philosophy and politics themselves shaped the realization of the danger of excessive "supernumerariness" as threatening and catastrophic and contributed to the development of an intersubjectively structured concept of reason. In the Federal Republic of Germany, the establishment of this concept of reason owes much to the transcendental pragmatics of Jürgen Habermas and Karl-Otto Apel. And yet, we believe that Kant—as well as Hegel and Lacan—thematizes this dimension of the supernumerary ethical as a factor that can also represent the actual process of the expansion of ethics.

Key to our interpretation is the moment of noncoincidence between the theorem of the categorical imperative, so central in Kant's ethics, and the agent's self-imposed duty to act morally. This noncoincidence, which we aim to capture in a theory of the *split subject of ethical agency*, following Lacan's intuition, has been relatively neglected in the earlier-mentioned schools of interpretation. Those schools of thought that interpret Kant as a metaethical realist often cannot accept this split due to their premise of the subject's unbroken autonomy and self-identity.[23] Those schools of thought that move Kant's solipsistic self-legitization into the outlying social arena often consider it unnecessary or impossible to thematize a split moral subject and to conceptualize a supernumerary ethic, because autonomy itself is almost purely the effect of socially structured processes of recognition that may not leave any room for the nonrational, not even from a structural perspective. In the first case, the subject must be autonomous due to the necessary reductionist simplification; in the second case, autonomy has to be socially conditioned. Whoever reduces the tensions inherent in Kant by seeking continuity in his earlier and later works also falls short, in my opinion, in recognizing for herself the intentionally constructed paradoxical tension within Kant's ethics.[24]

Our thesis is, therefore, that the Kantian moral subject has to shape itself each time anew in a moral act and bridge the hiatus of her own split toward a future morality. The normativity (that is, the supernumerary ethical) that results from this process can be discerned only recursively and the subject can then act each time toward herself based on the "signs/indicators" it sets. In this regard then, there is indeed a transfer of *is* and *ought* in Kant, but not in the sense of an analogous or causal conclusion, but rather insofar as *is* and *ought* coincide in the very moment of the ethical act, after the act will have retrospectively let develop a "disposition," or, metaphorically speaking, will have "ratified" it. The normativity of an ethical subject's disposition needs to be understood as a recursive moment from the perspective of the act-deed, for which act the subject can always only be understood too late as the true guarantor.

After we have, as a first step, exemplified this thesis with the help of Kant's theory of the "revolution of disposition" (often quoted as "revolution in the disposition"), this seemingly neglected idiosyncrasy in Kant shall further be made clear through a contrastive comparison with two contemporary, explicitly Kantian ethical theories. By expanding on the studies by Henrik Joker Bjerre,[25] I will mainly refer to the two contemporary Kantian scholars Robert Brandom and John McDowell. Oriented to late Wittgenstein, their Kantianism frequently reduces the ethical to an aspect within the "space of reasons," which needs to be understood through intersubjectivity, against which Kant understands the ethical in its *incommensurability* with this space of reasons. In order to understand this topic within the complexity of the praxeological moral philosophy developed by Brandom and McDowell, we will thoroughly address relevant concepts of both authors such as that of "second nature" and that of "inferentialism" and "scorekeeping" that are central to both authors in their references to Wilfrid Sellars. Finally, we will make reference to the implicative norms of a "giving of and asking for reasons." In contrast to the orientation of this ethical view on Kant and the late Wittgenstein, we intend to emphasize that Kant goes beyond the normative inferentialism represented by McDowell and Brandom.

Against the backdrop of the paradox that deducing a moral act-deed from ethics is an impossibility, which we will further explicate, Kant pleads for a concept of the moral act as an almost godlike absolute of something universal collapsed to the level of the particular. Yet the Kantian subject, as an autonomous subject equipped with self-identity, can neither guarantee this collapse nor find a clear grounding for it in the social arena of shared norms. The subject has to venture on this collapse and embody it as if it were her uncanny destiny.

We will attempt to expand on this admittedly challenging thought in detail. We intend to take our thesis so far as to claim with Sean Drysdale Walsh that Kant never intended to develop an ethical system that would define a morally good act once and for all, as examples from the *Groundwork of the Metaphysics of Morals* suggest.[26] This aspect of our thesis does not mean though to paint Kant as an ethicist of *phronesis*, as Walsh does. For it is exactly in the hiatus spanning the unbridgeable chasm in the moral arena that Kant shows us an "absoluteness" that he lets stand as "inexplicable" and that he, in contrast to Fichte, for example, does not feel obligated to have to deduce metaphysically.[27] The Kantian moral subject, as discussed earlier, has to shape herself across the hiatus of her own split toward a future morality; and she must do so each time anew. Just as there is no guarantee of progress on the moral front in politics, the individual cannot be sure that she will not repeatedly fall into the lower depths of "radical evil," as Kant emphasizes in the *Religionsschrift*.[28] The ethical poses a challenge to subjectivity each time anew and therefore cannot be explicitly captured in an ethics as in a catechism of rules of application. "Certainty with respect to the latter [the good and pure disposition] is neither possible to the human being, nor, so far we can see, morally beneficial" (Rel. 112). Since a human being will never be able to look into her own disposition with the help of the intellect and penetrate herself, we "must at best infer it from the consequences that it [the disposition] has on the conduct of our life" (Rel. 112), that is, read indicators of a moral disposition only from the deeds that the individual—*believing herself to possess a good disposition*—has divested herself.[29]

However, there is no guarantee of a "reading" that is successful and gathers proof of one's own goodness. Consequently, Kant's ethics is presented here—analogous to the concept of "negative theology"—as a form of "negative ethics" that urges the individual neither to pragmatism nor to formalism, but rather puts her into a position of power for which she is responsible *via her own split subjectivity.* This power concerns the split nature of the moral act, as thematized by Kant, which is linked back to a locus of nondeducible excess of the ethical. Kant's ethical subject is to be understood as a singular universal whose duty is captured neither in discourse ethics (Habermas/Apel) nor in inferential normativity (Brandom/McDowell), nor under the premises of an unbroken autonomy (Korsgaard). The legal arena, which Kant also calls the realm of reforms, may undoubtedly, as has been said, influence the individual subject as in the realms of custom, tradition (*habitus*), and pedagogy. And, as is well known, Kant does thematize this in detail. Yet the moral realm is, as Kant repeatedly emphasizes, the extralegal. The Kantian subject acts morally *not* because she can provide good reasons for doing so, and not because this explanation provides her with the final guarantee of her ethical decision; rather, *because the subject has acted ethically based on a maxim that determined her will*, she can provide an explanation to others. Moreover the Kantian subject can still do so even if others (for example, the majority of those involved in the discourse) consider her to be *out of her mind.*

OF DISPOSITION AND REVOLUTION

For Jacques Lacan, Kant represents the contrastive exception in the entire intellectual history of ethics. According to him, Kant's practical philosophy scorns any morals that reduce action to an "insofar as it is possible" (S.VII 315). The moral imperative for Lacan stands for an ethics of "transgression," an ethics of "the impossibility in which we recognize the topology of our desire" (S.VII 315).

Many well-known motifs in Kant's writings support this pointed, if not new, reading: the "absolute necessity" of the moral will (in, among others works, GrMM 44); the unattainable yet nevertheless attracting goal of holiness (CPrR 243; Rel. 107n); the subsumption of the propensity toward "happiness" in favor of moral laws (GrMM 54); and Kant's often-emphasized skepticism that the individual can never be sure that she has ever performed *even one* moral act (Rel. 95). One might further consider the horizon of the kingdom of ends as the final goal of desire. Even in a life after death, this final goal is to be pursued with the unquenchable desire of the soul separated from the body as unending progress.[30] As such, the world of appearances, in which the human being perfects herself, and apparently even the realm where immortal souls dwell are forever and ever subordinated to this absolute horizon—the kingdom of ends. The exact shape of this subordination is of concern to the majority of Kant studies: whether this process happens via a radical separation, anchored in the pure law of duty between the intelligible area of the *ought* in differentiation to that of the *is*, conditioned on propensities and natural causalities, or whether this occurs via more nuanced transitions of broader and narrower duties and gradations of certain virtues.

The concept "disposition" stands out as an unwieldy term in Kant's ethics of duty.

In our interpretation, Kant develops this third option, which exemplifies the supernumerariness of the ethical and which breaks through both the strict division of *is* and *ought* and the gradual intermingling of the two brought about by the transition created in the moment wherein their difference collapses. For this reason, I intend to examine this term "disposition" closely and to view Kant's moral philosophy from this perspective.

Kant mentions the terms *disposition* and *revolution of disposition* with particular prominence in his *Religionsschrift*. Synonymously, he uses terms such as *change of heart* and *rebirth*, or *new creation* to "[put] on a 'new man'" (Rel. 92). Since, according to Kant, man's choices are always partially determined by inclinations (of pleasure or displeasure), which, in addition to practical reason, are the main source of motivation for our acts, man's will is not constant. As a result, in the course of his existence, man finds himself "between his *a priori* principle, which is formal, and his *a posteriori* incentive, which is material, as at a crossroads" (GrMM 55).

Our arbitrary choice, that is, the factual will of man, is challenged, despite its brokenness, to define itself through a will based on rational maxims, particularly in morally problematic situations. This locus of a crossroads at which the human being chooses herself to be either a being of pleasure/displeasure or an autonomous being is what Kant conceptualizes with the term *disposition*. Disposition is the path that attempts to exclude inclinations.

However, that a human being should become not merely *lawfully* good but *morally* good (pleasing to God), that is, virtuous according to the intelligible character of virtue (*virtus noumenon*) and incentivized to recognize a duty only by the representation of the duty itself—that possibility, so long as the foundation of the maxims of the human being remains impure, cannot be effected through gradual *reform* but must rather be effected through a *revolution* of the disposition of the human being (a transition to the maxim of holiness of disposition). A "new man" can come about only through a kind of rebirth, as it were a new creation (John 3:5; compare with Genesis 1:2) and a "change of heart" (Rel. 91–92).

It is disposition that, like a compass, guides man on his way to reason, according to his choice. Disposition determines the hierarchical ordering of the moral law and sensory incentives. For its own part, however, disposition cannot make reference to a higher disposition that could assist in its own self-definition. Disposition is its own *causa sui* as the adoption of the highest maxim and cannot be linked back to a motive. It stands for a radically arbitrary being-as-such of a basic moral disposition and provides direction for the practically contingent human. Disposition, however, cannot completely prevent man from acting against his dispositional tendencies, and this is its limitation.[31]

Kant thematizes (at least) three concepts of disposition. Differentiating among them, in the context of our analysis, helps us to emphasize the motif of the Kantian split moral subject. All three concepts of disposition conceive of it as distinct from reform and legality. They highlight two motifs in Kant's image of the man: the self-legitimization of the moral will, and the noumenality or respective intelligibility, untouched by any natural causality, of the free and reasonable human will. Disposition, then, is the theoretical hybrid that unites these aspects within it and that Kant wants to use to link both moral absoluteness and the contingency of reform. The "revolution of disposition" is not to be confused with "reformation in the mode of sense" (Rel. 92). The former stands for a *causa sui* conversion, the latter for practical-pedagogical self-improvement via instruction, pedagogy, practice, and ritual. Kant sees a mutual influence here that—for the sake of morality itself—does not however allow for causal relationships.

DISPOSITION AS "SUBJECTIVE GROUND" FOR A "PROPENSITY TOWARD EVIL"

The first of Kant's concepts of disposition of interest to us here signals a pretemporal noumenal "disposition" as the "highest ground" that cannot be deduced from a "first-time *actus* of arbitrary choice." Kant names this "first subjective ground of the adoption of moral maxims" (Rel. 71n) "disposition" and he needs this term, as we will see, to provide man with the attribute of an original freedom of which man, literally, cannot rid himself.[32] As the destiny of all human beings, this disposition is something for which man opted as not-responsible-and-yet-to-be-taking-responsibility-for. Even if the original ground of this concept of disposition cannot be located in a clear responsibility, the person is fully and pragmatically exposed to the freedom emanating from this disposition, namely, her own freedom, and she cannot renounce it retrospectively. The maxims that form the origin of the acts carried out in her life demonstrate the "subjective ground" of her character, although this original ground paradoxically still rests in the *suspension of its having-taken-place*. But let us take a look at the details of Kant's deduction.

When Kant speaks of this first type of disposition as a highest "ground" that cannot be deduced from a "first time-*actus* of arbitrary choice," he makes clear how far the definition of disposition is not yet to be understood, as it will be in the subsequent concepts of disposition, as an "establishment of a character" (Rel. 92). Character only realizes itself in the human being educated via various pedagogical stages. Character is not yet the center of concern here. This initial concept of disposition that specifies mankind's determination a priori is a transcendental-noumenal factor with which Kant attempts to determine man's freedom—similar to squaring a circle—and which at the same time does function as an introduction to the topic of the split subject.[33] Following this initial concept of disposition, man is ascribed—as in the fall of man—the responsibility for his "propensity to evil" (Rel. 92). Adopting his disposition through free arbitrary choice expresses itself in a subjective maxim, that is, in a choice of either the metamaxim of evil or the metamaxim of good. The metamaxim of good or evil, which does not allow for further inquiry into why one versus the other was opted for, is the ground for all morally evil maxims (Rel. 69–70). If the original choice of the metamaxim of good or evil were *not* grounded in an a priori concept of free choice (located outside of time), then, according to Kant, the educated human being would never be responsible for her maxims at all. She could always refer to her pathological tendencies as something that she unfortunately inherited from nature and for which she cannot assume any responsibility. "I am just a human being," she could claim as a permanent excuse.

Kant's highest maxim as "subjective first ground" (Rel. 95) therefore serves as the final subjective basis for the definition of humanity's freedom to choose for all the bad maxims of arbitrary choices that *must* be ascribed to man—in order that he can be treated as a free being. Therefore, this act-deed of freedom is a paradoxical choice a priori (= Kant's teachings on original sin). From here on man can no longer opt for pathology or the maxim of evil. He must be reasonable by being human. As Kant emphasizes repeatedly: reason, once it exists, can no longer turn against moral law. Only the initial option of disposition has the power to choose devilish evil, if only—as Kant admits—as an explanatory crutch for man's freedom.

The highest maxim of this a priori original choice of the initial disposition is responsible for the *propensity* toward evil in the entire human race, and not only in the individual, according to Kant.[34] It distinguishes itself from that which he conceptualizes as the *predisposition* to good (Rel. 70; Anthro. 419). This *predisposition* toward good is the basis for good will and makes it possible that man is not completely at the mercy of his propensity toward evil.

It is precisely because the human has accepted this maxim and is neither innately evil nor constrained by a propensity for which she cannot be held responsible that she is called upon and singled out to act morally. In this sense, disposition is to be understood noumenally. It stands for an initial orientation of the subject outside of time. As a noumenal factor, disposition is not directly accessible to the subject; rather, for Kant it manifests itself as an empirical fact in a world in which objectively bad actions abound. In contrast to recognizing disposition as noumenal, for Kant the empirical effects of disposition manifest themselves in the world.

Kant thematizes the revolution of disposition under the heading "Concerning the Restoration to Its Power of the Original Predisposition to the Good" (Rel. 89). He himself admits that he cannot provide an explanation for how it is possible "that a naturally evil human being should make himself into a good human being." He states: "[this] surpasses every concept of ours. For how can an evil tree bear good fruit?" (Rel. 90). Nevertheless, the fact of such a reversal "cannot be disputed" (Rel. 90), because, as Kant claims, "in spite of that fall, the command that we *ought* to become better human beings still resounds unabated in our souls" (Rel. 90). This, in turn, is only possible for Kant because "there is still a germ of goodness left in its entire purity" (Rel. 90). He later defines this germ as "the incentive for the good," which "we were never able to lose" and which he also calls "respect for the moral law" (Rel. 91).

A much commented on problem and one that, in the final analysis, codetermines the split moral subject is the fact that Kant simultaneously speaks of the "predisposition to the good" (Rel. 95) and the "propensity to evil" (Rel. 107n) in man. For if man has chosen evil, from where then does the option to choose the "new heart" (Rel. 95) stem?[35] Kant can only make this claim if we indirectly assume that he splits the moral identity of man into subsets. The propensity toward evil stands for the natural persistence of man against his rational will. What is absolutely key to our analysis, however, is the fact that the concept of disposition itself is divided in Kant: first, as the destiny of the human for which she opted, without taking responsibility, and for which she nevertheless has to assume responsibility, and, second, as we will see in the concept of disposition that follows, as a spontaneous act in the realm of moral behavior that, ex nihilo, comes to the subject as if it was simply thrust upon her.

DISPOSITION AND ITS SPONTANEITY

Hegel is convinced that there is a cumulative retrospective cognitive recognition of morality in the sense of a successive progress toward the highest good for the human genus. This forms to a large extent the basis of his teleology of history as he presents it in his *Lectures on the History of Philosophy*, his *Elements on the Philosophy of Right*, and his *Philosophy of History*. Kant, on the other hand, does not think this possible due to his individualization of morality that appears cut off from legality, especially in the early writings of the critical Kant. For Kant, morals generally encompass the area of law. Morality consists for him in an unending task that "can be fully accomplished only in an eternity" (CPrR 240). The reason for this lies in "the distance between the goodness which we ought to effect in ourselves and the evil from which we start . . . it is not exhaustible in any time" (Rel. 108).

If Kant's initial concept of disposition, as presented earlier, points to a transcendental-noumenal character, which Kant requires so as to explain how one can ascribe to man a freedom for which he has to be responsible despite his malice, then Kant's second concept of disposition signals an answer to the question of how far man, due to his inner-worldly striving for true morality, as discussed earlier, must turn away from evil again and again anew in his lifetime.

The inner-temporal revolution of disposition can be in this sense understood as a moment of *kairos* that cuts through the earlier-mentioned infinitude of progress without dissolving it, and as such integrates a moment that can be called messianic into temporal sequences. This disposition in particular concerns a human being at the end of her pedagogical education and coincides with the choice of character that Kant in his *Anthropology* describes as an "explosion" (Anthro. 392) and that he curiously associates with the fortieth year of life. Conversion stories of religious leaders (saints, prophets, apostles) but also of political fighters, revolutionaries, and activists report on this, even if Kant does not specifically turn to such examples. When in his *Anthropology* Kant speaks of disposition with regard to a "kind of rebirth, a certain solemnity of making a vow to oneself" (Anthro. 392), he emphasizes that, in this context, no motivation appropriate for moral reform could have been sufficient *before* the inner-worldly revolution of disposition. Here, too, disposition is *causa sui*. And if, as we have seen, Kant presupposes that man possesses an immoral disposition from birth on, then his "revolution of the mode of thought" (*Revolution der Denkungsart*) describes a conversion away from evil. This revolution, however, is equally "completely inscrutable," because it consists of an absolutely free act of "revaluing all values."

Whoever "clothes himself as a new man" no longer "wears" the old clothing. While man can be trained, the reversal itself has the characteristics of an invasion by a foreign power. In his second *Critique*, Kant calls this "a consistent practical cast of mind in accordance with unchangeable maxims" (CPrR 262). This second, inner-temporal disposition constitutes for Kant a condition for a coherent concept of reason that conceives of acting morally as breaking through the metamaxim of evil.

Christoph Horn sees a conflict in Kant's argumentation in which the idea of a revolution of disposition renders subsequent reforms pointless.[36] Horn asks why reform would be necessary when "all that is crucial" was accomplished with the revolution.[37] Consequently, Horn interprets the revolution of disposition as a "successful initial anticipation of complete revolution."[38] This interpretation corresponds partially to ours. For, when Kant quite clearly does not conceive of a "revolution of disposition" (Rel. 92) as the final state of conversion but only as one part of the unending path toward holiness, one cannot but describe it in the sense of an interim step. This should, however, not relativize the revolutionary aspect as "an initial anticipation" toward the "complete revolution," as Horn ends up doing. Revolution marks every ethical decision per se. A revolution in the disposition does not have to accomplish "all that is crucial," and it does not have to coincide with reform in a causal relationship.

THE REVOLUTION OF DISPOSITION IN ETHICAL BORDERLINE SITUATIONS

The understanding of disposition explicated in the previous section underlines a thought in Kant's ethics that is important for deducing our concept of split subjectivity, namely that a revolution in disposition is a constant moment of challenge for the ethical subject, a moment for which the subject herself cannot provide a final guarantee. The revolution of disposition marks progress on the unending path toward holiness for Kant, yet he has to admit that man will still lack holiness even after this revolution of disposition. The revolution of disposition may have "trained" a particular ethical attitude (for example, I always give alms), but as soon as this attitude no longer fully embodies the moral disposition (for example, giving alms for the sake of giving alms, a pure, nonpathological deed) and instead has become a mechanistic and passive routine, it degenerates into habit or legality. In his *Religion Within the Bounds of Mere Reason*, Kant employs a comparison of numbers to illustrate an example of such a routine act that can be good yet demonstrates "mere lack of a ground of the good" (Rel. 72n). The mechanically passive routine deed is, as he writes, "= 0," in contrast to a truly moral deed "= a" and a "positive evil" deed "= -a." The good deed that has degenerated into a legality, as the reference to "= 0" makes clear, is not even in the slightest comparable to the good deed "= a." It is only a form of "indifference" (Rel. 72) and therefore, as the zero demonstrates, not a moral achievement at all.

Similarly, moral failure *after* the revolution of disposition cannot be defined as merely a minor infraction according to Kant, as each omission of the categorical imperative coincides for him with the absolute fall, unable to be stopped by a safety net, into the nether regions of "radical evil." This means that even the person who, in the revolution of disposition, has decided on the moral law is not protected from having to start at "zero" again in a morally difficult situation and having to again make a decision as if the revolution of disposition had *never* taken place. Therefore, this third concept of disposition, as presented here, marks every ethical act in which the individual directly experiences a loss of happiness and has to once again "put on the clothes of a new man" so that, for instance, she is in a position to give alms to even the fifth beggar for the sake of giving alms. This includes every ethical act that we perform not (only) as legality. As mentioned, when Kant speaks of a "first subjective ground of the adoption of the maxims" (Rel. 74), he constructs a logically necessary metamaxim of the good and likewise of the evil.[39] Yet as an extratemporal maxim, this option is still *in the suspension of its status as having had happened.* Metaphorically speaking, God could show me only at the Last Judgment which "subjective ground of the adoption of the maxims" I had really chosen freely. Despite this atemporal original choice for the maxim of the good or evil, which will have only found confirmation retrospectively, the individual who finds herself in a situation of moral dilemma will reach the point each time anew whereupon she has a retrospective recourse to this pretemporal deed of freedom. The "subjective ground" has always already been posited, and yet—as paradoxical as it may sound—in this *having been posited* is the suspension of its very occurrence. This theory is intuitively very convincing, as it seems to place the individual into a peculiar teaching of predestination while anchoring its validity in a *kairos*-like present time for which the same individual, and precisely not a divine destiny, is responsible.

Kant provides two examples in the *Groundwork* for the suddenness of the conversion under discussion here as a kind of overcoming: First, he introduces a philanthropist, who, plagued by the blows of fate, barely has the strength to empathize with the needs of others amid his own propensities and emotions. In suddenly becoming aware of this "deadly insensibility," he is overcome by a sense of duty and pulls himself out of the nether regions of his inclination-oriented way of being by his own strength: "And suppose that now, when no longer incited to it by any inclination, he nevertheless tears himself out of this deadly insensibility and does the action without any inclination, simply from duty" (GrMM 54). According to the second example, something similar could happen to a man whom "nature had not properly fashioned . . . for a philanthropist." This man, too, could be overcome by the power of duty and "give himself a far higher worth. . . . It is just then that the worth of character comes out" (GrMM 54).

These examples respectively demonstrate for us the suddenness with which a disposition can occur at the level of daily life. The unspecified threshold from a premoral to an extramoral status refers us to a place of noncoincidence where the subject is suddenly positioning himself via a kind of forced choice. Here we encounter disposition as a fact, which, coming from a noncoincidence of the revolutionary, autocreates itself only *after* the act-deed. In other words, the subject constitutes herself as a subject of disposition only after her agency. Kant makes this clearer when he focuses on the "consequences" of the deeds that for him are the only *indicators* (that is, proofs that cannot be objectified) of a revolution of disposition. He writes that since man cannot "see through" his disposition, he can "best infer it from the consequence that it has on the conduct of one's life" (Rel. 112). Yet Kant also adds: "one is never more easily deceived than in what promotes a good opinion of oneself" (Rel. 109). This means that where one could find objective proof in consequences, man deceives himself with particular ease.

The revolution of disposition can truly mean conversion and be indicative of a "conduct of life," and yet when encountering ethically dilemmatic situations, man can arrive each time anew at the initial question of disposition and find himself confronted by the question of whether he ever *truly chose* a disposition. The discussion of this reactualization for each new event dramatizes the importance of the deed and also the focus on a *kairos*-like, nearly messianic present moment. While he has always already begun to act freely, from the point of view of ethics, man must begin each time anew. In case he falls into "radical evil," the individual not only demonstrates "weakness" for which he shows "remorse"; he *is* evil. In this sense, then, each new failure in daily life on the path to holiness is "radically evil" and not a minor infraction of an almost saint. Only the deed opens retrospectively the possibility of having had a disposition, as the disposition will have been created as *causa sui* in the performance of the deed. This explains why disposition, in the moment of its overcoming, that is, as the moral maxim that completely changes man all the way to his "way of thinking" is always a *too much*. Disposition is suddenly responsible for too much of what one can be responsible for. It requires the excess of an ad hoc: it will have required too much of man, and is provoked precisely by having man lift himself out of the lowest regions of the legal realm, thus positioning himself into the noumenal realm.

FORM *FORMING ITSELF*: THE CATEGORICAL IMPERATIVE

As is widely known, the fundamental insight of Kant's moral philosophy is the thesis that pure practical reason can act morally, independent of any type of inclination, self-love, or self conceit, and thereby proves its absolute power of will and the freedom of man as a rational being. Pure reason wants to act morally because it *must* act morally. In situations in which the morally correct act is in doubt, the categorical imperative assists in forming maxims.

Yet Kant knows very well that the insight into a moral act does not yet constitute the moral act itself. It requires an incentive that he conceptualizes as the incentive of "*respect*" (CPrR 199). So that it is not again inclination or sensibility, the moral act originates from the same source at the same time with the cognition of duty, the maxim of the act, and the purpose of the act. In a best-case scenario, moral law then truly succeeds in practical life in a decision-making situation to diminish self-love and to place an intelligible, almost holy, and absolute moral act into a world determined by natural causes. The act "presents me in a world which has true infinity" (CPrR 269).[40]

Kant's ethics have drawn criticism from his first drafts of the categorical imperative in the *Groundwork of the Metaphysics of Morals* to the present day. Pistorius counts among the first who formulated such a critique and faults Kant's semantics of morally and ethically "good" as void of context and meaning. As Hume's translator, Pistorious was familiar with the British empiricist's theory of rationality, and he objected that Kant's idea of an absolute good will "was a nice, but impossible idea."[41]

Ernst Tugendhat indirectly takes up this critique again. Similar to Pistorius, he critiques Kant's universalistic use of the concepts of "good" and "reasonable" in the sense of the categorical imperative as void of meaning and points to a grounding of moral verdicts as oriented in the use of language.[42] According to Tugendhat, there is no "directly understandable meaning of the grammatically absolute usage of 'good.'"[43] With regard to the categorical imperative, he writes: "Talking of a moral act that is supposed to be rational in and of itself makes no sense. This kind of talk runs counter to logical reasoning."[44] Tugendhat tosses out the notion of an absolute good and suggests a path to a solution that is to determine the semantic implications of the word *good* via a discourse of objective criteria of reasons. If Tugendhat's moral subject calls an act ethically good, then one can cite all kinds of reasons in the usage of the word *good* for why the value judgment "ethically good" was justified. Alenka Zupančič, however, in her reading of Kant, points out that in this case Kant's philosophy of ethics is not yet sufficiently captured. And when Tugendhat writes: "This much we . . . can say: . . . this concept of reason [in Kant's ethics] no longer orients itself on the usual/customary notion of rationality,"[45] then Zupančič views this precisely as Kant's achievement. If one subtracts all elements that are "pathological," that is, associated with inclinations, linked to the usage of "good" through everyday practices stemming from an act, then, according to Zupančič, there is still a remainder that Tugendhat does not see. This remainder, as the moment of supernumerariness, is what she calls the pure form of the ethical act, which, we could say echoing Tugendhat, seems not to orient itself "on the usual/customary notion of rationality."[46] For Zupančič, acting *for the sake of duty*, in contrast to acting "in accordance with duty," means to make precisely this remainder the ground of our acts, to understand this "remainder" as something unconditioned that cannot be rationalized. From Tugendhat's perspective, no further grounds can be provided for this remainder. This remainder is, for Zupančič, the pure form *forming itself* or *the form "outside" content*. Zupančič believes herself able to show that Kant's portrayal of the ethical lies on the plane of this form and therefore on the plane of the *production* of the good and not on the plane of its application or instantiation. Exactly how Zupančič adduces this difficult thought will be laid out in detail, as it is an important catalyst for our reading of Kant.

Zupančič claims that Kant's supposedly formalistic ethics is not simply to be understood as an "empty" form or an "empty formalism," as one reads frequently, and to some extent also in Tugendhat. It is a "surplus in terms of *form*" itself. [47] Employing Kant's dichotomy of acting *in accordance with duty* and acting *for the sake of duty*, she explains what she means by this surplus. It is common knowledge that an act carried out in accordance with duty may, from the perspective of a third party, not be distinguishable from an act carried out for the sake of duty. For instance, if I incriminate a friend accused of treason during a trial, I fulfill my duty as a citizen, and it makes no difference to the court whether I submitted the incriminating proof *for the sake of duty* or only *in accordance with duty*. Zupančič's thoughts are instructive here.

With this initially confounding paraphrase, Zupančič aims to articulate the following: the act carried out "for the sake of duty" is not simply grafted onto the one done "in accordance with duty," along the lines of: "yes, I turned my friend over to the prosecutor; that was my duty as a citizen, and of course I did so, in as far as it was my duty as a citizen, also as a rational being *for the sake of duty*." Zupančič instead sees a "form" at work in this ethical act that all of a sudden is "no longer the form of anything, of some content or other."[48] Instead, it is "a form 'outside' content, a form that provides form only for itself."[49] In this manner, Zupančič wants to emphasize the generally acknowledged fact in Kant's ethics that the act *for the sake of duty* cannot, metaphorically speaking, be simply poured into the engine of the act done *in accordance with duty* like motor oil. For Kant, the act performed *for the sake of duty* is not even remotely on the same level as the act carried out *in accordance with duty.* It is "different *in kind*" (CS 284) because it, the ethical act, is known to posit the subject into a world of the absolute that is diametrically opposed to being in accordance with duty: it (the ethical act) removes the subject from the arena of values that are legally and intersubjectively acknowledged and places the subject into an arena in which the norm, out of pure will in combination with its incentive, makes the subject into an ethical one. Simultaneously, this ethical act allows the subject to become a vessel of instantiation of the universal on the level of the particular. I already touched on this when I deduced the revolution of disposition as a nondeducible excess of the subject's ethical self-creation ex nihilo.

With regard to the formality of the categorical imperative, Zupančič strengthens this concept. In this way, she aims to argue against a representation of the categorical imperative that has become too banal, and in contrast to which the moral could correspond to an easily established catechism of conduct.[50] (No serious Kant expert takes this position, to my knowledge.) Zupančič wants to do justice to the excess of the ethical act that has no other content or incentive, respectively, than the form of the pure will, which, as well as providing the motivation for the moral law, in turn *constitutes* the law. Insofar as the incentive of the ethical must not contain any pathological object, this implies for Zupančič that this incentive is its own formal, as well as material, form-content principle.

When Bernard Williams in his book on *Moral Luck* argues that Kant's ethics provides the moral agent with one level of reflection *too many*,[51] Zupančič does not see one moral deliberation too many at work, but rather the "form 'outside' content" of the moral. Williams presents a hypothetical scenario that he took from Charles Fried. A husband distinguishes whom he is allowed to save in Kantian terms: his drowning wife or another drowning person. Williams claims that any kind of moral algorithm, as Kant (supposedly) designed it, ignores the emotional basis of being human. A morality that would first force the loving husband to morally weigh whom he will save is exactly one thought too many, according to Williams. What Zupančič wants to get at is that Kant is not interested in questioning human passions, love among them, but rather that the "form 'outside' content" of the moral introduces a new relationship of universalization as it relates to the particular as well as to the universal. If one wanted to object to Williams, one could point out that it is indeed possible to imagine a husband who would perform the "surplus-thought" in the scenario mentioned and still not show himself as inhuman. This then would not necessarily have to imply a lack of love, as Susan Wolf claims.[52]

Zupančič attempts to lay open the radicality of the ethical that Kant upholds, by showing how seemingly impossible it is to define the freedom of the moral will in Kant.[53] In her reading, this freedom takes the shape of a purely negatively determined distance to established inferential norms in the arena of practical reason, in which, for instance, cooperative and discursive subjects interact as free and rational agents. In all likelihood, Axel Honneth would not share Zupančič's reading, yet he too describes the characteristic of moral freedom as some kind of "disturbing 'interruption.'"[54] Honneth: "Whoever exercises moral freedom seeks to gain reflexive distance, in order to reconnect to a social praxis that has faced him or her with unreasonable or irreconcilable demands in a publicly justified way. However this imbues moral freedom with a transformable power that legal freedom does not have. . . . The value of moral freedom thus goes beyond that of legal freedom."[55]

Zupančič would agree with these sentences, except for the reference to moral freedom retreating from a so-called unjustified practice with the goal "to reconnect to a social praxis in a publicly justified way." What is of interest to Zupančič is the fact that moral freedom in certain cases can no longer present itself in a manner that is publicly justifiable, although it unites "the entire reason of mankind" in itself via the application of its maxim of action. This is why political crises between the particular and the universal exist. Incidentally, Hegel too will use this surplus force of certainty through absoluteness of the pure "form 'outside' content" for his own practical philosophy, as I will show, despite all of his criticism of Kant's concept of conscience. This means that Hegel not only critiques Kant's concept of freedom with respect to the ethical-moral will, which he holds partially responsible for modern aberrations of reason, for instance, in the context of the French Revolution. Hegel also attributes to Kant, as the successor to Rousseau, the unique importance of having provided the necessary principle that catapulted reason in the eighteenth century into new extremes of practical philosophy.

For Zupančič, the absence of a concrete, pathological incentive takes over the *function* of the incentive. As such then, Kant's pure moral will appears as "form 'outside' content." Along with Hegel's critique of "conscience" articulated in his *Philosophy of Right*, one could say that Kant's moral will is almost a *pre-Kantian* metaphysically laden godlike moral principle because, as such, it is its own creation. For this reason, Zupančič compares Kant's ethical incentive with Alain Badiou's notion of a "singular multiplicity."[56] This singular multiplicity is a dimension that for Badiou "presents" something as yet unknown, whereby the new cannot yet be "*re*presented" in the canon of options of ethical acts. In this sense, Kant's understanding of an ethical act has formal elective affinities with Badiou's understanding of an event.[57] As a "genuine event," the act will have opened up the future space of its representation proceeding from its own indeterminacy. For Zupančič, this structure corresponds to a singularity that unites both the universal and the particular into itself and, as such, defines the moral act as a supernumerary singularity.

If, as stated earlier, Tugendhat's moral subject calls an act "ethically good," then one can cite all kinds of reasons for this usage of the word *good* that explain why the value judgment is justified. Yet Zupančič's "form 'outside' content" of the ethical, its surplus, which she believes she is able to demonstrate, does not come into view in this traditional understanding of ethics. Additionally, Zupančič observes very fittingly (and, apparently without knowing it, taking recourse to an old conflict between Kant and Karl Leonhard Reinhold) that the act out of "pure form" has also the form of a properly evil and "diabolical" act, that is, an act that, according to Kant, opposes the moral law out of principle and not for pathological reasons. Whoever follows the categorical imperative can no longer violate the law, because she *instantiates* the law. The difference between the moral law and what Kant calls "diabolical evil" (*das teuflisch Böse*) no longer makes any sense. And, as already mentioned, this is precisely where Hegel finds Kant's powerful modernity, as well as the terrifying abyss of the pure moral conscience. It can do anything—even call the world in its bliss-conditioned entirety into question—for the sake of its own seeming unconditional absoluteness, and in the name of the kingdom of ends.

Kant's ethics, then, for Zupančič mean the extent to which situations in daily life depend again and again only on the particular subject, in her definition of what the ethical is. It is, one could say, *the subject's* revolution of disposition, *her* fundamental attitude and character, for which one must take responsibility despite being fundamentally unable to, which will have determined what the subject will have considered her responsibility (or to what extent she will have shirked this responsibility). In a certain sense, Zupančič turns a critique of Kant by Reiner Wimmer into something positive.[58] When Wimmer claims that Kant's concept of universal human reason is only monologic, and that the universal does not refer to a *genuine* intersubjectivity—with the real will of potentially also unreasonable seeming people—then Zupančič sees precisely in this the power of an ethics that instantiates the concept of the universal coming from the subject and its monologic positing of the "reasonable." Zupančič does not want to propagate a relativistic "anything goes." She wants to tie the absoluteness of the moral act back to a rationality in which the individual guarantees the collapse of the universal and the particular and, turning Tugendhat's reproach into something positive, is strictly speaking "no longer oriented to the traditional sense of rationality." Against the thesis supported by a number of Kant scholars that Kant's categorical imperative had always been oriented toward intersubjectivity, Zupančič emphasizes the thought that this externalization is only apparently intentional. While it is true that the principle of generalizability is at the core of Kant's ethics, this generalizability remains necessarily monologic, as this is the only way for it to ensure its absoluteness.

Incidentally, a judge appointed by the public does indeed indirectly have this power to posit a law. Her authority is the "system-immanent" embodiment of the positing of the exception, and she is awarded this authority as authority by the symbolic order of the polity. While it is true that the judge refers to statutory provisions of the polity's legal traditions in proclaiming her verdicts, she then has to somewhat move beyond this tradition, that is, by overcoming it through taking office, in order to pass *her* judgment.[59] She is the authority accepted by society that has the power to define exceptions and with it "scores" (Brandom) in the area of "external freedom." Her decisions mark the occurrence of the momentary state of exception, that is, the positing of a particular as a universal in the tradition of the universal, which needs to be accepted as the condition for the legal regulation in the context of the social contract. The particular individual, however, who is not equipped with a similar symbolic investiture of positing an exception, yet according to Kant's ethics embodies the same performative power, may well risk her life if she feels called to pass judgment like the judge.[60] If this subject in her certainty then is also prepared to endanger the social bond with the community, she may be considered by outsiders as a troublemaker who is a stickler for details and fails to align her own convictions with "common sense," that is, with the established practices of the reigning order. Yet those familiar with the conventional way of doing things may then not share the opinion of the ethical subject simply because they lacked the decision that excessive subjectivity, or the revolution of disposition, had made in a given situation. Maybe, however, they also lacked the *talent* necessary to make an ethical, perhaps scandalous, irrational, and monologic-seeming decision. The fact that talent is a critical category for our analysis is explicitly mentioned in Kant's definition of the faculty of judgment. In the following section, we intend to look in detail at this definition in order to link it with the question of the determination of ethical judgments.

TALENT AS THE "EXCESS" OF THE POWER OF JUDGMENT

As Kant emphasizes in a variety of contexts such as epistemology, practical philosophy, and aesthetics, man's power of cognition and reason is defined by the fitting linkage of the particular and the universal. Judgments follow rules, and for Kant all knowledge implies the subsumption of a given object under a general concept. Thought articulates itself in judgments and in the process of judging.[61] The judgment is the connection of the subject (that is, something particular) to a universal (that is, the predicate). In his *Critique of Pure Reason*, Kant defines the "power of judgment" as a specific faculty, since the power of judgment as the ground for man's intellectual activity is also of import for evaluating situations in daily life that challenge the ethical will of man. It is advisable to take a closer look at Kant's definition. He writes:

> If the understanding in general is explained as the faculty of rules, then the power of judgment is the faculty of subsuming under rules, i.e., of determining whether something stands under a given rule (*casus datae legis*) or not. General logic contains no precepts at all for the faculty of

> judgment, and moreover cannot contain them. For since it abstracts from all content of cognition, nothing remains to it but the business of analytically dividing the mere form of cognition into concepts, judgments, and inferences, and thereby achieving formal rules for all use(s) of the understanding. Now if it wanted to show generally how one ought to subsume under these rules, i.e., distinguish whether something stands under them or not, this could not happen except once again through a rule. But just because this is a rule, it would demand another instruction for the faculty of judgment, and so it becomes clear that although the understanding is certainly capable of being instructed and equipped through rules, the power of judgment is a special talent that cannot be taught but only practiced. (CPR 268)

Here, Kant articulates the problem of determining the mechanism for the *application* of rules, whereby he shows that man's use of rules is underdetermined with regard to structures of knowing and judging. This usage of rules is underdetermined because the power of judgment, as the "faculty of subsuming under rules" (CPR, 268), is confronted each time with entirely new situations in daily life. It is evident that no life situation at point *t1* in time is identical to point *t2* and so it is for all cases in subsequent points in time *tn*. With regard to these constantly new everyday situations, the power of judgment was never able to build up a repertoire of rules—as it were, never able to preempt the future of its application options. The power of judgment is a finite faculty of man and respectively therefore the responsibility of a recourse to rules. Wittgenstein's dilemmatic analysis of rule-justification and rule-following is anticipated here.[62]

The finitude of a potential repertoire of rules for making judgments also concerns the moral act and the categorical imperative that Kant anchors in it. For if Kant attempts to provide man with a medium to test the application of rules (with the categorical imperative), that is, the rule of a maxim, in regard to a situation in daily life that challenges his acting ethically, he is well aware that even here the problem or paradox of rule-following continues to be present. What is required *before* an ethical maxim of action can be tested at all, for instance, is the fundamental evaluation of a situation in daily life brought about by the power of judgment. This evaluation first implies a decision about whether the individual finds himself in a situation that is to be judged ethically or not. If my power of judgment comes to the conclusion that it is impossible for me to come to the rescue of a man drowning in the ocean, it will not pose the unpleasant question of whether, in this case, the rescue attempt is an absolute law of free will or not. The faculty of judgment might then determine in the case of the drowning man that an ethical act is not an option of moral will. Yet could it not be that the lack of a clear rule of judgment had after all wrongly judged the distance from the shore to the drowning man? The problem of rule-following and rule application shows, as mentioned, that the faculty of judgment itself brings with it a rule repertoire that in the final analysis will also remain insufficient for subsuming particular situations of daily life under a universal.[63] The faculty of judgment then resembles, metaphorically speaking, a very wide-meshed net that is, in only a very limited way, able to do justice to each new flow of daily situations that it tries to order. This also has consequences for acting ethically. The faculty of judgment is not only necessary for evaluating a situation that may require acting ethically; it is also a requirement for finding the correct maxim of action that is then being tested by the categorical imperative. Kant himself knows this, which is why the faculty of judgment (*Einbildungskraft*) contains its central decision-making moment precisely in its meaning: *Kraft*, "force," "power."

Wittgenstein, for his part, provides an argument for the question of how far the problem of the ethical act, together with the categorical imperative, requires an "ad hoc" moment, as was pointed out for our ethically excessive act-deed exemplified with the revolution of disposition. This "ad hoc" moment cannot be prescribed clearly and absolutely by the power of judgment itself as instantiating a rule: it is as nondeducible as the revolution of disposition itself. The faculty of judgment has rather to posit this moment ex nihilo, as it were, through *Kraft*.[64] This positing allows the power of judgment to create its own parameters of application. Precisely herein lies freedom, the main topic of German idealism for the human being who is called to the power of judgment and equipped with the power of judgment. However, the faculty of judgment may not be reduced to an unconquerable stability of rule-following and rule-application. The subject's freedom in the power of judgment consists precisely in not only "representing" the universal but positing it, instantiating it as the collapse of the difference between the general and the particular, as Kant states in the quotation earlier.[65] What is particularly insightful is the final sentence of the quotation. There, he defines the power of judgment as a "particular talent" that cannot be taught by rule-following, due to the paradox of a nontotalizable number of all potential applications under one rule. Judgment requires talent so that it can emerge as an idiosyncratic interweaving of an underdetermined rule application and an "ad hoc"-like and overdetermined rule-instantiation, respectively, in a specific, nongeneralizable situation in daily life.

In our reading, then, Kant's mention of talent indicates how far he externalizes the problem of rule application to an enigmatic signifier: that is, talent. The latter is supposed to solve the paradox with the help of a surplus factor. Speaking of talent is problematic because this wholly unspecific term, which reminds us of the Kantian concept of genius in his aesthetics, opens a nonspecifiable difference into the multitude of all beings equipped with reason. If the power of judgment is more tied to "talent," in contrast to the generalizable structures of reason available to all beings equipped with reason without having to be talented at the same time, then it is not clear how Kant can declare the power of judgment a universal power of intellect and one that determines ethical judgment. Is the universality of man's power of reason not indirectly relativized by having one part of mankind equipped with talent and the other part not? To speak of relativization in this case misses the key point of the problem. I would like to argue that with respect to the concept of talent, Kant intentionally articulates an excess, a surplus-form, that precisely neither renders the power of judgment as a universal factor to be generalized nor unites everyone under a universal faculty.[66] Rather, with Kant, one has to consider the power of judgment as a power that "posits" the general and the specific, and creates an ad hoc link between them where the general and the specific do not establish themselves according to rules. And one could argue that the power of talent is all the stronger the more unexpected this gesture of linkage is, that is, of positing a particular on the level of the universal. As indicated, the power of judgment has to posit the application where the universal and the individual collapse.[67] In this positing, the power of judgment articulates a freedom for itself for which it is paradoxically never entirely responsible, similar to the "subjective ground" of the disposition in Kant's concept, that is, whoever is talented is so precisely *not* because of himself, and for which he *nevertheless* has to take responsibility. What Kant conceptualizes as talent is less what we understand as the productive application of a general rule to a particular case; rather, it is to be understood as productive instantiation of the universal to the level of the particular, and therefore as *positing*. Understood in this way, the power of judgment would be accorded to the truly *talented* philosopher who can immediately grasp the solution to a problem, for example, in the field of the science of philosophy, and precisely in doing so cuts through the limitations of the old and familiar, that is, the old applications of rules, in his discipline as through a Gordian knot.[68] Similarly, the "talented" natural scientist would be the one who, along the lines of Thomas Kuhn and Michael Friedman, has contributed to revolutionary breaks in epistemic justifications of the natural sciences by replacing the established models and their assumptions with something seemingly new.[69] Can one not draw the same conclusions for the person who acts ethically? Would this not imply an incommensurability that would take the form of exploding the application of the rule through something new that was discovered "by talent," something seemingly event-like in which the subject "posits" incommensurable subjectivity and risks being appreciated for this positing too late, or not at all? Understood this way, the truly ethical man, similar to the artist or the genius equipped with artistic spontaneity, would be the one who grasps the challenge of an ethical situation even without clear rule applications and in the ad hoc moment of positing through nondeducible spontaneity cuts through the limits of outdated rule applications.[70]

KANT AND "INFERENTIAL" KANTIANISM: McDOWELL AND BRANDOM

In order to move deeper into the paradoxical entanglements of Kant's ethics and deduce from it a split subjectivity and its structures of ethical excess, we will bring two contemporary Kantian ethics, namely, those of John McDowell and Robert Brandom, contrastively into play in the following section. The topics discussed so far—disposition, supernumerariness, excess, revolution, talent, and belatedness—emerge here in new contexts. Our intent is to show that while the divide that exists in the Kantian subject, as it is thematized in the earlier terms, concerns only a marginal aspect of his ethics, it nevertheless provokes important consequences for our deducing an ethics of excessive subjectivity. Similarly, we intend to demonstrate that the Kantian split subject cannot easily combine with the concept of rationality so prevalent in today's philosophical debates about the pragmatic and Wittgensteinian inferentialism propagated by these two representatives of the Pittsburgh School. If Kant's concept of disposition is to make any sense at all, then it does so because of the tension between reform and revolution in his understanding of an ethical subject that emerges as ethical in a retrospective belatedness. The noumenal moment repeatedly evoked by Kant is here not to be understood as guarantor of freedom and reason, in the sense of a classical humanistic (pre-Kantian) understanding of self-identity, but can only be theorized under the concept of noncoincidence.

John McDowell and Robert Brandom view Kant as a founder of the moral-philosophical linguistic turn and, by combining Ludwig Wittgenstein's late philosophy and German idealism, they tie the question of ethical normativity back to man's capacity for language and action within a space of reasons that has always already been shared with others.[71] In brief, they see a mutual referentiality between theoretical and practical reason in Kant. For Brandom's and McDowell's interpretations of Kant, the veridicality of moral judgments is analogous to epistemological justifications of propositions. In their view, Kant's teachings on categories recognized, as a predicative theory of judgment, the binding validity structure of meaning in the propositional epistemological structure of judgments. With this foundational insight, Brandom attempts to overcome Kant's threefold concept of reason—divided into morality, epistemology, and aesthetics—which Karl Leonhard Reinhold had already lamented. To do so, he tries to transform this concept of reason into a praxeological ontology called functionalism. According to Brandom, Kant falls short when speaking of the "thing-in-itself" and holds on to a "myth of the given," as deconstructed by Wilfrid Sellars, which can presumably find its locus in a world beyond of conceptual understanding.

Brandom's socially conveyed and normatively driven theory of language has become known as "inferentialism." Employing the word *inferential* and the term *inferentiality* refers to the fact that concepts are integrated into not only semantic but also normative fields which lead to the recognition that, for example, Pittsburgh is located west of Philadelphia, which at the same time normatively implies that "Philadelphia is to the East of Pittsburgh."[72] Only truthful speakers know of normative meanings of concepts they employ, since as sapient beings they are immediately placed into an indirect "scorekeeping," that is, a space where reasons are constantly exchanged. A parrot may shriek "Hegel" when shown a picture. Yet the sound produced by the parrot is a linkage of stimulus and reaction, whereas a being endowed with language and reason will immediately be able to produce such "inferential" associations to "Hegel" such as "human being," "male," "mortal," author of *Phenomenology of Spirit*, and so on.[73] In opposition to a representationalist theory of meaning, Brandom develops a purely inferentialist logic of linguistically expressive and pragmatic meaning. A nonrepresentationalist intentionality of thinking and moral judgment is at the core of his theory.

For his part, Brandom venerates Kant for having recognized the function of judgment as the "fundamental unit of awareness or cognition."[74] However, a central flaw in Kant, according to Brandom, is that, despite this insight, Kant interprets the categories of human thought processes in the sense of eternally valid "intellectual" structures.[75] In the context of the linguistic turn and discourse pragmatics, Brandom, referring to Kant, puts forward the deontic commitments that are implicitly normative for language. They are the result of their inferential character and defined by normative references. Brandom wants to establish the inferential logical structures of language not as formal/formalistic but as "material-inferential" and pragmatic. "Material proprieties of inference" are central, such as that, for instance, Hamburg is located west of Berlin and that therefore Berlin is east of Hamburg.[76] Brandom speaks of *commitments* and *entitlements* as "discursive" practices. They are to be assigned conceptual content in deontic scorekeeping. Uttering a statement is a performance that implies a commitment to the statement. Brandom calls this "doxastic commitment."[77] These commitments refer to a *social* situatedness in the discursive practice with which he aims to overcome the concept of conviction with its connotations of interiority and inner-psychological representation. Being convinced of circumstances and passing judgments of all kinds mean entering the play of scorekeeping in the giving of and asking for reasons whereby conviction, according to Brandom's thesis, depends much more on the external.[78]

It is characteristic of pragmatism that the concept and theory with which we describe and explain reality are interpreted as a means conditioned by convention and less, following Gottlob Frege, as given reflections of the unchangeable condition of reality. Meaning shows itself as externalized by a metastructure that language itself is hiding. According to Frege's ontological thesis, there exists, strictly speaking, a generality of concepts that is used and instantiated in our individual speech acts. Understanding the world as if it consisted of entities such as objects with properties and relationships between them, which exist independently of our knowledge of them, fails to recognize the integration of truth-values into a space of reasons that itself requires these truth-values to be constantly challenged and reevaluated. What exist for this praxeology oriented to Kant are linguistic plays of various normative structures that justify themselves through practices and linguistic communities. This leads to an opposition between an objectivist conception of the definition of content, following Frege, on the one hand, and to a position that claims that there are no objective limits to the definition of a concept, on the other.

Brandom views Kant as the philosopher who saw a relationship between theoretical and practical philosophy in language. For "what is made explicit by normative concepts is already implicit in the idea of action. If that is true, then these are pure concepts: concepts whose implicit understanding is a prerequisite to dispose of explicit concepts at all. This idea belongs to what was most important to Sellars in Kant's theory."[79]

Consequently, Brandom understands his philosophy as a moral-philosophical one because he, similar to McDowell, believes it bridges the respective realms of theoretical and practical philosophy, which for Kant were still separated by chasms. For our line of inquiry, concerning the analysis of a normative judgment of excessive subjectivity, Brandom's philosophy is an important point of reference since we, in recourse to Kant and later also Hegel, precisely do *not* understand this subjectivity as inferentially deducible. The "infrastructure of daily communication" is, as Habermas so fittingly says, the object of Brandom's inquiry.[80] Brandom writes: "Rationality consists in both being subject to (assessment according to) conceptual norms and being sensitive to them—being both bound by and able to feel the force of, the better reason."[81]

Brandom's interpretations of Kant can be retraced through Kant's teachings of categories in the *Critique of Pure Reason* as well as through Kant's comments on language recorded in his *Lectures on Metaphysics Recorded by Mrongovius* and in the notes from his lectures recovered by Pölitz.[82] The question remains, however, whether Kant's comments on language allow for abstracting a transcendental logic. This epistemological question is also relevant for our initial question that, in essence, is of a practical nature.

THE FORCED CHOICE OF MORAL OBLIGATION

When Kant develops the notion of phenomena as situated in intersubjective objectifiable structures aided by the transcendental deduction of pure concepts of understanding in his *Critique of Pure Reason*, he emphasizes language as the central medium in his theory of judgment, with all the consequences that this entails for his practical philosophy. Language is the medium with which man recognizes the world of appearances, as well as the medium of training in education and pedagogy. Similarly, in his *Metaphysics Lectures Recorded by Mrongovius* (1782–83),[83] he identifies, as mentioned, the ability to speak, guided by reason, as a condition for acting morally. Nevertheless, it is not quite clear when and according to which criteria exactly we declare a human being that is able to speak to have moral power of judgment. At which point in time, for instance, do we judge actions by children who are in command of language according to moral criteria applied to adults? The age of consent is, up to a certain degree, a pragmatic instrument of the legislative powers. Yet it only marks an arbitrary moment in time, deduced from pragmatic necessity, located at the nondeterminable threshold between premoral and moral accountability. How can the sudden change from the one to the other be determined when it is linked to language acquisition and linguistic competence yet linguistic competence is only a necessary condition? A fifteen year old may speak well and yet, for instance, according to the law, he is not—morally speaking—fully accountable. In his "Conjectural Beginning of Human History," Kant circumvents this question when he presupposes linguistic ability as a condition for man's moral judgment without addressing at which exact point command of language can be the criterion for moral consciousness (CBHH 110–11).

In this context, Robert Brandom points to a sudden retrospective change when he writes that a deed which, through the capability for language, requires moral responsibility shows itself at the moment when one has made "*enough* of the right moves—but how much is enough is quite flexible."[84] This change takes place gradually and yet, one day, it is simply there. Brandom marks this change by contrasting the terms *salient* and *sapient*.[85] By distinguishing between these two terms, he points to the scenario in which a child acts morally exactly at that moment when she recognizes that she really has always been thrust into a normative field that has, to a large extent, determined the criteria of her identity. Therefore, the sudden discovery that the child has made the "right moves" and the sudden discovery that she behaved in an erring, immoral, or age-inappropriate way toward her parents when she pulled the chair out from under her father are comparable to that which Slavoj Žižek interprets, in recourse to Lacan, as the appeal of a superego mediated by the unconscious or, in recourse to Louis Althusser, as "ideological-interpellation."[86] This mechanism of setting aside the self by allowing the normative to penetrate into our consciousness, which is turned away from intentionality, is not a slavish submission that forces us to something against our will. In Brandom and similarly in Althusser, the subject experiences himself as the target of an interpellation while he simultaneously and from the same source determines the entity that he believes is the legitimate origin of the interpellation of his own morality. Interpellation, then, marks the tipping point at which submission, identity formation, and the determining of an inferential entity of recognition and interpellation collapse.[87] Suddenly, in the "appeal" of an ideological self-imposed normative interpellation, the child experiences herself as active in her forced decision made by the self, for the first time.[88] The normative external area has become internalized. One could interpret this tipping point as essential to the paradox of autonomy.

It is exactly this problem of the paradox of autonomy that Kant and Hegel, via Rousseau, thematize and which refers to the subject's being woven into a real-life semantics that, as the external condition of our being, is always already involved in one's inner world: the psyche. The inferential web of practiced norms allows us to perceive "evidences," and such evidence, as Brandom suggests, may appear both in a moral deed and in a missed chance of adequate behavior. Retrospective recognitions in particular lay bare how a structurally determined space of norms *eccentric* to the individual is of importance. In these cases the subject discovers her ability for moral duty only from the retrospective discovery of having missed it. If the child interprets this "having missed" in the sense that, for instance, before she pulled the chair from her father, she is doing something funny, then she has proven that she was not yet able to perform the right "moves," according to Brandom. Only once the child truly feels responsible for pulling the chair, as an act that she was *not* allowed to perform, does she possess moral responsibility.

John McDowell develops his philosophy in a similar context proceeding from Wilfrid Sellars and developing Hegel's notion of the "second nature" of man.[89] This second nature also initially finds expression in Brandom's notion of the self's asking for and giving reasons. So, when we one day notice that a child can understand our arguments, can respond to and follow them, even if not with absolute agreement, but with references to facts and values, we judge her as having the ability of justification that incorporates moral criteria as well.[90] The adolescent will not view her own process of education as one moving from a premoral level to a moral level of self-assessment. This would already presume the cognitive ability to judge. Rather, the adolescent will one day perceive a difference in her understanding of herself, for instance, when she, as mentioned earlier, does not simply passively accept a reproach but experiences it as justified based on a retrospective understanding of acting improperly. In this context, guilt signals that she could have acted differently, even if this guilt, by coming too late, retrospectively structures the moments before becoming guilty toward the guilt.

With regard to Brandom, and—as we will see—to Lacan as well, one could say: a child experiences herself as moral when, in the interpellation of an ideologically compelled choice of existing value judgments, she suddenly experiences her understanding of herself in relationship with, for instance, her parents. This might be the moment when the child no longer ignores the words "you should be ashamed of yourself" with bored indifference but rather is now truly ashamed of herself. One could then say with Niklas Luhmann's systemic-functional moral theory: the child has learned the "expectation of expectations" and this does include her moral behavior. Luhmann argues for a functional understanding of morals that is to a certain degree analogous to Brandom. Such an understanding affords that "expectations can be expected" and that therefore reductions in contingencies, stabilization of equilibrium in the system, and development of trust can be generated.[91]

As we saw with the example of being able to make the right "moves," the moral subject does not enter into the realm of normative judgments, but rather experiences himself as *already* in this realm, which is experienced retrospectively. In that moment, the feeling of guilt is the emotive state of a *forced and simultaneously self-imposed choice*. Having linguistic abilities means that an individual has accepted certain obligations in what Žižek terms "forced choice"[92] and to execute or fail to execute certain performances, which, according to Brandom's philosophy, appear on the "scorecard" mentioned earlier as, figuratively speaking, hanging above the space of reasons. In the intersubjective exchange of practices and claims, participants assign one another "commitments" that are automatically recorded. This accounting is done individually and transindividually in the sense of a regulative idea in order to allow for the possibility of reconciling the performance-related obligations of the linguistic participant: "For someone to *undertake* a commitment . . . is to do something that makes it appropriate to *attribute* the commitment to that individual."[93]

In this manner, then, participants in discourse and practice are mutually aware of the normative status of their exchange and for their part behave according to the respective score that, in their view, is assigned to them, and that they in turn assign to others. We are tied to the "difference between status and attitude, between commitment and its attribution, between what is correct and what is merely taken to be correct, between objective content and subjective view of it" exactly for this reason.[94] Brandom defines mutual scorekeeping as a fundamental structure of social practices that can be normative even before they are made "explicit."[95]

This matrix of transindividual modes within the reconciling of scores, however, does not, at least not for Brandom, confront the individual like a foreign encroachment, though for our study it does precisely that. As memory of the social with universalistic validity, this matrix has always already left its traces on the *ability* of man to recognize commitments and entitlements, not only in concrete insights but in unconscious, propositional content-lacking practices as well. In the end, this is what the paradox of autonomy rests on. For Brandom being a participant in linguistic play means to always already have been involved in performance-related relational events in which an institutional dimension is always of relevance. Brandom's "scorekeeping," therefore, resembles a Kantian notion, which as simultaneously virtual and "mandatory," that is, logically linked, concerns the transcendental necessity of the structure of language as the realm of the "big Other" (Lacan) that has its real present instantion in the concrete other whom one faces. All linguistic participants are necessarily subject to this "big Other" who keeps score as the virtual authority of the social contract as the condition for the possibility of claims of truth and *oughts*, but also subject to establish one's own self-knowledge. Norms result from structures of acknowledging mutuality in a shared culture.[96] These determinations can even go so far that others assign assertions to us of which we, to this point, did not even know that *we ourselves* are their true guarantors and authorities.

Brandom's analytic pragmatism has the utopian goal of making the inferential-normative content of discourses and practices ever more explicit.[97] The discursive practice is always part of a totality of acts for which we similarly can require a retracing of reasons. In many of our shared practices, we automatically accept the authority of "assertions" as a given, assuming that there is a hidden option of making them "more explicit" if necessary. Nevertheless it is hard to imagine a community where each custom, practice, or action would first have to deduce itself from the authority of the normative and social-pragmatic and inferential chain of reasons. As Wittgenstein shows in his theory of the forms of life, communities would not come into existence in the first place because each chain of reasons for an "assertion" cannot be explained when the chain itself in turn does not rest on particular "certainties" of forms of life or morality. Only certainties of established customs enable—as shared virtualities—the normativity of practices in a space of reasons. The use of "virtuality," which will be more prominent in the chapter on Lacan later on, shall indicate that, in the colloquial sense, one expects to be able to demand details at any time about assertions that have been given or received. But if this were really done, then the practice of communication would be permanently overstraining. Language therefore seems to work only when several assertions in a conversation are *not* made "explicit."

The intensity of public expressions of indignation, which sometimes starts with minor crises and then often increases, demonstrates how quickly virtual assumptions about the practices of another, be it an institution or an individual, can all of a sudden be regarded with strong skepticism if and when this other has begun to fall behind the score. Suddenly, one discovers by looking beyond the virtual moments of the entire inferential area that a politician not only may have too much supplemental income, but—now that the society views him with the scoreboard in hand—is also cheating on his wife or doing something similar. This underlines to what degree the area of giving of and asking for reasons is always strongly determined by virtual gestures and repressed antagonisms, assertions, and determinations that may never be made absolutely explicit as a condition of the body politic. In this context, Žižek and Robert Pfaller provide us with the enlightening reference to paranoia in public space, to be discussed in the chapter on Lacan where, on the one hand, the "illusions of others" create the stability of the public space that, on the other, can be revealed as truly "virtual" when presumably perfect public persons or financial or legal systems suddenly and almost out of the blue lack justification and reputation.

As soon as man "becomes a being who has mastered language," he finds himself as existing in another, always also symbolic-virtual world. In a fundamental sense, man is *ex-tim* (Lacan, vs. *intim*, see chapter 4) by virtue of being enmeshed in an always-also-overdetermined frame of normativity that makes the sharp distinction between hypothetical and categorical imperatives porous. In the moment at which the human being, in his process of education, becomes a full citizen of the realm of the second nature, this second nature penetrates his entire being, whether he wants it or not. Only medical confirmations of a lack of accountability on his part liberate him from the grip of the whim that determines normativity.

KANT'S CRITIQUE OF INFERENTIALISM

We have dealt with the two philosophers Brandom and McDowell and their Kant-inspired pragmatism in such detail because they see themselves as indebted to Kant, particularly where they work out the justification of moral principles as transcendental-pragmatic ones. At times, though, the setting aside of moral principles and their praxeological justification brings them into partial conflict with Kant's conception of self-legislation, particularly as it concerns his *Groundwork* and the second *Critique*. Brandom and McDowell, for their part, represent the recent American strand of research of a "new Kant"[98] whose position is interpreted from the vantage point of contemporary value theory.[99] While these interpretations admittedly find their references in Kant's work, an ethics based on value theory and inferentialism neglects the moment in Kant's moral philosophy that is central to our argument. For although Kant sees the necessary link to linguistic ability as a condition for the possibility of man's ability to reason and similarly sees the necessary motivational integration of humanity in moral and legal forms of life, it is doubtful whether Kant truly ties logic, categories, and pure morality—*the* ethical as opposed to ethics—to a linguistic-pragmatic fundamental ontology, or to a moralism or system of observation of the second order (Luhmann), as Brandom and, as pertains to Luhmann, Caroline Sommerfeld-Lethen,[100] for instance, suggest. Brandom's and McDowell's Kantianism leaves open the question of the moment of the absolute, which we briefly addressed at the beginning of the chapter, and which is of central importance to Kant in *Groundwork* and the *Critique of Practical Reason*. While Brandom allows for a conflict with the scorekeeping of normative reconciliation processes to be seen as an illegal act, we notice that for Kant, on the other hand, "the illegal still falls within the category of legality,"[101] as Alenka Zupančič suggests. As Kant also makes clear when he initially talks about the revolution of disposition, the moral law in its pure form is always an expression of *im*moderation. Acting out of duty means not acting, strictly speaking, based on a scoreboard, as opposed to acting dutifully. Kant's theory of the excessive gesture of the revolution of disposition cannot be integrated without objection into Brandom's notion of normative inferentiality. As we have seen, the disposition is *causa sui*. As revolution, it will have been recognized by the effects of the deed in retrospect. In the moment of its performance, it cannot provide absolute accountability, but only what Badiou calls a supernumerary "coming-to-being"[102] in opposition to the natural coming-forth. Badiou also speaks of a "unifying scission" of a supernumerary act that represents but is not being represented.[103] What does it represent? *Itself.* A moral act, as unifying scission, is "singular" in the sense that it is an element that belongs to the situation without, however, being represented in it. One could say: the ethical gesture is an act-deed that crisscrosses the "scoreboard" within the body politic through counterfacts perceived by the individual at the level of its (paranoid?) particularity. In this case the individual is not bound by the scoreboard but sublates the scoreboard under the singularity of its normative surplus.

Kant's great achievement in his basic works on ethics (*Groundwork*, *Critique of Practical Reason*) was after all to reverse the hierarchy between the concept of the good, equivalent to Brandom's scoreboard, and the moral law in such a way that the concept of the good is defined at the level of the ethical law and not, as it was common in the philosophical tradition over centuries, from within the materiality of lived and shared imaginations of the good. Even though, as Kant knows, the entanglement of norms into time-specific contexts of forms of life always plays a role in choosing maxims, since man develops his maxims out of his shared lifeworld with others, Kant nevertheless tries to avoid any form of pragmatic reduction of the ethical. This radical priority of the ethical, as represented in the *Groundwork*, over and above the concept of a good anchored in practical life, needs to be emphasized even when Kant, due to numerous objections by contemporaries, tries to weaken this priority in later works (for example, in the "Doctrine of Virtue"), which in turn contributes to new problems in the coherence of his system. For his early, critical works there is above all the moral good. No other good has a concrete space in the ethical. The ethical actor can precisely *not* simply unburden himself in reference to the happiness of his fellow man. Neither can he, as Zupančič points out, hide behind his duty like Adolf Eichmann along the lines of: I "only" did my duty. Zupančič writes in this regard: "The subject is fully responsible for what he refers to as his duty."[104] Whoever acts according to the moral law can never say: "Sorry, I know it was unpleasant, but I couldn't help it. The moral law imposed that act on me as my unconditional duty!"[105]

Kant repeatedly refers to the fact that man, as a being endowed with language, is always already situated in an inferential space of reasons. And in this sense, Brandom and McDowell are justified in referring to Kant and perceiving his comments on language as essential. Yet his

Groundwork emphasizes just as clearly that the determination of man as an intelligible being does not exhaust itself in Sellar's "space of reasons." The human being becomes moral only at the threshold upon which her responsibility no longer stands in a causal relationship with the normativity of her education, with its goal of ongoing reformation and discipline. Put more pointedly, one could say: Kant's subject is either premoral or extramoral but never only inferentially moral, as Brandom and McDowell suggest.[106] McDowell comments both on the Aristotelian understanding of "the virtue of character," which refers the human being to the realm of moral judgments distinct "from a merely habitual propensity to act,"[107] and on Wittgenstein's theory of meaning as a bridge between theoretical-empirical and moral knowledge.[108] For Aristotle, a moral norm is a *polis norm* that is in and of itself already reasonable, whereby virtue is a purposive disposition for the good. As exemplified in the figure of Pericles, the best in the state appear as the epitome of moral reason.[109] In Kant, however, it is precisely the reference to the "best," that is, those who master the norms of the polis, that is *not sufficient* because he insists that the moral act—if it is not to be merely legal—cannot be learned. Moral-legal behavior can be practiced but moral-ethical behavior can only be realized when the individual herself decides to act as such. While it may sound paradoxical, this means that a moral act, in the sense of the *Groundwork* and the *Critique of Practical Reason*, can be understood precisely as the overfulfillment of that "which one simply does."[110] The moral act is incommensurable, really a type of erroneous interpretation, because it can never be mastered as a rule. The ethical act posits its own law performatively in the application with which it only then reveals the criteria of its implementation.[111]

For instance, when on December 1, 1955, the African American Rosa Louise Parks refused to vacate her seat in the whites-only section of the public bus against the established normativity of rules for local public transportation, legitimized by practices, it was not yet conclusively decided in the horizon of collective "scorekeeping," in Brandom's articulation, whether her deed was a fundamentally erroneous interpretation of the local public transportation rules of the state of Alabama or whether it was an expression of moral courage against segregation.

The essential question is now: Who decides on the authority of interpretation in this situation, that is, on the "score" of the virtual scoreboard, and therefore hazards certain consequences?[112] Rosa Parks lacked the symbolic investiture of a judge who, enforcing his verdict on the same matter in the legal arena, would have embodied a calculated suspension of the established scoring practices with regard to transportation rules. Rosa Parks was not a comparable institutionalized instantiation of the universal, but rather a singular representative of her opinion (or that of her fellow activists) on the matter. She may have shared this opinion with like-minded civil rights activists and she may have claimed many arguments for civil disobedience for herself. Yet to then transform these arguments into the on-the-ground reality of an act-deed based on her own performance of a decision that challenges others immediately on a practical level and not only theoretically can be interpreted as a form of spontaneous revolution of disposition. Therefore, the point that is of interest to us here is that only the act of breaking through a practice (for example, the act by Rosa Parks) retrospectively reveals the amoral nature of that same practice, while many participants in the practice were unable to see its moral failure *before* the breakthrough because the practice was the established norm of that which one simply does as a citizen based on the general understanding of the established "scorekeeping."[113] The practice was, as argued in late Hegel, the "lived good" of morality.

As mentioned in the introduction, Terry Pinkard points to the meaning of practices in Hegel as conditions for subjects to become autonomous through contextualized acts.[114] Being part of a practice, as Robert Pippin describes as well,[115] means having a certain status in this practice and having been cognitively "formatted" through this status in one's own interiority. Established practices generate the ability to judge them and vice versa. It is not always possible to say to what extent subjects determine the practices that they perform, or whether it is the practices that predetermine the subject's faculty of judgment. If the "spirit of a nation" is for Hegel in his understanding of *Sittlichkeit* the true ground of (our) moral duties (PhR §274), then this leads to the spirit being able to provide the individual with not only the epitome of moral duties but also their application criteria (LHPH 432–32). This means that the established practice *as* practice has always already had, in accordance with Lacan, the "big Other" on its side, that is, the semantic-normative field of that which "one" simply does in a particular way.[116] And not infrequently, this provides the right to do it. If a problem of the categorical imperative for Hegel lies in the fact that its maxims are tied to the premises of established practices (an aspect of unimportance to Kant), then from the point of view of the white passengers on the bus, Rosa Parks cannot claim the categorical imperative to explain her provocative act, because a separation of bus seats, just like a separation of bathrooms for men and women, does not per se have to be a manifestation of racism.[117]

The example of Rosa Parks lays open therefore how far it is simply not possible to find empirically verifiable examples of excessive subjectivity, in addition to the question just discussed of a definition of the ethical as unambiguous and free from distortions when switching the perspective to a specific situation. This is the case because excessive subjectivity describes a structure, or better a structural moment, in certain constellations of acts that cannot always be determined inferentially. This means that when successful individual examples of excessive subjectivity are mentioned, such as that which Rosa Parks unambiguously represents for the contemporary United States, we are always already interpreting Rosa Parks from the perspective of the success of her deed, which in retrospect does not seem excessive at all to us anymore, but rather quite matter of fact—as normative. For future generations, her act-deed has always already been situated on the level of the universal from which we retrospectively interpret it from the horizon of the civil rights movement that has, in the meantime, become socially accepted.

In the aftermath of Nelson Mandela's death and his memorial at Johannesburg on December 10, 2013, Žižek depicts, in an insightful article published in the *Guardian*, how the socially accepted *universal* can provoke even bitterness when it is celebrated one day *by all* (but not recognized as an unacceptable act-deed, which it once was).[118] It was for Žižek the scandal-provoking fake and schizophrenically ill interpreter for the deaf, Thamsanqa Jantjie, who—by pseudotranslating international celebrities from Barack Obama to the UN secretary-general Ban Ki Moon into sign language—laid open the inner meaningless of their talks. What the ceremony left uncommented was exactly the traumatic effect of a particular, not yet universal excessive subjectivity: the fact that the real Mandela was a defender of violence in his political fight of the African National Congress. Dick Cheney, the former US vice president, did not support Mandela's release from prison in 1986 and Margaret Thatcher, who branded the ANC "terrorist," was reluctant to meet him in London.

Now, on December 10, 2013, Mandela, the aggressive and politically incorrect agent provocateur seems to have been displaced by a universal Mandela that everybody apparently could agree on: the Mandela of passive resistance. Žižek describes the ceremony with irony as "a self-congratulatory exercise, and Jangtjie [the schizophrenic pseudotranslator] translated them into what they effectively were: nonsense." Žižek finishes his article with a political diagnosis: "What the world leaders were celebrating was the successful postponement of the true crisis which will explode when poor, black South Africans effectively become a collective political agent. . . . Through his fake translation, Jantjie rendered palpable the fake of the entire ceremony."[119]

Excessive subjectivity points to the structural moment *before* the acceptance into the universal, that is, when the "scorekeeper" really has not yet virtually decided which side she is on, and where the higher score (of what might one day be explicit) might lie. Looking for a perfect example of excessive subjectivity, one would have to hark back to a moment in time when the universal was not yet realized on the level of the particular and when the retrospective appropriation had not yet happened. Since this is impossible, it only refers us to the impossibility of bringing to a close the ethical as the question which the subject has to answer each time anew for himself: At what point in time, where, and how does he opt for his world?

The retrospective appropriation, which, based on premises of reason, has to push aside the tipping point due to premises of reason that cannot consider contingency as worthy of reason, renders each individual example opaque, almost as if it were part of an uncanny twilight zone. To a certain extent, then, the truth-value of the moral judgment of excessive subjectivity remains undecided as long as the subject moves within the boundaries of the prevailing doxa. Frequently, subsequent generations find edification in these individuals. Those generations edify themselves without realizing how the historical distortion of their judgment is conditioned by their place in time through its being anchored in a genealogical metastructure—a time that is at the prevailing level of what Hegel calls "experience." To realize this without restriction would cause irreparable damage to reason in its self-reflective understanding of autonomy. This means that reason here has an embedded interior level of self-protection that has to ignore the relative and contingent course of experience, according to Hegel. This is why an ethics of inferentialism can maintain that Rosa Park's act-deed only made more "explicit" what was already established as normative. What this interpretation misses, however, is the moment of the *breakthrough* that our discussion of excessive subjectivity attempts to describe. The fact that concrete individual examples for the explication of this theory are not to be found in the true sense once again underlines that there are no "excessive subjects" but only "excessive subjectivity."[120] We cannot think excessive subjects as ethically justified ones since, no matter their ethical tradition, they have to appear to us as lacking responsibility. One would have to imagine oneself back to a point in time when the universal had not yet realized itself on the level of the particular, and when the retrospective appropriation is not yet distorting the tipping point as such from which these subjects appeared. Yet this is precisely what seems impossible for reason due its limitation by its own structural temporality.

In the wake of periods of social upheaval, attempts to "work through" history often represent a similar situation marked by a paradoxical entanglement of empirical-variable and seemingly simultaneous transcendental-invariable normativity. The collectively guaranteed virtuality of Brandom's scorekeeping becomes evident, for instance, in the political crises of the twentieth century. If we look at the German Democratic Republic (East Germany) as an example, we see a regime coming to an end finding itself being judged from 1989 onward in a "superstructure" by a neglected and combated scoreboard: that of the Federal Republic of Germany (West Germany). The new legal system, as the victorious one in the genealogy of normativity, disclosed, for example, to individual members of the State Security that their lives were always already valued under the sovereignty of a "Western" scoreboard. The constructive moment of this positing of the victors has to be structurally shut out of the victorious legal system to reassure the system's ability not to destabilize its own agency with too much insight into the historical contingency of normativity.

Contemporary historical conditions, under which we once acted as presumably morally justified, can indeed be rewritten each time anew by historical upheavals such as the one that Rosa Parks initiated. It can reveal us as having failed. The scoreboard in and above the space of reasons then appears personified as a transcendental scorekeeper almost in the mask of the Cartesian *Deus Deceptor* (evil demon) since it can retrospectively declare something as having existed earlier without the accused being able to extricate himself or being able to become an equal in the process. Kant indirectly thematizes this in his *Metaphysics of Morals*, in which he stingingly interprets the revolutionary tribunal's verdict on Louis XVI as suicide of the communal will, the social contract (MM 464n). At the same time, however, Kant has to admit that after a coup of the "common will" by illegal revolt, the new powers are immediately legitimized as the highest authority in the now newly founded common will.

The aporias of human subjectivity are nourished in a certain sense by being at the mercy of an overdetermined, enigmatic realm of that which normativity *has* always already *been* or—coming from the future—*will have been*.[121] This realm then retrospectively posits the act of a Rosa Parks as the cause for the application of commitments and entitlements as one that can now be applied generally to the concrete situations of the local transportation conditions. It is as if some kind of Wittgensteinian "aspect-seeing" or Heideggerian "viewpoint" (*Gesichtspunkt*) had suddenly channeled a steadfast stream of normative judgments into a new riverbed. A decision like Parks's might then be precisely neither unambiguously inferentially deducible nor able to be described via an objective third-person perspective or, with Thomas Nagel, from an "agent-neutral" viewpoint.[122] Suddenly the chain of causation of the established normativity of morals is no longer acceptable because now, after the deed, it is (apparently) racist.

This interpretation is supported by Terry Lovell,[123] who points to the contingent interplay of such actions that cause social irritation and crises within certain social circumstances, based on her reading of Pierre Bourdieu's analysis of the development of social classes against Judith Butler's thesis of a "performative authority of speech." Only a contingent interplay of an individual act-deed within a context that then strengthens this act into a societal crisis retrospectively produces the authority envisaged by Butler. The very subject that embodies authority in the final analysis has to be declared not accountable for her authority. Lovell writes: "In other words, the authority of Rosa Parks' act was retrospective."[124] This is not to preclude that Parks, based on certain arguments, on intuitions of justice, and on certain experiences, would not also have had reasons to interpret the separation of seating areas on the bus as racist. Yet precisely because such a separation is not intrinsically racist, the act is needed, as it pushes Parks's reasons of agency suddenly into a *new* context not necessarily visible beforehand. This means that the subject at this point breaks out of the established practice with her deed and as such "conjures up" and makes visible the context to all. Earlier, many people had not considered it necessary to commit such an act; one might say in order not to cause a scandal and the like. Yet one might also say that because earlier the separation of seating areas as established practice seemed moral "to all" and seemed to be what "one" simply does. With Wittgenstein one could argue: "This is simply how we act" or this is how we accept "separate seating areas." This is simply how we act until, maybe, one day a subject is overcome by an act and no longer acts in this way and then risks introducing a new perspective. Yet, were there then not always reasons for this perspective? *Yes and no.* Yes, because there are, so to speak, always countless reasons to question a political situation, once one has distanced oneself from the "common sense" within the situation; and no, for the practice makes clear as practice that there are empirically verifiable "lived reasons" for keeping it, because otherwise the practice would obviously not be what all are doing: performatively sanctioning the established good by that "which one simply does." The fact that Parks's act-deed was undeniably one of the sparks of a civil rights movement can then be interpreted in such a way that, with Hegel, the spirit of the people had become a mere "shell" as "a shadow of its former self,"[125] or in other words, a "shell, which contains the wrong kind of kernel."[126]

What is needed—and this is the crux of the matter—is a contingent subject that comes out of this spirit of the people and that declares the "shell" to be performatively empty, that is, truly *posits* a new perspective against that of the majority. As long as this does not happen as a true "deed" and, for example, remains only in the imagination of a *beautiful soul*, the "shell" of the spirit of the people is not "hollow" in the strict sense. Or, to put it another way: the shell of the spirit of the people was empty for a few months but could then again resolidify its "wrong kernel" into the "right one" with its old shape, for instance, through reactionary forces. And is this not what we see today in Abd al-Fattah as-Sissi's Egypt of 2017, after the suppression of the Arab spring and his coup d'état against the elected president Mohamed Morsi?

In this sense, then, one can also understand Rosa Parks's act-deed in the context of Badiou's discussion of a performative naming of a truth-'referent' that only comes into existence in an act of naming or of performative declaring. Badiou shows this with the example of the French Revolution in *Being and Event*.[127] In this work, he emphasizes that speaking of the French Revolution takes recourse to a number of events, gestures, acts, and words that took place between 1789 and 1794. Yet the ability to *posit* these multiple facts and circumstances as a unified event depends on the moment from which the revolution, as represented by the revolutionaries, performatively generates and declares itself *as* event. Analogously, Rosa Parks's act-deed is one that is needed, an act that out of certain, seemingly underrepresented facts and circumstances posits certain representative facts (of a racist practice?) in an almost performative way. Only her performative positing, her speech act, *changes* reality by placing it in a new representational frame, which is initially legitimized solely by her act-deed. According to Florian Klinger's theory of judgment and from his discussion of the "temporal particularity" (*Jeweiligkeit*) of the judgment, one could say: Rosa Parks's thought and judgment of temporal particularity lead as if to a new, "kairotic" image of the world in the immediate proximity to now newly grouped facts. Klinger fittingly describes this as a decisionist act in which positing and personalization coincide.[128] Rosa Parks's act-deed is to be understood as a formal-logical principle of an interruption of inferentialist chains. The act-deed then, once it experiences its representation in the legal arena, creates its own cause. Through the act, one could say that Parks retroactively recognized a plurality of moral reasons for her act. Through the act she saw something that other blacks and whites who were part of the same practice were potentially not able to see in the preceding decades, because the act was missing, that is, the moment of decision that only creates the perspective as a condition of moral judgment in a *revolution of disposition*.

Generally speaking, what Hegel defines as "morality" rests on the functioning of a practice defined as *Sittlichkeit*, or, according to Kant, on legality as an expression of the idea of communal will (MM 375–76). In this context, morality (*Sittlichkeit*) is to a significant extent dependent on the *displacement* of the moral for *Sittlichkeit* to exist at all, as Hegel so comprehensibly suggests in his *Philosophy of Right*. This process of displacement is accentuated by processes of collective misperceptions, in the context of Robert Pfaller's analysis in *On the Pleasure Principle in Culture: Illusions Without Owners*.[129] This means that established practices are permanently suggesting to us that they are legal-moral—even if not purely moral. The practice of the legal, for Kant, is the juridical-moral idea of the general will, independent of the shortcomings with which it is concretely applied. The practice of the legal generally tends to produce preemptive obedience in its subjects due to its appellative-ideological basic character with which it *must* force subjects into bondage, in order to continue existing within the bounds of its legality. Subjects are nothing more than sub-jected ones. It is precisely the dependence of the individual on the *illusions of the others* that can—and this is the other side of legality's coin—contribute to everyone believing in the legal practice as the "idea of the general will," from the democratic system of law to the obedience to the *Führer*, although everyone might have misgivings that there is something wrong with the agreement between idea and reality.

Rosa Parks's breakout from the inferential fills the gap between established knowledge and a justified decision. Her act-deed is an event that can fittingly be understood through Heidegger's discussion in his texts on *the Event* where the event is defined as "de-cision" (*Ent-scheidung*), "re-ply/counter" (*Ent-gegnung*), "uniqueness" (*Einzigkeit*), and "solitude" (*Verlorenheit*).[130] Consequently, the freedom of decision provokes as groundless ground an urgency: "*eine Not*."[131]

Rosa Parks retrospectively made visible the gap that she filled with the performativity of her act-deed.[132] Her act performatively *hollowed out* the "shell" of legality. Similarly, one could say in the political arena that the bloody course of the French Revolution announced the historical necessity of transitioning to the empire of Napoleon Bonaparte. A political leader or a political party had to bring an end to the "chaos" of the years 1789–99, so one could assume. One could say that the French Revolution needed a person *such as* Napoleon. However, the fact that this person *turned out to be* Napoleon is pure coincidence. As Žižek points out, this description still has the necessity preceding the coincidence.[133] As we will see in the next chapter on Hegel, however, this process also takes place partially in reverse. Only once Napoleon has seized power or an act-deed such as Rosa Parks's has taken place are the conditions that allowed it to happen retrospectively complete. This means that a temporal-progressive order is always accompanied by a transcendental-regressive movement of appropriating historical events. With regard to Napoleon: Only through the appearance of the real Napoleon are the events read retrospectively with an eye toward his usurpation of power. This implies that things could have turned out differently. It also implies at the same time a shockingly high degree of contingency that, through an individual who got his way, establishes an apparently virtual space of necessity. The necessity appears as a retroactive effect that "legitimizes" a contingent process after the fact through future events in the sense of a causal chain. Necessity is then in this sense a belated effect of a transcendental-aggressive appropriation of meaning.[134] This means that necessity itself is contingent in such a way that the meaning that transforms the contingent into the necessary is precisely not always visible in the sequence of accidental conditions, but rather that these conditions, only after their having been posited, become necessary conditions for that which they have posited.

Excessive subjectivity appears as a formal-logical structural instant where particularity and universality decide to equate form and content, from which point of disposition the subject looks at her environment and allows new judgments to arise. This place is inaccessible to the subject. In this moment, the subject only experiences herself after the act. The act-decision is a positing of premises before judgments, not the result of judgments. This thought is meant to illustrate the basic idea that permeates this analysis, namely, that of excessive subjectivity that cannot be interpreted inferentially and stands against the earlier-mentioned pragmatic Kantianism.

The case of Rosa Parks is here representative for situations in which Brandom's "scorekeeper" will have revealed itself retroactively through a positing provoked by the excessive subject only in its embodiment of a normative authority that, without the subject, could have been understood very differently as justified, for instance, as a political misinterpretation of a given circumstance. Rosa Parks's act occurred at a symbolic tipping point (or evoked it), which, through her provocation, led to the sudden setting in motion of a human rights movement that might have missed out on itself, or might not have been realized, without the contingency of the event in the state of Alabama. Through her act, Rosa Parks brought the culture of the Southern states over to her side, a perspective that was separated from the other side by a parallactic gap and therefore not even able to be perceived as such. Rosa Parks's example stands for an act-deed that forces Brandom's scorekeeper to reset his account. With this, Parks succeeded in breaking through a legality on the level of the particular and thus embodies Kant's understanding of the overdetermined power of the ethical as the universal.

THE IRRESPONSIBLE IMMATURITY FOR WHICH RESPONSIBILITY NEEDS TO BE TAKEN

As Kant makes clear in his theory of the revolution of disposition, as well as in individual comments in his writings on pedagogy, on anthropology, and on the philosophy of history, neither as an individual nor as a collective can man arrive at the point where he says that the reform process of his education has enabled him on day x at time y to act morally. The discussion of conversion and revolution explains the circumstance in which the individual is overcome by the moment of decision, or in which the individual suddenly will have found himself in the moral arena.[135] To pinpoint the moment at which the individual arrives at the point in her moral development where she says that she will now decide on a moral disposition necessitates that the disposition exist a priori for one to be able to opt for it. This idiosyncratic entanglement also appears in Kant's famous essay "What Is Enlightenment?" When he speaks in this text of a "self-incurred minority" (En. 17), it is at first glance not clear how to understand this oxymoron. One way to interpret it would be to see the inability to use one's reason without the direction of another as something self-incurred because, as Kant claims, reason does not make a decision "without direction from another" (En. 17).[136] Yet how should an immature being, albeit one capable of reason, convert to responsibility for which it cannot yet be responsible, due to its very minority or lack of maturity? Kant's famous paradoxical statement makes sense in light of the paradox discussed earlier of a moral act that legitimizes itself retroactively as an expression of the disposition that legitimizes itself too late. From his discussion of disposition and of "deciding" on a moral character, it also becomes clear what Kant means, namely, that minority marks a status that contains a responsibility which always proceeds the subject's awareness of it even if it is only retroactively recognized. For this reason, Kant can claim that the status of minority has always been "self-incurred."

Man becomes man at the point where he is responsible for something for which he erroneously considered himself *not* responsible. Accordingly, one could also say in the reverse that self-imposed immaturity equally implies a maturity that is no fault of one's own. For us the act-deed is of this kind: an agency of maturity without a subject or, better, with the subject coming too late. Maturity is a status that is primarily outside of one's responsibility and for which one must take responsibility nevertheless (retrospectively). Immaturity is a status that is primarily to be taken responsibility for and then, from the perspective of maturity, seems to be the mirage of responsibility. Accordingly, immaturity persists always too long in a human being and maturity always comes to the fore slightly too late. In a sense, Kant urges us to consider that man is also responsible for things for which he only belatedly recognizes his responsibility. Again, then, we encounter here the split of the moral subject that, in an excess of his decisions, as *causa sui* retroactively proves his disposition.

If there were a reasonable being that only lived in the legal arena, then we would not need the paradox of two nonsimultaneities that is tied to Kant's moral philosophy. Yet because Kant ties the moral duty to an absolute that does not legitimize itself through any natural law except in its form, he pays the price: precisely that only from a blind spot in his philosophy can this absolute be conceived in the final analysis. The ethically excessive subject comes into existence out of this noncoincidence between *is* and *ought*. The normativity of disposition needs to be understood as a recursive concept. To that extent, there is very well a transfer of *is* and *ought*, not through analogy, but rather in the sense that *being* and *ought*, the particular and the universal, coincide in the moment of the ethical deed on the level of the particular itself.

HABITUS LIBERTATIS: CHANGE OF DISPOSITION AND GESTURE

In his *Anthropology*, Kant describes the revolution of the disposition as "an explosion that happens *one time* as a result of weariness at the unstable condition of instinct" (Anthro. 392, emphasis added). The revolution of disposition concerns acting as on a noumenal level according the "mode of thinking." In contrast, for the "mode of sensing," the empirical character, a "gradual reform" is necessary. Is a revolution of disposition conceivable for Kant only once?[137] This would mean that once the revolution has occurred, all other moral acts would only have a "habitual" character. Yet it is exactly such an understanding of habitual moral maxims that Kant rejects in the philosophy of Christian Wolff.

Kant provides what seems to be a solution to the tension between the noumenal revolution of the mode of thinking and empirical reform on the level of the "mode of sensing" in his theory of *habitus*: "An *aptitude* (*habitus*) is a facility in acting and a subjective perfection of *choice.*—But not every such *facility* is a *free* aptitude (*habitus libertatis*); for if it is a *habit* (*assuetudo*), that is, an uniformity in action that has become a *necessity* through frequent repetition, it is not one that proceeds from freedom, and therefore not a moral aptitude. Hence virtue cannot be *defined* as an aptitude to perform free actions in conformity with law unless there is added 'to determine oneself to act through the thought of the law'" (MM 535).

Here, as in other passages, Kant claims that moral-reformatory motivation and revolution of the disposition can approach each other where "the way to acquire it is to enhance the moral *incentive* (the thought of the law), both by contemplating the dignity of the pure rational law in us (*contemplatione*) and by *practicing* virtue (*exercitio*)" (MM 527). He writes that gestures that remain purely external can influence man's disposition. And in his *Anthropology* we read: "On the whole, the more civilized human beings are, the more they are actors. They adopt the illusion of affection, of respect for others, of modesty, and of unselfishness without deceiving anyone at all, because it is understood by everyone that nothing is sincerely meant by this. And it is also very good that this happens in the world. For when human beings play these roles, eventually the virtues, whose illusion they have merely affected for a considerable length of time, *will gradually really be aroused and merge into the disposition*" (Anthro. 263, emphasis added). What Kant suggests here anticipates a theme in behavioral therapy: behavior has an effect on attitude instead of vice versa. Through his physical behavior, man strengthens his inner disposition, which he then defines as born from freedom and autonomy. (This would be a brief definition of "ideology." More on this in chapter 4.)

In order to uphold this last thought, however, Kant must not declare the influence of ritual pseudomorality as a condition. As a factor of influence, ritualization cannot mean causality. For, as we know, for Kant a deed is only warranted by its intention, not by its effect.[138]

Yet how can Kant repeatedly emphasize the noncoincidence of morality and *habitus* and at the same time pretend that there nevertheless exists a magical sphere of influence? Or does Kant, in the vein of a slew of moralists such as Montaigne, Bacon, Descartes, and Gracián, who focus on habitual performances in moral actions, signal here an ethics of virtue whose particular feature is that man is always already pragmatically "interwoven" with the forms of life of the external world? This is not so, as he who does not yet possess the correct moral disposition cannot act morally according to Kant, even if he commits seemingly good deeds. Yet the question arises: How should behavior truly influence moral attitude within a fraud-like *habit* of a pure "as if" that lacks inner conviction? For in his "Doctrine of Virtue," Kant writes that virtue cannot be a habit but "results from considered, firm, and continually purified principles" (MM 516), that is, moral maxims. Habit stands in direct contradiction to inner freedom (MM 535, 537; LP 454; Anthro. 261).

Acting according to moral maxims cannot become a habit either, because the tendencies to apply them oppose this notion.[139] Kant can only ascribe a life according to habitual maxims of established socially warranted morals, as Wolff understands it, to the arena of a virtue of legality (*virtus phaenomenon*) (Rel. 65).[140] He contrasts this with "actions from *duty*" that are "(because of their morality) . . . called *virtus noumenon*" (Rel. 65).

Nevertheless, acting on a purely symbolic-external level presumably trains one's interiority. Therefore, Kant has to integrate another split into his comments on *habitus* in order to guarantee the cohesion of his theory. The term *habitus libertatis* is therefore only a seemingly coherent concept, for what kind of habit is it that has to deny itself in order to become habit through permanently imagining a law?[141] Only with this solution, which cannot be called anything but paradoxical, does Kant succeed in combining his ethics with a life shaped by habit.[142]

Let us summarize what we have said so far: Man can overcome himself, that is, his habitual and pragmatic limits. Disposition is not something one chooses like a good among other goods in certain hypothetical ends-and-means relations. Choosing the disposition, for Kant, is the moment of a sudden conversion. It is the moment that Heidegger repeatedly describes as a moment of fear: it is the choice of existence before the possibility of a perspective that can only be experienced retrospectively.[143] This is why Kant, in his reply to Reinhold, insists, for the sake of maintaining the topic of fear-inducing distress to existence, that the only freedom which the subject has is a forced choice that has *always already been made*.[144] Here lies the freedom of a rational being who (1) knows *not* to possess the freedom of God—meaning a holy will—to be not identical with himself during the "revolution of a mode of thinking" in a moral act, but who (2) chooses freedom *despite* his noncoincidence with himself, "as if" freedom were, in the final analysis, guaranteed by him as through an almost godlike being in spite of all empirical counterevidence.[145] The only freedom that Kant's subject possesses is consequently that of the forced choice of her nonidentity with herself as a rational *and* sensory being, and of having to act morally despite this split *as if she were not split*.

The forced choice as a split subject structurally corresponds to Kant's discussion of the *focus imaginarius* from his first *Critique*. It marks a logically necessary illusion that the subject in the moral act has of herself as if from an external position in the distorted image of a godlike absoluteness. Kant interprets this absoluteness as one that is inscribed into man's understanding of autonomy. There exists no empirically guaranteed proof of this autonomy, as Kant emphasizes repeatedly. While this view into nature shows indications for moral acts that suggest freedom and allow for a hermeneutic (subjective) reading of progress in history, much more than that, it is the case here that nature bears witness to a deterministic chain of cause and effect.[146]

This means that the subject as split is allowed to "deceive" himself so that he has through this and through the resulting "revolution of disposition" a retroactive proof for a moral act in the world, which in turn transforms his original illusion into an indication of moral action. Kant articulates an *ought* condemned to a *must* in the sense of "Here I stand, I can do no other." Yet the authority that stands there, to exaggerate slightly, is not truly responsible for standing there, exactly because of a disposition that remains hidden in the "inexplicable." The subject might then even experience himself as schizophrenic insofar as he sees himself within a *focus imaginarius* from an outside perspective of his noumenal being.

Only due to the affirmation of this schizophrenia does Kant believe himself able to defend the morally absolute in a world permeated with natural causalities against any eudemonistic, pragmatic, or communitaristic concept of life. (As we will see, this comes close to Lacan's own ethics of psychoanalysis.) Kant even claims that man, in the forced choice that he will have made, always will have *had* to choose this split resulting in the unbearable consequence, that is, that he chooses the absolute in each moral plight for the sake of the eternity of the realm of ends—and not for the sake of a concrete situation in daily life. The result is an ethical act that, with its partially paradoxical remaining plea for the absoluteness of the ethical, goes beyond contemporary ethics such as Brandom's and McDowell's neopragmatic or Habermas's and Apel's discourse-theoretical forms of ethics.

The ethical person authenticates the recognition that she is *not* God and yet acts as if the realm of ends depends on her, as from a singular-universal authority that God has, as his *only* representative on earth.[147] If one wanted to phrase the paradox of such autonomy *in heteronomy* in a pithy statement, one could say: "Act as if everything depended on you, yet in the knowledge that in reality everything depends on God [as a virtual idea]." The phrasing "as if" reflects Kant's teleological power of judgment. One could then interpret the sentence that follows a famous statement by Ignatius of Loyola in such a way that man has to accept his being split, as he has no holy will, and nevertheless out of this noncoincidence with himself should pretend "as if"—through his acts alone—the realm of ends would be empirically realized. Yet he may only understand this belief as motivational virtuality of an absolute, which enables him to the revolution of disposition. He cannot consider it as objectively proven. At the same time, he *may not only* view it as virtual. For he who wanted to even just slightly relativize the goal of holiness, for example, in the sense that this goal is only virtual, "degrade[s] the moral law from its *holiness* by making it out to be *lenient* (indulgent) and thus conformed to our convenience" (CPrR 238).

If the individual acted morally out of his state of being split in the hiatus between being and ought, which he leaped across with the motivational virtuality of his freedom, then he may take this leap retrospectively as an indication of moral acts in the world, but as *no more than an indication*. He may not boast that the act he performed was truly free. In this sense, the moral law of the *Critique of Practical Reason* does not present a godlike "view from nowhere" from which the freedom of man can be measured.

KANT'S "DOCTRINE OF VIRTUE"

Frequently, Kant's second part of the *The Metaphysics of Morals*, his "Doctrine of Virtue," with its focus on the quest for "active perfect[ion]" (MM 545) of oneself and the quest for the "happiness of others" (MM 517) is treated as the theoretical area of Kant's ethics that, in contrast to the *Groundwork* or the *Critique of Practical Reason*, succeeds in defining the ethical orientation of self-determination under the conditions of human nature as one that accounts considerably more for the public arena, that is, the arena of "external freedom." As Andrea Esser writes, Kant's "Doctrine of Virtue" addresses "the general structure of the practical law . . . considered under the concrete conditions of human existence: . . . its physical existence in time and space, the limitations of its abilities, and the fact that man's purposes are not only determined by his thoughts but also by his fundamental needs. The initially formal general structure [of Kant's early ethics] thus obtains a specific configuration in special principles of realization, the so-called 'virtues.' "[148]

Like several other interpretations of Kant in the last decades (by Wood, Korsgaard, Nussbaum, O'Neill, and Sherman),[149] Esser's analysis has as its goal to indirectly absorb Kant's early ethics into his "Doctrine of Virtue," or to let it be absorbed in such a way that its diffusion in the late Kant was already planted from the beginning. For Esser then, maxims become "structures realized in our acts"[150] that in their descriptions allow for deciphering them in their empirical moments and for freeing them from their individual moral isolation. The intelligible world of the absolute moral proves in this context to be a construct of mutual commitments by rational beings. Yet Kant had already received a fundamental critique of his *Groundwork* from Pistorius, which did not keep him from writing his *Critique of Practical Reason* shortly thereafter, and not his "Doctrine of Virtue" or his "Doctrine of Right." One can read this as an indication that the early critical Kant was truly aware of the radicality of his position, and very consciously wanted to leave an (insurmountable?) tension between the spheres of right, virtue, and the moral, for the sake of the impossibility of integrating *the ethical* into ethics.[151]

Esser points out that the repeated critique of Kant's ethics with regard to his discussion of an "ought" that implies a "can" (that is, a possibility) ignores the difference between the determination of the moral *will* and the concrete act. The determination of the will can very well be self-determined while the concrete act has to be interpreted as determined through circumstances and possibilities of realization. The purity of the determination of will is maintained by externalizing the act in the area of "external freedom"[152] as its pragmatic corrective. What remains problematic in the differentiation between will and act that Kant introduced in the "Doctrine of Virtue" is, however, that the will would have to determine itself twice: once as moral will and once as an acting moral will.[153] Yet, what remains of the moral will when it is always pragmatically relativized by the pragmatically acting will anyway?

If the will then knows how one should act properly, it can in turn subordinate the *ought* under pragmatic viewpoints. Even if Esser emphasizes that "at any time" newly arising circumstances can compromise a situation that needs to be evaluated in terms of its ethics, this does not necessarily mean that the determination of the will would be different from the determination of the act. It means that the ethical agent in the new circumstances has, as always, to take account of them in finding the ethical motivation for her deed. If a drowning person is so far out in the ocean that a rescue is no longer possible, then the ethical will of the subject does not first have to consider whether the drowning man can be helped or not. The rules of prudence forbid this in any case. The truly interesting motif of Kant's early ethics that is to be found in a paradoxically excessive self-determination is now dissolved. Therefore, Esser necessarily has to define the moral will as one that is always and already codetermining the ethical problem for each case in the context of the possibility of realizing it within the frame of established reasons. Esser attempts to take this problem into account in the course of her book when she does indeed refer to Kant's categorical imperative (GrMM 73), underlining that a moral will without a deed remains "an empty wish." Yet when she includes acts in contexts that are each expanded by modern sciences (sociology and the like), which according to the will are precisely not "motivational grounds" for the moral law, it is unclear how Esser can still define an inherent unity of will and act without declaring Kant to be Hegel avant la lettre. Similarly, Esser unfortunately does not address Kant's "Doctrine of Right."[154] In this context, it is the question of the exact definition of morality and legality, of interior and exterior motivations for the moral will, in Kant that in particular arises again. It is this question in which it becomes evident that for the love of maintaining his theory of the ethical (and not his theory of ethics) Kant precisely can*not* be allowed to succeed in harmonizing the two spheres, that of the public law and that of morals. Generally, Esser's position makes it very clear how Kant's ethics in the *Groundwork* is to be "rescued" with the help of his "Doctrine of Virtue," whereby in general the real tension—presumably consciously emphasized by Kant—between his theorem of the revolution of disposition and his later "Doctrine of Virtue" is dissolved. Yet the theory of the revolution of disposition unfortunately plays barely any role in Esser's analysis.

ENDS-DRIVEN DUTIES OF VIRTUE

Kant views his "Doctrine of Virtue" as the expansion of the formal principle of ethics and extends the categorical imperative as follows: "Act in accordance with a maxim of *ends* that it can be a universal law for everyone to have" (MM 525). Kant stresses here how far the maxim is to correspond to ends that in themselves have to be able to be universalized. The noncontradictory universality of the formalistic categorical imperative is here expanded into an area where the moral principle, besides the *purity* of its reason, can now also find its motivation, at least partially, when taking into account the welfare of other subjects and find the relationship to them. The end is here in each case an intersubjectively shared one. Such a reference to the "maxim of *ends*" was not allowed by the *Critique of Practical Reason.* And in the ends formulation of the categorical imperative in the *Groundwork* (GrMM 87) the end was phrased in a universal-formal manner in the intelligible "kingdom of ends" (GrMM 87), that is, a realm in which *not concrete* empirical human beings live and therefore exist without any concrete *content-related* determination of an end too. The imperative of the moral will can only be attained here by excluding a purposive relationship of a real and existing interhuman area of shared morals.[155] Kant then in part explicitly excludes the categorical imperative from the duties of virtue. "Not all ethical duties are . . . duties of virtue" (MM 515). The odd *ends*-driven concept of the "Doctrine of Virtue" that initially contradicts the (pure/formal) ethics of duty and that does not explicitly have to correspond to the categorical imperative comes into being because Kant mentions a plurality of duties of virtue that in their plurality, as he says, do not all have to correspond to a "duty" precept. In this context, Kant speaks of "broad duties" where he now suddenly also declares the attentiveness to morals as a "broad duty." In the *Groundwork*, the concept of duty did not differentiate between "broad" and "narrow." Kant does in fact introduce new problems through this differentiation. While he introduces the term *broad duty* in his late ethics in order to underline to what extent several duties of virtue can exist simultaneously (for example, parental love, love of one's neighbor), the question arises which duty corresponds more closely to which maxim of acting. However, the question as to the criteria according to which the interpretation of various duties must be held remains unanswered, for the categorical imperative continues to be valid and does not simply become dependent on pragmatic judgments in the description of problematic situations.[156]

Kant then writes, "the *concept of duty* will lead to ends and will have to establish *maxims* with respect to ends we *ought* to set ourselves, grounding them in accordance with moral principles" (MM 515). Yet in the final analysis, Kant here presupposes a recognition of duty as the condition for the possibility of retroactively applying it to an interhuman interpretation of the positing of means. The question then remains, however: From whence are the determinations of the concrete ends to come? If from experience, ethics would no longer be pure. As mentioned, the ends formula of the categorical imperative of the *Groundwork*—"*So act that you use humanity, whether in your own person or in the person of any other, always at the same time as an end, never merely as a means*" (GrMM 80)—is no solution here because it is itself finally only a formal determination, insofar as the means addressed here are always that which is to realize itself against the background of the kingdom of ends. This realm of ends, however, is the hollow form of the universal where the concrete content of an end is precisely *not* to be determined. Therefore, Kant writes in his "Doctrine of Virtue": "But pure reason can prescribe no ends *a priori* without setting them forth as also duties, and such duties are then called duties of virtue" (MM 526).

The determination of the universal ends of virtue therefore itself remains in turn abstract: "*one's own perfection* and *the happiness of others*" (MM 517). The reference to the "happiness of others" remains an enigmatic signifier. After all, there are various conceptions of happiness and a "good life." In our analysis on Lacan, we will furthermore see that the individual subject can be sure of neither his own desire nor his own happiness because this is always located precisely eccentrically, in the hallucinatory desire of another.

Only a content-related determination of these ends could free the "Doctrine of Virtue" from its formalism. There is, as Michael Städler describes so aptly, room to maneuver, "with regard to the manner and scope of performing the duties of virtue."[157] Yet this only moves the problem around. For in order to interpret partially competing duties of virtue, as the general discussion of "broad duties" suggests, what is needed is a criterion for distinction, itself anchored in pure duty, a criterion that for its part cannot only be covered through empiricism, because otherwise the purity of the ethical claim is lost. With this, the "Doctrine of Virtue" moves the formalism toward a less-formalistic formulation (for example, one's own perfection, the happiness of others), which upon close inspection remains itself undefined. Self-cultivation is, to the largest degree possible, a determination, yet because Kant himself says, "No rational principle prescribes specifically *how* far one should go in cultivating one's capacities (in enlarging or correcting one's capacity for understanding, i.e., in acquiring knowledge or skill)" (MM 523), the concretization necessarily does *not* take place. In a polemic sense, one could say that even a Jean Marat or a Mao Zedong saw himself duty-bound to achieve his own perfection and the happiness of others; and as we know a majority of political discourses concerns itself with the content-related definition of these enigmatic categories.

A further regress results when Kant conceives of aesthetic and "*subjective* conditions of receptiveness to the concept of duty" in his "Doctrine of Virtue," about which he claims that they could not be "objective conditions of morality" (MM 528). These aesthetic conditions are "*moral feeling, conscience, love* of one's neighbor, and *respect* for oneself

(*self-esteem*)" (MM 528).[158] Yet Kant sees the reason for their validity in moral consciousness. If the consciousness of law is the condition for the moral feeling, conscience, and the like, yet the consciousness of law, for its part, is in turn the condition for the receptivity of the consciousness of law, then we enter into an unending circle. Similarly, it remains unclear how the mentioned "subjective conditions" are to be understood as criteria, since they assure moments orientated toward inclination.

In one aspect, however, Kant remains true to his theorem of the revolution of the disposition even in his "Doctrine of Virtue." For even though Kant emphasizes *exercises* of virtue, for example, in the methodology of his "Doctrine of Virtue" (MM 591–92), he sticks with the idea that the moral decision has to continue to be understood in the sense of a nondeducible decision. The true ethical power of decision-making is excessive here as well.

3

HEGEL

The Split Ethical Life and the Subject

The crisis consists precisely in the fact that the old is dying and the new cannot be born; in this interregnum a great variety of morbid symptoms appear.

—A. GRAMSCI

Hegel's philosophy has been criticized, especially in the philosophical discourse of the twentieth century, for incapacitating individual subjectivity. In particular, the later *Philosophy of Right* has been read as a self-reflective ontotheological metatheory of normativity that in the name of a metaphysical monism leads ultimately to a totalitarian state. This interpretation of Hegel as a foster father of totalitarianism, going back to Karl Popper among others, can in fact already be found growing in the nineteenth century with Schelling and Kierkegaard. The late twentieth century, however, has successfully established a new and more complex understanding of Hegel with the analyses of Charles Taylor, Terry Pinkard, Robert B. Pippin, Allen Wood, und John McDowell[1] in the Anglo-Saxon tradition and those of Dieter Henrich, Ludwig Siep, Herbert Schnädelbach, Vittorio Hösle, Jürgen Habermas, Axel Honneth, Christoph Menke,[2] and others in the German tradition. Yet even these divergent interpretations of Hegel preserve a fundamental dichotomy: Repeatedly, these interpretations appreciate Hegel as a theorist of the social and of dialectical structures of recognition, but just as commonly, he is suspected also of having developed no more than an insufficient reconciliation between the individual's right to freedom and an understanding of state and society. Habermas represents this school of thought on Hegel. In his early book *Knowledge and Human Interests* he acknowledges Hegel's achievement of transforming epistemology into social theory; at the same time, though, he critiques Hegel for not providing the crucial step from the analysis of objective knowledge to an analysis of the communicative and ethical interactions of language-based discourse between free responsible agents.[3]

The tension mentioned here is indeed obvious in Hegel's work. For if Hegel's *Philosophy of Right* emphasizes that the ethical substance, understood as an intersubjectively shared, normative life-world of a given time period and a given culture, is nothing but a "mere abstraction"[4]—that is, without the individual—and if the ethical life needs the accidental properties of "vain form[s] of subjectivity,"[5] then we could understand Hegel's philosophy as one that brings moral conscience together with ethical life. If, however, we analyze how an individuality is to be understood, when institutions express this individuality, as Hegel also writes, as the "substantiality of the individual" and "the general essence of the individual,"[6] then we have to wonder: What remains of this individuality? Even Siep's reference to the theory-immanent condition of the possibility of freedom in Hegel's own understanding of the ethical life (presented in response to Ernst Tugendhat's critique of Hegel) does not solve the problem entirely.[7] For if Hegel considers only an ethical life as a universality (*Allgemeinheit*), in which all individual wills freely and self-determinedly desire and recognize this ethical life, and therefore the freedom of individuals *is* the universality of the ethically institutionalized (freedom), then one wonders if this idea can be anything more than a utopian fantasy. (It sounds identical to the transformation of Kant's "kingdom of ends" into the empirical world as Marx and Engels at times conceptualized it in their proclamation of a communist state.)

Furthermore, these conflicts surrounding Hegel's legacy also culminate in the context of the definition of "conscience" as deployed in the *Philosophy of Right* (§§129–40). If, for example, as one interpreter of Hegel states, "the individual may not insist too unilaterally on its inner court of law in order to play it against the customs and laws of the commonwealth,"[8] and the conscience is only a good one when it has made a habit out of the ethical disposition, then the question remains unanswered: Which perspective determines whether the individual is insisting too one-sidedly on her "inner court of law" or whether it is the "ethical habit" of the persons living in a body politic that does so? Is the conscience more naturally convicted of delusion due to *Sittlichkeit's* prerogative to define the ratio behind established facts and values? This seems to be Siep's claim when he writes, in reference to Hegel's chapters "Reason" and "Spirit" in the *Phenomenology*, that within the subject matter of the "conscience" negotiated there, "he who acts based on his conscience must accept that his decisions *need to be recognizable* as interpretations of generally-accepted laws, values, and institutions. This acceptance requires, first of all, a sufficient understanding of the internal logic and the history of a moral culture."[9] The conscience must admit to what degree "it can err in its subjective certainty."[10]

But what if conscience does not err? Or, to put the question more precisely: From where originates the criteria to judge whether the conscience has strayed into utopian fantasies or whether it is not rather the ethical life, as the totality of collectively internalized social norms, that errs due to solidified delusions? Is it the ethical life that is deciding here *by definition* according to which premises the particular conscience of the individual is interpreted as either good or bad/paranoid?

Here, Hegel's analysis of the conscience, which we will take up later in his interpretation of Socrates, is valuable for our interpretation of a theory of excessive subjectivity, as Hegel's theory of conscience positions itself in opposition to both ethical traditions: the ethics of the moral judgment in the Kantian tradition and a consensus-oriented universalism of mutual recognition.[11] While traditional ethics suggests that the individual is pulled into a space of reasons essentially determined by a collectively warranted giving of and asking for reasons, Hegel focuses on individual examples which indicate that those who represent the space of giving of and asking for reasons can also be "called to order" by the excessive subject, which is positioned beyond this space. How else could the conscience at all possess the certainty of being "sacrosanct" (PR §137)—an idea that continued to fascinate Hegel in spite of all criticism—given that the province of the ethical life per se would be at all times and places already the "sacrosanct" as it contains the criteria that have always already determined the error of each conscience? Is the majority of a body politic less prone to delusion because those forming this majority ascribe rationality to one another through the power of the established "scorekeeping" (in Brandom's sense of the term) and its underlying premises? The question is whether Hegel sees it this way.

Siep seems to suggest so in his interpretation of Hegel. Therefore, he can only assign a role to the conscience that is subordinate to the role of the ethical life. The inverse, that is, that the province of the ethical life could be subordinate to the conscience, seems to embody for him the justified and not to be underestimated danger of a lawless positing.

We, on the other hand, wish to show that Siep, here representing widely prevalent interpretations of Hegel as a theorist of paradoxless and undistorted structures of recognition, neglects a tension deliberately provoked by Hegel. The questions that emerge in the conflict between established norms legitimated in practices and particular convictions bordering illegality have gained political meaning in recent years. Authors like Ernesto Laclau, Chantal Mouffe, Alain Badiou, and Slavoj Žižek but also Robert Brandom (in some parts of his work) point, from within very different theoretical frameworks, to the fact that the inferentialist space of established normativity is not safe from being caught in a fundamental error.[12] Given the experiences of the twentieth century, this theory is not hard to comprehend. Yet if this is indeed the case, then conscience as a particular objection to ethical life might free the latter from its error.

Siep admits that the role of a "divergent conscience" is difficult to grasp within the registers of the *Philosophy of Right*. He mentions instances in which the "divergent conscience" is nevertheless honored by Hegel: in the right of the sovereign to pardon, in the passionate undertaking of social roles instead of blind obedience, in the revolutionary (who, from the world-historical perspective, affects the next step of constitutional development), in the duty of inner emigration.[13] Yet Siep's interpretation, no matter how closely related it seems to ours, differs from our position in one aspect. For he conceives of the revolutionary only in the context of a future stage in the normative development of world-spirit, as if this stage was already a potentiality *before* its occurrence. Hegel defines "world-spirit" as the genealogy of truth and determination in what he calls the *Begriff*, "the *concept*." It is through self-reflexive moments within the process of the world-spirit's coming-into-being that this entity-in-process defines itself toward its "ground." The *Begriff*, understood as the process of its retrospective self-legitimization, articulates its infinite continuum and in doing so generates a unity of necessity, contingency, and reality. For Hegel, though, world-spirit is in essence only subsequently manifested as that which it was prior to its antecedent realization. In this sense world-spirit is not a ghost-like noumenality floating somewhere above empirical reality but a second-order narrative by which human beings reconstruct through historically transmitted memes and justified reasons their historical experiences according to teleological sequels. Siep does not ask how it is possible to conceive of the revolutionary actor or from which structure of retrospective verification it emerges. Crucial questions arising from Hegel's genealogy of self-consciousness as one that progresses through fractures, contingencies, noncoincidences, revolutions, and missed chances are too seldom analyzed—or not analyzed at all. For this reason, Siep's conclusion is unsatisfactory when he writes that Hegel had allegedly viewed the tension "in the modern European state as essentially overcome."[14] Was Hegel really so naïve?

Similarly, Juliane Rebentisch sees Hegel primarily as the theorist of a totalitarian state who hazards the marginalization of the individual: "Here, subjective freedom seems to be allowed in ethical life only to the extent to which ethical life identifies with the status quo."[15] Rebentisch offers a counter interpretation of an ultimately discourse-ethical intersubjectivity, which for her is best articulated by Romantic irony as an expression of self-reflexive freedom. She claims that Hegel missed this aspect of Romantic irony in his critique of Romanticism. Subsequently, Rebentisch reproaches Hegel for displacing subjective freedom from the ethical life.

In defense of Hegel, one could mention that Hegel's understanding of the universal (objectivity, ethical life, state) leads to a dialectical integration of the particular into the universal in such a way that the universal particularizes itself. However, when looking at history, it remains unclear what kind of state this is supposed to be, or even where the glimpses of such a state could be found, that is, a state that particularizes itself in particularities, as it were, while simultaneously embodying the universal without antagonism. As political science, political philosophy, and Luhmann's general system theory show, the political order always constitutes itself in the empirical world through delimitation, suppression, and exclusion, both internally within its own positing (obedience to the law as obedience to what "is posited": that is utmost civic duty) and externally in relation to other communities from which it needs to differentiate itself. A universal that designs itself as an entity only insofar as it is absolutely self-particularizing refers at most to a regulative ideal.[16]

The theory of excessive subjectivity therefore seems incompatible with both the theoretical framework of primarily a priori oriented ethical traditions (Habermas, Rawls, and in part McDowell) and the primarily a posteriori oriented ethical models (Siep, Honneth, Pippin).[17] These traditions assume subjectivity's freedom to be dependent, in one way or another, on the social realm. Subjectivity here means, more or less, responsibility in an inferentialist network of direct or indirect standards of justification. Whether these standards exist in the Kantian sense a priori or emanate a posteriori from social processes is secondary in an analysis of excessive subjectivity, since normativity here is thought of as something stemming from a solipsistic insistence, with the effect that it will have retrospectively legitimized itself as lawful. The analysis of exactly this issue can be resolved neither in the absurd image of Hegel as a thinker of totality (or totalitarianism) nor in the modern image of Hegel as a *theorist of the social*, originating in particular in the context of liberal democratic, Western societies.

We wish to highlight a way out of this tension within the Hegelian practical philosophy by drawing on Hegel's recurring references to the political fates of Socrates and Antigone. The goal is to make clear how Hegel rephrases the theorem of individual morality contained in the Kantian revolution of disposition (*Gesinnungsrevolution*) as a theory of revolution in the realm of politics. To this end I will draw on Ido Geiger's brilliant interpretation.[18] This will illustrate how Hegel employs the references to Antigone in the *Phenomenology*, both at the end of the chapter "Reason" and at the beginning of the chapter "Spirit," in order to understand Oedipus's daughter as stepping out of the world of heroes and becoming a political agent whose deed causes the spirit of Greek ethical life to disintegrate. Antigone acts to a certain degree on behalf of her unreflected desire for a different (political) reality—that is, she acts unconsciously for a polis that is yet to come.

The aspect of unconsciousness is partially characteristic of the ethical act in the political realm, and it is unmistakable that this is where its persistent modernity lies to this day, irritating political as well as ethical philosophies.[19] Antigone embodies a relentless and an almost pathological will for duty (her duty), which she can neither relativize inferentialistically by negotiating with the polis nor bring into a relationship of exchange of different negotiating interests. Her challenging of certain norms of the polis, as well as the insistence of her political desire, is represented in deontological speech acts that go beyond established constraints of the "daylight of consciousness" (PhS §473).

Instead of engaging further with the repetitive definitions of conscience, morality, and ethical life in the Hegel literature, we shall focus our attention on those places where Hegel quite explicitly presents "vain form[s] of subjectivity," [20] as this leads us, after Antigone, also to Hegel's interpretation of Socrates. Hegel uses Socrates's "tragedy" to exemplify the intrusion of a supernumerary normativity into the space of the "healthy understanding" of common sense (LHPh 379) in Greek culture. It is especially Socrates's "conscience" that will be legitimized as an always-already having-been-lawful dimension of subsequent normativity.[21] As mentioned at the outset, we hold that Hegel seizes upon the individual moral theorem of Kant's concept of disposition to develop his theory of the "revolution of disposition" for the space of politics and he does so in order to theoretically penetrate the societal-structural split of ethical life. In the context of his practical philosophy he shows in several of his writings how the symbolic orders, which over the course of centuries follow upon one another as sociocultural manifestations of human history, are forced into a new shape at key points by rebellious political agents.

These subjects draw their strength from a partly delusional and partly holy certainty that will belatedly derive its legitimacy from the future. To discover this Kantian trace in Hegel's own theory of excessive subjectivity, it will be necessary to bring Hegel's complex relationship with Kant more precisely into the focus of our inquiry.

HEGEL vs. KANT?

As we have seen in the previous chapter, in a twist that can only be understood as paradoxical, Kant places the source of the law of the moral will within its own form, so that form and content are indistinguishably intertwined. In contrast, Hegel will object that the purely formalistic grounds for motivation, as Kant conceives them, ultimately leave the moral law and its motivation void and powerless. In this sense, he is indirectly repeating a criticism that Aristotle offered against Plato in his *Nicomachean Ethics.* Aristotle criticized the "chorismos," that is, the gap that separated the Platonic idea of the Good from the goodness of concrete objects, tools, and practices in the empirical world.[22] The priority of true being, the "ousia," the essence, is for Aristotle to be seen as inherent in concrete things, actions, and performances. Analogously, for Hegel, the universal is to be read from the factual strivings of life forms through history. Inside them lives a source of motivation for laws as *laws-having-been-set*, guaranteed by the facticity of their validity in communal practices. What represents the universal in the individual is always already established as "*universal determinations of thought*," and he mentions "i.e. the form of *laws* and *principles*" (PR §137). Specifically, this means that practical reasons are in a strict sense inseparable from morality given their embedding within an order of the objectively good in established life forms. Reasons stem from the practices of established norms and institutions. Norms are not exclusively externally imposed structures of order but also the internalized conditions of human beings for sharing a communal space of normativity.[23] Oddly enough, Kant had recognized in a different context that the question "What is truth?" could not be answered by logic without ridiculing logic or the logician itself.[24] However, as Hegel's argument continues, Kant gives a similarly reductionist answer with his theory of free will, which misses the topic of practical philosophy because it "abstracts completely from all material [aspects] of the will" (NL 123–24).[25] Just as Aristotle denotes the good as that for the sake of which everything is done in good and concrete actions,[26] so too Hegel interprets the ever-established good as something that can't be separated from the effective strivings embodied in practices. If it is separated and distilled as something confronting this pursuit, then such a separation ignores how morality has always been living in "*universal determinations of thought*" (*allgemeinen, gedachten Bestimmungen*) (PR §137). In the breadth of his metaphysics, Hegel thus suggests that the recognition of the gap between *being* and *moral obligation* (as well as the recognition of the gap between the "thing-in-itself" and the phenomenon) is already part of that which the absolute is itself capable of overcoming and reintegrating as an inner harmony—though with antagonistic proportions.

One could say then that, for Hegel, Kant resembles the "Unhappy Consciousness" (PhS §206) mentioned in the *Phenomenology*, a consciousness that is still partially blind to the dialectical movement of Spirit. Why? Because Kant does not recognize that the presupposed separation from the absolute (that is, from the highest good) has its cause in the absolute being mistakenly thought of as *independent* from the empirical (the lived legality). For Hegel it is not; for him the absolute is, so to speak, the historically conditioned *ex*timity of an entanglement of the categorical form of moral thought (ethics, cast into laws) and the material content (the established practices), which is always already conditioning the same form of thought as practical forms of life.[27] Legality is saturated and imbued with morality. The absolute (that is, theoretically the "thing-in-itself" and practically the "highest good"), from which the "unhappy consciousness" believes itself to be isolated, cannot be absolute for Hegel, because the absolute is within Hegel's speculations dependent on the "unhappy consciousness" itself. For Hegel, a look at history shows how being (nature) and morality (the will) have brought each other into new complementary structures throughout the centuries. Consequently, the dualism supposedly stressed by Kant between an "I shall" and nature (that is, that which simply *is*) is not an absolute dualism that can remain the same across all epochs. Subject and object historically put each other categorically into new inferential relations. These relate not only to theoretical questions concerning the cognition of the external world (empirical research), but also to questions concerning normative behavior (ethics/the ethical life). For Hegel, this history of thought and action is a process (guided by subjects) of ethical lives constantly reestablishing themselves autocreatively and prestructuring what Kant defines a priori as the law of the pure will. Thinking/logos is not an a priori medium, but sustained by, with, and through itself due to its teleological history. The state especially is the political realm of a felt rationality, imbued with inclinations. In this sense, Hegel combines insights of the early Enlightenment period (Rousseau), the early Romantic period (F. Schlegel, Novalis), and the late Romantic ideal (H. v. Kleist). These periods of reason also understood the state not as a machine, but as the organic and emotional unity of a common will.[28]

THE DEED AS A BREAKING OUT OF UNDEFINED INTERIORITY

Hegel adopts the Kantian motif of self-legislation without following Kant's understanding of an absolute purity of the will. In his understanding of a world of shared life forms always predetermined by ethics, tracing back to Aristotle, Hegel considers this purity to be untenable. The purity of the will nevertheless fascinated Hegel as an intense idea, because he sees in it the unconditional potential of an agency from which the subject can recognize itself *after* the consequences of his agency play(ed) out. When Hegel describes the freedom of the will in the *Philosophy of Right* as the most radical power of man and as the ability to question everything that exists, even man's own well-being, his respect for this source of unlimited violence, resonates: "The human being alone is able to abandon all things, even his own life: he can commit suicide. The animal cannot do this. . . . The human being is pure thinking of himself, and only in thinking he is this power to give himself universality, that is, to extinguish all particularity, all determinacy. This negative freedom . . . is one-sided, but this one-sidedness always contains within itself an essential determination and should therefore not be dismissed" (PR §5A).

Hegel sees in this Kantian power of freedom (originating in Rousseau) a radicalism that—as necessarily conditioned by modernity—affects man fundamentally and especially in the aftermath of the French Revolution. In fact, Hegel assigns to man even a "*privilege* of folly and madness" in his *Philosophy of Mind* (part three of his *Encyclopedia*, PM 119). As we will see in chapter 4, Lacan develops from this "privilege" an entire ethics of psychoanalysis in his understanding of subjectivity. For Hegel, man has the ability "to capture himself in that perfect abstraction of the 'I' " (PM 119). He describes madness as "throw[ing] off the yoke of the *ethical* laws" (PM 126). Madness is, to him, a figuration of freedom.

The pure will therefore embodies, for Hegel, an enigmatic potential of an act-deed. And Hegel already makes it clear in the *Phenomenology* why the deed—even before it reforms itself into a responsible action in its true sense[29]—is crucial for a process of self-awareness locked in empty self-reflection. While the theory of a "pure will" separated from its empirical effects is crucial for Kant (in Hegel's understanding of Kant), Hegel emphasizes the need for a deed that—overcoming a misunderstanding of interiority—actually gives birth to a subjectivity as an effect in the outside world, in which this subjectivity can then act toward itself. The deed is not only determined exclusively by the motivating reason, upon which Kant so heavily relies, as a crucial criterion for the purity of the will; Hegel rather emphasizes that the deed makes possible the retrospective identification, or indeed the first appearance at all, of a motivating reason.

Hegel describes this dialectic of deed and its consequences on several occasions in his works (and unfortunately partially and imprecisely overshadows it with his comments on actions). Examples include his remarks in the "Introduction" of *The Philosophy of History* on arson. Hegel uses the example not only to scrutinize the question of responsibility for practices and actions, but also to demonstrate "that in a simple act, something further may be implicated than lies in the intention and consciousness of the agent" (PH 28). He says this not only for the sake of the self-evident fact that one action can result in unexpected causal chains. He mentions it primarily to clarify the way in which an act—in addition to its unforeseen consequences—can retrospectively reinforce or even "create" the intention, which is at first only rudimentarily formed. He also mentions this idea in the *Philosophy of Right* in the chapter "Purpose and Responsibility" (PR §§115–18). Even if Hegel asserts here that the person who acts has to take responsibility primarily for the foreseeable consequences, he dialecticizes the results of an action as interplay of necessity and accident, which manifest "the proper and *immanent* shape of the action." The consequences of the action are "its nature and . . . nothing other than the action itself." Therefore, his conclusion is trenchant: "The development in the realm of existence of the contradiction which is contained in the *necessity of the infinite* is simply the transformation of necessity into contingency and vice versa. From this point of view, to act therefore means *to submit oneself to this law*" (PR §118). Acting, for Hegel, is always partially involved in the dialectic of necessity and contingency, which is its "nature" and even its "law." This is hardly comparable to the concept of an act in Kantian ethics. For Kant, after all, a good act is one that originates from a good intention, detached from its consequences. Žižek comments on this aptly:

> What is . . . crucial for Hegel's notion of *act* is that an act always, by definition, involves a moment of externalization, self-objectivization, of the jump into the unknown. To "pass to the act" means to assume the risk that what I am about to do will be inscribed into a framework whose contours elude my grasp, that it may set in motion an unforeseeable train of events, that it will acquire a meaning different from or even totally opposed to what I intended to accomplish—in short, it means to assume one's role in the game of the "cunning of reason."[30]

One could say that the collective ground of an act as a moment of externalization of a still indefinable internalization is that both the act, with its partly unpredictable effects in the outside world, and the subject are related to each other around a blind "point of failure."[31] Subject and action relate to each other because they are two moments of an underlying antagonism that relates to the substance as an "outside" of the subject and the subject as a particular "inside" of the substance. I emphasize Hegel's motives for the multifaceted meaning of deed and act because the potential of excessive subjectivity for the act-deed, and the normativity that lies within it, can be understood neither in a clearly justifiable intention nor from a third-party perspective.[32] The deed is part of an eccentricity that reacts back to the acting subject.

For Kant, the goal of practical philosophy is the distillation of willpower from pure reason. In his chapter "Reason" in the *Phenomenology*, Hegel, in an indirect reference to Kant, confronts "observing reason" (*beobachtende Vernunft*) with its failure to see itself as realized in the encountered actuality. As a result, reason is thrown back onto its "inner essence" (*inneres Wesen*). As such, its properties are reduced to negativity, self-distinction, and self-legislation. Reason therefore, at this place in the *Phenomenology*, is defined as "the *practical* consciousness, which steps into its world . . . with the aim of . . . becoming conscious of this unity of its own actuality with the objective being of the world" (PhS §356). Hegel calls these attempts the "ethical experience of the world."

While the first part of the *Phenomenology* deals with the genesis of a consciousness that, with ever more complexity, discloses the objective world and engages in epistemology, in the second half of the "Reason" chapter Hegel turns to the questions of the True and the Good. A clearly recognizable switch is evident after the sections on physiognomy and Gall's phrenology in the "Ac" section of the *Phenomenology.* From the failed logic of one's self-observation, in which the self-observing reason realizes that it isn't "immediately to be found" in an objective nature independent of reason itself, the rational self-consciousness tries to translate its certainty of being reality in entirety through *activity.* For the self-consciousness recognizes: "The *true being* of a man is rather his deed.... It is murder, theft, or a good action, a brave deed, and so on, and what it *is* can be *said* of it" (PhS §322).

Self-consciousness is no longer concerned with the explanation of dialectical processes of understanding between subject and object. It "no longer wants to *find* itself *immediately*, but to produce itself by its own activity" (PhS §344). Now, consciousness is "*itself* the End at which its action aims, whereas in its role of observer it was concerned only with things" (PhS §344).

It is thus crucial for Hegel's genealogy of consciousness in the *Phenomenology* that self-consciousness must generate itself through its *deed*,[33] since it cannot yet grasp itself theoretically. Interiority does not have the power to affect history, as it cannot step out of itself at the risk of a confrontation with the outside world's negativity and subsequently act toward itself on the effects of its actions. Thus, Hegel begins to present individual versions of agencies/interventions as though they were rehearsals of the same effort of acting out. On this level, unlike in his chapter "Spirit," he wants to make clear the extent to which the shapes of individual, philosophic-practical acts do not yet possess "inner spirit," of which consciousness becomes nevertheless finally aware. Consciousness then becomes in the end "*itself* the End of its own activity" (PhS §344). The transition from a self-observing consciousness to a practical one—which takes place in the transition from section A of the chapter "Reason" to sections B and C—goes hand in hand with a switch from the epistemic attitude of the logical idea of truth to that of the good.[34]

We have addressed this change of perspective in the *Phenomenology* to make it clear once again why, according to Hegel, a "pure will" cannot yet enter into a truth of the good. A pure will, as articulated in Kant's early moral philosophy, is still (at least for Hegel) too much indebted to an epistemology of a truth of knowledge rather than to a truth of the good, which, according to Hegel, has to risk itself in the deed, for example, in a deed that pours its effects into the semantic web of the life-world each time anew. The will can precisely not extract itself from the effects of an act, Hegel claims, because it can experience itself only retrospectively as determined or influenced by them as its motivation.

The fact that consequences are hard to predict does not acquit the deed of its responsibility, but only emphasizes how the deed and some of its motivation always already seem to be located apart—due to the space in which the deed occurs, and from which it retroactively shows the acting subject in her normativity. (In a certain sense, we find ourselves back at the topic of the chapter on Kant, in which the moral subject was only retrospectively able to find herself as a moral subject in her misconduct. For us, it was an indication of a fundamental dichotomy within that very subject. This dichotomy also occurs in Hegel's work, specifically in the relationship of the subject to her act-deed.)

Where Hegel's *Phenomenology* goes through models of ethical life (the "pure heart," the "beautiful soul," "the conscience"), which are reminiscent of Kant, it is not yet concerned with a unified concept of a deed within the notion of ethical life. Hegel develops experimental models in which individual positions of practical reason are examined as in the form of a "phenomenological treatise."[35] In the "Spirit" chapter, he attempts to synthesize these positions into a higher form, but, at the level of reason, we still have to deal with inquiries that make clear how Kant's theories of practical reason are still held captive by an "inner spirit," of which consciousness is not yet aware. Either consciousness sees the only source of reasonable insight in the ethical order in its individual reason, or "it abstracts," as Siep aptly comments, "reason's being-in-itself up to an 'intellection law,'"[36] and this particularly concerns the Kantian ethical law.

Hegel thus criticizes Kant not so much for the latter's formalism being "empty," but for not explicitly recognizing the extent to which this formalism *is just a vanishing moment, an excess, through which the subject emerges from a false interiority.* An interiority that recognizes neither how it is influenced by ethical life nor how it can be shaped too late through both positive and negative consequences of its deeds persists in a blindness that, for its purity's sake, wants to see neither its own historical power nor the lack thereof.

THE REVOLUTION OF DISPOSITION AND SOCIAL SPACE

Hegel uses Kant's concept of the moral will to think about the way an ethical founding act may relate conflictual-generatively and normative-creatively to the established sphere of value in the guise of a "revolution of disposition." Ethical life thus for Hegel does not disintegrate into a model of rigid totality, and its spheres of value do not merely linger for all eternity in their normative categories, which have become self-evident through their practices. Both the (uncomprehended) ethical founding act and the shared ethical life form in the state turn out to be the moments—standing in tension to each other—that are needed to break open the static, dominating system of ethical life through conflicts (between the universal and the particular) that entangle themselves in aporias each time anew.

For Kant, there is no other motivation for a moral act, unless it is based on the submission of the maxim under the universal law that governs it. Similarly, as Ido Geiger has so aptly shown, Hegel thinks that a radically autonomous act is a necessary condition of a moral action.[37] Yet, for Hegel, the characterization of an act as a radically autonomous one concerns the revolutionary action, which is at the origin of a new form of ethical life.[38] On the one hand, he criticizes Kant's moral philosophy because it seems to be unaware of the influence of the life-world in each case. On the other hand, Hegel accepts the radical nature of Kant's understanding of morality, and he uses the Kantian formalism of freedom (that is, duty for duty's sake) to conceive the autonomy of a moral act as a force that crisscrosses the established *Sittlichkeit* of a polity. Hegel will therefore adopt the Kantian theme of moral motivation for his theory of the creation of a new life form at the point where Kant cites the motives of pure will, fraction, event, and revolution. Hegel adopts these motifs in order to explicate how a new life form creates a space for itself through a rupture that may have previously lacked the appearance of a potentiality.

Does such a Hegelian theory of ethical-revolutionary founding gestures not imply a retreat into the irrational? According to the reading of Hegel presented here, it does not; this thesis is to be interpreted much more materialistically than, for example, Kant's own perspective on the infinite approximation of the moral subject and of society to the ethical ideal. It is more materialistic insofar as the ethical ideal can also realize itself in (revolutionary/epistemic) ruptures of self-consciousness that constitute its path. The individual, the particular, is given the outlet of behaving as the proper medium *behind the back of the universal*, and without any self-reassuring recourse to an abstract idea or a separated universality (out there in the heavens of "real" moral universals). In this process the true and thus the universal will have recognized itself. This goal of the particular depends on its specific achievement to actualize that which still awaits the "determination of the essence" of the universal. Thus, a respective goal and a specific power to posit the normative are assigned to the particular (and therefore also to the individual subject), that is, a specific power of the normative to actualize itself behind the back of the universal as the universal's "vanishing mediator." This is the central idea in Hegel's comment that "the living Substance is the being that is in truth *Subject*, or, what is to the same thing, is in truth actual only insofar as it is the movement of positing itself, that is, that it is the mediation of its self-othering with itself" (PhS §18).

The absoluteness of the ethical is something that Hegel seems to share with Kant. It can be represented by a subject that is always already shaped by inclinations and yet realizes that its conscience "sees" or intuitively feels a truth that the established doxa cannot represent and comprehend. The strength of the ground of these convictions may then not be able to be integrated into the logical space of normative practices and their justifications. That, however, does not mean that these convictions give up their own rational character.[39]

We shall illustrate this theory with the example of Antigone. Hegel portrays her conflict as one that at no point promises a potential solution via a *tertium datur*, and nevertheless the downfall of the polis gives rise to an ethical origin of a new stage of consciousness of the spirit. Antigone's legal claim cannot take recourse to any "scorekeeper," in Brandom's terminology, as a guarantor of a giving of and asking for reasons, as Antigone's own certainty slumbers in the "Stygian water" (PhS §467), as Hegel writes, or in the "waters of forgetfulness" (PhS §474), where the laws of the underworld lay hidden.

HEGEL'S ANTIGONE: THE TRAGIC vs. TRAGEDY

A great man wants to be guilty, and takes on the great collision.

—G. W. F. HEGEL

In a variety of his writings, Hegel refers to ancient tragedy as a stalemate-like conflict of rights with equal claims and interprets it, in contrast to the epic, the comedy, the modern and romantic tragedy, in each case comparing its relation to certain forms of consciousness. Especially in the *Phenomenology* an important distinction is presented with the difference between the tragedy as a literary genre and the tragic as a historical conflict of the hero. The latter thematizes the tragic with the example of Antigone and Oedipus in the chapter "The Ethical Order" as a form of consciousness, which is not equated to the literary genre of tragedy, which occurs much later in the *Phenomenology.* Not until the chapter "Religion" does Hegel refer to the artistic genre of tragedy as the modern, antiarchaic shape of consciousness in the classical Greek era, in which form and content are a dialectical reflective determination of the structure of (self-) consciousness. In the *Phenomenology,* Hegel repeatedly defines "life" as the entirety of intellectual-material historical processes and thus as a unity that renders itself asunder. The sundering of life during the ancient ethical life, as it is triggered by Antigone ("*das schöne Wesen*"), implies a separation in Being that in ancient times is nevertheless unified for Hegel and therefore not comparable to his own epoch shaped by antagonisms of (Kantian) modernity. The tragedy of Antigone as commented on in the chapter "The Ethical Order" marks the decisive conflict between the hero and the polis. "Hero" refers to the level of consciousness that is aware of itself as being in an undivided entirety of an understanding ethical life. The outcome of this conflict is politically (in the sense of Realpolitik) no less disastrous for the polis than that of any crisis. Yet, the sundering, as it is represented by Antigone's individual will as the voice of the "divine law" (PhS §449) as opposed to "human law" (PhS §447), is, on the level of consciousness on which it appears in Hegel's genealogy, established not as remote from everyday life with the divine, but rather as part of a divine universality (of life) that tears itself apart. Here the universal and the particular do not yet stand opposed to each other as estranged and modern-antagonistic, despite an inherent division. The hero embodies an ethical-divine power in her acts as a subjective wanting (*Wollen*), which comes into conflict with an equally legitimate counterpower, as it is represented in the very same ethical order as well. For Hegel, the Absolute stages this division in the unity of itself as a tragic play, because it rises, as Hegel already writes in *On the Scientific Ways of Treating Natural Law*, after separation, collision, duty, and death "from its ashes up to glory" (NL 151). The ethical consciousness has "forgotten all the one-sidedness of being-for-itself" (PhS §467). If it divides itself, the ethical other of Being recognizes that its reality is a double one, whereby consciousness becomes "guilt" through deed, "for the deed is its own doing" (PhS §468).

Hegel thematizes the unity-in-division in the age of heroes against the backdrop of the experience of division in his own time. Yet he already knows during his time in Frankfurt, contrary to his theory of reconciliation that is characteristic at least for the essay on natural law, namely, of "tragedy in the ethical life," that a return to the ethical unity (as he constructs it) in the ancient sense is impossible. Even the Greek division, for which Socrates's conflictual-unassimilable subjectivity will stand, is no longer a unity. Numerous other figures of "modern" or "romantic" tragic heroes from Shakespeare's Hamlet to Schiller's Karl Moor, which Hegel references in the *Phenomenology* and his lectures on *Aesthetics*, are not heroes, even if the modern tragedy tries to establish these figures as tragic ones under modern conditions.[40]

In the tragic life of Antigone (in contrast to tragedy as a genre), the daughter of Oedipus appears as an individual destined for certain substantive ethical purposes. Her actions provoke a conflict with other substantive ethical purposes that are part of the same "cup of substance" (PhS §467). Hegel upholds the dominating ideal of ancient Greece, where the conflict, be it the conflict of knowledge (Orestes) or the conflict of the deed (Antigone),[41] is not yet the modern dilemma of subjectivity and universality. In the ethical age of the tragic, Hegel is not yet interested in the audience of the tragedy who by viewing the play reflect on themselves.[42] In this sense, the culpability within the tragic fate is a guiltless and at once unconscious guilt (*felix culpa*). The tragic nature of Antigone is, according to the (self-)reflexivity that makes this opus superior to Aeschylus's *Oresteia*, not analogous with the reflexivity, which spectators will at a later stage of consciousness interpret as part of the resolution of the tragic conflict. The tragic nature of Antigone is her deed alone.[43] What distinguishes the tragedy in general from the epic, and makes the former a higher form of art, is the fact that subjects are represented as "*actual* human beings" (PhS §733), namely, in actual speech "not in the form of a narrative" (PhS §733).

While the deed in the epic, according to Hegel's comments in his *Aesthetics*, stays an external one in opposition to the experience of subjectivity, the deed in the tragedy emerges from "the private will, from the morality or immorality, of the individual characters" (Aesth. 2:1038). The tragedy's tragic conflict becomes a moment of realization in the relationship of the audience to itself.[44] Thus, the level of consciousness contained in the tragic, in contrast to the tragedy, can no longer be revived, even during the era of the tragedy. It also cannot be revived during the era of comedy or during that of Socrates.[45]

The tragedy of *Antigone* needs to be judged differently than that of Schiller's Karl Moor. The former is tragic (despite a lack of consciousness), while the latter is skeptically interpreted by Hegel as "only" an ultimately banal and uninteresting individual delusion. Hegel states in the *Aesthetic* that Karl Moor lacks the greatness of the ancient heroes. His "private revenge," "tiny and isolated," fails and can "only lead to crime, for it incorporates the wrong which it intends to destroy" (Aesth. 1:195). Such comments make clear that Hegel does not see the drama of the late eighteenth and early nineteenth century as a rebirth of antiquity.

How then are we to judge conflicts after antiquity or after the ancient concept of the "tragic fate"? As not at all tragic anymore? Are there no more tragic human fates, since they are possible only in the ancient form of life, in the ancient "ethical order" as defined by Hegel? These questions arise in light of the everyday use of the word *tragic*. Conflicts and strokes of fate are colloquially interpreted as "tragic" to the extent that those concerned have to accept them as unwarranted and as resigned to certain fateful or contingent circumstances. Hegel's concept of the tragic fate has nothing in common with this sense of the word. For him, the word *tragic* marks the condition of a very closely defined concept of an ancient form of consciousness. This, nevertheless, does not mean that the potential of a conflict between universal and particular is resolved for Hegel. This conflict is, after all, the basic structure of the *Phenomenology* as a whole. Therefore, one can argue that the conflict between the particular (will) and the universal (norm) experiences a new form of drama in modern times due to the disappearance of ethical unity, which the ancient world still contained. Hegel notes in the subsequent chapters after "The Ethical Order," "Culture" and "Enlightenment," and finally in reference to the French Revolution, that the dialectical upheavals that create enlightened modernity, contrary to its original intention, generate brutality and reigns of terror, against which the ancient concept of the tragic appears almost as a harmless and banal history of suffering. Cutting off heads in the manner of a "cutting off a head of cabbage" (PhS §590) is not something of which the ancient world was capable. In its "primitivity," one could say cynically, antiquity had not yet "matured" this far genealogically, and was not as diseased in its consciousness by *self*-consciousness.

ANTIGONE'S ACT

Hegel understands subjective freedom to be dependent upon a deed and its effects.[46] This freedom has different levels of reflection, but for Hegel, as a "passion" (since the Greeks at the latest) it can be a form of acting that strives for the establishment of an unseen deontological dimension of reality. The subject—however much blinded—experiences the form of a paradoxical future retrospectively in the outburst of its acting. The entanglement of "ought" and "being," which the subject realizes in its potentiality, sets free something eternal—the idea—and this occurs precisely at the moment in which it is realized in its contingency as what, at the level of the idea, it has retrospectively and virtually always been. When Hegel talks about freedom as "self-contained existence" (*Bei-sich-selbst-Sein*) in the introduction to his *Philosophy of History* (17), for instance, he does not mean it in the sense that freedom can be mistaken with static resting, like matter, which possesses the property of resting well balanced in itself. Rather, freedom is in a sense "being-with-oneself" insofar as it is experienced in expending oneself through deeds. A transubstantiation takes place: being "with-oneself" is becoming what one retrospectively has always been. Only through the deed and its consequences can freedom recognize itself looking back as that which will have always been "with-itself." If we understand this "being-with-itself"/"being-with-oneself" only as a harmless transformation of potentiality into actuality, then the paradox, which Hegel struggles with in his theory of the deed and which he puts forward in his Antigone interpretation, slips away. For what characterizes Antigone is precisely that through her a detail emerges, which, as part of the ethical substance, brings this substance into a discrepancy with itself through a sacrilegious "deed."

Hegel articulates, similar to Kant's theory of the moral act as an act of spontaneous freedom, an absoluteness that realizes itself within its own form. This means that the moral subject can be determined by contingencies and yet also be a representative of an absolute. As such, it is the embodiment of an idea, a "beyond," an "abstract universal" in the here and now. Hegel, like Kant, therefore sees the absolute as going time and time again through contingencies, absurd personifications, and incarnations. The idea needs the contingence of material-historical reality, so far as the determinants in matter (which, as Hegel writes in the introduction to the *Philosophy of History*, "strive after the realization of [the] Idea" [LHPh 17]) can only articulate themselves *through* matter. If Jesus of Nazareth, for example, had not been subject to the contingent fact of being a Jew in the first century of his becoming the principle and the idea of *the Christ*, then the contingency of the existence of this itinerant preacher would not have entered the world in (about) the year eight *post Christum natum*. Idea and contingency are mutually dependent while at the same time indicative of a nonsufficient structure of the conditionality of both moments.[47] Thus freedom realizes its potentiality in a loop of performance, where the contingency of an act will have established itself as "being-with-itself." Hegel speaks of "activity." As "activity," the deed is "the middle term of the Syllogism, one of whose extremes is the Universal essence, the *Idea*, which reposes in the penetralia of Spirit; and the other, the complex of external things—objective matter. That activity is the medium by which the universal latent principle is translated into the domain of objectivity" (LHPh 27).

Hegel had already emphasized the "deed" in the chapter "Reason" as an escape from a self-consciousness, entangled in epistemological questions, that had to step out of itself (PhS §322). However, the deed in the context of Greek ethical life goes one step further: it not only overcomes the introversion of self-reflexive, epistemological consciousness; it also reflects a level of consciousness of freedom in the polis. As Antigone shows, the deed risks a catastrophe for the community for the benefit of the universality of the so-called ethical substance. The hero's deed provokes an imbalance. As the deed as such represents the law of the substance opposite an *equally* substantive countervailing power, the conflict is still part of the unity of the ethical substance. Yet the ethical substance of Greek antiquity will also perish, because the principle of the particularity will not be respected until the emergence of Roman law and Christianity.[48] Hegel writes, "the deed is the *actual self*," and through it the former order experiences "a transition of opposing" (PhS §464) forces. Yet the reason for this "opposition" is still, as mentioned, the realm of ethical life. So the deed is itself part of this ethical life and as such the "duty" upon which the ethical life calls itself. Therefore, in this deed, there is "no indecision" (PhS §465). The deed knows no weighing, no arbitrariness. In the Kantian sense, it is a duty, because, as a wanting to (*Wollen*), it is an absolute must. Therefore, Antigone's deed cannot, as Hegel says referring to Kant, take place in the form of a "collision between passion and duty" (PhS §467), because it is not a "struggle" (PhS §467) but rather "*the simple, pure direction* towards ethical essentiality, i.e. duty" (PhS §467).

Heidegger was fascinated by the nonpropositional knowledge at the root of Antigone's deed as well. In his Freiburg lecture in 1942, concerning the Greek interpretation of man in Sophocles's *Antigone*,[49] he emphasizes that the original oppositionality to the polis and the uncanniness/foreignness (*Unheimlichkeit*) of Antigone lie in her deed. Heidegger develops a phenomenological study of the uncanny and nonhomely essence (das *nicht-heimische Wesen*) of Antigone. According to him, the power of this essence rests on the fact that it does not integrate itself into the world of that which "is" (*das Seiende*). "Yet because those who seek to explain this tragedy are always eager to find in Antigone's words *an explanation of her actions*, that is, a statement about whatever it is that causes her deeds, they are concerned only with finding some reference to beings, whether the prevailing or ancient cult of the dead, or the familial blood-relatedness. They fail to recognize that in her words, Antigone speaks of neither of theses. One is still unable to see that she is not speaking of a being at all."[50] Heidegger translates verses 450ff., which fascinated both Hegel and Hölderlin, as follows: "Antigone: It was no Zeus that bade me this, / Nor was it Dike, at home amongst the gods below, / who ordained this law for humans, / And your command seemed not so powerful to me / That it could ever override by human wit / The immutable, unwritten edict divine. / Not just now, nor since yesterday, but ever steadfast / this prevails. And no one knows from whence it once appeared."[51]

Heidegger concludes mystically that Antigone had been "unhomely" (which is how Heidegger translates *deinon*), "because she properly is the most uncanny in the supreme manner."[52] The uncanny, or the "nonpropositional" in contemporary jargon, receives here its own power to reveal "that which is" (*seinsoffenbarende Gewalt*), according to Heidegger as well as to Hegel. Both Hegel and Heidegger are interested in an "empty space," which, as a kind of ontological gap, has consciousness-expanding (and that also means normativity-expanding) dimensions. Antigone articulates a counterplay inherent in herself "between being unhomely in the sense of being driven about amid beings without any way out, and being unhomely as becoming homely from out of a belonging to being."[53] As with Hegel, one could say: Antigone represents a gap in being, in which being recognizes itself in its own noncoincidence in favor of its new form, which will have resulted from "tarrying in the negative" (PhS §32).

Antigone's legal claim cannot appeal to a "scorekeeper," the guarantor of a giving of and asking for reasons, since her own certainty slumbers in the "Stygian water," in the "waters of forgetfulness" where the laws of the underworld lie hidden. Yet what sounds mysterious and mythical here can also be interpreted systematically within the meaning of two contiguous subsets whose coherence is dependent on the boundary between them. The crisis consists then in the fact that the old (burial) rituals are not dying and the modern polis cannot be born. In this interregnum a "great variety of morbid symptoms" (Gramsci) must appear and Antigone is one of them. The possibility of the existence of the modern state depends upon the suppression of old forms of life and when they come back, the force of the repressed can be fatal. The forgetfulness and unconsciousness of the normativity that Antigone advocates then represent a normativity whose arguments should not at all be allowed to be valid in the actuality of the polis. This is not, however, because the propositional content of normativity is lost in the mysterious fabric of tradition, but because this content, given the premises of "the established representation of reality" (via the state), is per se already in its stubbornness "of the nether world" and must be pushed back into "forgetfulness."

Sophocles's *Antigone* thus stands as a systemic allegory of two political subsets (the old vs. the new) whose respective coherence within the conflict requires the boundaries of the other and where only the collapse of both subsets through a political catastrophe provokes a new origin for ethics: the Roman legal order and a Christian understanding of individuality. Hence, it is not important whether rights and normativities lie here "in the waters of forgetfulness" or not. Even if Antigone were conscious of them (that is, would understand the rights and normativities self-reflexively), they would not be automatically understandable to the polis. Hegel's talk of "the waters of forgetfulness" refers to a plunging of old premises into the deep that, due to forgetfulness, the polis as modern political community had established. So only Antigone's ethical-catastrophic founding gesture brings a suppressed particularity into a new relationship with the universal.

The ethical deed as a violation and sundering of the ethical substance is part of the ethical substance. Human law and divine law complement each other like the two sides of the Möbius strip, where the exterior side of the one turns out to be the interior side of the other. Through the deed, however, this interwovenness is conflictually brought into the "actuality" of the ethical substance and then appears provocatively as a collision. Hegel wants to express here once again that the ethical deed, as violation and sundering, strives through the struggle between human law and divine law to bring into "actuality" that which the ethical substance harbors in itself as its own "being." Thus, it realizes itself in its demise as a new figure of consciousness, which can now, after all, produce the right of the individual in a new corpus of law, albeit at the cost of the old substance of ethical life.

One can understand the excessive subjectivity of Antigone as well as an "acratic act" in the sense of Donald Davidson's "Medea-Principle."[54] The excess of an "alien force" hereby forges its path and determines the subject's act-deed. This "force" is insistent even when in practical conflicts the motivation of the will ought to be appeased following the demonstration of logical contradictions. Davidson's thesis of irrationality is based on the assumption that there may be a mental origin of the deed, which, in the strict sense of the word, is not a propositional justification for the deed. He explains this with a Freud-inspired division of consciousness into different levels. Bernard Williams shows for his part in his article on "ethical consistency" that a difference between practical and cognitive conflicts is discernible in cases where the losing side in practical conflicts does not abandon its willpower, even if the reason for the deed is weakened relative to other reasons.[55] The conflict therefore continues, as it is not exclusively reducible to logical relations. As Dirk Setton reveals in his insightful analysis of the approaches of Davidson and Williams, this insistence on a willpower that transcends its logical disempowerment corresponds to the shape of a "syllogistic bastard," which Aristotle illustrates using the example of "thymos." Setton writes: "The undecidability of the conflict: that is, the 'both-and' (*sowohl-als auch*) as opposed to the 'either-or' (*entweder-oder*) logic of prohairesis [that is, choice/decision] is retained beneath the surface. Here, in the latency of the will, a counter-decision can occur, a decision that does not take place in the self-presence of the exercise of the rational will, but rather in its shadow. It is a virtual act that the self-conscious subject may neither attribute nor not attribute to herself."[56] Setton interprets such an "acratic act" using the example of Medea, whereby he assigns this act two alternatives (similar to our approach to the example of Hegel's Antigone): the way of irrational failure and the way "of a rationality to come."[57]

THE TRAGIC AND TRAGEDY IN THE CONTEXT OF KNOWLEDGE AND TRUTH

While, according to Hegel, the ethical substance in ancient Greece can still unite the opposition of particularity and universality as a *unity in disunity* (present in the tragedies *Oedipus* and *Oresteia*), this unity perishes finally in the emergence of Antigone's sacrilegious deed, represented by a new form of freedom, however unreflected it is. The deed alone as willingly sacrilegious is of importance. Further of interest is the fact that the conflict between the particular and the universal, which the *Phenomenology* addresses, is situated as well within an epistemological metatheory that affects the relationship between knowledge and truth from their first stages of consciousness up to their last. This means that the principle conflict in terms of practical philosophy that characterizes *Antigone* as one between the particular and the universal goes hand in hand with a conflict between knowledge and truth, as Tilo Wesche convincingly suggests.[58] Knowledge (= justified belief) and truth stand for equally valid claims and constitute a necessary contrast within the genealogy of the Hegelian concept. Wesche writes: "The unity of knowledge and truth in this case takes the form of mutual recognition. Knowledge is recognized as true, based on general standards, which in turn have to be able to be recognized by knowledge."[59] What situates Antigone's conflict within the earlier-mentioned dichotomy of knowledge and truth is that the political collision between the particular and the universal also points to the codependence of values, norms, and facts, which has been repeatedly thematized in recent practical philosophical and epistemological discussions. The debate between Jürgen Habermas and Hilary Putnam is worth mentioning, for example, in this context, which, in turn, refers to a similar conflict between William James and John Dewey within the first generation of American pragmatism.[60]

So, Antigone's struggle is not exclusively a battle for forms of life in between the domains of ancient myth and modern politics, but, like all forms of consciousness in the *Phenomenology*, always relates to epistemological moments of the recognition of truth in the dialectical turns of the *Begriff* as well. In his *Phenomenology*, Hegel emphasizes precisely how theoretical and practical philosophy and even aesthetics cannot be examined as separate domains of reason in the Kantian sense. The *Phenomenology* always incorporates a theory that considers a strict separation of facts, norms, and values to be a misperception of reason's scope and range. It is important to emphasize this point: not only to recognize the conflict between more or less arbitrary forms of life in *Antigone*, but to appreciate in it the question of and the quest for objectivity. In this context, knowledge, as it is carried within excessive subjectivity, needs a universal to reassure it of its potential veridicality, because it is only from this universal that it can assure itself that its convictions can (one day) be integrated into a web of belief, into a holistic structure of justifications.[61] Due to the fact that this is not what we see in Sophocles's play, we experience the tragedy as unfolding. This leads up to the current collapse of the entire relationship between truth and knowledge inside the polis.

So again: Knowledge as it is claimed by the particular—by the "being-for-itself"—needs an approving authority of justification and validity. It needs "being-in-itself" to achieve veridicality even if the approval comes from the future. For Hegel the dichotomy between "being-for-itself" and "being-in-itself" guarantees the interdependence of subject and object within the development of Spirit, inscribed into the intentionality of consciousness and its misperceptions within the folds of its era-contingent reflexivity. To test its own inconsistency, knowledge requires a universal that unfolds within the historical process of self-legitimation that is the *Phenomenology*.[62] In this process, the particular and the universal—or, with regard to our topic, excessive subjectivity (embodied by knowledge, conscience, and certainty) and established universality (common sense, *Sittlichkeit*)—face each other within the conflict of recognition in a mutually dependent manner. This conflict is tragic because, according to Hegel's definition of tragedy, two contradictory legal claims challenge each other irreconcilably.[63] Excessive subjectivity provokes the "estrangement" (*Entzweiung*) of the concept by not recognizing in the form of the ruling doxa the realm of validity of the universal. However, at the same time, for its own advantage, it needs the universal, as the latter, of course, exceeds the particular. This universal must "be able to legitimize itself to knowledge, even though it exceeds this very knowledge,"[64] as Tilo Wesche observes. This crisis-prone dichotomy substantiates itself in political constellations between established normative practices and those practices struggling for legitimization. Indeed, for Hegel, the conflict over Antigone's defense of funerary practices is in this sense an epistemological conflict between knowledge and truth. If, at the level of the particular, a funeral rite is being defended against the universal, which sees its political authority threatened by this very insistence, then, from the position of Antigone's knowledge, a belief is defended that claims validity over the world in its "being-in-itself," that is, in the objectivity of how it has to "be" at all as a condition for the possibility of judgments.

A prohibition on burying one's own brother is a propositional judgment that, from the perspective of the particular (that is, from Antigone's perspective), may never relate to "being-in-itself." Doing so would violate the concept of truth, which, as a transcendental condition, affects science, culture, and politics, and thus the objectivity of the realm of the political. Therefore, Antigone is not just fighting for a ritual, but for a truth that must be defended normatively—a truth in which the polis has to locate itself necessarily *as a polis for her.* Advocating for the funeral of the brother means defending the objectivity of the world as a condition of the possibility of propositional judgments. To refrain from a specific funeral ritual is, at the level of the particular (that is, Antigone), not one of many insignificant value judgments, where certain normative preferences prevail. From Antigone's perspective, the entire world, her life-world, is violated in an absolute manner, if the ancient laws are rejected. With their violation and neglect the objectivity of the space of reasons dissolves.

However, since reason necessarily misperceives itself in the conflict between Antigone and Creon, reason's excessive subjectivity is a potential medium toward a possible transformation of that which in its current state is not yet understood, prior to the tragedy.

Separating judgments based on values, norms, and facts is not possible for Hegel. The entire *Phenomenology* is an argument to prove to what extent judgments based on values, norms, and facts unfold in one and the same area of normativity, an area that is torn in the conflict between knowledge and truth. Antigone fights in order to save the legitimacy of universality as a condition (of her understanding) of giving of and asking for reasons.[65] It is obvious that her agency does not adopt a traditional Kantian first-person perspective of the moral will. However, not because Antigone—as Christine M. Korsgaard might put it—is not "certain" of her maxim, but because her maxim, even from the perspective of the established law (that is, from the third-person perspective), would mean an interruption of the ethical life, from which her reasons cannot be viewed as anything but "private." If one takes up this position of Korsgaard, who draws on Wittgenstein to reject private reasons just as Wittgenstein rejects a private language, one will miss the conflict.[66] Robert Pippin makes this point clear when he writes with regard to *Antigone*: "The painfulness and irresolvability of their [Creon and Antigone's] disagreement . . . indicates that there is . . . something basically wrong with the roles of the divine and human, private and public boundaries. . . . There are breakdowns and failures in ethical life of a sort that reveal the limitations and inconsistencies *in a value claim itself*."[67]

The ethical lives opposing each other with hostility do not occur as a crucial test of Spirit; they tear the Spirit apart as a necessary condition for its rebirth "from the ashes." In this way, Antigone takes an *a*moral (not *im*moral) position with regard to the polis's understanding of ethical life.[68] It is precisely the unconsciousness of her deed and the noncoincidence of her certainty[69] with respect to the ethical life of the polis that lead to her political act, seemingly stemming from an indefinable in-between realm, and to the staging of the tragic conflict as a subject's path through the "night of the world." Antigone incarnates the insight that humanity is situated always within an anonymous process of liberation that precedes the individual human being but that, nevertheless, calls upon him—like Antigone—to struggle for autonomy. Autonomy might then manifest itself in breaking up the matrix of the law in favor of an unpredictable future to come, where the subject only in the act can reach to herself—even if this act is a "sacrilegious" one.

THE RATIONALE THAT WILL HAVE ACTUALIZED ITSELF

At the beginning of his *Encyclopedia Logic*, Hegel admits that his famous dictum from the preface of the *Philosophy of Right* ("what is rational is actual, and what is actual is rational") had provoked much opposition. Yet as he writes in section 6, one must not understand this sentence in such a way that the rational of what is actually here and now in actuality, that is, in the "living spirit" of the present, would fill this spirit at its present age entirely. This is impossible, as, for Hegel, every presence or every present age becomes drawn into the horizon of a teleological process exactly *through* the division of every presence into a part of its rational actualization (the result of its prehistory as an instance of its freedom here and now), and into another part of its outstanding future, the still-to-come realization of actuality. The latter part robs every present age necessarily of its self-presence, as it is not yet and never will be in its own future. If we would see through all that is finite, Hegel writes, then "this transparency of the finite . . . ends up in complete disappearance, for there is nothing in the finite which would retain for it a difference over against the absolute; as medium, it is absorbed by that through which it shines" (SL 468). Thus, the truth of what Hegel calls substance progresses forward through ever-new, reflexive moments in the process of its formation, and it paradoxically comes in this development back to its true ground. Along with Robert Brandom, one might say that, historically, the rational steadily becomes "more explicit" without ever being able to become completely explicit.[70] This is simply impossible.

In explicating this process and its impairment by contingency, Hegel distinguishes in the *Encyclopedia Logic* between "contingent concrete existence" on the one hand and "actual" existence on the other (ESL §6/p. 33). He then underlines that contingent existence has "no greater value than that which something *possible* has" (ESL §6/pp. 33–34). Even if Hegel wants to justify the fact that whatever exists by chance exists precisely *through its existence*, he nevertheless sees in contingency an inferior status. (The existence of the contingent endures as something possible, "which may just as well *not exist* as exist" [ESL §6/p. 34]). Contingency includes, for example, whether a certain year's harvest has turned out well or badly. Similarly, the disease that someone catches through an infectious virus might be contingent, or it might be the result of the outbreak of a collective epidemic that threatens a village. The foreign policy of a king may be bad; the Roman law may be bad in terms of the construction of the "pater familias" compared to the actual legal progress it represents. These actualities as possibilities simply exist because they *are*. Actuality, by contrast, is understood in Hegel's text differently. The existence of the actual exceeds the existence of the contingent in the sense that the rational has let itself become expressed in it. Examples may include the constitution of a nation-state that grants more freedom to its citizens than the old constitution allowed for. Similarly, an economic system might be "rational" by creating structures of freedom for a bourgeois society, as Hegel points out in the *Philosophy of Right*. That does not mean that the existence of the actual encompasses all of reality. Concerning the capitalistic structures of the bourgeois society in particular, Hegel has to admit, for instance, that a part of society—"the rabble"—arises simultaneously with a social class that revels in luxury.[71] Or: The legal system of a society's judiciary branch may be good, yet that does not rule out the possibility that the executive branch simultaneously still has a "contingent" character, that is, the character of something that's only "possible."[72] But, as we've said, the actual has *more* historical ground, because past moments of freedom express themselves in a more concentrated fashion in the actual than in the contingent or in the possible.

Nevertheless, contingency and actuality must exist simultaneously. This is of relevance for our understanding of excessive subjectivity.[73] Next to the provocation that it triggers in "what men call healthy understanding" (LHPh 379), the nonnegotiable claim of excessive subjectivity will seem normatively contingent and even shockingly arbitrary. Solipsistic certainty can justify neither its necessity nor the possibility of its normative claim, since the possibility of the normative would appear as an option only through a shifting of the established norms. The emergence of certainty thus seems initially radically arbitrary, as in the case of Rosa Parks too. Why, for example, was Parks not willing to discuss the matter of segregation long before entering the bus? Why the sudden breach of rule? Why this bus, why this year and day? Is such an abrupt civil disobedience in a more than trivial context—public transportation—something that truly educated people would do?

Hegel understands contingency as an unsubstantiated actuality, which, on account of its pure being, is more than what he calls a pure "formal possibility." Excessive subjectivity enters the realm of the political with demands: it does not remain a formal possibility, as one might say with regard to the political impact of the "beautiful soul." Thus, contingency stands in our interpretation also in relation to the category of necessity.[74] This is one of the most profound thoughts that Hegel develops in his chapter "Actuality" at the end of book 2 of "The Doctrine of Essence" in his *Science of Logic*.[75] Hegel defines various categories of modality and explains how the actuality of reality differs from formal temporality and possibility, and he places contingency in a relation to necessity. That which is contingent is grounded and groundless at the same time. It is grounded in the simple fact that *it is* here and actual. In this sense, it is more than "formal actuality" or "possibility." It is groundless in the sense that this actuality is not—or is not yet—reflected in itself.[76] According to Hegel, this is a characteristic proper to what is contingent. It can, but does not have to be.

With reference to the forms of modality exemplified in the *Encyclopedia Logic* and in the "Actuality" chapter of the *Logic*, we can answer the aforementioned questions. We can, since we understand excessive subjectivity as future necessity *in the suspension* of contingency. The contingent, as Karin Ng aptly puts it, is a unilateral "determination of actuality," which (as of yet) fails to grasp its own reflected character. Excessive subjectivity would then be a (seemingly) one-sided determination.[77] While it seems to be contingent, noncomprehensible, and nongeneralizable, its second reflected half will nevertheless have shown itself retroactively. In its contingency as a potential empty value of the nonrepresented, the freedom of the ethical deed imposes a grid upon reality that determines, in the form of a performative act, what actuality is about from a future perspective and what it is lacking here and now. It defines within a performative act "contingent concrete existence" and "actual existence," even if the latter is perceived and instantiated via the individual herself. It is the seemingly contingent choice of the Kantian revolution of disposition, or—in psychoanalytic terms—the "choice of neurosis" that defines the normative frame of rationality in which actuality then appears.

With regard to Antigone, one could, for example, claim that she uses the appeal of the unwritten, ultimately enigmatic, and unspecified laws of the underworld as the starting point of her "disposition" (*Gesinnung*). She precisely does not choose her sister Ismene's cooperative path within the body politic but posits herself in opposition to any kind of cooperation. Accordingly, as a consequence of this decision, her life-world orders itself along the lines of this positing. Similar to what Heidegger calls in a different but analogous context the "viewpoint" (*Gesichtspunkt*)[78] as a template of perception and agency, Antigone's deed prestructures the actuality within a new system of coordinates that now redefines what is actual, possible, and contingent.

The possible consequences of such a deed are illustrated by Žižek with reference to the Marxist teleology of history in an exemplary manner. He suggests that "If, for example, we are Marxists"—or, better, if we declare ourselves as orthodox Marxists—"the entire past is perceived as one long narrative whose constant theme is the class struggle and whose plot strives toward that classless society." By contrast, though,

> if we are liberals, the past tells the story of the gradual emancipation of the individual from the constraints of collectivity and Fate. . . . And it is *here* that freedom and the subject intervene: freedom is *stricto sensu* the contingency of necessity—that is, it is contained in the initial "if . . . ," in the (contingent) choice of the modality by means of which we symbolize the contingent real or impose some narrative necessity upon it. "Substance as subject" means that the very necessity that sublates contingency by positing it as its ideal moment is itself contingent.[79]

In the performative acknowledgment of a "viewpoint" (*Gesichtspunkt*), certain moments of actuality fall into possibility, similar to a kaleidoscope, while others fall into contingency and necessity. We can cite numerous examples for this. One of the most famous is Žižek's Marxist interpretation of history, just mentioned, as an antagonistic struggle between the social classes. One could also take into consideration Steven Pinker's more recent interpretation of historical progress from the "viewpoint" of "maximizing human flourishing" in his book *The Better Angels of Our Nature.*[80] Such a narrative as presented by Pinker within the contemporary naturalism that he is affiliated with suppresses various difficulties, for instance, the most obvious one: How to draw up a general definition of "human flourishing" in the first place? Viewpoints presented as neutral and scientific obscure other aspects of reality while simultaneously urging us to accept their perspective (for instance, Pinker's) on reality as normatively secured and thus as determining the spirit of our time. In Utz's words, excessive subjectivity could, in the context of Hegel's interpretation of contingency, be defined as an incident, which "in an ingressive context stands in a negative referentiality to a given."[81]

Rosa Parks's negative referentiality with regard to her interpretation of established normativity within the public transport service of Alabama may well appear contingent at first sight or from a third-person perspective. Yet with regard to the normative frame that—from the performative acknowledgment of her viewpoint—then changes the whole situation like a kaleidoscope, this contingency is no longer the case from a retrospective viewpoint. This again underlines how a performative deed intervenes in forms of practical life and new aspects come to light that for many people were not actual (or possible) at all.

Excessive subjectivity understood as such contrasts with "precociousness" (ESL §6/p. 34), which, as Hegel says, considers the "ideas and ideals" of philosophy as being "much too exquisite to be actual." They are nothing but "chimeras" and "phantasms" (ESL §6/p. 34). Precociousness possesses an intellectual "severance of actuality from the idea" (ESL §6/p. 34). Here, Hegel sees a type of vanity at work, which ultimately remains historically impotent. Its dream of an "ought" in a better world can never become actual since it declares every ideal as a figment of one's imagination. Precociousness appears here as the aged version of the "beautiful soul" having become embittered and morose.[82]

If, as Hegel remarks in section 6 of the *Encyclopedia Logic*, we may assume that in every age the modalities of "contingency" and "actuality" are always intertwined, then this also raises the question of who acknowledges at which point in time and place something as actual while others perceive the very same as possible or contingent. In other words, it takes in certain situations a subject's performative deed to enact what is actual, even when many others declare *this* actuality to be purely contingent. Antigone's attitude can be interpreted in this light, but so can Hegel's Socrates. In what follows, we will expand on the latter. It is in Hegel's analyses of "conscience" in particular that Socrates's attitude distinguishes itself from the uncertain, unreflected, and indeed almost "empty" certainty of Antigone.

HEGEL AND CONSCIENCE

Hegel repeatedly mentions the concept of "conscience" as a factor that can object to common sense, or to "what men call healthy human understanding" (LHPh 379). Certain contemporary "maxims" are simply not shared; conscience, for example, does not deduce its maxims from the premises of the established order. Here, the noncomprehension of conscience/morality on the one hand and ethical life/"common sense" on the other leads to a tragic impasse. Hegel presents his discussion of the "conscience" explicitly within the context of Greek tragedy (LHPh 390, 446) and—emphasizing the danger of delusion inherent in conscience's structure—takes Socrates as an example. Hegel sees in him a "major turning point of the spirit in itself," which prefigures many of the dominant philosophical questions of Hegel's own time. Thus, Socrates appears both as an opponent of Romantic irony and as a pioneer of Kant's transcendental philosophy (LHPh 385). His main contribution was that "the substantial, although eternal and in and for itself, must as truly be produced through me" (LHPh 386), that is, through the individual human being and its consciousness. With Anaxagoras, thought was raised to an "all-powerful notion," the "negative power of all that is definite and existent," while for Protagoras, the "I" was "the unrest of the notion" with "moments of movement outside [of the 'I']" (LHPh 385). With Socrates, in contrast, the "I" emerges in the form of a reflected universal.[83] In an analogy saturated with allusions to Kant, Hegel assigns to Socrates the world-historical point where "infinite subjectivity" and "the freedom of self-consciousness . . . break out" (LHPh 386).

What Kant says about the perception of facts or states of affairs as pending veridically on a priori structures of the mind is applied to Socrates's understanding of the good.[84] Plato had understood the good as a "form." For Socrates, the good determines the act, and thus, Hegel claims, Socrates had always already mediated epistemology through practical philosophy. As mentioned earlier, it is in particular Kant's principle of morality that shapes Hegel's understanding of Socrates's practical philosophy. While the ethical surrounding Socrates concerns only a form of life, wherein shared maxims define "common sense" ("Common sense contains the maxims of its time"), the claims of morality now emerge with Socrates and his stubborn subjectivity.[85] Hegel defines this morality as a "reflexive morality" (LHPh 388) since the "I" becomes an authority through the autonomy of its own thinking. This subjectivity is not relative. It does not mean particularity or the arbitrariness of solipsistic individuality. If this were the case, then Socrates would not have overcome the Sophists, in Hegel's reading. Hegel understands the individuality and subjectivity of the Socratic "I" as "being-in-itself-and-for-it-self universal." Here, truth is understood in the recognition of the good "as a product mediated through thought" (LHPh 386).

Even though the Sophists were already given the "principle of subjective reflection" of free interiority, this principle was characterized by "ambiguity" and "indeterminacy" (LHPh 373). "The principle comes forth only as the peculiar possession of one individual" (LHPh 445). Man was the Sophists' measure of all things, but it was man "as the undetermined and many-sided" (LHPh 373) who was their yardstick. For Socrates, on the other hand, mankind is able to recognize not only what is right and good, but also that this right and good, by its very nature, must be universal.[86] Yet even Socrates could no longer defend the maxims of the Athenian life-world and its adherence to the old gods, mocked by Aristophanes. After all, many of the Socratic dialogues end in confusion about the concept under discussion. Although maieutics are supposed to lead "to the *true* good, to the universal Idea" (LHPh 402), it cannot provide a positive content of its subject matters under discussion.

For the Greeks, individuality was a part of ethics within the entire context of a system of actuality, where the individual is "unconsciously" doing the "right" thing (LHPh 411). The ethical human being "*is* like this," "without prior considerations about" *how* or *what* he is, and without behaving self-reflectively toward this being or trying to objectively "shine a light" on himself out of the conceptuality of his thought, as Socrates does. This exact moment "of an individuality of mind" (LHPh 422) emerges with him: autonomous thinking as an active determination against all "unconscious" ethical life.

However, strictly speaking, Socrates's subjectivity becomes "excessive" when he does not submit himself to Athens's judgment and rejects—"disdain[ing] the juridical power of the people" (LHPh 442)—a voluntary exile.[87] Thus, similar to Antigone, he represents a kind of "death drive," as an insistence that accepts death for the sake of a higher normative value. Socrates's affront is "a moral autonomy" (LHPh 442) that is aware of its rights. It is in this context that Hegel mentions the concept of conscience. "Socrates thus," he writes, "set his conscience in opposition to the judges' sentence" (LHPh 442).

SOCRATES'S CONSCIENCE

The criminal who knows that he has committed an injustice with his action has performed an illegal act. This kind of illegality is not evil in the same sense as the inviolability of conscience can be evil. In the latter, that is, in conscience, lies a much stronger force of negativity, provoking world-historical collisions between a moral-formal certainty and an established life form. Hegel refers to the French Revolution and interprets the Kantian moral law in this context as an instrument of modern violence. The events of 1789 incarnate this violence with a radicality never seen before. Since the concept of the moral will can resist in the name of a kingdom of ends, exhausting and gratifying itself within a particular way of life, an "infinite injury" (PR §218/p. 250) can be the effect, as exemplified for Hegel in the bloody years between 1789 and 1799.

Hegel considered the terror of the French Revolution the spawn of such context-free reason beholden to freedom, in which he sees a structural tragedy of modernity. The standpoint of morality underdetermines the historicity of morality itself. However, Hegel—in spite of his radical critique—nevertheless reserves the individual's right to question the power of social norms and behaviors over and over again before the "law of the subjective will." For the "highest right of the subject" is to "recognize nothing that I do not perceive as rational" (PR §132/p. 159).[88] If Hegel therefore locates conscience at the end of the chapter "Morality" in the *Philosophy of Right* as a radical step of a solipsistic self-legislation, then we must assume the extent to which conscience must overcome its formality and self-legislation and pass into the realm of the living good, precisely because the risk of blindness is greatest in context-free self-reflexive self-confidence, according to Hegel. However, when Hegel applies this conscience likewise to Socrates as someone whose outstanding self-consciousness articulates a new stage of communal reason in (and against) Athenian society, then conscience is in turn indispensable for provoking ethical life into a respectively new form. Therefore, it is not easy to integrate the concept of conscience into ethical life in such a way that, in each case, the conscience acts in freedom the way it has always wanted to act. And it is this tension between morality and ethical life that contributes to the irreconcilable contradictions in Hegel's work that are the subject of countless commentaries. These irreconcilable contradictions are symptomatic of the controversial questions in the literature about the extent to which Hegel (1) destroys the concept of morality in the concept of ethical life (Arnolf Ruge, Tugendhat, Theunissen),[89] (2) lets it persist as a protest against ethical life, (3) lets it emerge constructively (Siep, Taylor, Schnädelbach, Neuhouser),[90] or, in close analogy to the latter, (4) understands it as an "ideal" that must be continuously conceptualized anew (Karl Rosenkranz, Peperzak, Ottmann, Wood).[91] I will adopt in the following option (2). For if Hegel can escape the accusation repeatedly raised against him in the twentieth century, namely, that his metaphysics embodies a totalitarian dialectic at its purest, then he can do so only if one shows how and in what contexts his work allows morality to persist as a nonsublatable objection to the all-incorporating tendencies of ethical life. Socrates appears to be a good example in this context, as Hegel repeatedly uses him to indicate the topic of conscience, which received little consideration in our interpretation of Antigone.

Does Hegel's treatment of conscience relocate him into the Kantian tradition? For many interpreters, this is not the case, as the concept of "conscience" cannot be claimed for an ethics of a first-person internalism of rational motivation. On the contrary, according to these interpreters, Hegel thematizes conscience critically in the ambivalence of solipsism, which cannot positively be evaluated. According to Christine M. Korsgaard, Hegel distances himself from Kantian "internalism" when he binds morality to practices in shared forms of life.[92] Frederick Neuhouser understands conscience as a concession to the individual that an advanced society can—from a patronizing perspective—*permit* itself, in the sense of a sophisticated understanding of modern tolerance.[93] Ludwig Siep interprets conscience as a stage that overcomes the confrontation between solipsistic beliefs and social normativity via a "step coming from both sides."[94]

Dean Moyar demonstrates, however, that conscience is presented in a positive ethical dimension in Hegel's thought when it is linked to Hegel's theory of the inference (*Schlusslehre*) in the *Encyclopedia Logic* (ESL §§131–93).[95] I wish to join this interpretation in what follows, because it helps us to think of certainty within excessive subjectivity not simply as "primitive" (Halbig)[96] or as a negativity geared toward reconciliation (Siep).[97]

Hegel develops his theory of syllogistic inference in response to an epistemological problem inherited from Hölderlin and Fichte in the context of the theory of judgment. In his remarks in *Judgment and Being* (*Urtheil und Seyn*), Hölderlin—playing on the German word for judgment, *Ur-Teilung* (primordial division)—directs attention to the idea that any propositional content of a given judgment presupposes an absolute Being in order to ascribe veridically a subject to a predicate. This process of an *Ur-Teilung* presupposes in turn a One and All in which every human being finds itself and shows to what extent the form of judgment is "inseparably connected to the schema of substance and accident or thing and property," as Georg Sans puts it. He adds: "As soon as we judge, we cannot help but imagine reality as a set of substances in which certain determinations are inherent."[98] In a judgment or a proposition, the subject will necessarily particularize, and in the predicate it will be attributed a *universal* property. The result is that the judgment abstracts from the subject's particularities, and as such no longer satisfies the particularity in an absolute manner. The theory of the inference is to remedy this primordial division (*Ur-Teilung*) in the judgment (*Urteil*), the separation of subject and predicate, without presupposing, as Hölderlin does, an understanding of the Absolute in the light of an antagonism-free concept of Being. So Hegel's *Schlusslehre* attempts to go beyond Hölderlin. For Hegel judgment is not to be understood as a primordial division, but embodies the claim of a totality *without* an original division (*Ur-Teilung*). Judgment does not abstract from Being—triggering the question of how to bring subject and predicate back together again within the confines of truth and objectivity. Judgment rather—as overcoming *Teilung*—incorporates a momentum of absoluteness in itself. Moyar relates this insight to Hegel's theorem of conscience in comparison to the Kantian structure of a moral judgment. For conscience embodies the claim of an objectivity without a primordial division (*ohne zu "ur-teilen"*).

When Hegel writes in the *Logic* of his *Encyclopedia* that "everything is a syllogism," he refers, according to Moyar's complex linkage between the *Schlusslehre* and Hegel's theory of conscience, to the extent to which inference is so bound up in a real-world context that we are granted objectivity not through, for example, chains of syllogistic reasoning, but, for example, by certain exclusions of options for deeds. About these options, Moyar with his claim about conscience as judgment holds that they say something essential about the inference with respect to conscience. "A is either B or C or D / But A is B, / Therefore, A is neither C nor D" (SL 622–23).[99] Moyar sees this inferential process of elimination as a moment of conscience. He writes, "The basic move here is to individuate a term (e.g., a right action = A), and thereby specify its *content*, through determinate *exclusion*."[100] Moyar thus points to the extent that conscience stands for a certainty that situates itself *beyond explanation* for Hegel, and this circumstance relates to our topic of excessive subjectivity. It is, in Hegel's words, a "self-referring determination," and it is made possible, according to Moyar, through "the determinate exclusions . . . by the exhaustive 'either-or' of the particulars."[101] Other scholars have already addressed this point (critically), but for Moyar the decisive factor is that conscience *could* very well provide reasons for its acts. However, compared with a Kantian moral judgment that finds its maxim according to the categorical imperative, it does not act based on these reasons.[102]

The subjectivity present in conscience cannot be exhausted by descriptions or interpretations of the world. This helps Hegel to conceptualize an entity whose claim to validity is *not derived* from judgmental and inferential contexts. If A, B, and C are the alternatives, then there are immediate rejections within conscience. What then remains is, for example, A. But A is not the result of a judgment in which the conscience has the entire scaffolding of an inferential world- and value-interpretation nonthematically in store, which it could unpack at any time. Conscience's process of deliberation through determinate exclusions can precisely *not* invoke a general judgment, but it can evoke *certainty.*

One could derive conscience also from the Kantian understanding of reflective judgment, as Will Dudley does.[103] An individual thus finds in the reflective judgment "the unique combination of particulars" as the "ultimate justification" of its judgment, according to Dudley. For Moyar, however, this reasoning falls short. What he wants to demonstrate instead is that the traditional model of judgment "is *at no stage* in a position to fully grasp conscience, for conscience is a figure of the autonomous act and not merely the conscious judgment that an act X was good due to such and such properties."[104] The goal that Hegel envisages in conscience is not a denial of reasons in favor of primitive feelings. (Yet he declines to grant conscience the lack of justification too.) What he is interested in is the development of transitional figures of morality that go beyond standard understandings of moral agency and justification.[105]

Even if one cannot exclude the possibility that conscience could cite reasons for its conduct, these reasons are not present in conscience's certainty. Therefore, conscience is metaphorically speaking "empty." Reasons are part of another inferential system of determination, another life form, to use Wittgenstein's term, to which conscience is not bound. Therefore, Hegel cannot switch from his concept of conscience to a third-person perspective, such that an immediate certainty may become an actualized universality evident for all. This is impossible—and this is precisely the basis for the fact that conscience makes a ludicrous claim, at which one could almost laugh, if it were not so tragic as the examples of Antigone and Socrates show.

Conscience can only explain itself in a negative manner. If it could explain itself positively, then it would be part of shared reasons, and could no longer expand the rational space of commonality from its nonplace.

Yet it is precisely this expansion of the sociality of reason through an antisocietal lack or gap directed against reason that concerns us here. Conscience is empty, in the sense that it does not contain an interpretation of the world anchored in judgment.[106] The subjectivity associated with it is nonetheless indeed universal, but crucially *not universalizable*. At most, this subjectivity is universalizable *too late*.

In regard to Kant's highly controversial example in *On a Supposed Right to Lie from Philanthropy*,[107] Hegel would certainly not disagree with Kant that lying is immoral and reprehensible. Hegel would reject lying no less than Kant. It would also be wrong to interpret Hegel as though he favored a utilitarian assessment of the issue and would rescind the prohibition on lying in the process of weighing the goods, so to speak. Hegel's discussion of conscience, against and only against the background of which we judge this example, does not mean to say that. With regard to Kant's example, Hegel would grant conscience the right to deny telling the murderer the truth about the whereabouts of the friend only from its lack of reasoning, its emptiness. Conscience is empty. It is empty insofar as it is not equipped with an ability to judge in the Kantian sense and so, with the help of the categorical imperative, will not impose a maxim upon its will. The particular (the concrete situation presented by Kant with a murderer at the door) and the universal (the duty not to lie) are *not*, according to Hegel, in conflict in the conscience. Precisely for that reason, particularity and universality do not set themselves apart either, an idea central to our understanding of excessive subjectivity. This idea of a self-referring determination of particularity and universality proceeds from a false understanding, in Hegel's understanding of conscience and justification. When Socrates, as Hegel writes, opposes with his conscience "the juridical power of the people" (LHPh 442), this could be interpreted according to the line of reasoning presented earlier that, for Socrates, particularity and universality coincide free of judgment and that there is no other alternative for him than to represent his freedom of "being-in-and-for-itself," that is, universal within his particularity, even if this includes exactly the end of this universality, that is, his death. Hegel's arguments even suggest that we consider Socrates's fate within the tragedy of ancient Greece as a *condition* of the political. For it is only through tragedy that a "principle" can "elevate itself," according to Hegel, "into a form of the world-spirit" (LHPh 444). Immediately afterward, he refers to the retrospectivity of that very same principle when he writes that it as principle "penetrate[s] later" into actuality. And he continues: "His own world could not comprehend Socrates, but posterity can, in as far as it stands above both" (LHPh 444).

With this Hegel indirectly rejects the idea that Socrates's teachings, as a collection of abstract, universalizable propositions, could have been spread by his students purely in the form of formal teachings (that is, detached from Socrates). For the "principle," the particular-universal, advocated by Socrates, has again only "through the manner of that event [the end of Socrates's life]" experienced that "this principle became so highly honored" (LHPh 445). Only the normativity, recognized too late, shows that this principle is "totality" and as such stands "in direct and even hostile and destructive relation to the actuality," and not merely as an "opinion and doctrine" (LHPh 445), among others. The principle as actuality needs the embodiment of a concrete personality. The latter gathers the love of his disciples "against the actuality of the Greek mind" (LHPh 445). The disciples are the ones who receive the teachings of their master from the horizon of his personality—and only from here: from the particular place where he articulated them. Therefore a radical teaching requires the contingent-existential incarnation of a subject and not simply the formula of doctrine.

Hegel grants the Athenians the "honor" to sentence Socrates to death, but in the same breath records without irony that the same people "repented of their condemnation, . . . and punished some of his accusers with death itself, and others with banishment" (LHPh 445). In both cases they acted lawfully. The Athenians' remorse precisely does not imply for Hegel that "it should not have happened." Only the tragic liquidation of an excessive subjectivity and the certainty of no longer being able to hear its enigmatic invocations allow the descendants, via the ensuing gap, to recognize a new consciousness that previously had been unable to establish any normativity in the realm of "common sense."

It would be wrong to limit the "principle" made visible through Socrates's fate solely to the latter's ability to question established definitions of general concepts/ideas when he starts asking "What is X?" Even if this is what Socrates's dialectical reasoning is most famous for, Hegel's discussion of the "principle" cannot be reduced to universal skills. The "principle" as a totality goes beyond universal teachings as it is bound to particularity, that is, to a concrete individual, not just a teaching. This is historically significant for excessive subjectivity. Going beyond Socrates, Hegel writes: "So the heroes appear as violent, the laws as harmful. Individually they find their downfall; but this principle penetrates, though in another form, and undermines that which exists."[108] The principle, once it has entered actuality, necessarily vanishes. It becomes the unconscious maxims of a new epoch. It nevertheless required excessive subjectivity, as a "great man wants to be guilty, and takes on the great collision" (LHPh 446, translation changed).

THE UNIVERSAL AND THE PARTICULAR

As seen earlier, Hegel understands the "spirit of a nation" as the epistemic-normative framework within which specific acts, situated among universal practices of application, gain their validity. This universal dimension of the national spirit specifies the uniting principle of moral obligations and subsumes particular acts under its authority. The national spirit can be compared here with the relationship between the universal and the particular in Hegel's *Logic*. There, the universal is interpreted as the entity, which is tautologically *itself* even in crossing over into an otherness within itself. (It is "at rest in its other as *in its own*" [SL 532].) The universal does so "without *doing violence*" (SL 532) to itself.

The universal embodies in this very abstract context of Hegelian thought a "free power" (*freie Macht*), by integrating the particular "other" into itself, into its universality (SL 532). In the words of Klaus Düsing: "In this 'free power' of *particularity* [*Einzelheit*] lies the 'principle of individuality and personality.' Particularity is the conceptual determination of subjectivity. . . . It is concrete universality itself."[109] The universal can integrate the "free power" of the particular, yet the process does not always proceed without crisis for the individual existing subject, who only lets the universal be universal within the limitations of his concrete life.

The universal can integrate the free power of the individual only because it is situated *in time* and, therefore, on the horizon of its *ever-newly-evolving* formative idea. This idea will then be inscribed into it from eternity onward, and prior to its ever-new and future shape. Through its temporality, the universal as the "spirit of the people" is always also a condition of the occurrence of a particular, which not only confirms the universal, but also can endanger it as concrete universality, at least from the perspective of the universality of (ethical) living. Socrates embodies such an occurrence. As the embodiment of a new consciousness falling out of the established common sense of his age, he is more than just an (ordinary) particularity under the universal rule of *Sittlichkeit*. As a "supernumerary" particularity that incorporates within its self-consciousness its own universality, he represents humanity in an enlightened but threatening form. With reference to Žižek's use of the terms *genus* and *species*, with which the Slovene philosopher describes the crumbling hierarchy of a set and its included subsets,[110] one could say that Socrates is the embodiment of "concrete universality" insofar as he is not one philosopher/Athenian among many other philosophers/Athenians of the same "species," but negates all the positive properties of the others with his outstanding superiority/singularity. As such, he establishes a new "genus": the enlightened mankind of modernity. So the universal does not become concrete when it incorporates itself into a certain member of its instantiation (that is, into a certain species), but when it becomes the singularity that negates all positive species that traditionally defined the genus as such. Only through this enactment of a retotalization of the genus from a singular point of exception (or excess) inside of it, we have true universality as it is at the same time *substance and subject*. This enactment threatens established forms of inferential differentiations. Why? Because the place of superiority marks—in the vocabulary of Badiou—a void in the "state of a situation" or in "the state of a world."[111] A potency presents itself as illegal as it cannot be determined with regard to the potency of the "state of a situation." An individual has the right to be recognized as one on an equal footing with others, but to recognize in it concrete universality, that is, to see in her one *beyond* all the others, is (almost) too much to ask for common sense. This holds for antiquity as it holds for our present age.

In the *Philosophy of Right*, section 279A, Hegel relates Socrates's firmness to his "demon," and calls his decisiveness "pure insight." He develops this line of thought in the context of his comments on the monarch's power to form the body politic via the rule of his will (often with the help of his magicians). From the individual peak of the monarch's rule, Hegel sees the unity of a community guaranteed. He stresses that the sovereign decision brings an end to semantic fluctuations of justifications between contradicting arguments. In relation to this kind of decision via the monarch, Socrates's "demon" overcomes through consciousness mythical insight. The "pure decision" that, from the beginnings of the formation of human society, was divined from auguring the flights of birds and from the "entrails of animals," is overcome by him. Hegel still sanctions the pre-Socratic forms of decision-making as an expression of all "actuality's" necessity of a fundamental choice "in the decided unity of its beginning and its completion." Socrates, however, overcomes this arbitrary choice. In his "*daemon* . . . we can see how the will which in the past had simply projected itself *beyond* itself began to turn in upon itself and to recognize itself from within, which is the beginning of a *self-knowing* and hence, genuine freedom" (PR §279/p. 320). Therefore Socrates's exception is justified.

In the *Philosophy of Right* as well, Hegel does not reject the "exceptions" of a socially prescribed universal, even if they contradict the established ethical life (PR §150A). Klaus Erich Kaehler aptly identifies, in relation to Hegel's *Logic*, a similar structure in Hegel's notion of tolerance. He writes that "letting the contingent and particular be . . . is also part of the ethical task. . . . But *how* that willing and doing in the concrete existence of the individual will come about must be left to him [the single individual, in our case, Socrates]." Kaehler continues: "In the system of speculative philosophy it logically follows that nothing can be said about it [that is, about this particular exception], as it concerns precisely the sphere of the difference between [Hegel's understanding of] substance and subject."[112]

If a people's spirit embodies its idea of ethical life, yet allows for moments of differentiation and levels of valence (that is, it lets the contingent and the particular be) through its genealogical anchoring in the time of world-spirit and in its respective embodiment, then the universal of the people's spirit can always be rewritten from an unfinished future with new legitimacy (via the contingent and particular), despite the real presence of the idea *in it—in the spirit of the people.*

When Hegel therefore speaks of "the spirit of the people" as a "true ground of established norms and values," he does so with the conviction that this ground can be violated by individuals. The emergence of individuals in world history as retrospectively acting instances of the particular in the universal brings then the world-spirit "to consciousness and self-consciousness, and thus to the revelation and actuality of its essence, the essence that is in and for itself" (PM §549/p. 246). "Socrates' universal" therefore has the power to see through the "nullity of the laws of the particular good" insofar as its dialectic is capable of overturning the existing laws.[113]

According to the reading proposed here, for Hegel, excessive subjectivity generally embodies a "singularity," which is "not being imported . . . from the outside" of the universal into the universal, but "as negativity in general, . . . as *a second universal*, as the negation of negation" (SL 532) affect it from within. As such "singularity" is "absolute determinateness" (SL 532). The "universal concept" specifies itself from immanent necessity via concrete universality, which may occur first as contingency, as an event and then as an "exception in terms of ethical meaning."[114] Yet Hegel does not surpass Socrates, as Smail Rapic claims, by exerting control over "a conscientious decision of intersubjective control."[115] Rapic holds that the Socratic method is "in so far inferior, according to Hegel's self-understanding of the conceptual theory of his logic, as the structure of the people's spirit can be reconstructed with logic as a joint framework for the application of abstract ethical rules to individual cases."[116] If this were true, then the particular would play its role only ever under the sovereignty of the universal *again*, and could not break through to an "other" of itself. Yet the eruption of the ethical in an illegitimate founding act is exactly what Hegel repeatedly emphasizes with figures such as Socrates.

Therefore, it is also incorrect to claim that the grounding ethical principle, in the sense of the *Logic*, can only be understood as the way in which the "demand that is to be directed toward an ethical justification" is possible only when it justifies "the validity claim of the ethical rules *at the same* time" and "in a controllable sense sublates"[117] them. Hegel goes beyond Socrates's subjective-remaining universality because his philosophy can raise the particular into the universal, taking into account that this universal will be determined through a genealogy of its unfinished future.

MADNESS AND DISASOCIABILITY OF THE HUMAN SOUL

In his *Anthropology*, developed in the chapter on Subjective Spirit (also called Subjective Mind) within the third part of the *Encyclopedia* (*Philosophy of Mind* [PM §§388–412]), Hegel offers some important observations on madness that touch upon our subject matter. Here, his analyses, as part of his comments on the genealogy of the soul (*Seele*), assert the previously described relationship of the subject's interiority to be dependent on the world of the universal (out there) as a medium of the individual's relationship to herself (in me). Now Hegel's remarks on madness show how the dividing line between madness and consciousness must not be understood as a sharply drawn boundary. This is due to the fact that the human "soul," as we shall see also in reference to Lacan, can exhibit eccentricity, which means that it cannot be understood to be synonymous with a traditional understanding of the Cartesian *res cogitans*. Hegel's remarks are also particularly beholden to the goal of understanding the soul not as part of a *world-soul*, but exclusively as "individuality, subjectivity" (PM §391). The individual soul is not a derivative of a cosmic soul-substance. On the contrary, its modern role is grounded in independence.

Hegel elaborates his anthropology as a generative development of consciousness through emotive states. These states are, in each case, in a mutually referential relationship with the objectivity of a natural environment of the soul that—from the outside, so to speak—coinstantiates its interiority. The increase of conscious subjectivity out of pure states of emotions in reference to an environment is understood here in particular as a procedural self-molting. The sentient, still mollusk-like soul of the ego evades more and more the interference of its emotional nature. It does so in a reciprocal relationship with an institutionally mediated outside world that always finds itself shaped by the universal (PM §§409–10).[118] Through habit then, the soul experiences itself finally, to use the apt words of Rometsch, "as that which stays constant in the transformation of its emotional content through repetition. . . . The self has not just simply become used to something; it is able to discern gradually [*tendenziell*] to *what* it has become accustomed and to what not. By ordering the emotional content in the act of imagining, the entire emotional life opens up as the horizon of that which can be experienced."[119] At the end of this procedural maturation-through-alienation, with which Hegel indicates his response to the mind-body problem of his time inherited from Descartes and indebted to the Zeitgeist of mesmerism and magnetism, consciousness can conceive of itself *as* consciousness in a reflective and, as mentioned, alienated relationship.[120] Hegel views stages, such as animal magnetism and madness, as necessary steps in this self-alienating process of the soul/ego intended to solidify and strengthen it via guided habitual processes. The emotive constitution of man is not simply the passive basis of a higher rational faculty, which at some future point in time will take over the rule of agency. Hegel's understanding of the emotive soul, on the contrary, refuses to countenance a precise boundary between rational and emotional parts of it, even if rational parts of the soul finally take on the supposed reign over consciousness through the process of habituation.[121] (Hegel indirectly anticipates a debate concerning the Freudian legacy, led by Marcia Cavell and Sebastian Gardner about the status of nonpropositional contents of human consciousness in the context of the debate on "the heterogeneity of the mental.")[122]

For Hegel, the awakening of the soul is not the appearance of a consciousness that is already self-referential and self-reflexive. The soul does not simply grow "from" nature. The activity of the soul is rather the "sleep of mind" (PM §389/p. 29) awakening slowly by gradually growing into the "identity- and continuity-providing instance of the social existence of man,"[123] according to Dieter Sturma. Sturma underlines how the soul in its own self-reflexivity precisely *cannot* refer only to itself. The soul is self-reflexivity through externalization. Its origin is tied to instances of a societal context. It exists "in itself" only insofar as it exists "in others" or in "an other" as its unconscious flip side. The soul stands also for a magical relationship to be one *and* dissolved into another at the same time. On the lowest level of embodiment, as Hegel notes, this is represented by the embryo and the womb.

The ability of the soul to ultimately grow into rational self-positing and self-reflexive intelligibility, as mentioned earlier, can also be lost again. We refer to this as an illness or, in contemporary jargon, as a psychopathology. The disease does not attack the substance of the soul, but it is understood in part by Hegel as essentially a relapse to an outdated mode of consciousness that was overcome through the disciplinary adaptation of habits. In the relevant sections of the *Encyclopedia*, Hegel calls madness that state in which subjectively created visions and imaginations can no longer be confirmed through reference to the external world, for the ability of having access to objectivity is restrained.[124] When Hegel speaks of madness, he means not only our common understanding of madness, but also particularly strong and unreflective emotional mental states that "color" our life-world, our way of "what it is like to be me." To describe it as distortion as opposed to a distortion-free perception suggests falsely that the soul could cast off the being-for-itself of its emotional life, with the effect of finding a "neutral" experience and an emotion-free access to reality.[125] Hegel rejects this understanding in his genealogy.[126] In extraordinary cases the soul falls prey to madness and separates itself "from its *substance*" (PH §408Z/p. 116). It "comes into *direct opposition* . . . into complete *contradiction* with the *objective*, thereby becoming a purely *formal, empty, abstract* subjectivity." In this "its *one-sidedness* claims for itself the significance of a veritable unity of the *subjective and objective*" (PH §408Z/p. 116).

Lacan calls this a state of psychosis-related mania with reference to his so-called imaginary register. The imaginary, as the subject's realm of autopoietic self-relations filled with fantasies, becomes almost absolute and fills the outside world, because it can no longer adjust itself through the world of others (for Lacan, it is the world of the symbolic). Particularity no longer has access to the universal so to speak (or only very little), which might then also provoke a countereffect, namely, a new form of universal certainty within this particularity. Just remember Hegel's comments on Socrates. The Greek philosopher leaves the symbolic world of common sense, developing a self-consciousness that, as "supernumerary" force, brings him beyond all standards of reason. Can this not also be called a kind of madness, a higher-order faculty of madness? Let us go back to Hegel's comments on the soul or respectively on the mind. He writes: "In order to reach this perfect separation" of the soul from its environment—or, in the language of psychoanalysis, in order to ultimately express an ego-function—"the *feeling soul* must overcome its *immediacy*, its *naturalness*, its *bodiliness*" (PM §408Z/p. 117). It must posit itself "ideally," thereby transforming the properties just mentioned "into an objective unity of the subjective and the objective, and thus discharging its Other from its immediate identity with the feeling soul as well as at the same time freeing itself from this Other" (PM §408Z/p. 117).

Hegel describes the soul in the moment of its self-grasping and emphasizes the act as being performative and hyperbolic. The positing is the instantiation of a unity of the subjective and the object in subjectivity itself. It appears as if this performative act of self-assertion incorporates a quanta of madness. In contrast to this self-assertion of an ego-function, incorporating phantasmagoric ideals, madness appears in Hegel's words as a regression out of the ego-forming process of alienation. The subject falls back into the past where emotions and partial drives reign. Precisely by not recognizing the *Allgemeines* (universal) in the outside world as an entity codependent on itself, the subject runs the risk of taking the actuality of the reality around her—that is now legitimated by herself, by her ego—*as too real.* In this way, the soul/mind can get lost in its own emotional life. Yet that which is understood here as an illness and as madness is, for Hegel, *always* a potential condition of the increasing reflexivity of the mind. It is only because the mind can fall into madness that it can also posit and self-referentially instantiate itself as self-consciousness. (Take again the case of Socrates: his exceptionality is described by Hegel as hyperbolic.) This is so because in "magical relationships," as seen in "female friends with delicate nerves" (PH §405/p. 90), the soul can find itself in itself *at the moment of being set apart from itself,* and the absolute empathic bond is a good example of an externalization. The soul/mind can determine itself as having "posited" itself in reference to a *beyond* of itself. The self-grasping *is*—as we've already seen in Kant—a magical and paradoxical act: taking one's own split upon oneself and acknowledging something alien within that which is one's own.

The soul needs habits because of its fundamental eccentricity. Hegel calls the body the "sign for the mind" (PM §411/p. 137). Habit is the corset that helps the sentient soul grasp itself even if this self-seizing remains imperfect and incomplete.[127] If this incompleteness were not the case, the soul could neither lose itself in madness nor posit or grasp itself via madness. Hegel's reference to madness puts him at a distance from a Fichtean understanding of the performative self-assertion of the "I" and from the concept of the transcendental apperception of the "I" in Kant's philosophy. The ego is for him always more fragile and more dependent on normative bindings, on hyperbolic acts of self-instauration, and on societal relationships (which determine the emotional life at the level of individual experience) than Fichte and Kant saw themselves obliged to examine.[128] As such, then, the soul embodies a potentiality and differentiality that according to Catherine Malabou is at the center of Hegel's understanding of "plasticity."[129]

The tension into which the soul may relapse—between, on the one hand, madness, magical emphatic relationships of duality, and, on the other hand, habitual autonomous self-determination through integration into identity-creating instances—shows that the "*fundamentum*" of the soul can be determined neither in reference to interiority nor in reference to the exterior world.[130] So, Hegel, too, cannot mark the origin of the soul or fix it forever in an established doxa through the habitual structures of morality. The soul is always already split in Hegel's Subjective Spirit of the *Encyclopedia*. It is split between an inner realm and an outer space where the boundary between both is itself *split yet again*. Jens Rometsch seems therefore to underestimate "madness" in Hegel's understanding of the soul when he interprets it in his otherwise brilliant commentary on Hegel's Subjective Spirit as "an intrusion of corporality and therefore of Nature [*Natürlichkeit*] into spirit."[131] He writes: "Instead of obeying reason, the mad person obeys a certain emotional disposition."[132] However, at the decisive point at which Hegel thematizes "madness," Rometsch fails to appreciate that Hegel locates something nonspiritual and alien in mind itself, which is misunderstood when interpreted in terms of a hierarchy, that is, from the perspective of a "subordination under reason," as if reason were independent of the soul's emotivity. Therefore, Gerhard Gamm's interpretation seems more convincing. In his study *Der Wahnsinn der Vernunft* (*The Insanity of Reason*), published in 1981, he shows how, in Hegel's emphasis of the atemporality of the "sentient soul" in contrast to the temporality of consciousness, neither the soul nor consciousness can be dissolved into each other without a disturbing remainder.[133] For Gamm, the "other" of reason (*das Andere der Vernunft*) lives in reason's consciousness, and does so without being subject to time. (Freud also understands the unconscious as an entity that is not to be subjected to the temporality of the ego.) Madness is not an intrusion of corporeality. Corporeality splits the soul/body (or mind/body) dichotomy itself at its origin, when spirit comes on the scene.

Let us return to Antigone one more time: Why, in the vocabulary of Hegel's Subjective Spirit, should a "soul" like that of Antigone not fall back into the embodiment of an emotional content (on the level of sentience) as the ultimate line of defense when the outside world has turned the space of reasons upside down? In a way, she has to do exactly this. Her mind no longer has recourse to a space of reference for truth and reason beyond herself. Does this alleged "relapse" into sentience necessarily ascribe to Antigone the judgment of being hysterical or insane because her actions include "emotive" symptoms such as emotional outbursts? One could diagnose Antigone as suffering from some form of schizophrenia, as characterized by Marianne Krüll in her book on the topic.[134] Krüll defines schizophrenia as the inclusion of society's antagonisms into the emotional world of the subject. She shows how the insane schizophrenic is characterized mainly by the lack of repression-capacities that are necessary for the mind to diminish confrontations with apparent contradictions that are immanent in every society. Repression-capacities are essential in forming "common sense" within a body politic and as such are indispensible for the establishment of a "healthy" human mind. The person who may appear as mentally disturbed, then, would be in this assessment he (or she) who absorbs *too much* reality in the perception of reality. Collectively practiced mechanisms of repression are lacking. Hegel's definition of madness strikingly resembles this modern diagnosis by Krüll. In the anthropology section of the *Encyclopedia*, he describes the soul as a fragile entity in its slow genealogy of emanation out of emotional states that adopts through habits more and more the capacity of a central perspective and, finally, self-reflexivity. In this process of different formations of emotional moments in interplay with an outside world that seems just as amorphous, habit offers structures of repetition that gradually force the feeling soul into a corset of the ego-function. The latter is thereby codepending on an intersubjective space of norms and values.[135]

Madness stands, in Hegel's genealogy of the soul, for the danger of sinking back into the mollusk-like absence of differentiation and into the particularity of individual instincts and emotions. The repression-capacities acquired by habit may nevertheless one day fail—perhaps in view of an external world that is no longer comprehensible. As such, the external world cannot be any longer a guarantor of habit and repression. It cannot no longer unite the "I" with an image of itself or a feeling of itself. Antigone may have had an experience like this. If she embodies madness from the perspective of the polis, then this might be so as "the subject finds itself in the *contradiction* between its totality systematized in its consciousness, and the particular determinacy in that consciousness, which is not pliable and integrated into an overarching order. This is *derangement*" (PM §408/p. 115). If one states this as such, one neglects another explanation for individual madness, namely, that the "systematized totality" of the polis may prove *itself* to be paranoid, for example, due to what Robert Pfaller calls "illusions without owners,"[136] illusions that make reality without there being "minds at home" with justified beliefs in facts and values. This is what Antigone experiences in relation to her polis. In the case of collective paranoia caught in illusions without owners, *Sittlichkeit* may have no other option to perceive everything that is *truly reasonable* (like Antigone's deed) more or less as mad. The individual subject then can no longer accept the ideological map of the "healthy men" of common sense, which is "transmitted through education and cultural activities."[137] Put in other words, she can no longer situate herself on the map according to the routes depicted.

Thus for their part, the healthy men of common sense may suffer from a systemic blindness of their health (the doxa of their certainty). They fail to recognize that the contradictions that the subject embodies are, as Krüll notes, the contradictions of society itself. The emotionally excited and hysterically acting subject seems then to do harm (to herself and others) in contrast to the external view of third parties, who remain calm and composed in the protective apparatus of shared universality, and recognize in the rage of the individual the strengthening of their own righteousness. Therefore, one can interpret Antigone's deed as based on not being able to share the displacement of the funeral rite from the polis in favor of a collective will (or illusion) that confirms (almost unanimously) that this displacement is necessary. It is this will/illusion that the choir as the embodiment of the vacillating moment of public opinion submits itself to.

Consequently, from the perspective of society, the will just mentioned is the condition of one's own health (which in certain situations may also be the health of the illusions without owners). From this perspective, excessive subjectivity has to appear in the disguise of mania. If the subject sees madness on the side of institutionalized practices of the polis—practices that are inconsistent with the unwritten laws—then, in a system-conditional reverse, the institutions diagnose "madness" in the particular subject.

Excessive subjectivity, as Hegel presents it in the examples of Antigone and Socrates, articulates an empty space in the political codes of norms and values. Hegel shows how this space is challenged by the moment of otherness that is radically "external." One's own limits are shaken, in part, by the underrepresentation of this external other in a political crisis through a subject as "concrete universality." Excessive subjectivity can thus reveal that the existence of the political system of differences, specifically in the establishment of their structures of justified normative beliefs, rests upon an Other that simply cannot be recognized. This Other bursts in and then, at best, forces differences to readjust their premises of differentiation.

Hegel's theory of excessive subjectivity ultimately advances its own model of mutual recognition by demonstrating that this recognition is not all that the systematicity of the political community rests upon. It also rests on an unrepresented external otherness, which Alain Badiou calls the "void" inherent in every situation of political representation. In this sense, Hegel indirectly anticipates Badiou's insight, but also Ernesto Laclau's theory of a radical antagonism of the social.[138] The possible objection of an alien and antagonistic other is the condition for the possibility of a future that overwrites and reshapes the realm of society.

4

LACAN

Subjectivity and the Autonominal Force of Lawgiving

We grasp one thing after another, and when we have grasped a thing, it is as if it possessed us. Not we possess it, but the opposite: whatever we have apparently acquired rules over us then. . . . The law which commands, the discipline which compels, and the many unmerciful rules which give us a direction and give us good taste: that is the big thing, not us pupils.

—R. WALSER, *JAKOB VON GUNTEN*

METAPSYCHOLOGY AND ITS POLITICAL DIMENSIONS

Subjects often appear to be, metaphorically speaking, "evasive answers" to a diverse array of inquiries and question-begging appellations that, emanating from society's institutions, have influenced these very subjects from early childhood on. Kant and Hegel interpret these appellations differently depending on their respective philosophical investigations. Kant does so, for example, in his *Pedagogy* and *Anthropology*, given that we leave the terror-inducing "call" of the moral law aside. Hegel, for his part, does so in exemplary manner in his master-slave dialectic of the *Phenomenology*. Lacan became interested in these appellations and calls due to his work in the psychiatric clinic Sainte-Anne in Paris's fourteenth arrondissement. Here he witnessed psychological impediments, when, for instance, in early childhood, certain calls were not received or certain appellations were misinterpreted by the evolving mind. The reference to Freud's term of the unconscious is crucial in the following sections of this chapter, since, for Lacan, the appellations transmitted by societal institutions, from parents to police and even visible in every advertisement we encounter in the subway, concern permanently the relationship of the subject to herself. They can be linked to intimate longings and inner fantasies of idealized images of the self. Due to an inherent shortcoming and a fundamental eccentricity, interiority turns out to be a foreign body for Lacan, invaded by an Other. It stems from a semantic field that, because it is overdetermined, always overtaxes us and does so especially at night, when rational thoughts ("secondary processes," as Freud calls them) are waning. This *Other in the own* often prevents us from finding peace in our dreams and accompanies the subject throughout her life. It also concerns the political order in which the subject lives as *zoon politikon*, since she expects this order, among other things, to compensate for her own shortcomings. The subject is haunted by an insatiable insistence of desire to be inscribed into the political order that, for its part, renders itself impossible due to its own deficiencies. To comprehend this aspect in its relevance for philosophy, it is important to take a look at Lacan's concept of subjectivity and its dependency on the force of law. As will be demonstrated, Kant and Hegel are of great importance for Lacan. Their works anticipate crucial insights of psychoanalysis. Therefore it is no surprise when Lacan explicitly states in his *Seminar X* that if there was anyone in his generation who had understood the contribution of the *Phenomenology of the Spirit* in an exemplary manner, it was *he himself* (S.X 22).[1]

Lacan's philosophy will assist us in this final stage of our study to comprehend the motif of the subject's constitution in the context of his social-societal alterity. It will also give us the opportunity to shine some light on the various motifs of appellation, incommensurability, and "split identity" of the ethical subject, already discussed in the chapters on Kant and Hegel. The conceptual instruments of psychoanalysis give insight into the societal relevance of the individual psychological anchoring of subjectivity as a secondary effect of normative appeals as well as of enigmatic ones.

If we speak of an autonominal force of law of subjectivity in the context of Lacan's oeuvre, we do so in order to find theoretical support for the importance of excessive subjectivity, not only in the development of the individual's act of freedom, but also in setting the structurally immanent conditions for the symbolic life-world that every subject shares with others of his kind. In the chapter on the aporias in Kant's moral theory, such an excessive subjectivity was already present in our analysis of the split subject. The idiosyncratic aporias of the moral act proceeded from a subject who retrospectively discovers himself each time anew and who, in the moral act, simultaneously withdraws and prefigures himself in relation to the extremes of holiness and radical evil. Subsequently and corresponding to the Kant chapter, we discussed Hegel's philosophy by analyzing his understanding of the ethical life as split in itself. Lacan's work allows us now to provide a psychoanalytic foundation for these two theoretical moments in idealism (the split subject in Kant and the split ethical life in Hegel). Excessive subjectivity thus emerges from our analysis of Lacan's writings both as fundamentally socially relevant and, under certain premises in the philosophy of psychoanalysis, as constituting its own branch of ethics.

Lacan shows repeatedly that the subject's self-understanding and the reality that surrounds him are shaped by collectively guaranteed virtualities, idealizations, and repressed contradictions. For Lacan, Jeremy Bentham's analyses of the virtual moments of the social contract (S.VII 12; S.XX 3, 58) are as responsible for the subject's perception of reality as Hegel's theory of recognition. Subjects are both the beneficiaries of the virtualities of the social contract and the source of energy for its maintenance. Living in these virtualities nevertheless also produces a certain discontent, which Freud described long before Lacan, as early as 1930, in his text *Civilization and Its Discontents*. Our topic here is Lacan's detailed analysis of this discontent; we wish to show how his metapsychology profoundly enriches our theory of excessive subjectivity.

We will begin with a simple example to illustrate what is meant by stating that virtualities are the condition for subjectivity to the law. We encounter one such example in our daily lives prominently in the form of paper currency.[2] It has, as we all know, a symbolic (and, indirectly, also normative) value through the number printed on it. This value is not comparable to the value of, let's say, one hundred rolls of bread that one can purchase with the bill. The rolls of bread have a use value in an empirically pure form, whereas the bill has no analogous value or, as such, it could only be as paper. Yet that does not prevent it from yielding an empirical effect, namely, buying rolls of bread. Things can change dramatically. If, for example, doubts appear suddenly in the collective agreement of faith as to the incarnation of the value printed on a piece of paper, then a sudden recognition of the collective fantasy as an illusion of the value of this or other pieces of paper (for example, stocks and bonds) emerges. Precipitous drops in international stock market values repeatedly demonstrate this virtual game of recognition or misrecognition of trust in the trust of others who, in turn, trust in others yet again.[3] Social upheavals as caused by a loss of faith in political institutions can be interpreted in this manner. This brings us to the context of our previous analyses of morality, conscience, the ethical life, and revolution. For the loss of trust in institutions can occur in a body politic abruptly. It can do so through the emergence of inner antagonisms, with citizens only belatedly recognizing their responsibility for something that already lay within their culpability. Simply replace the paper bill with the authority of a parliament, a financial system, or the faith in the state derived only from the seal on official documents. Just as a customer believes on any given day that his paper bill can be exchanged for one hundred rolls of bread, but receives only fifty for it, the law-abiding citizen may one day feel similarly deluded by the doxa of those ruling "from above" and suddenly feel no allegiance to the law. Who, then, is responsible when the question of responsibility proves itself necessary for readjusting the law, and when responsibility cannot simply be repressed?

It is precisely these mechanisms of collective virtuality that not only have an impact but even constitute our daily lives and political landscape. They are at the center of Lacan's analyses on the symbolic-imaginary networks in which both subjectivity itself and subjectivity to the law appear as answers of imaginary autopoiesis through appellations of normative communal structures. The virtual world of symbols structures empirical reality, permeates all aspects of daily life, and burrows into the abysses of the psyche. It is therefore premature to claim that after the demise of the "grand narratives" or ideologies of the twentieth century, our twenty-first century is a nonideological one. For Lacan, we human beings are, as individuals, always subjects of ideological appellation in a matrix of determinants that are our "second nature." This "second nature" is, for Lacan, not the epitome of mankind's reason, capable of truth-apt justifications in the context of an inferential and normatively structured life-world, as represented, for instance, by McDowell. Rather, for Lacan the "second nature" stands for the subject's embeddedness in another inferentiality that, in the final analysis, always escapes reason and entangles itself in aporias. This can repeatedly result in the psyche tossing aside its convictions and manipulating its autopoietic self-relations simply because the world out there, the big Other, says so. In the long run, no subject can refuse the ideological corset of her "second nature" and the respective accompanying idealizations and legal-theoretical phantasms that support it. If this nevertheless happens, then mental illness can easily be the result. In these cases the subject misses what Habermas calls "life-world . . . background knowledge"[4] and it will immediately feel the consequences.

Similarly to Hegel, Lacan considers human beings capable within their second nature of a complete phantasmatical surrender to the most bizarre authority, due to their lack of being. This lack haunts the subject in its search for completeness. A polis's culture and its politics form a semantic field that aims to compensate for this lack of order to guarantee stability through competing desires within the community. However, the subject's lack transfers to the social order in return, and it can only conceal but never remedy it. Lacan's polyvalent talk of the "Real"[5] as the unrepresentable abyss that the symbolic order cannot denote and yet upon which it rests (as much as the psyche rests on the unconscious) underlines antagonistic conflicts in the realm of politics. This manifests itself both in inner-psychological terms (via the unconscious as the locus of repressed facets of identity) and in intersubjective terms in the area of the political doxa. The latter is unable to represent all of its subjects' desires. The subject attempts to escape this Lacanian Real by inscribing herself into a phantasmatic and communal reality. This reality is always of a constructivist character, or, in Louis Althusser's and Slavoj Žižek's terms, of an ideological-interpellative form.[6] What Lacan then calls the phantasm conceals the inadequacies and disproportions of meaning construction beyond the Real. The phantasm wards off the Real yet does not annihilate it. Lacan's Real is to be understood, in the terminology borrowed from Kant, as the "transcendental object X" and consequently the condition of and correlative to the "I" of pure apperception. This already hints at the artificiality of the concept of the Real, a concept that will nevertheless prove central for our theory of excessive subjectivity. The Real can be understood as the "transcendental object, that is, the completely indeterminate thought of something in general" ("[als der] transzendentale Gegenstand, d.i. der gänzlich unbestimmte Gedanke von etwas überhaupt").[7] Without this paradoxical object, which Lacan asserts is repressed through language and the symbolic order, and which moreover can only be understood from its effects much like the vortex of a maelstrom, neither the subject nor society would be able to reconstitute herself or itself each time anew. There would be no "world" against the backdrop of the subject's constructivist eccentricity, which is alienated from herself through the symbolic and occasionally caught in his own delusions. In this context, we will discover in Lacan an aspect central to our inquiry, namely, that a "distortion"—to be understood as a performative act of freedom—of the phantasmatic frame of subject constitution can have salvific effects on the symbolic order. This performative and autonominal act of freedom, which also echoes Kant's talk of the "determination of character" (*Charakterwahl*) and the revolution of disposition, is the medium of a transgressive self-positing. It initiates for Lacan a readjustment of the individual's coordinates of appellation within the big Other, and in doing so re-creates conditions for the big Other. (Remember: the big Other is not exclusively beyond or outside of subjects, but within them.) When, for example, a subject such as Martin Luther states on April 18, 1521, at the Diet of Worms, "Here I stand. I can do no other. God help me, Amen," such an autonominal exclamation can be read as shifting or breaking through a phantasmatic frame that can have epoch-making consequences, as it did in the sixteenth century.[8]

A community's culture and its body politic need to prevent such a self-positing and must exclude it as illegal. Culture and politics are employed in a ceaseless loop of compensatory compromises that have to, on the one hand, maintain the political-libidinal desire of the subject according to its mandate and, on the other, at the same time minimize excesses of that very same desire. The political dispute instantiates an always newly self-generating loop of desire for inner coherence and stability. In this process, the political realm, as a conglomerate of historically mediated symbolic forms, circulates around a nonsymbolizable traumatic core, an inner antagonism. Around this core, myths, narratives, and political rituals establish a network of authority within which subjects recognize themselves. As such, then, the community's political discourse is also in the process of constantly failing itself, of missing a final reconciliation of immanence with transcendence. This discourse is both a creative and also creationist process that attempts to conceal the trauma of its own split and yet cannot achieve a lasting recovery. Nevertheless, as both Hegel and Lacan point out, the subject has the potential to stretch the existing virtualities across ever-new horizons of meaning and to always vitalize the body politic anew.

Consequently, for Lacan, the subject does not harmoniously grow into its environment as, for instance, Marcia Cavell suggests in her book *The Psychoanalytic Mind: From Freud to Philosophy*. For Cavell, the prelinguistic character of the unconscious with its hidden secrets and repressions has to be integrated harmoniously into a coherent overall image of the "I" and her world; the subject, having been cleansed through a cognitive clarification of repressed wishes, desires, traumata, and so on, is called to enter into an authentic relationship with herself and her environment.[9] For Lacan, this harmony is impossible. The subject is always in haste, damned to be ahead of herself, to miss herself, and to never enter into a pleasant relationship with herself and her environment. Yet it is precisely in this misrecognition or distortion that Lacan locates an ethical power, which is why he combines psychoanalysis with ethics in the first place and repeatedly refers to Kant and Hegel. The subject seems to Lacan to be less the "crown of creation," or the most precious link in the chain of being. Rather, he sees the subject as the weak link in the chain, or, more precisely, as the gap and hiatus in being.

As we attempt to pull the various strands of our inquiry together, it will be necessary to provide a more detailed introduction to Lacan's theory of subjectivity than was given in the chapters on Kant and Hegel. This is so because Lacan's elective affinities to German idealism reveal themselves through numerous references to the works of Kant and Hegel, as the representatives of the Ljubljana Lacan School have also shown in recent years. These references to Kant and Hegel gain explanatory strength when their complex entanglements with linguistics, phenomenology, set theory, and Lévi-Strauss's structuralism are simultaneously laid bare. This is what we wish to do.

Such an approach opens up areas of investigation that, though they may seem foreign to Kant and Hegel at first glance, upon closer inspection make the illuminating connections to idealism and Lacan's enthusiasm for Kant and Hegel even clearer.

KANT AND HEGEL IN LACAN'S THEORY OF THE LAW

In contrast to modern psychology and neuroscience, Freud's psychoanalysis and its further elaboration by Lacan are not interested in biological life. Rather, it focuses on the symbolic-representational relatedness in which the psyche anchors itself with respect to the world around it. In this context of the psyche's intentional orientation, questions of normativity and authorization arise. Psychoanalysis uncovers to what extent the question of authorization within a given order is put under pressure by the twin enigmas of appellation and the quest of the individual for his own legitimacy. These same questions are also of key concern in German idealism. In the chapter on Kant, for instance, we analyzed how the subject of the moral will is simultaneously the subject-in-question. The subject's splitness is due to an intentionally nonassimilable foreign core, the precondition for the radical absoluteness of his moral will. The moral subject's calling, according to Kant, is carried out by the resounding voice of conscience: it cannot be deduced further. In an unending approximation toward perfection (Kant speaks of holiness), it carries its own absoluteness in the autonominal assertion that it (the will) truly exists. Kant can explain neither why this call resounds nor why it should be binding; he can only posit it as a premise. He suggests locating the source of this calling in a foreign agency of the *completely Other* within man's inclinational and pathological egotism. He describes this agency *both* as a threatening foreignness[10] and as the true core of man's striving for (an almost divine) absoluteness. Psychoanalysis, on the other hand, came into existence precisely in the confrontation with such a threatening, nondeducible foreignness, or, more precisely, with an alterity's unbridled insistence, or, even more precisely, with its commands and desires. In extreme cases, these commands and desires forge their way forward into pathological obsessive-compulsive disorders or psychopathological symptoms that are life threatening. As such, then, psychoanalysis is also the science of that which in human beings escapes satisfaction or inner pacification and which, according to Freud and Lacan, cannot simply be reduced to man's instincts and animalistic leftovers, such as drives that have not yet been cleansed by human reason.[11] As Lacan puts it in his *Seminar VII*, the *Ethics of Psychoanalysis*: "The ethics of psychoanalysis has nothing to do with speculation about prescriptions for, or the regulation of, what I have called the service of goods. Properly speaking, that ethics implies the dimension that is expressed in what we call the tragic sense of life" (S.VII 313).

According to Lacan, Kant's ethics discovered the intractable interplay of Final Judgment, insatiable desire, and permanent failure. While "traditional morality," as Lacan discusses in recourse to Aristotle, "concerns itself with what one was supposed to do 'insofar as it is possible,'" Kant unmasks the fact that the dimension of the possible precisely does *not* touch "the topology of our [that is, human] desire" (S.VII 315).[12]

Psychoanalysis devotes itself to this desire but, as mentioned, does so repeatedly in light of the paradoxical knowledge that this desire *does not want to be satisfied* and that it proves structurally (that is, without the intentional consciousness of a purpose) resistant to the option of a life guided by virtue or reason.[13]

The insistence of such a foreign agency inside the subject ("whose center is absent" [S.VII 236]) had been precisely the discovery that gave rise to psychoanalysis. It was this confrontation with the enigma of psychosomatic symptoms from which the psyche, with regard to a pleasure-in-pain economy, could not abstain, and which escaped the cognitive reflection of an intentional consciousness. Psychoanalysis sought to provide an answer to this with the help of the theory of the unconscious as an entity hiding behind intentionality.[14] This is why Freud, from the beginning of psychoanalysis in 1895, that is, since his *Project for a Scientific Psychology*, coauthored with Wilhelm Fließ,[15] always emphasized the consistency of a nonsemantic core within the dynamics of symptom formation.[16] While we generally speak of life-threatening pathologies caused, for instance, by traumata, is it not so that, to a certain degree, Kant's ideal of the moral will, under the transcendental condition of what it means to be human, embodies such a pathology as well? Béatrice Longuenesse and Sebastian Gardner have shown this convincingly.[17] This makes clear again how the philosophy of subjectivity in psychoanalysis affords us a look into the Kantian moral will and reveals inscrutable psychointernal aporias. As Kant lacks the discovery of various layers of the psyche achieved by psychoanalysis in painstakingly developed theses, he never directly questions his ideal of autonomy and psychological self-identity. (He does so only indirectly, as the chapter on him attempts to show.) For Kant, there is no subject of the unconscious qua cybernetic machine to which man is attached and which coordinates masses of input data or stimuli on its own. Nor is there a superego.[18] What Kant nevertheless acknowledges, however, is this foreign body: an Other in the self, inside the subject's core, an Other dimension of the Other that is at the same time as unknowable as it is absolute.

For instance, Lacan likens Kant's discussion of "pain" in the pure moral will, in the third section of the *Critique of Practical Reason*, to an "outer extremity of pleasure" (S.VII 80), a feeling that, in Lacan's reading of Kant, correlates to the moral law in its purity. He comes to the conclusion that "Kant is of one opinion with de Sade," (S.VII 80) insofar as all "flood gates of desire" (S.VII 80) lead the moral subject into the horizon of the pleasure of pain in its attempt to touch on the phantasmatic limits of the unattainable (for example, holiness in Kant).[19] Here Lacan, contrary to many assumptions, is not saying that Kant's ethics in its presumed formalism is on the same level as de Sade's catalogue of perversions and human torture. However, he does see an analogy between both authors through an excessive surplus value or an *enjoyment in pain*, which psychic-economically is anchored in the phantasm of the unattainability of sexually multiperverse satisfaction or morality. For Kant, the moral act with its renunciation of happiness in combination with the infinite distance toward the kingdom of ends, a distance that despite man's failure to ever live up to holiness *has* to be bridged (though it cannot be bridged), stands in obvious relation to pain. For Lacan, this economy of pain is not per se pathological. On the contrary, it is both life-causing and life-affirming because it is tied to a peculiar form of enjoyment—*jouissance*, as Lacan calls it.[20]

In the context of the theory of excessive subjectivity, Lacan assists us in deducing the aporias of desire via psychologically described structures of normativity, at whose limits the individual (torn between different inner-psychic dynamisms) finds her place. As we have seen, Hegel too thematizes these limits as places where individual desires, in their unruliness and partial unconditional blindness, bring the process of the world-spirit into new stages of self-understanding. It is not that the world-spirit is self-reflexively aware of how excessive desires (for example, Antigone's) might be intermediaries and vanishing mediators of new horizons of consciousness. Hegel repeatedly thematizes desire, excess, mania, and strength as unruly powers that the Spirit in its increasing self-penetration genealogically requires, like a fuel necessary for its existence. If then, for Lacan, culture, political community, and the community's political doxa as instable "chains of signifiers" are never all—more precisely, they are "non-All" (*pas-tous*)—then for him, as for Hegel, it is precisely the subject's deficiency, her being driven by a normatively unattainable and unpacifiable excess (as for questionable burial laws in earlier times), that can take on antinormative power *and finally be normative for all.* This power then can only appear as offensive, unthinkable, heretical, or illegal, as it is able to attain from the deficient political structure something that in the phantasmatic reality of the general public is anathema. What Lacan calls the "Real" breaks into the political space as the exposure of the limits of meaning through an insatiable desire—a desire that for Lacan, similar to Hegel, is embodied in exemplary manner by Antigone.

Since for Lacan the subject is called upon to moderate her own destructive moments of desire through defense mechanisms, she seeks stability via the symbolic identifications of language and culture. Yet the deficient structure in the subject and in the social order can only be concealed and not completely remedied. In this sense then, the subject is necessarily a legal and political subject, even as she can never be such in absolute or autonomous terms. Here, Lacan's discussion of the Real marks the structural moments of antagonistic conflicts/noncoincidences, both inner-psychologically and intersubjectively.

When Lacan speaks of the Real, he is referring to a category that precedes the "reality principle" and impedes the attempt to distance that principle from the "pleasure principle" through a clear-cut dichotomy. The Real is at work, so to speak, not only in pleasure, but in reality itself. It is more external to us than the external world itself insofar as we can only establish both our self-image and the external world—intersubjectively structured and conveyed through signifiers—as a harmonic whole, by excluding the Real. This exclusion nevertheless leaves its traces and resists with unexpected effects. In this sense, psychoanalysis believes that it attends to something that precedes concepts such as virtue, duty, purpose, or the "service of the good." As such, then, the concept of the Real is one of Lacan's three "registers," in which subjectivity comes to be and which also include the Symbolic and the Imaginary. Inner-psychologically, the Real marks a kind of wound that we suffered through being driven out of our "pre-oedipal Eden" and that we carry forward like an original sin: apparent, for example, in the guilt of being unable to truly be oneself because the locus of the self is a phantasma of the wound that the subject tore open in the formation of its *I*-function and is necessarily unable to reclose. The Real marks the lack that emerges in the moment of required detachment from the so-called Mother-Thing. It is the trauma of the paternal prohibition that cannot be located precisely in the genealogy of the *I*-function. It is the castrating power forced upon us by laws, words, desires, and repressions of desires that format the unconscious. The latter, as a condition of subjectivity that cannot see through itself, is that locus "whose center is absent" (S.VII 236). It is "that fundamental omission in which the subject is situated" (S.VII 236). It also concerns the "foreign body in me" that Kant mentions and that, as part of "validity" without "meaning," exceeds that which cannot be stored reflexively in the self-image of the *I*-function. It is the power of a rousing Other in one's *Own* that may make itself known in desire.[21] For, as Lacan shows, man's desire is not something personal. As "desire of the other," it is an effect of the external pressure that we carry in us. In this sense then, the Real would also be this "desire of a foreign desire in me." It is the place of a "*felix culpa*" (S.VII 6), as Lacan says in his *Seminar VII*, "puisque c'est d'elle que proviendrait la loi originelle."[22] Similar to Hegel's concept of the negative, the Real marks a structural form of reversal that can, in addition, also appear in social structures.[23]

ORIGINS: FREUD'S PLEASURE COORDINATES OF APPELLATION

In his seminar *The Ethics of Psychoanalysis*, Lacan investigates whether psychoanalysis, similar to philosophy, can found an ethics, and if so, what kind of ethics it would have to be. He chooses to approach the topic with Freud's *Project for a Scientific Psychology* of 1895.[24] This *Project* can be considered the foundational text of psychoanalysis since it, similar to Hegel's *Anthropology*, links the question of legal subjectivity with the generic formation of the psyche in processes of internal and external energetic stimuli compensation. One of the theses that Lacan derives from this text, and that animates him to interpret it ever new, is that the subject emerges as a psychosomatic-compromise structure made up of various, not propositionally deducible forces. Subjectivity to the law becomes conceivable under the conditions of "another scene" (*ein anderer Schauplatz*, as Freud/Fechner have it), which ascribes a noncoincidence to the "I." In Kant, we interpreted this noncoincidence as of central importance for the moral act. In Lacan, we see how this noncoincidence concerns the subject far more profoundly than merely in the context of morality and conscience.

Freud claims in his *Project* that the perception of the external world takes place in the horizon of experiences of pleasure because the external world is necessarily mediated through the body. The human body is not the medium between sensual perception and reason; rather, for Freud, reason/mind are the result of a compromise-like formation of symptoms through traces of discharged or retained energy that have shaped the entire body but especially, of course, the mind with its separate layers. Freud describes these traces of energy as quantities of various strengths. Out of the chaotic multitude of sensual impressions (coming from the body itself or the outside world), the cognitive apparatus generates itself as a symptomatic compromise in between them. Energy quanta pass through the neuronal network where some quanta are passed through, some diverted, and some stored, in the process of building the mental prepropositional constants that combine into more and more layers of memory. Lacan aptly speaks of "pleasureable associations" within which the genesis of the psyche unfolds (S.VII 52). This paraphrase makes clear how this is more than just a neutral mechanism of spreading quantum of information, as with the semiconductors of computer chips. Discharges, diversions, and storage of quantities are physical processes accompanied by feelings of pleasure or displeasure, respectively impregnated with or accompanied by libido. In addition to these events, there is a further aspect of importance for Lacan. Freud explains how these energetic flows take place in the presence and under the conditions of the so-called *Nebenmensch*, or the *fellow human-being.* Lacan writes: "The subject's experience of satisfaction depends entirely . . . on the other, on the one whom Freud designates . . . the *Nebenmensch*" (S.VII 39). Freud mentions this *Nebenmensch* only briefly, in the last section of his *Project.*[25] Lacan, on the other hand, develops the concept of the *Nebenmensch* as the center of his theory of desire.

Upon first hearing the term *Nebenmensch* in the context of Freud's explication of the development of the psyche, one might think, for instance, of a toddler's parents. Yet the fact that Freud precisely does *not* talk of parents suggests that the *Nebenmensch* embodies another instance of alterity that is beyond the familiarity of father or mother and yet still necessarily an external point of reference. The psyche is precariously dependent on finding stability in coordinates of acknowledgment. "It is in relation to a fellow human-being that a human being learns to cognize."[26] The fellow human being is an external authority of the subject and underlines his "eccentricity" as the condition of his subjectivity. Freud also speaks of the "fellow-human being as 'Ding,'" "thing," whereby "Ding"[27] is to be understood here as a nonpropositional moment that renders the fellow being foreign once again. He cannot even be recovered in the "work of memory" as someone.[28]

The subject lacks any self-reflexive access to either herself or the external world without this fellow human being, however foreign and opaque, however "thing"-like this other human being may initially be. The fellow being is the first source for psychosomatic experiences of tactility, and for Freud that means libidinal energy. At the same time, the fellow being is in his inadequacy the "thing" of which Lacan, interpreting Freud, will say that the human world will build itself around, "as dependent on that fundamental *hallucination* without which there would be no attention available" (S.VII 53, my emphasis). The fellow human being emerges at the place "in which the whole hallucinatory phenomenon of perception occurs, of that false reality to which, in brief, the human organism is predestined" (S.VII 41). Lacan unmasks the Other as the structurally necessary coordinate for the "hallucinations," or the false reality for which the human organism is predestined.

The societal consequence of subjectivity already shows itself here, that is, in the unstable status of reality. "Reality" is precarious. It guarantees disjuncts between the individual subject and intersubjectively guaranteed metastructures of the symbolic order that cannot simply be uncovered, because were that to occur, reality as a whole—as the location of inferential reasons (for that which is)—may get lost. Human beings are predestined to live in "hallucinations," that is, in realities with inner-virtual deposits.[29]

Žižek so aptly emphasizes how the fellow human being through overly close proximity pressures the child. "It is this intrusive presence which is then interpreted as an 'enigma,' as an obscure 'message' from the other who 'wants something' from me. In this sense, the 'Neighbor' refers not primarily to the abyss of the Other's desire . . . but to an intruder who is always and by definition too near."[30]

If we now ask where the subject is located according to Freud's neuroscientific *Project*—Descartes, for example, located it in the pineal gland—Freud's answer is that it is a secondary effect of conflicting forces in the neuronal network where a foreign desire, enigmatically remaining in the *Nebenmensch*, has always already helped trigger certain phantasmagorias.[31] "All of the needs of speaking beings," says Lacan, "are contaminated by the fact of being involved in an other satisfaction . . . that those needs may not live up to" (S.XX 49). Or to phrase it more pointedly: the subject is a vortex of resentments organized by neurons that in his dependence on the Ding, that is, in his dependence on an enigmatically desiring and absolute Other, needs to constantly retain its blurry boundaries. Similarities to the master-slave dialectic of Hegel's *Phenomenology* stand out here: In their dependency of mutual recognition, both master and slave need the other and (for their own self-assurance) the conflict with the other in order to increase self-consciousness. This self-consciousness is not a fixed universal entity that, once acquired, remains with the subject for the rest of his life. Self-consciousness seems to always hide its center, the locus of "my true self," precisely where one is *not*, but where the other has taken one's place. Self-consciousness, therefore, can also collapse. Behind the master's back, as Hegel shows, it can unfold as the effect of the working slave precisely through an incorporation of the outside world through labor. Yet self-consciousness also can, as clinical psychoanalysts know, lose itself psychotically in traumas or find itself betrayed by desires, wishes, and hopes, which perhaps have never been truly its own. Political implications are omnipresent here. Consider, for instance,

Karl Marx's reinterpretation of Hegel's dialectics of recognition in the context of his metaphysics of history. Marx calls for the toppling of the bourgeois-capitalist society, which he denounces as hallucinatory due to commodity fetishism and which is characterized by the acquisition of surplus value and surplus enjoyment at the expense of the working class.

In Kantian terms, one could also interpret the energy quanta that affect the psyche from the outside and from the body's instinctual drives as the yet-unfiltered effects of sense perception. As such, these quanta are the basic material of symbolic claims. They spread their effects, and they shape the psyche and evoke normativities, even if the child's psyche can neither propositionally nor self-reflexively react yet to symbols as *symbols*.[32] Quanta of energy leave behind traces of validity on their pathways, through discharge, storage, or diversion, yet they cannot be harmoniously integrated into references of propositional meanings. This means that in this foundational text of psychoanalysis a rudimentary reflection on the force of law in the generic development of subjectivity is already omnipresent.[33] The true core of Freud's *Ding am Nebenmenschen* for Lacan is that the quanta of energy as basic material always already possess an enigmatic quality that is determinate for the psyche, at the level of neurons. Human beings set themselves apart from the *Ding am Nebenmenschen* while at the same time they appear to be addicted to the Ding as the source of a (or their) foreign desire. The fellow human being carries responsibility for the pathways that have shaped the mind in its emergence. "The Ding am Nebenmenschen as *Fremde*, strange and even hostile on occasion," is "in any case the first outside" (S.VII 52). Yet since Lacan proceeds from the assumption that this orientation is one that leads the subject into the "world of desires" (S.VII 52), it is also tied to hallucination as the foundation of perception and therefore destined to always be oriented "in relation to the world of wishes and expectations." To attempt to "reach *das Ding*" (S.VII 52) has therefore always been the fate of human beings because the *Nebenmensch*, as indefinable as he may and must be, is its source.[34]

To summarize what we have said so far: For Lacan, subjectivity, as perceived through Freud's discoveries, is established in a space of enigmatic structures of desire and legitimacy. The psyche must react to quanta of energy (external and internal) and this is precisely what makes the psyche ambiguous and shows the gaps in its self-understanding, through foreign desire, claims, appellations, and coded messages. Since these quanta of energy can never fully be cognitively metabolized by the psyche, they play a decisive role in the development of the unconscious, both according to Freud's first topical model of the psyche in *Interpretation of Dreams* and to the second model from 1923 in *The Ego and the Id*. Where these quanta of energy are able to injure or enigmatize the psyche, they bring forth neurotic symptoms that greatly impair life and can barely be kept under control. These symptoms constitute, on the one hand, a compromise that the psyche establishes in order not to collapse for good. On the other hand, the symptoms also represent an insistence on the nonmental, nonintentional, which once put a spell of too many demands on the psyche and which now will not let it get out from under this spell. As we will see, this spell-like structure can be used in political-ideological ways, particularly via ideological appeals whose power of subjection (subjugation) is stronger the more enigmatic those appeals seem to be, even if this seems initially paradoxical.

THE SUBJECT, HIS SUBJECTIVIZATION, AND THE SUBLIME SIGNIFIER

The formation of subjectivity is shaped by appellations, from which certain coordinates of reality, coupled with hallucinatory moments, are injected "under the skin" of the excentric human being. The subject builds her reality in a state of irritation mediated by the fellow human being. The fact that appellations include legal-normative dimensions was one of our central arguments for employing the philosophy of psychoanalysis in explicating Kant and Hegel. By turning to another student of Lacan's, Louis Althusser, we will push even further into this territory.

Althusser compares the "eternity of ideology" with the timelessness of the unconscious in Freud. He writes: "If eternal means, not transcendent to all (temporal) history, but omnipresent, trans-historical and therefore immutable in form throughout all history, I will go so far as to adopt Freud's formulation word for word, and write *ideology is eternal*, just like the unconscious."[35] Althusser, for his part, is referring to a thesis by Marx, who wrote in the *German Ideology* that ideology had no history.[36] His discussion of "eternity of ideology" should be understood against the backdrop of our interpretations of psychoanalysis so far. What Althusser articulates here is a relatively easy-to-understand objection to the idea that there is ever a nonideological, neutral relationship of the subject to the world.[37] If ideology, as Althusser writes, "interpellates individuals as subjects,"[38] just as for Marx the economic substructure shapes their consciousness, then the "category of the subject is constitutive of all ideology . . . as all ideology has the function (which defines it) of 'constituting' concrete subjects."[39] As each ideology has the function (which defines it) to "constitute" specific individuals into subjects, ideology succeeds in doing so via two terms shaped by Althusser: "Evidence" and "recognition/misrecognition [*reconnaissance, méconnaissance*]."[40] The subject is such a piece of "evidence," for it is "an ideological effect" in and of itself.[41] As Althusser puts it: "I shall then suggest that ideology 'acts' or 'functions' in such a way that it 'recruits' subjects among the individuals (it recruits them all), or 'transforms' the individuals into subjects (it transforms them all) by that very precise operation which I have called interpellation or hailing, and which can be imagined along the lines of the most commonplace everyday police (or other) hailing: 'Hey, you there!' "[42]

Terry Eagleton builds on Althusser's insights and, in his *The Ideology of the Aesthetic*, refers to the parallels between Althusser's understanding of ideology and Kant's analysis of aesthetic experience. Just as for Kant the aesthetic experience mysteriously bridges the gap in his first two *Critiques* between necessity and freedom, Althusser likewise understands ideology as bridging the gap between the forced external "interpellation" and the inner freedom of the subject to accept it by having the subject believe that the acceptance of the interpellation is a free decision (that is, coming from inside). Eagleton's alternating reading of Kant and Althusser provides an explanatory model for the nature and function of ideology per se. What aesthetic experience and ideological interpellation have in common might be called *servitude volontaire*, a term coined by the French writer of the sixteenth century Étienne de La Boétie. Aesthetic experience in its combination of immediacy and intuition, lawful order, and sensual pleasure represents for Eagleton a model for the way in which a new type of hegemonic authority *idealiter* interpellates the subject: "in a condition where neither civil society nor the political state would seem to provide (uniting) values with a particularly plausible foundation."[43] The decisive factor for Eagleton's interpretation of ideology in Kant's analysis of the Beautiful is not the feeling of harmony in the subject's aesthetic experience on the occasion of encountering the object considered beautiful; rather, the key is the dimension that goes beyond the individual and that declares the aesthetic experience simultaneously as *subjective* and *universally valid.* Kant employs the term *sensus communis* to express this and develops it in his second and third definition of the Beautiful.[44] If we claim that something is beautiful, then, according to Kant, we demand a universal agreement on that which we consider beautiful. We are convinced that we have the universal right to employ the judgment "X is beautiful" for this object. The point of interest to Eagleton is precisely the fact that this is both a "subjective" and a "felt" universality. This aspect of the "felt" universality is in turn exactly what Althusser has excavated when he redefines the problem of ideology "from a cognitive to an affective theory of ideology."[45] After this change in the inquiry's perspective, according to Eagleton, the question of the propositional "truth" or "falsehood" of a particular ideological claim can no longer be considered the decisive criterion. Instead, the key factor is how ideologies situate subjects into the world and how they do so in an emotional context of "mood" or of being attuned, or in reference to the previous section on Lacan's reading of Freud's *Project*, according to associations of pleasure and displeasure. Borrowing from John L. Austin, Eagleton states that ideological claims "[are] primarily a matter of performative utterances"[46] that evoke a naturalization of circumstances that are presumed as *sensus communis.* An ideology's success is measured not by being recognized as such but rather by intuitively being understood as that which one simply does. For Eagleton, Kant's analysis of the beautiful as a judgment of taste (*Geschmacksurteil*) is the best analytical matrix to assist us in formalizing this noncognitive but rather "emotive" mechanism of subjectivization in legal terms. Ideology aims at neither compromise nor dialogue; rather, it aims for phrases along the lines of "but everyone knows that."

It is evident that Eagleton's emotive-libidinal analysis of ideology, based on Althusser, is also close to Lacan's theory of the subject. For in this lies the value of Freud's *Project* for Lacan: it shows how consciousness unfolds in emotive coordinates of appellation and irritation. "Ideology" can be translated into Lacan's symbolic order of the big Other. This order interrelates with the unconscious as the exterior place inside the "I," outside of time. The big Other would then be present in the timelessness of the primary processes of the unconscious before the "I" of the secondary processes encounters itself as a phenomenon in the flow of time of its designs. What Althusser describes in his theory of ideology as imaginary distortions is of fundamental import for Lacan. For there is no legal subject that, in a given phantasmatic distortion to its environment, does not find itself reflected back on itself by this environment in imaginary ways. One could call this a part of Hegel's legacy, which Lacan adopted from Alexandre Kojève's lectures on Hegel.[47] For this process, Lacan employs the term *phantasm*, understood as the result of a phantasmagorical filling in of gaps in the moments of subjectivization, which always remain enigmatic.[48] We will see later that a distortion of the phantasmatic frame which is to be understood as a performative act of freedom is contingent on excessive subjectivity. This performative act of freedom, which also rings through Kant's theorems of character choice and the revolution of disposition, is the medium for the act of transgressive self-positing that particularly interests us in Lacan. This self-positing commences for him the process of newly aligning the subject in the coordinates of appellation and attempts to transform society, the big Other, or the universal from the level of particularity. Yet despite the similarities in Lacan and Althusser, at key moments Lacan's theory stands in opposition to Althusser's concept of ideology. For Lacan, the central aspect is precisely the "going astray" of the appellation that determines the ideological "suturing."[49] Lacan exemplifies this in the "Graph of Desire,"[50] which we reproduce here up to its so-called second level (figure 4.1).

The split subject (on the bottom right of the image) has to cross the symbolic order of the big Other (O = society, morals, culture, the others, and so on) in such a way that at the end of this crossing, the subject will have been able to interiorize the idealizations with which (O) and its semantic field of authority (s (O)-O) have exerted influence on the split subject.[51] In Žižek's words: "To refer to the terms of speech act theory, the illusion proper to the process of interpellation consists in the overlooking of its *performative* dimension: when I recognize myself as the addressee of the call of the ideological big Other (Nation, Democracy, Party, God, and so forth), when this call 'arrives at its destination' in me, I automatically misrecoginze that it is this very act of recognition which makes me what I have recognized myself as—I don't recognize myself in

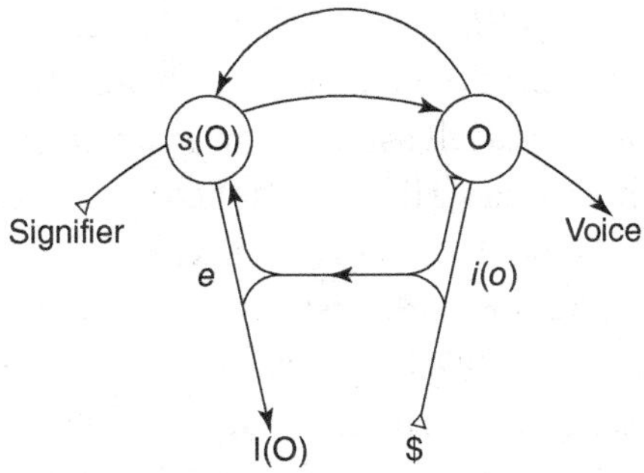

FIGURE 4.1. Graph of Desire.

it because I'm its addressee, I become its addressee the moment I recognize myself in it."[52] As a being of lack, the split subject ($) is the embodied question of herself. She is dependent on others, or, as the case may be, on the big Other as the source of knowledge that brings her to a partial enlightenment of herself. The split subject is confronted by the big Other (O). This big Other, represented for the toddler by the educators, is the locus of the symbolic order, as it is embodied by language as a web of signifiers (the expressive side of linguistic signs) in particular. (See figure 4.2.)[53]

The big Other does not exclusively represent language on a grammatical level, in terms of *how* one has to speak: it stands for *the word* in its monistic dimension as the creationist unity of sense and meaning. Similarly, in addition to language, the locus of the big Other stands for the inferential web of norms of the impersonal "one" ("man") in which the subject, as we have seen in the chapter on Kant, needs to have retrospectively recognized herself in order to be able to serve as a mirror for herself, as if viewing herself from the outside perspective of the social realm, for instance, as a legitimately acting subject in the course of her education. The big Other neither stands alone nor is reducible to an individual subject, even if it incarnates itself in individual subjects (parents, teachers, judges, the pope). This is due to the fact that the big Other is an effect of the symbolic order's sphere of power and field of knowledge that Lacan makes dependent on the intersections s(O) as "the signifier of the Other." In vectors s(O)-O, with its corresponding direction from left to right and in the reverse crossing of the vector ($-I(O)) from right to left, Lacan underlines that the meaning, or the fullness of knowledge that is

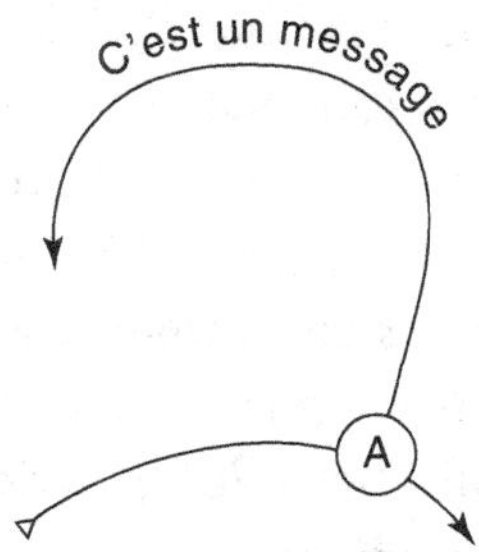

FIGURE 4.2. C'est un message.

concentrated in O, can be comprehended by the split subject only retrospectively.[54] With Hegel, we could speak here of the "spirit of a people/nation," which is the "true ground" for the moral duties of the subject. Or to exemplify with a quotation from Hegel's time in Bern: " 'Is' is the synthesis of subject and object, in which subject and object" and also ought and reality "have lost their opposition."[55] The particular will appears to be culturally legitimized since it has (retrospectively) been part of practical life and factual reality. Being part of this practice also means, as Pippin notes with regard to Hegel,[56] having a certain status in this practice and through it having been cognitively "formatted" in one's own interiority. Only once the split subject has immersed herself into the world of the big Other and—galvanized by it—reemerges will she have understood the normative web based on which the big Other (in Kant's terms, for instance, the moral law) will have always already justified its power.

Brandom describes this, as we have seen, as analogous. The human being is trained in the giving and taking of reasons until she has learned to perform the "correct moves" autonomously and seemingly out of her own sense of responsibility in the symbolic order, which structures itself around O. Simultaneously, the subject will have experienced (in Brandom, in Hegel, and finally in Lacan) how the power of normativity, looming behind his back during his own recognition of himself within normativity, has always been present. For Freud and Lacan, this power of normativity, as part of the subject's unconscious, has been closer to him than his intentional consciousness had been able to comprehend.[57] With regard to Lacan, one could therefore say that the subject will have retrospectively accessed the big Other O, according to the graph's thesis of subjectivization, *in such a way* that he will have, in the course of this process, unconsciously posited O and, as Kant's moral subject, will one day have felt responsible for his present immaturity, for which he has always been belatedly responsible.[58] Upon entering the symbolic order, the subject almost mechanistically learns the "certainties" that are simultaneously criteria *for* justifications and practical applications as well as those that are already *in* the applications at work. The human being learns certain language games, such as arithmetic. She learns that this arithmetic is absolutely certain, but she does so without having to learn the property of certainty of arithmetic as well.[59] The subject also teaches and learns what Heidegger points out in section 17 of *Being and Time*, that is, the reading of signs and what it means to comprehend a sign from a practice of reception.[60] Yet the subject learns this without teaching and learning both the certainty and guarantees of this particular learning process, as elements that are needed to make signs in the external world comprehensible. As Heidegger repeatedly states, for the subject, the factual practice of certainty in perception and linguistic practice constitutes the *practices themselves*. In the words of Wilhelm Lütterfelds, the symbolic order is "[itself an] application criterion, and yet it obtains only *through* the application its (new) critical subject matter [*kriteriellen Gehalt*], thereby loosing its property of being a criterion."[61] For Lacan, similar to the late Wittgenstein and to Heidegger, certainty is a pragmatic function of practices mediated by language. Enumerating these foundational aspects of a Lacanian epistemology brings us to the core of the topic of excessive subjectivity. Understanding these circumstances will allow us to grasp all of the implications of Lacan's epistemology, with which he describes the self-transcendence of the subject as a *self-positing* accomplished by breaking through the coordinates of appellation as a new choice of phantasm. The subject is the locus of rule-following, for instance, in adapting certain language games or practices. Yet he is potentially also the source of rule-*positing against* rule-following.

Speech acts such as those guaranteed by the symbolic order are primary, according to Lacan's seemingly antirealistic position: nothing precedes them. (Lacan never differentiates between the need to justify a language game through its practice and a statement capable of presenting the truth via practice-independent truth conditions.) Searching for necessity and justifiability behind situations of application implies for Lacan the desire for a foundation that precedes the linguistic act, which, as the primary original ground, vouches for the necessity itself. In this context, Lacan would claim that he follows neither Cartesianism nor skepticism. For him, the speech acts form part of one and the same commensurability and incommensurability that language necessarily carries within itself as medium and frame of the subject's phantasmatic self-reflection, always already rooted in the big Other. Precisely because of this, Lacan endows the subject with an autonomous subversive performative power of imposing norms and values, the reasoning for which will be highlighted later in a discussion of his philosophy of language.

Lacan was well aware that appellations never occur in "pure form," that is, without leftovers of meaning being worked through in the psyche. He develops the Graph of Desire primarily in its seemingly ideal form of subjectivization with the goal of laying bare subjectivity to the law, in contrast to Althusser, precisely from the gaps in the appellations, from those inherently disturbing distortions that in turn *precisely* concern subjugation and constitute excessive subjectivity as the structural characteristic of any subjectivization.[62]

The gaps, distortions, and enigmatic "leftovers" fulfill a dual function: they force the subject to iron out the distortions, with the help of phantasm, in a preemptive obedience so that she can nevertheless position herself concretely a propos a law that does not always sound its call very clearly. At the same time, the "stain of traumatic irrationality" (Žižek), which protrudes from the ideological appellation like a foreign body, marks the subject in such a way that she can free herself, in turn, from this appellation through the "stain." From this gap, this "stain" or "leftover," the subject can free herself despite necessarily having to move through the process of subjectivization, which is why, as Lacan will say, the subject does not quite dissolve herself in the appeal.[63] This aspect becomes crucial for Lacan's theory of the subject's self-positing and self-transcendence in his phrase "la traversée du fantasme,"[64] or traversing the fantasy.

Hegel explicitly describes this impasse of harmoniously dissolving in the symbolic appellation with the example of the symbolic roles of "being father" and "being son." In his *Wesenslogik*, Hegel writes: " 'Father' is the other of 'son' and the 'son' the other of 'father,' and each is only as this other of the other; and the one determination is at the same time only with reference to the other" (SL 383). [65] Here, Hegel accentuates the antagonistic circumstance of symbolic identification and shows this precisely in the state of being father *for the son* and of being son *for the father.* This seeming tautology becomes illuminating when, in the mutual relationship of father and son and in the symbolizing of being father and being son, a hidden difference emerges in being "for oneself." Hegel writes: "The father is indeed something for itself outside this reference to the son, but then, he is not 'father' but a 'man' in general. . . . Opposites entail contradiction inasmuch as, in negatively *referring* to each other, they *sublate each other reciprocally* and are *indifferent* to each other" (SL 383). As mentioned, Lacan, too, refers to the gap that appears in the moment of symbolization (being father vs. being "for oneself"): in the web of symbolic relationships the subject is something for the other—his symbolic determination as father or son. Yet at the same time, the subject is what he is "for himself" "abstracted. . . . from my relations to others."[66] Or again in Žižek's terms: only in the world of symbolic forms does "the contradiction between the void of the subject's pure 'being-for-himself' and the signifying feature which represents him for the others"[67] emerge. "It is my very 'alienation' in the symbolic mandate, in S1, which retroactively makes $—the void that eludes the hold of the mandate—out of my brute reality."[68] Yet it is precisely from this understanding of one's own "being for oneself" that the subject's self-transcendence can emerge in her act of freedom.

Lacan develops this thought once more in *Seminar IX* (*L'identification*), when he differentiates between the indexical use of a term and its simultaneous symbolic-linguistic use. "When I say: 'My grandfather is my grandfather' you should . . . capture clearly that this is absolutely not a tautology: that the first term 'my grandfather' expresses an indexical use of the second term 'my grandfather,' the latter, in turn, is not noticeably different from his proper names, for example, Émile Lacan. . . . This applies to all tautologies, . . . because it concerns the question of the relationship between the Real and the Symbolic. When I say that a tautology cannot impossibly exist, then I do not mean to say that the first A and the second A want to say two different things. I do not mean that when I say that a tautology does not exist. [What I mean is] that in the status of A itself is inscribed that A can not be equal to A."[69]

The famous equation of identity A = A is for Lacan exactly the equation of A's being split in itself as part of a chain of signifiers. (If A were *not* split, the propositional structure that confirms that the subject A is truly *the predicate* would not make sense.) This concerns the psyche's subjectivity to the law. The subject has to be subjectivized, yet precisely through the web of symbolic relationships, the I/Ego is thrown back onto itself as that which through *self-reference* to this order can create a distancing caveat. The subject can determine the manner in which others have determined and shaped him behind his back, so to speak, and into the layers of his unconscious.[70] This has political consequences that are reminiscent of Hegel's description of the dangerous potential in Kant's free will, which is capable *of anything* and can disregard anything. Based on the awareness of this Lacanian difference, the subject can reach the point where he "turns himself off" within the old coordinates, and if only because the difference mentioned comes to the fore in disturbing psychosomatic symptoms, neurotic ticks, or seemingly never-ending nightmares. Axel Honneth, for instance, sees this instantiated in the biography of Ulrike Meinhof, the famous German left-wing militant who cofounded the Red Army Faction in 1970 with Andreas Baader and Gudrun Ensslin.[71] Similarly, Bernward Vesper's collected letters to his wife, Gudrun Ensslin, published under the fitting title *State of Emergency Laws from Your Own Hand*,[72] express this moment of splitting oneself off from the coordinates of a former subjectivization. Here, the subject is autonominally reconstituted as an instance of authority in the state of emergency from its apparently paranoiac particularity.

This differentiation in Lacan marks the difference from Althusser's theory of subjectivity through "evidence of felt experience" and "identification/misrecognition." Unlike in Althusser, subjectivization for Lacan is not to be understood as the totalitarian transformation of the "individuum" into the "subject" who has finally *identified* herself in the symbolic form. Subjectivization integrates the subject into the normativity while at the same time evoking a withdrawal of the self *from itself* (or, better, from its traditional self). This enables the ego to at least try to see itself "for itself." This ego, then, can radically put into question the subjectivization through the big Other and, in this process of dissociating itself from the given phantasmatical frames of subjectivization, can bring itself into an oppositional position in which the "I" appears as a political and dangerous outsider. Precisely because the subject is seemingly "nothing" outside of social relationships, this "nothing" can become an upper-case Nothing. In the "Nothing of a pure self-relating,"[73] a potentiality can unfold that may pose an extreme challenge to the world of the big Other. Hegel's great figures of world history (Caesar, Napoleon, and the like) can only partially be cited at this point since they do not quite meet the situational context of the theory of excessive subjectivity developed here. For these great figures are often imbued with insignia of symbolic power, while excessive subjectivity aims at this power precisely from the Nothing of symbolic valence and from the Nothing of pure self-reference. This means that excessive subjectivity is particularly relevant for the political fight in which the lack of symbolic meaning and radical self-reference develop into a political effect. Martin Luther is such an example. By repudiating the phantasmatic frame of the Roman-papal theology of salvation, he metaphorically drops out of the soteriological appellation structure of the Aristotelian-Thomistic episteme of the sixteenth century into an abyss of godless heresy. Confronted with this step into the Nothing that he accepts, Luther likewise steps into the earlier-mentioned "Nothing of pure self-relating" in a certain sense. This forces him to design a new universal frame of subjectivization and a new theology, with its well-known cosmological consequences for the sixteenth century, which also fascinated Walter Benjamin in his book *The Origin of German Tragic Drama*.[74] Felix Ensslin, Gudrun Ensslin's son, subdivides this frame in his comments on Luther using Lacanian terminology into four individual moments: "since a.) I [Martin Luther] am structured by the Other, and b.) I have no access to the Other, and c.) I can only exist in the Other, it is d.) fully my responsibility to articulate my place in the Other without recourse to knowledge (of the absolute, of what the Other wants from me)." Ensslin continues: "Only a confrontation with the designified signifier and its ghostly productions allows for a new subject to emerge in the process of working through by taking up a truly designified signifier from the rubble of the reservoir of the Other."[75]

At the intersection of s(O) in the Graph of Desire, the subject will be interwoven into signifiers and established norms. One could say with Robert Brandom: against the backdrop of mutual scorekeeping, the subject has learned how to deal with the chain of signifiers, considered as justified through practices and pragmatics. Moreover, Lacan, in recourse to Hegel's master-slave dialectic, speaks of a normative effectiveness of the master-signifier. Lacan's mention of the master-signifier underlines, in recourse to Lévi-Strauss's study on the elementary structures of kinship,[76] that the giving of and asking for reasons can only be claimed when there is a social network that, as, for example, in the incest taboo analyzed by Lévi-Strauss, is structured around norms and makes possible in the first place that "the exchange of words" can take place. With regard to Lévi-Strauss's incest taboo, Lacan writes: "This law [the prohibition of incest], then, reveals itself clearly enough as identical to a language order. For without names for kinship relations, no power can institute the order of preferences and taboos that knot and braid the thread of lineage through the generations."[77] With the term *master-signifier*, Lacan highlights the fact that the interplay of signifiers cannot posit its own origin and has to proceed from a center of signification (called *point de capiton*)[78] where the signifier literally falls into the signified.[79] What is required is the moment of subordination of signification under an Other of itself, which in turn cannot be part of signification. Since any order of law is based on a certain interweaving of signifiers, Lacan shows how the subject integrates herself into a normative reference field of interrelated inferentialities. Yet beyond that he shows how the symbolic structure of the chain of signifiers, for its part, rests on a concrete point of departure, namely, the master-signifier mentioned just earlier. Due to the symbolic function from which this signifier spreads its effects, Lacan also calls it the *phallic signifier*, or the "name-of-the-father."[80] The resulting word play in French of "nom du père" und "non du père" illustrates how for Lacan, fully in the Freudian tradition, the legal structure moves from family constellation into society itself, and in this way rests on a repressed origin, or, better, on the internal antagonism at the original illegal imposition of the law. One might think here of the "social contract" (Hobbes, Locke), the myth of the "volonté générale" (Rousseau), or, in a more modern vein, the theory of the "veil of ignorance" (Rawls). These theorems structure the societal field through normative speech acts that simultaneously create and depict the source of norms and values through themselves. Lacan's "nom du père" represents a "non du père" for the kind of negation "by virtue of which," according to Welsen, "the symbolic order excludes from itself the existence of subjects as standing in relation to the symbolic."[81] Welsen states here that the subjects only emerge at all when the symbolic order eliminates the "true being" of the individual (think of Freud's laconic mention of "Our Majesty the baby"). The subject has to pass through the Oedipal complex as through a bottleneck if she wishes to be become a subject at all.

The law of the chain of signifiers posits its own origin and at the same time "splits" the "authentic subject" from the subject of consciousness. Consequently, the true meaning of the Oedipal complex—employing the name-of-the-father—lies in introducing the human being via "the metaphor of the father considered as a principle of separation"[82] into the symbolic order (self-alienating in favor of identity).[83]

Kant, too, thematizes, at least indirectly, this taboo of the "non du père" at the origin of the legal order, when he forbids speculating about the origin of the law itself.[84] As such, then, Kant confirms what Lacan terms the repression of S1 as a foundational grounding of the world of chains of signifiers, called S2, namely, that there is no *founding* but only an imposition at the origin of law.[85] S1 is ground without justification. A simple illustration of this thought might be that for a newborn child, language as the locus *of the word* is the overarching structure of meanings (S1 in Lacan's terminology). S1, which lies in the power of the parents who force their language onto the child, is simply unshakable in its foundation. No justification can be provided for it; and yet it is the ground. In this sense, S1 in its omnipotence is necessarily dimmed and structurally repressed. Wittgenstein, for his part, articulates this point when he emphasizes that rule-following does not imply judgment. In his prominent comments in the *Philosophical Investigations* (§§185–202), he underlines the hidden aporetic relationships of universal norms and individual application in a unique situation of application. When a human being judges that he followed this or that rule when judging a situation, according to Wittgenstein, in this reference to judging he again follows another rule of judging and so on ad infinitum. For this reason, Wittgenstein suggests that we understand language in such a way that the judging associated with it at one point is no longer understood in the rule-following paradigm. This means that we necessarily have to assume a structural incommensurability in language's discursive structure that we humans, as beings who know through language, are in turn unable to comprehend because this comprehension is conditioned by a discourse that is always already finite. As such, then, S1, in Lacan's parlance, is to be understood as the law-like condition for the possibility of speaking and reasoning, which is structurally masked. This is highly relevant for the topic of excessive subjectivity, because the recognition that there is a lack of legal justifications for the established legal and linguistically decoded order can bring a political subject (we are reminded of Martin Luther) to rebel against the existing order and its phantasmatic frame, a rebellion that Kant considers absolutely unacceptable as a threat to the communal will. Precisely because no legal order can provide a sufficient ground for its justification—neither a kingdom by the grace of God nor a "volonté générale"—is it at all possible to conceive always and everywhere of excessive subjectivity as moral objection against the establishment.

The master-signifier's operative task consists of "anchoring" or, better, "sewing together" (Lacan speaks explicitly of "suturing") the field of signifiers, the field of the Hegelian *morality*, and the field of the Kantian teachings of law and virtue so as to create a coherent field in the first place.[86] In Wittgenstein's terms: "We do not learn the practice of making empirical judgments by learning rules"; rather, with it, S1, "[a] totality of judgments is made plausible to us."[87] Theologically speaking, S1 is *the word* at the beginning of creation that enables the multitude of words and languages. The establishing of this totality, over which "light dawns gradually,"[88] is represented for Lacan by the master-signifier.

The foundation of this totality is familiar to us through religious creation narratives as well as through gestures of political founding. A polity sees itself, as, for instance, in the American Declaration of Independence, as "counted as one" with the words *We the People*. It hopes to declaratively "suture together" a unity with this excessive-revolutionary self-creation. It is almost a mythical gesture of a kind of *emergency laws from one's own hands* with a master-signifier (S1) that in the act of its performance can, in the final analysis, no longer be scrutinized and, as such, dims the questioning of its foundation itself. The new order performatively creates subjects in the declaration "We the People." The "play of signifiers" (S2), which constitutes culture and morality, takes its course from the origin of this positing. The prelegality/illegality of this suturing (or, to bring in Badiou, of this "count-as-one")[89] has to be dimmed or repressed. S1, as the condition of the possibility of S2, falls out of the play of signifiers, which *is* S2 (S.XX 80). In concrete terms, this means: only because, for example, one day the polity of the United States declaratively formed itself as "We the People," individuals in the subjectivization process as US Americans were able to retrospectively recognize themselves from a phantasmatic future perspective, and this process allowed at least some of them to be more than just a colony of the British Empire.[90] These "US Americans" only became US Americans in the performative act of an ideal phantasmatic form for their political representability, that is, retrospectively through the excess of their self-declaration. Under the aegis of this "suture" of "We the People," several semantic chains, in the terminology of Lacan, were able to unfold (S2a, S2b, S2c), exchange (S2a + S2b = S2ab), and develop further (S2a1 and so on). The stability of each of these individual formations is part of a differential web, S2, that is to be tolerated as long as its origin, S1, is not questioned.

The suturing of "We the People" is on the one hand impossible, as Kant explicitly says in his critique of any form of revolutionary upheaval, because it stands outside a conceivable, reasonable normativity of the common will. (It *is* declaratively S1. How should an ultimate and undisputed ground be provided beyond that?) At the same time, as Lacan discusses and as Kant has to admit in view of human history, this suture seems unavoidable from time to time. One neither can provide an ultimate ground for the *momentum* of suture—which Lacan, by the way, called (before Badiou) "*count-as-one*" in his Baltimore lecture of 1966—[91] beyond its decisionistic performance, nor can one escape the empirical reality of these moments in history vouched for, again and again, by seemingly excessive subjects (Paul, the Founding Fathers, Lenin, Mao, and so on). In this act of imposition of S1, an encounter occurs between the whole and the exception, the interior (content) and exterior (political form) at the same place and the same time.[92] In this manner, put in a more exaggerated manner, a paradox element, or, to use Hegel's thought, "a meaningless sound" (PhS §23), which in its simple identity may appear as a pure glossolalia with the sound sequence "We the People," becomes the beginning of something new and does so—again calling on Hegel—in the explicit "movement of positing itself" (PhS §18). As such, then, S1 corresponds to the condition of the possibility of the continuous sequence of signifiers within a systemic structure that in each instance undergoes a new differentiation of itself. Or, to return to Kant, S1 is the condition of the possibility of the social contract itself, because it opens up subjectivity to the law without being able to unite subjects in it *completely*. The subject's remaining deficits—of potentially being driven by her own excessivity that cannot be contained or pacified in normative terms—might then also constitute the antinormative power. It is precisely this power that might be able to benefit from the lacking political structure, which in the phantasmatic reality of the general populace cannot fail to seem offensive, heretical, or illegal.

Here, the Real collapses the political realm and lays bare the limits of meaning. Excessive subjectivity articulates this collapse of that which the established political doxa considers nonrepresentable within the limits of that which is represented. In this context, it is obvious that the premises of the ruling "hallucination" of reality or representation cannot cover all that they tried to achieve through subjectivization. An excessive subject such as Martin Luther, who, for instance, declared his conscience to be an overly powerful signifier ("Here I stand, I can do no other") and who succeeded in establishing the "fear of God," may then in its defense of the Reformation bring the Hegelian world-spirit into a new Gestalt that the ancien régime, with its concept of salvation so foreign to modernity, could not accommodate within its theological premises.

In his *Seminar VII*, Lacan repeatedly refers to the German theologian. He is interested in Luther's annihilation of the subject as proclaimed specifically in the Heidelberg Disputation of 1518 and in the commentary of the Magnificat of 1521.[93] Luther succeeded in directing "God's eternal hatred" that "existed even before the world was created" (S.VII 97) onto humanity, which can no longer lay claim to the grace of God as it could within the classical Thomistic-Aristotelian ontology. Luther evokes a fear that requires one to be "poet or prophet" in order "to invent a thing like this . . . the fear of God . . . [as] primordial signifier" (S.III 267). Lacan advises his students: "Read a little Luther; . . . if you want to see to what extent the power of images may be affirmed, images that are very familiar to us because they have been invested with the quality of scientific authentication on a daily basis, through our psychoanalytic experience. It is to those images that the thought of a prophet refers, whose influence was such a powerful one, and who renewed the very basis of Christian teaching when he sought to express our dereliction, our fall in a world where we let ourselves go. . . . Luther says literally, 'You are that waste matter which falls into the world from the devil's anus'" (S.VII 92–93).

From Freud and Breuer's *Studies on Hysteria*, Lacan borrows the idea that memories absorbed by the psyche can mutually reshape one another. Freud and Breuer had shown how the latency period between a traumatic event and its real traumatic experience can be of an accidental nature for the psyche.[94] This results in a paradoxical shift of temporality and causality, which was ultimately also thematized in our interpretation of Hegel. For Freud and Lacan, latency, or the retrospective loop of causality, can reshape the layers of memory in such a way that the "ego," similar to the Hegelian "spirit of the people," accidentally and suddenly finds itself in other narrative contexts of its own history of emanation.[95]

Just like the social structure in its originary moment (S1 = "We the People"/ "Here I stand, I can do no other"), the subject in Lacan's *mirror stage* sees himself as a "virtual" entity in a projection, necessarily distorting his *Dasein* onto a future that can only be fulfilled retrospectively.[96] The imaginary-phantasmatical and narcissistic exaltation of the subject herself represses the experience of a factually still-fragmentary body in the vision of his Gestalt (a vision that is like a promise from the future). For Lacan, the subject is caught unconsciously by this vision, as if by an inner incentive to catch up with his ideal in the mirror. Because this vision has left its traces, the subject tries asymptotically to cross the gap that the mirror opens. The fact that the establishment of norms and values rests both in the *mirror stage* and in the earlier-mentioned examples of "We the People" and "Here I stand, I can do no other" on (hallucinatory) performative acts is the key point of Lacan's structural analysis of ethical agency. Metaphysical or metaethical justifications are lacking, as there is no *master-signifier of the master-signifier*, just as there is no metalanguage that could bring to a halt the movement of signifiers through prefixed "truth-makers." Hegel writes about the moment of such a performance in a prominent passage: "The living Substance is being which is in truth *Subject*, or, what is the same, is in truth actual only in so far as it is the movement of positing itself, or is the mediation of its self-othering with itself. This Substance is, as Subject, pure, *simple negativity* . . . not an *original* or *immediate* unity as such—is the True. It is the process of its own becoming, the circle that presupposes its end as its goal, having its end also as its beginning, and only by being worked out to its end, is it actual" (PhS 10). If a performative imposition attempts to take over the discursive field and to totalize it according to its performance, this act may be a "*meaningless* sound" (PhS 13, emphasis in original). The positing then becomes a Lacanian quilting point that marks the structure of the discursive field with a surplus element.[97] While this element then ends up being one element *too many*, it nevertheless aims at concealing the void. It indicates that a field cannot overcome its fundamental antagonism as the "articulation of the inconsistency of the One."[98] And yet, reality changes fundamentally as soon as this element appears and leaves behind its effect, as soon as a new order comes into power "in one flash" (PhS §11), as Hegel says, for example, through the phrase "We the People."

SIGNIFIERS AND THE "FORCE OF LAW"

For Lacan, the master-signifier in each chain of signifiers is the signifier that totalizes the chain from a nonvisible background.[99] Its function in the signification marks its absence. The signifier brings order to the dispersed field in which innumerable justifications move through an act of imposition that lacks any ultimate justification or ground. With regard to this lack of legitimacy within legality, several twentieth-century philosophers have repeatedly used the term *force of law* to refer to the structural act of violence at the core of normativity.[100] Lacan describes this process of a performative positing precisely as a way of leaping over the barrier that Ferdinand de Saussure uncovered within the linguistic sign separating signifier and signified as the two sides of the same coin.[101] While Saussure, according to his *Course in General Linguistics*, proceeds from the sign as signifier *and* signified in one, while nevertheless ascribing a priority in this dichotomy to the signified as the carrier of meaning (= concept/reference), Lacan is particularly interested in the very non-deducibility of reference in a metaphysical sense. For him, the signified (= content/reference) is a secondary effect within a discursive field safeguarded by signifiers and master-signifiers, and only this.[102] On the content side of the meaning, Lacan does not see any reference to a truth-value that lies beyond the inferential network of semantic itself. He sees in it a (fleeting) effect on a chain of signifiers that can never be brought to a close and can only temporarily be stabilized via master-signifiers with different status-functions of veridicality. This has political relevance as ideological status-functions with their invocations/appellations can never achieve unlimited success in the subjugation of subjects, because every ideology's language is lacking a master-signifier of a master-signifier, or, to use the terminology of Gottlob Frege's referential-semantic realism, it is lacking "the True" as the ultimate ground of reference for its propositions.[103] Ideology can never "say it all" and chain the subject to an unshakeable web of belief. This means as well that ideologies cannot get rid of a "stain of traumatic irrationality and senselessness sticking to them"[104] as they can never make transparent the normative procedures of their machineries entirely, no matter if we refer to democratic or totalitarian state apparatuses. This was the dilemma of the "force of law," mentioned earlier. The stain of senselessness harbors now an interesting dialectical dual function within every political web of belief. It can prevent the subject from completely submitting to the Other; yet it is also able to evoke the opposite and cause the subject to fall under the spell and be particularly devoted to the big Other. Žižek examines this latter aspect, and shows that through the enigma of appellation (present in the various revelations that are proclaimed in the name of "God," "King," "Fatherland," "Democracy"), the subject might be tempted to bridge the enigma of his call, as necessitated by the "stain of traumatic irrationality and senselessness" through phantasmas of her own and a preemptive obedience. This may result in the subject's willingness to subjugate herself even more and to unconditionally surrender to the big Other.[105] A positive effect is simply the reduction of cognitive stress, as the big Other will probably have justified true belief.

Bertrand Russell had been able to defuse the problem of self-referentiality in his critique of Frege with an axiomatic "prohibition" on the self-inclusion of sets within their own limits, as such a self-inclusion can lead to paradox. Lacan considers this interdiction futile with regard to language and also with regard to ideological languages that constitute a certain web of belief. In what else should a symbolic order ground its authority if not in its master-signifiers? Language cannot but aim time and time again at its own self-inclusion, even if that leads to paradoxes. If a metalanguage were to exist at all, it would not be an ideal language (cleansed from nonsensical propositions of the natural languages) as developed for example in early twentieth century's Logicism, but rather it would be the metalanguage that natural languages carry in their folds, just as the so-called Klein bottle (*Kleinsche Flasche*) described by the German mathematician Felix Klein in 1892 encompasses its content in its external form. Language develops metalanguage-like within itself, within different forms of veridicality conditions. Language circles around a nonrecoverable void, as Lacan says. New meanings emerge unendingly, whereby these emerging meanings can be claimed by an excessive subjectivity as well.

To summarize what we have discussed so far: the so-called split subject $ has to cross through the symbolic order of the big Other (O) at its neuralgic coordinates of power (master-signifiers/*points de capiton*) so that it can develop its own ego-identity. The corresponding "symbolic castration," represented by Lacan's linguistic interpretation of the Freudian Oedipal complex, simultaneously renders visible the loss of an object of the I, often psychoanalytically associated with the metaphor of the loss of the mother as the "Other of one's own." This loss positions the subject, in her experience of lack, even closer to the conditions of the culturally transmitted regime of meaning. If *mother* is not all and *father* frustrates the subject's desire, then the desire has to be pacified through the order of society (symbolic order, rites, knowledge), that is, with the help of a delay toward an Other (for example, to culture as the location of sublimation). The subject as one that is traumatically impossible and continuing to desire thus emerges out of the very same origin as the symbolic order that has simultaneously built itself up for this subject. A dialectic of desire sets in, in which the subject is the excess of more than the political order can uncover as compensation, since she is at the same time the medium that keeps the symbolic order alive both with her own substance and with her lack of substance. Only through the breaking in of what Lacan calls the Real, a breaking in that is possible both inner-psychologically and intersubjectively, can the tendentiously conservative structures of order be crossed toward imaginary and illegal horizons. In this sense, then, the pathological desire of a subject (think of Antigone, of Martin Luther) can itself become a Real for the symbolic order and pull the subject into an upheaval of her order, which, inferentially, is seemingly secured for eternity. Indirectly, the inferential normative structure of society "profits" in part from excesses of the subject. These insights are, as we have shown, already present in Kant and Hegel. Nevertheless, Lacan offers more profound explanations in the given interplay of language, chains of signifiers, phantasmatic breakthroughs, and conditions of appellation, from which an ethically excessive desire then emerges. Lacan's Real can mark a dimension that opposes subjectivization and can also in turn further subjectivization. It can allow the individual to rebel against its mandate and against the mandate's authorities in the superstructure of the big Other. To do so, it does not necessarily need inferentially secured, comprehensible reasons as from a neutral observer, but rather self-references and self-transgression.

ANTIGONE, ROSA PARKS, AND THE "DISCOURSE OF THE HYSTERIC"

Which positing manages to become a condition?

—DIETER HENRICH

As we have seen, Lacan interprets the subject as essentially limited in *being herself* in relation to the symbolic roles that she will attempt to fill as compensation for this lack. The symbolic order, for its part, has, as a differential chain of signifiers, a deficit structure such that the mandates that it claims remain fragile, questionable structures. The predicament of a nonirreconcilable difference between the particular being-in-and-of-itself (*An-und-für-sich-Sein*) and the mandates in the foreign (the big Other, society) opens up an insatiable dialectic of desire. This dialectic expresses how far "the wound can be healed only by the spear that smote it."[106] Healing a wound through the medium that caused the wound (the spear) nourishes via deferral the lack in the subject that has always already experienced her being (*Dasein*) from the wound. Lacan illustrates this loop of desire in what is called his "discourse of the hysteric," which relates to our comments on Antigone's desire in Hegel, as well as to the Graph of Desire analyzed earlier. This discourse, which Lacan explicates in *Seminars XVII* (*L'envers de la psychanalyse*), *XX* (*Encore*), and *XXI* (*Les non-dupes errent*), is one of four examples of discourses with which he renders the psyche's structures of desire legible—according to their mandates and depending on the symbolic order—with the help of four different coordinates.[107] All discourses (of the university, the hysteric, the master, the analyst) are contingent on the subject as *zoon politikon*, since they respectively thematize the nonharmonizable interplay of the symbolic-inferential normative superstructure (the symbolic order of the big Other) as well as depict the subject that is split due to a noncoincidence and her desire for the phantasmatic fullness of one's own "calling," with regard to Lacan's *objet petit a*. Of these four discourses, the stability of political doxa can be particularly threatened by the third one, the "discourse of the hysteric." For it shows how the reflexive self-understanding of autonominal subjectivity is provoked by an affront on the part of the law. In contradistinction to the other three discourses (that is, master, university, and analyst), the discourse of the hysteric is marked for Lacan by the guess or the presumption that the big Other, due to a concealed fundamental lack, is an impostor and that this has become obvious to the hysterical subject, thereby provoking her on behalf of her own mandate. This discourse fittingly describes the fate of Antigone, because if the big Other is not a point of intersection for a guarantee of meaning/veridicality, then the subject is, in a radical search, tied to the phantasmatic object of the true, still-to-be-discovered fullness of meaning: *objet petit a*.

For a better understanding of the discourse of the hysteric, it may be useful to start with Lacan's first model of discourse, the "discourse of the master." It provides us with the originary form of the four coordinates crucial for Lacan, which exchange their variables clockwise. The discourse of the master describes the basic structure of an insatiable desire in the subject combined with a dependence on a phantasmatic remainder of an object (*objet petit a*) that stems from the subject's very origin.[108]

$$\frac{S1}{\$} \rightarrow \frac{S2}{a}$$

This illustration of the "discourse of the master" reads as follows: S1 marks the totality of knowledge that appears as an "entire system of sentences in which consequences and premises support each other mutually."[109] This is contrasted with S2, which stands for the propositions that are being formulated in the system as a whole. Lacan here speaks of knowledge or of the battery of knowledge. The split subject is located below S1 because the "entirety of judgments," despite its axiomatic totality, does not capture, depict, or completely represent the subject. (As we mentioned earlier, ideology cannot simply say it all.) The subject can never be completely subjectivized, which is, after all, the condition of the unconscious.[110] Therefore, for Lacan, the subject is directed toward a remainder (*objet petit a*) that guarantees a structural void, which is in turn covered through the *écran* [111](screen) of a phantasmatic fullness of being. The *objet petit a* comes to the fore where the noncoincidence with S1 ties the subject phantasmatically to a quest for the desire to attain her autonomous selfhood. The *objet petit a* is phantasmatic because the "I," in confrontation with its symbolic roles (being a father, daughter, judge, and so on), necessarily experiences itself as *more* than what others see in it.[112] Thus, the subject is both *in* this tension and *is* this tension: it is the gap between foreign roles and the undefined identity.

The *objet petit a* phantasmatically deflects the repeatedly lurking possibility of a collapse of the meanings of these symbolic roles through the encounter with the Real. It does so by reversing the groundless abyss of the Real—its negativity—as with a photographic negative turning positively into white, into the seemingly desire-quenching Identifiable. The phantasm distorts the Nothing that threatens the meanings at which the subject has arrived into a "Something," which is then available as an imaginary construct of meaning that is concretely desired, for example, in an author, a new partner, or a new profession.[113]

If, as the sociologist Yong Wang points out in his article "Agency: The Internal Split of Structure,"[114] a homosexual man or woman escapes the heterosexual norms of society by remaining "in the closet," then this refuge allows them to experience how far they are *more* than what the others see in them, according to Wang. The closet may make possible, *even in its concealing*, an identitary normativity *before* it becomes represented in the established *doxa*. Only once this nonplace, this void, emerges from the beyond of being excluded can a social order develop that is now expanded by this very void.[115] For this to occur, the subject necessarily has to want to posit the nonrepresentable as representation. Or to put it differently, the subject must know that that which (for herself) was initially "only" nonrepresentable ("this is my closet") has in the true sense always already been representation before the horizon of a future of its victorious imposition/positing. The subject needs a certainty that is linked to her own phantasmatic "Ding," that is, to this "thing" that she, in contrast to all others, must be convinced is *real*, this "thing" that embodies an absolutely certain objective maxim, for instance, one's own sexual orientation as objective norm of the universal, or, with regard to Antigone, the burial ritual for her brother that has to be performed, because it simply *has* to be performed. If the nonpresentable is truly normatively represented while simultaneously lacking confirmation through scorekeeping on the level of representation, then one could say that in order to have the power to self-posit as a reversal from nonrepresentation to representation, what is needed up to a certain point is a paranoid distortion and a certain excess on the part of the subject who posits. For which "deontic scoreboard" should the positor make use of, in order to know for certain whether the norm that she defends, such as sexual orientation or the burial of her brother, will indeed possess validity on the level of representation? In Antigone, we discover such a distortion that fascinates Lacan as well as Hegel. Yet as we attempted to show in chapter 2, Kant himself is already well aware of this distortion when he mentions the *distortion of the distortion* as that which is in the center of the moral will, namely, the revolution of disposition as the locus of a gap in the reform-trained consciousness. Precisely at this locus of its *positing* of disposition, consciousness is at its seemingly most exalted position, a gap that Kant intentionally leaves open. The revolution of disposition is a paranoid distortion of a daily situation in which pathological tendencies would permanently have the upper hand, *if not for this distortion.* It is a self-deducing positing that transgresses itself performatively and overcomes the subject.

As Hegel has shown, the laws under which Antigone claims objective validity can only demonstrate insufficient scorekeeping "in the light of the day" of the polis. The majority of the polis is *for good reason, that is, with justified beliefs*, in opposition to Antigone. That does not keep her from sticking to her desire in an almost paranoid manner and this is because Antigone, according to the "discourse of the hysteric," possesses certainty (and not knowledge) that the big Other lacks the anchoring center of its legitimacy. For Lacan, it is of relevance that Antigone's attitude toward Creon leads her beyond a rational discourse in which reasonable collective norms of the polis could be exchanged. The play transcends the binary alternatives of an antithesis of the individual's freedom, on the one hand, and tyranny and the sober reason of the state, on the other. Antigone does not let herself be dissuaded from her "Ding," from her object of desire, even if it seems to be located outside the symbolic order as an indefinable and life-threatening good. Antigone is incapable of accepting the *objet petit a*, which is being pushed at her as alternatively and metonymically functioning objects of desire that could render her life so much more pleasant. For Lacan, the "Ding" is a combination of Kant's "thing-in-itself" and Freud's discussion of the "Thing" as standing in an irritating and enigmatic relation to the fellow human being (*Nebenmensch*). It is that which, though forever separated from us, makes the symbolic order come into being in the first place, *within* this very separation. In this way, for Lacan, Oedipus's daughter becomes exemplary of a mental illness that is at the core of the excessive dimension of human existence and that therefore expresses the true tragedy of all life. One could also say: Antigone desires the *Real*. With his concept of the Real, Lacan refers as mentioned to a nonrepresentable underside that nevertheless constitutes the world of phenomena; this underside is both its abyss and its ground of being. Antigone's desire marks a nonnegotiable, almost blindly radical claim to unilaterally overstretch reality to her horizon of meaning. For Lacan, Antigone has a particular, tragic authority due to her excessive desire. When we read the term *desire* in Lacan, it is important to take into account the Freudian distinction between *Trieb* (drive) and *Instinkt* (instinct). Only the drive intersects with Lacan's term *desire*. Instincts are biological needs such as hunger or thirst and refer to a relatively fixed and inherent relationship to the desired object. Drives are not immediately tied to certain objects. Freud writes in the *New Introductory Lectures on Psycho-Analysis*, "The drives are like mythical creatures, magnificent in their indefiniteness."[116]

For Lacan, Antigone is a great tragic figure because she refuses to be dissuaded from her great desire. By pursuing it without compromise, she separates herself from the symbolic order of Thebes. As Freud makes clear in his cultural-political texts (*Civilization and Its Discontents, Totem and Taboo*), culture contains within it a network of interdependent laws that attempts to conquer this drive. In the case of Antigone, this corset no longer works in its original sense of disciplining her. Why should that be so? According to Lacan, it is because her position has transcended the idea of a supreme good that is reasonable from the perspective of the symbolic order. Antigone's position lays bare that her desire, as a gesture of excess, as an attitude that cannot be reintegrated into the symbolic order, is actually not of this world. Antigone's desire is directed beyond the limits of human desire, "beyond this ἄτη," beyond this catastrophe (S.VII 262–63).

In an expanded sense, Lacan understands the Greek word *ἄτη* in the sense of misfortune and lament. Antigone positions herself beyond the pleasure principle. Preferring to be dead in life thus becomes the singular apotheosis of tragic transgression for Lacan. He writes: "Antigone appears as αυτόνομος, as a pure and simple relationship of the human being to that of which he miraculously happens to be the bearer, namely, the signifying cut that confers on him the indomitable power of being what he is in the face of everything that may oppose him. . . . She pushes to the limit the realization of something that might be called the pure and simple desire of death as such" (S.VII 282). Antigone's deed goes beyond an ethics of a good life in the Aristotelian sense. What makes her deed nevertheless ethical for Lacan is that she remains true to her desire and suspends those meaning-structuring schemata of behavior that are guaranteed via the symbolic order. In doing so, she takes a paradoxical position that Lacan describes in his *Seminar VII* as "entre-deux-morts," between-two-deaths (S.VII 270). While it is true that Antigone lives in the temporal space between her decision not to subjugate herself to Creon's will and her suicide at the end of the play, it is precisely the life that she leads between these two points that for Lacan resembles a life that is led as from an *outside of symbolic place.* It is this very life "between-two-deaths" that awards her with a terrifying beauty, as Lacan phrases it, that the audience cannot grasp.

From a Kantian perspective, one could defend Antigone's deed in the sense that she could very well refer to Brandomian scorekeeping for her deed, even if the burial laws stem from the primal grounds of an archaic time and even if she, Antigone, obviously acts against the order of the highest authority in defending these Ur-grounds. In this, Antigone could (1) claim for herself an absence of inclinations and pathologies by referring to the fact that the burial ritual was tested as a generalizable maxim of agency based on reason, not on the power of a religious or political authority, which should be available to all humans (*ius quia iustum* and not *quia iussum*). Similarly, Antigone could (2) recognize Creon not as king but as tyrant. As such, then, the tyrant's goal would not be the general good of the city (and the state) but rather his own self-interest, in this case, revenge on a political enemy. Following this interpretation, one could claim that Antigone acts in civil disobedience against a sacrilegious tyrannical law and that her action is therefore morally justified.[117]

However, it remains ambiguous in Kant's ethics how far Antigone is authorized to commit an act of active civil disobedience.[118] (This question leads to numerous problems that have been discussed in secondary literature.)[119] Regardless though, one can defend Antigone along the lines that the tragic consequences of Creon's prohibition and the ensuing number of dead ultimately prove that reason in no way owes obedience to a sacrilegious figure such as Creon. Creon had no right to prohibit Antigone from burying her brother, and Antigone had a duty to terminate her obedience to Creon.

Objections to such a Kantian interpretation could include that one cannot precisely state at which point the sovereign conforms (or does not conform) to the definition of a tyrant. Does this definition not require the positing of a disposition, a way of aspect-seeing? Assuming that the sovereign is identified as tyrant, it remains ambiguous which form of civil disobedience Kant affords to the population or the individual political activist. Kant categorically renounces any form of revolutionary upheaval. Yet regardless of the specifics in Kant's philosophy, the crucial question remains: Who decides at what point the king, leader, minister, president, and so on has become a tyrant and traitor to the common will? [120] Doubtlessly, Polynices was the enemy of the polis and had therefore lost his rights as citizen. To refuse the burial of traitors of the city-state was legal. Therefore, the chorus expresses its opinion toward Antigone that obeying the law would not mean opposing the general good of the city.

A parallactic gap opens between the correct judgment of moral and legal duty that departs from the ideal model of a "third-person perspective."[121] The model of a neutral observer is phantasmatic because it constructs a locus outside the field of conflict; from this outside perspective then, the conflict no longer appears in its aporetics, which is what interested Kant and Lacan in the first place. The parallactic gap may prove to what extent a "positing" (by Antigone and by Creon), often dimmed by practices and traditions, is needed.[122] In a certain sense, one is betting here on the question of who will be the victor of history and who, due to the authority that comes with this victory, will be allowed to write those history books that subsequently determine the normative premises of the perspective from the victor's "viewpoint."[123] (Is this not similar to the Palestine-Israel conflict, where both sides try to conquer the victor's viewpoint to retrospectively legitimize themselves?) Similarly, one could ask with regard to the French Revolution whether the conquering of the Bastille was a form of civil courage against a tyrannical ancien régime, or perhaps rather an illegal attack on the royal dynasty, which as supreme authority was the condition of the possibility of political exchange. As Kant stresses in his "Doctrine of Right" within the *Metaphysics of Morals* (MM 375–76, 379–80), there is no legitimate form of civil disobedience if it endangers the state and the social contract, since both are conditions of any political dispute.[124] Therefore, one can assume that Kant would have judged Antigone's deed as disobedient and a danger to the state.[125] Similarly, one can ask whether the founding of the United States of America was a terrorist act against the British Empire or a sovereign act of freedom.[126] We mention these cases in order to tie the evaluation of a situation once more back to the appellation-structure of subjectivity highlighted by Lacan. Based on this aspect, certain premises of an evaluative situation can determine how the subject positions itself; these premises, due to the psychoindividual anchoring of the big Other in the unconscious, in the desire-creating appellation, make a "neutral" observation impossible and can bring the subject to adapt or rebel. For, as stated earlier, the subject never completely dissolves in its subjectivization. Antigone, as we have already seen in Hegel, takes on a revolution of disposition and decides that she will place her life in the "viewpoint" of a normativity arriving from the future.

Lacan terms this "the discourse of the hysteric": a subject who has his own excessive form of holding on to desire while at the same time questioning the "entire system of sentences in which consequences and premises support each other mutually," to paraphrase Wittgenstein once more.

$$\frac{\$}{a} \rightarrow \frac{S1}{S2}$$

The first two coordinates, $\$ \rightarrow S1$, illustrate how far the split subject does not accept the "system of entire sentences" as legal. If the split subject marks the initiation point in the upper left of the illustration, then for Lacan he becomes the true agent of the discourse despite his being split as the subject.[127] In the "discourse of the hysteric," the subject has a voice. S1 is experienced as having a lack. S1 may still have "validity" but no longer "meaning," to employ a phrase by Gershom Scholem, who, in a letter to Walter Benjamin, describes Franz Kafka's literary characters as having a hysterical desperation in view of the appellation of bureaucratic authorities such as S1 who do not want to justify themselves.[128] While S1 is "valid," the subject has recognized illegitimacy at the origin of the S1's performance of power and prefers to "tarry in the negative" as in a "magical power" (PhS §19). The hysterical split subject $ perceives the performative gestures of power as insufficient. If one equates the big Other with the positive ruling law, as Jeanne L. Schroeder does,[129] then the split subject, in her hysterical status, becomes aware that the positive law lacks an important object, namely, Lacan's *objet petit a*. Schroeder calls this encounter *the moral moment* that is precisely *not* covered by positive law.[130] According to Lacan's definition, the *objet petit a* marks a constitutive depravation, a lack within the subject as the ground of her desire. Neither the I nor the social order can transform this withdrawal into an object that can bring closure to a desire.[131] The subject develops a knowledge of her own out of the distress of suffering from the lack within the big Other. This is represented by S2 and can itself become a positive law. "In this discourse S2 is the barred subject's own knowledge which now, for the first time, becomes accessible."[132] What are the consequences of this for Antigone's case? One could argue that Sophocles stages Antigone as a subject of the conflict between the symbolic order (which affords her such roles as mother, sister, woman, citizen of the polis) and her phantasma: to be necessarily more than these roles permit, namely, the carrier of a law of the underworld that is as unfathomable and indefinable as *objet petit a* is phantasmatic and to which she *nevertheless* feels duty-bound.

Antigone is unable to render a propositional account for the true content of her "phantasma," as we have seen in Hegel. The laws dissipate into the prehistory of the modern polis and the paradigm of state reason: these laws are not considered worthy of recognition (for enemies of the state) since they are merely intuitively felt.[133] Antigone recognizes the void in Creon's positive law. The latter makes the repression of her moral claim, her object of desire, into the precondition of the so-called modern state. In this way, Sophocles stages the conflict as one between S1 as positive law and the hysterical will, which holds on to its object of desire *a* as something recognized with certainty. This object *a* as placeholder marks a universal identity precisely as that *which is excluded*. A nonentity transforms itself into a threatening entity for the state. Even if the conflict over a burial ritual holds the meaning of a contingent naught/nothing—particularly with regard to a polis that has just proven itself victorious in war—this particularity becomes an increasingly meaningful universal in the course of the play, due to the intransigence of the hysteric subject. At the end of the tragedy, this universal identity (that as *objet petit a* may always be a contingent nothing) has *on the whole* become objective as proof of the illegitimacy of positive law and now is also worthy of scorekeeping. Sophocles stresses this by having Creon regret his action at the end of the play and ceding the normativity of the burial ritual to the gods of the underworld. Before it comes to that, though, Antigone puts the entire normative law into question through her phantasmatic clinging to *objet petit a*; through her life-threatening *all-or-nothing* radicalness, she prepares, for Hegel, the transition to a higher stage of the Spirit.

In a similar vein, one can read the actions of Rosa Parks, which we analyzed in the Kant chapter, according to the "discourse of the hysteric."[134] She, too, questions the appellation of the symbolic order. This questioning can be phrased according to Lacan's terminology as follows, by Žižek, "'Why am I what you are telling me that I am?'—that is, what is that surplus-object in me that caused the Other to interpellate me, to 'hail' me as . . . [king, master, wife],"[135] and, I would like to add, *as terrorist*. By insisting on the position of the split subject, the actions of the hysteric can be read as those that reject a given identity and the social duties that arise from it.[136]

THE SUBJECT'S SELF-DESIGNATION OUT OF HER VOID (LACAN ON RUSSELL AND FREGE)

So far we have analyzed how subjectivity to the law is, for Lacan, genealogically situated in its various discourses and appellation structures. In doing so, we both discussed the dependence of the subject on "enigmatic signifiers" and thematized the subject's reflex-like reaction to appellations in overly hasty attitudes of obedience. What has proven central to the subject's self-understanding is that the paradoxical structure of recognition, posited by the subject himself *before* his *Dasein* and linked to self-reflexivity, can take on Gestalt *within* this structure. Similarly, by referring to Lacan's Graph of Desire, we have shown how the symbolic order is both the criterion of application for the subject, that is, of his language and reflexive self-understanding, and the way in which the symbolic order receives its first reasonable content *through* the application. The subject is defined by semantic practices of authority, from which she receives the application criteria of her own self-understanding: a forced, non-self-determined choice, not unlike a process of galvanization.[137] Similarly, we've repeatedly made visible the fact, important to this analysis due to its relation to the structural foundation of excessive subjectivity, that the Lacanian subject is always also the weak point of any symbolic order. Therefore, the subject can be tempted into a type of excessive self-positing to create a new phantasmatic frame of her own subjectivity to the law even against the seemingly unshakable premises of the ruling legal order that can always justify itself. Self-referentiality and self-transgression here appear on one and the same level.

In the following section, we will provide a more concrete interpretation of this aspect of self-referentiality and performance that plays such an important role in Kant's revolution of disposition in the subject. Self-referentiality and performance are not only part of the symbolic-political matrix against the backdrop of the collective constitutions of subjects (our example was the Declaration of Independence of the United States: "We the People"). Rather, for Lacan such self-referentiality also concerns the individual human being (Martin Luther served as our example here). Despite dependence on a world of others or of the big Other, human beings are called to self-referentiality. It is the ethical and excessive moment in this self-referentiality that will be analyzed in more depth here with regard to Lacan's reception of a set of problems from early analytic philosophy.

In Lacan's texts, we repeatedly encounter comments on mathematical formalism, especially with regard to the works of Bertrand Russell and Gottlob Frege.[138] It is well known that these two philosophers worked with David Hilbert and Kurt Gödel on the foundations for a mathematics anchored in logic. One reason for Lacan's interest in this foundational attempt lies in the motif of self-referentiality, which in turn lies at the heart of our topic of excessive subjectivity. Lacan realized to what extent his ethics of performative self-referentiality, which is to be defined in the course of this chapter, was impacted by early foundational debates on the universalization of axiomatic models of science in analytic philosophy. In what Russell prominently developed in a letter to Frege and subsequently in his *Principles of Mathematics* (§106) as the paradox of sets,[139] Lacan saw a cue for his own philosophy, namely that "chains of signifiers" in each case refer to their respective axiom and not to metalinguistic or ideal-linguistic, platonic forms in order to instantiate propositions, judgments, and justifications. Similarly, he recognized that "chains of signifiers" rested on imperatives, self-referentialities, and claims of exclusivity that fix a play of language in its use without being able to ensure the existence of a sufficient ground.

Lacan was never interested in establishing his own philosophy of language or an epistemology on a similar level as developed in orthodox analytical philosophy. Rather, he was only marginally interested in language in the context of axiomatic, ideal-linguistic, or ideal-formalistic questions of truth-value analysis in propositions. Language held his interest mainly as a medium of structuring the unconscious. For him, psychopathologies were proof of the psyche's inner turmoil that results from various functional roles of signifiers to be epistemologically uncovered, roles that the psyche forces into a compromise structure within its own self-understanding, which remains aporetic. Given this view of language as the structural medium both of consciousness and of the unconscious, Lacan nevertheless saw in the analyses of various language-philosophical aporias, as they were discussed in the works of Frege, Russell, and the late Heidegger,[140] clues to inconsistencies that, in his opinion, also shaped the subject living in semantics structured by language. This shaping in turn has consequences for the theme of transgressive subjectivity to the law because this subjectivity always remains in a precarious state due to its aporetic, language-contingent self-understanding. As we will try to show, Lacan's own ethics stand for a performative-excessive act of grounding, a self-grasping of the subject that he discovered in the themes of paradoxical self-referentiality within the analytic philosophy of language as an epistemological vehicle of his own thought process. As is easily evident, such self-referentiality is central to our explanation of the psychoanalytical foundation of excessive subjectivity: this excessive subjectivity repeatedly puts at risk, without sufficient grounds, the normative values of interpersonal morals, powered by a strength of its own "count-as-one."

Since language, as Lacan learned from the debates in analytical philosophy and naïve set theory, can be challenged by paradoxes of self-inclusion, self-referentiality, and non-sensical propositions like the liar's paradox, it seemed obvious to him that the human being and his "subject of the unconscious" are also affected by these aporias. Why? Because language is consciousness's medium in its self-reflexive autopoiesis and the mind is self-referential therefore to a certain degree in extenso. Lacan's remarks on the "paradox of lying" (S.XI 138–41)[141] address problems similar to Russell's set-theoretical antinomy of an aporetic nonbelonging in the act of considering a set of all sets that are not members of themselves. This example helped Lacan to understand how the speaking subject stands at the limit of her own self through the holistic structure of language. This limit asks her to potentially redraw this very limit time and time again (often without recourse to a big Other).

The representatives of early analytical philosophy used set theory as a model for formalizing linguistic operations. In *The Foundation of Arithmetics* (1884), Frege assumed, among other things, that each meaningful term has a corresponding defined object, with this object's class or set as its extension.[142] He developed this model of classes or sets in his wish to anchor arithmetic in logic, an intention steeped in his logicism of the *Begriffsschrift* (1879). His goal was to place mathematics on a basis of axioms from which all mathematical propositions could finally be derived. This included the attempt to see primarily antipsychological linguistic operations of truth-values disclosed through symbolic logic in operations of precise calculations. The source of objectivity toward "the True" was for him established neither in time nor in a Hegelian genealogy of concepts, memes, and ever-new notional determinations of the subject-object dichotomy, but through facts as entities existing independently of our mental lives. Facts verify propositional truths-claims—not the other way around—whereas truth-claims advocated by psychologism might be conceived (incorrectly for Frege) as mentally dependent entities. Thought does not (re)construct "the True" or "the False" but aligns itself with platonic entities of universal validity through "thoughts" (*Gedanken*), as Frege calls them, to "the True." *Gedanken* are the medium of truthful instantiations of facts. In *The Foundations of Arithmetic*, especially in the paragraphs on his doctrine of numbers, he shows how integers must be perceived as logical objects and ideal entities that thought adopts operationally insofar as numbers or numerical operations help the human mind to assign extensions to concepts. Logical laws are "the laws of truth,"[143] as Frege writes in his article "The Thought," and as such they are never subjective. Lacan's interest now lies in the fact that the operation of collecting elements under universal concepts is the fundamental operation of linguistic reference and, so, of language too.

Russell's set-theoretical antinomy, developed in his famous letter to Frege and in his *Principles of Mathematics*,[144] posited the illegitimacy of eliminatively reducing propositional reference through symbolic operations.[145] One reason why Russell analyzed the problem of a "class of all those classes which are not members of themselves"[146] in the first place was to question Frege's claim to subsume arithmetic under a limited number of universally valid laws of logic. To Lacan this vain goal of Frege's seemed analogous to the impossibility of a metalanguage or the subject's self-foundation. *Dasein*, Heidegger's famous term, depends for Lacan on linguistic performances in and through language, performances that—more or less neurotic—anticipate a certainty of oneself and at the same time a lack of certainty. Later, Kurt Gödel, Quine, and the late Wittgenstein categorically questioned the claim to conceive of an axiomatically founded, formalistic metaphysics in philosophic-analytical terms without contradictions. Russell saw, to Frege's horror, how the possibility of elements belonging to a universal set under which they are subsumed simultaneously implies in certain cases a paradoxical nonbelonging to the set according to its self-designation.

In the case of a "set of human beings" this does not happen, because the set is not a human being itself. And the self-inclusion of a set may not always be impossible and paradoxical, as the example of a "class of ideas" makes clear. This class may very well be understood as an "idea" itself. Russell, however, discovered that when the discussion of self-referentiality came to "the set of all sets" that do not contain themselves, an aporia occurs. If this set *is* a member of itself, then it is a member in contradiction with the definition of "not being a member." And if it is not a member, then it is not "the set of all sets that do not contain themselves," because a set—namely, itself—is not included. Frege's deduction of arithmetic from logic seemed untenable.[147]

Lacan writes with seemingly slight bemusement in his *Seminar IX* (*L'identification*): "And it is here that the logicians wrack their brains in order to understand the following: now does the set of all sets that do not belong to themselves contain itself, or does it not? In the first as in the second case you get a contradiction. . . . That may seem fairly childish to you but the fact that the logicians—up to the point where they give up—are haunted by this question . . . shows how this contradiction can bring their whole edifice tumbling down. So something needs truly to be solved here. And that relates to . . . nothing but the only thing that these logicians have not quite in view: *they do not know that the letter . . . is something that has forces in itself, a driving force, that logicians are not at all familiar with.*"[148]

According to Lacan, logicians, and Russell foremost among them, do not comprehend that the letter as signifier per se rips open a gap that concerns all signs within the holistic system of which they are part. For Lacan, there is no "predicating" of the letter behind the performance of its positing, as the signifier is—generally and metaphysically speaking—the application *criterion* and the application *case* in one, and can therefore instantiate form and content by itself. The holistic whole of the chain of signifiers has no ultimate ground. With reference to Hegel, one could say: the signifier as *Begriff en miniature* folds itself into itself, and becomes (like the Kleinian bottle), due to its very folds, both content and form in one. And because the signifier can never bring this form to an end, this nonclosure might exactly be the "force" of the letter mentioned earlier in Lacan.[149] Insofar, then, there is not *the* signifier as an abstractum that can be detached (from the *content-and-form* in semantic holism) and placed in a "beyond" of semantics, for example, in Fregian truth-values of the True. Semantics embodies this "beyondness" in itself. This is what Lacan seems to mean when he mentions the "force" of the letter ("la lettre . . . c'est quelque chose qui a en soi-même des pouvoirs").[150] Hegel emphatically explicated this nonclosurable process in his *Science of Logic* in the manifestation of categories that continuously disperse from one form of their intelligibility into another.[151]

Since language, with its own "holisticizing" absoluteness, provides the speaker with the internalized certainty that it is depicting facts in this process, it can always be recognized in its (language's) positings and the linguistic practices that result from it as well. The relationship of a rule to its application is, so to speak, analytic and synthetic in one. And to reiterate, understanding these positings/directives is the decisive factor for understanding the political potential of excessive subjectivity.[152]

For it is crucially bound to deontological speech acts, to positings and foundations of rules with regard to a future amenable to new commitments. Lacan considers it futile to search for a metalinguistic or ideal-linguistic ground as objectively sufficient beyond the processes within chains of signifiers and language games. The problems of Russell's antinomy can therefore not be erased by inventing new metalinguistic levels in search of an absolute reference as the idea of reference is, to paraphrase Willard V. O. Quine, "nonsense except relative to a coordinate system."[153]

It is here in the paradoxical nonbelonging in the act of designation that we can locate Lacan's interest in the linking of paradoxical-autonominal subjectivity to the law and set theory, which at first glance seem irrelevantly far removed from each other. He connects this to what he calls the "force" of the letter with which, as he states earlier, "the logicians are not familiar"—but the excessive subject, or, to be more precise, excessive subjectivity, indeed is. Lacan considers any attempt that tries to ground this power of the letter in a metalinguistic system erroneous, as does Russell in his book *An Inquiry Into Meaning and Truth*.[154] Yet paradoxically, language *invites* such misapprehension on its part in a transcendental manner, that is, paradoxically as a condition of its possibility. In his text "The Subversion of the Subject," Lacan writes about the concept of the big Other as the locus of the signifier: "No authoritative statement has any other guarantee here than its very enunciation, since it would be pointless for the statement to seek it in another signifier, which could in no way appear outside the locus. I formulate this by saying that there is no metalanguage that can be spoken, or, more aphoristically, that there is no Other of the Other."[155]

What makes the entire discussion of Russell productive for our topic of excessive subjectivity is that it led Lacan to realize that no axiomatic system can anchor its own founding in metaphysical universalia. Axioms bare no metaphysical guarantee. They are impositions of individuals, coordinate systems, or discourses of the master, the university, or the hysteric (Lacan calls Hegel "the most sublime of the hysterics").[156] Since there is no "Other of the Other," no universal ground of the symbolic order, excessive subjectivity incorporates the potentiality of disassembling established chains of signifiers through an alterity that is not represented, but that does come to the fore in excessive subjectivity. New performances of creative autonomy allow for something heretical to happen at the back the universal.

THERE IS NO METALANGUAGE

The set-theoretical antinomy stands for the impediment of an eliminative reduction of language through a metatheory (logic), or, as Lacan says, through a metalanguage. From here on Lacan develops the thesis, mentioned earlier, of the "force" (*le pouvoir*) of the letter. (Speaking is an act of interpreting based on practices and the retrospective grasping of that which has been interpreted as that which has been cognized.) The "essence" of language does not lie beyond its use in such a way that we can comprehend the application of language according to its respective linguistic rules only after having understood this essence. Language, for Lacan, carries in its expressive usage the application criteria in a paradoxicality that unites the commensurability and incommensurability of linguistic practices that shape the "chain of signifiers" as such, and through that enables the creative autonomy of a hysteric subject in the first place. The relevance of linguistic practice, in particular with regard to personal pronouns, was also analyzed by Émile Benveniste. Personal pronouns exhibit an interdependence of particular speech acts with linguistic representation and performance. This caught Lacan's interest as, even before John L. Austin developed his speech act theory, Benveniste exemplified the performance of the speaking subject with regard to the personal pronoun (the "I") in propositions. Building on Roman Jakobson's theory of the "shifter," Benveniste describes the linguistic function of personal pronouns as one that has to be categorized differently than objects such as "trees," "tables," "houses," and so on. Objects can be lexically labeled, defined, and classified through their meaning and use within a natural language, which is exactly what is *not* possible in the case of personal pronouns. Instead of referring to an object, the personal pronoun "I" refers to an individual who utters it in his discourse. As such, the first-person pronoun refers to his discursive performance, as do "the indicators of *deixis*, demonstrative pronouns, adverbs, adjectives which organize the spatial and temporal relationships around the 'subject.'"[157] Benveniste writes: "They [the personal pronouns] have in common the feature of being defined only with respect to the instances of discourse in which they occur, that is, in dependence upon the *I* which is proclaimed in the discourse."[158] Personal pronouns do not refer to a concept or to an individual. "There is no concept 'I' that incorporates all the *I's* that are uttered at every moment in the mouths of all speakers, in the sense that there is a concept 'tree' to which all the individual uses of *tree* refer."[159]

Demonstrative indicators help language solve the problem of "intersubjective communication," as each individual is offered the possibility to express the purely formal structure of language with her subjectivity and, as such, to occupy an ultimately *unique place* in the space of intersubjective communication. Only from this place can the structure of excessive subjectivity, as Lacan develops it, be thought: the uniqueness escapes "the status of all other signs of the language": "*I* refers to the *process of the individual discourse* in which it is pronounced."[160] This means that personal pronouns in a successful linguistic speech act become their own reality so to speak, a reality that cannot be objectified by a third authority. Through their own usage they enable a "conversion" of the language. They mark "the coincidence of the event described with the instance of discourse that describes it."[161] They transport the synchronic system of signifiers (Saussure's *langue*) into a concrete diachronic reality of the unfolding discursive practice. In this move, "language is so organized that it permits each speaker to *appropriate to himself* an entire language by designating himself as *I*."[162]

For our topic, what these discursive practices highlight are the performative dimensions of speech acts where personal pronouns play a role, such as in "We the People" or "Here I stand and can do no other." For Lacan, by using personal pronouns in political situations like these, subjects occupy a decisively unique place in language, from which a reality is installed that cannot be objectified through third-party authorities. Here, too, we encounter language as a tool of creation and not as a medium of representation. The subject constitutes herself in this performance insofar as she takes recourse to the entirety of language and allows this performance—against the entirety as a holistic stasis—*to happen* on the level of its particularity in a specific situation of application. The speaking subject is then, in her performance, the placeholder, so to speak, of *la langue*, that is, she is the synchronic entirety of language and at the same time, when she speaks in her own name, the diachronic refraction in a performative appropriation and simultaneously paradoxical universalization of her particularity. Lacan radicalizes the theories of his colleagues in such a way that he ties that which he calls the "act," that is, a deed of self-legitimization, back to the unconscious, back to an authority that, for instance, in the traversing of a burdening fantasy, empowers the individual to create itself anew. The act is the performance of a particularity that will have bared the extent of its own self-authorization in a *futur antérieur* (future perfect).

As has, I hope, become clear, the term *signifier* in Lacan stands for much more than only the formal sound-pattern of the linguistic sign. As the signified is an effect of signifiers, the signifier is medium of its praxeologically justified use. The content/concept side of meaning is the outcome of its expressive side.[163] Since the content of meaning cannot be brought to representation without the "chain of signifiers," Lacan considers the content, roughly speaking, secondary due to its inaccessibility. In Saussure's *Course in General Linguistics*, the signified still represents the referential truth-value in the linguistic sign as it stands as "content," "concept," and "referent" in opposition to the "sound-image" or "sound-pattern" of the signifier. For Lacan, this relationship is never reducible to "the True," as it is for Frege, or reducible to fixed contents of meaning, as it is for Saussure. "The signifier as such refers to nothing if not to a discourse, in other words, a mode of functioning or a utilization of language *qua* link. . . . The link . . . is a link between those who speak" (S.XX 18). When we talk about the world, we do not deal only with individual sentences or classes of individual sentences, as some of the founding fathers of the Wiener Kreis insisted, but rather with a holistic system of concepts that in its epistemic claim has to be considered as a whole (without having access to this whole).

As we are yet to see, this understanding of language is essential for Lacan's focus on the role of the subject both in speaking and in acting. He suggests that the "modus of functioning" depends on the performance of language whereby it may also be the (seemingly contingent) self-referential grounds for rules or the positing of rules which define all that language can express (for example, when the subject is equipped with the imperative of a "master"). Lacan establishes this frame of reference as an effect of discourse, that is, of the "chain of signifiers."[164] Referring to Jakobson's linguistics, Lacan speaks of the unstoppable flow of the meaning of speech. He writes that "that meaning effects [of language] seem not to bear any relation to what causes them" (S.XX 19). It is "not individual words that can ground the signifier. Words have no other place in which to form a collection than the dictionary, where they can be listed" (S.XX 18).

This understanding is also reflected in Lacan's question "What is a signifier?" He comes up with an answer that directly alludes to the set-theoretical paradox: "I must already stop, having posed the question in this form. 'A' (*Un*), placed before the term, is usually the indeterminate article. It already assumes that the signifier can be collectivized, that we can make a collection thereof and speak thereof as something that is totalized. Now the linguist would surely have trouble, it seems to me, grounding this collection, grounding it on a 'the' (*le*), because there is no predicate that permits that" (S.XX 18).[165] When Lacan says in this context that there is "no predicate" that encompasses the collection of all language forms, he is saying that there is no metalanguage, no metalinguistic signifier as the extrasymbolic truth-maker of a proposition.[166] What there is, though, is a supplemental gap that structures the web of language from a symbolically hidden void. Lévi-Strauss speaks of a "zero symbolic value," that is, of "a sign marking the necessity of a supplementary symbolic content over and above that which the signified already contains, which can be any value at all, provided it is still part of the available reserve, and is not already, as the phonologists say, a term in a set."[167] Language as the medium for acquiring knowledge of the outside world, as well as the medium of its own self-referential performance, is unrepresentable. This unrepresentability of language does not hinder the use of language. One might rather say with Wittgenstein that language can nevertheless point toward something with an unconcealed mysticism, especially when its limits are made clear. For Lacan, however, that to which language points is not "the mystical" (Wittgenstein) but rather the work of the unconscious, which cannot be positivistically captured, and which is "structured like a language." From Jakobson, he borrows the thesis that the metalinguistic function is one that befits all languages equally insofar as the function is always already in it. Lacan: "All language implies a meta-language, it's already a meta-language of its own register" (S.III 226).

Language is metalanguage in its antieliminative windings. Its unrepresentability reveals itself as a paradoxical condition of its use for Lacan. Wittgenstein, too, worked on this thesis when he underscored in his

Philosophical Investigations that the rule application of language in its use has to be completely repressed in practice so that it can succeed as language *at all.* For Lacan, one could analogously say that the impossibility of a metalanguage has to be repressed in language, just as the workings of the unconscious do, so that in the associative power of his "chatter," the speaker bares even more of that which shows "itself in it." Just as language seems necessarily to be in conflict with its own pretensions for describing the outside world, it also seems only indirectly able to answer the question "What is a signifier?" with both partial understanding and misunderstanding.[168]

LANGUAGE AS EVENT OF THE UNCONSCIOUS

Our discussion of the linguistic-philosophical implications of Lacan's philosophy was motivated by the fact that his theory locates autonominal subjectivity to the law in the linguistic theories of his time. Language, for Lacan, is at work on all levels of consciousness, preconsciousness, and unconsciousness, in the individual psychological imagination, and in the communal world of the symbolic alike. Since the unconscious is thinking "at another scene" (*Schauplatz*), no matter whether we are asleep or awake, daydreaming, or cogitating about philosophical topics, signifiers are always rotating. Lacan: "The question that the nature of the unconscious puts before us is, in a few words, that something always *thinks*."[169] Yet that which is doing the thinking can precisely *not* be put into an eliminative causal relationship with the kind of thinking taking place on a propositional level. "It [the unconscious] is a thinking with words, with thoughts that escape your vigilance, your state of watchfulness. . . . The question is to find a precise status for this other subject which is exactly the sort of subject that we can determine taking our point of departure in language."[170] It is this last sentence that should make clear why our psychoanalytic frame for the analysis of excessive subjectivity needs to follow Lacan's language-philosophical analysis so closely.

When Russell and Whitehead attempt to circumvent the set-theoretical paradox of a "class of all classes which are not members of themselves" by prohibiting the mention of "'all propositions' referr[ing] to some already definite collection,"[171] because such a mention gets entangled in the contraction of its universal self-inclusion, they repress the fact that natural languages are used not only to represent the world in the form of classes, relations, judgments, and propositions. In everyday life, we also refer metalinguistically and universally to the limits and effects, rules, and consequences of speaking itself, at least in certain contexts. And we do this despite various aporetics and paradoxes that such a metalinguistic shift might provoke. Language is always available to the speaker as a medium of a self-reflexive questioning of language's own limits within its medialization in reference to reality, despite certain aporia hidden in this second-order contemplation.[172] With a slight adjustment to Wittgenstein's famous dictum "This is simply what I do,"[173] one could say: "This is simply the way we speak," that is, the way we also speak metalinguistically from time to time.

The Wittgenstein of *Philosophical Investigations* analyzes the particular usage of language games, when in linguistic pragmatic terms he ties a peculiar interconnection of spontaneity, rule-following, and rule justification, seemingly ascribable to skepticism, back to language use and rejects any metalinguistic reduction of natural language as futile. Rule and application, concept and content cannot be separated from a spontaneous and self-referential use. When we speak, we do not choose a rule that is detached from what we want to do or say. As Wittgenstein writes in his *Philosophical Grammar*: the definition of a language game works only in as far as it is being applied: "A definition as a part of the calculus cannot act at a distance. It acts only by being applied."[174] What he means by this is that language does not transcend itself again beyond its application. In his *Philosophical Investigations*, he writes: "No course of action could be determined by a rule, because every course of action can be brought into accord with the rule."[175] A fundamental spontaneity of use cannot be logically grounded. Yet precisely for this reason, spontaneity *can* create something original, a fact that does not preclude that that which was newly created is in turn repeated in rules. The power of that which has been set as a rule is not dependent on past rule-following. In his *Remarks on the Foundations of Mathematics*, Wittgenstein underlines this relationship of spontaneity, rule-following, and concept-formation also central to Lacan, and in the final analysis to be understood politically, in a dialogue with a fictive interlocutor:

> "But am I not compelled, then, to go the way I do in a chain of inferences?"—"Compelled? After all I can presumably go as I choose!"—"But if you want to remain in accord with the rules you must go this way."—"Not at all, I call this 'accord.'"—"Then you have changed the meaning of the word 'accord,' or the meaning of the rule." "No; who says what 'change' and 'remaining the same' mean here? However many rules you give me—I give a rule which justifies my employment of your rules."[176]

The rule *is* the performance of the application of itself without the possibility of further justifications. Rule and application, concept and content can never be completely separated from a spontaneous and self-referential use of concepts.[177] Language reveals an alterity within itself where, for instance, a new rule or a new way of thinking "happens" spontaneously. Do these spontaneous events not occur again and again in the world of politics, philosophy, or art? Lacan locates subjectivity to the law precisely where a new concept-formation occurs in language, thinking, and consciousness. For him, excessive subjectivity comes to the fore exactly in the moment in which spontaneity, rule-breaking, and concept-formation articulate themselves without always having consciousness as the clear agent of this articulation. Giorgio Agamben expresses a similar conviction in his language-metaphysical meditation *Language and Death.* Due to language's failure in its totalitarian claims, a void dwells in language continuously.[178] It is the locus of a repressed noncoincidence in the totalitarian structure of language and as such is interpreted not only by Agamben, but also by Badiou and Lacan as a place of rescue.[179]

Our motivation for dealing here with the topic of spontaneity and rule-following in such detail stems from endeavoring to highlight Lacan's rejection of a "metalanguage" from the perspective also taken up by Lacan of language as "a mode of functioning . . . between those who speak" (S.XX 30). It reiterates the moment of language as a medium of an event that creates horizons of meaning that the subject can tear open almost ex nihilo (like a new rule), a moment that is in principle of interest to Lacan. If there is at all a meaning and an ethics of psychoanalysis, then

Lacan sees it precisely in the fact that the subject is able to call himself back into a new frame of subjectivity to the law from his own noncoincidence, similar to what we saw in the ethical act in Kant.[180]

IMPERATIVES

When Lacan speaks of signifiers (and thereby avoids the talk of Saussurean signs), he emphasizes how a subject is represented for another subject via the chain of signifiers and not by some kind of authenticity of its *Dasein*, its true being. As Brandom says in a similar way: I encounter the other in the game of the giving of and asking for reasons. For Lacan though, "scorekeeping" inside the mentioned "game" feigns a stability in the holistic web of signifiers that Brandom praxeologically would like to consider as something renegotiated from time to time. Yet for Lacan the virtuality of such a negotiation goes too far when thought of in terms of reliability, fixed commitments, and clear, defined entitlements. For Lacan to understand "scorekeeping" as a natural exchange between rational agents would be misleading, as *misunderstanding* is for him one of the essential features of communication. Scorekeeping dissipates in the subject's self-understanding due to her inner noncoincidence, just as it cannot be interpreted without aporias in her relationship to others, or to the big Other. Put simply: there are not scores that can be put in a coherent list as in an inventory.

Even more crucial for Lacan, however, is the libidinal dimension of language. "I will say that the signifier is situated at the level of enjoying substance (*substance jouissante*)" (S.XX 24).[181] He views any abstraction of language games toward clearly defined inventories of scores as a misrecognition of the libidinal dimension of language and as "a highly risky enterprise" (S.XX 19). He includes in such an abstraction the isolation and nominalization of the copula ("being") as signifier in the philosophy of Aristotle. This abstraction from the verb "to be" into "Being" evokes, according to Lacan, the "flickering" (S.XX 31)[182] of a meaning between sense and nonsense. "Being," in nominalized form, is pronounced "*it is what it is*" (*c'est ce que c'est*), and it could just as well be written "*idizwadidiz*" (*seskecé*) (S.XX 31). What Lacan means to illustrate with this ridiculous turn of words is that the performance of "c'est ce que c'est" is as meaning-full as "seskecé," and therefore as "stupid" as Parmenides's famous words—which he, Lacan, criticizes—that "being *is* and that non-being *is not*" (S.XX 22, my emphasis). The nominalization of the copula (for example, of speaking of "being" as if it were an object) for Lacan nevertheless makes sense *in the excessive imperative of an author* who believes himself able to speak of it meaningfully. (Aristotle truly does.) Lacan considers this possible, but only when taking into account that one recognizes that the objectivity and justifiability of language games and language rules are also always simultaneously dependent on the subject's fixed locus from which such words are uttered, at least in cases such as these. With this, Lacan is indirectly referring to the subject matter addressed in the *Entwurfsschrift*, in which subjectivity in the domain of radiating transmissions (desires) of an intrusive and meddlesome fellow human being (*Nebenmensch*) is always overstretched into a transcendentally understood *ex*-centricity. The imperative's effect of positing the talk of a nominalized copula through a subject is part of the condition of language that is at once totalitarian and antitotalitarian. Language includes an openness to the compatibility of meaning through subjects and their subjectivations (S.XX 32).[183] The nominalization of "to be" into "Being" does not lead to specifying an extrasymbolic truth, that is, "the True" of being. What it truly leads to is rather the question of human desire as we know it from the Graph of Desire, namely, *What is it in the end, this Being? Why is it of importance for me?* In these questions, one hears echoes of Lacan's "Che vuoi?" It is the question that refers us back to the interplay of desire, language, and the flow of signifiers marking the dependence on that which "is" and which, paradoxically speaking, fills its meaning via delay. This is why we can address the Lacanian "Che vuoi?" directly to Aristotle: *What kind of truth-apt propositions do you want me to grasp in relation to your talk on Being, master Aristotle? Do I have to desire finding sense in your talk?* Lacan underlines fallibility and infallibility here but in all likelihood also the *undecidability* between fallibility and infallibility in the use of "the signifier that commands." The signifier "is, first and foremost, imperative" (S.XX 32)—"the mode of functioning." And a signifier that commands does not only concern the philosophical question of being in Aristotle, but also the political struggle, such as the one by Vladimir I. Lenin, who, as Lacan puts it, "unleashed signifiers onto the world,"[184] and who demanded servitude and submission in regard to them. The signifier also bears on Antigone, who is prepared to fight and die for the signifier that determines her desire.

Lacan's concept of "phantasm" is dedicated to this thought. It is that which language evokes indirectly for the success of its own exchange of signs. One could also draw a parallel to Kant's earlier-mentioned transcendental idea of the *focus* as the Lacanian phantasm fulfills a similar function: to support the precarious state of reality in a regulatory manner and as a condition of the phenomenal appearance of objectivity. Lacan writes: "Language . . . is such that, as you see, I cannot but constantly slip back into this world, into this presupposition of a substance that is suffused with the function of being" (S.XX 44). Being is, as Lacan says in *Télévision*, the "screen" of language: "l'être fait écran."[185] Similarly, he emphasizes that man's fate not to be able to escape "being" is grounded in the effect of language's presupposed "substance." He adds that it is "provided by the sense each of us has of being part of his world" (S.XX 42). Although the concept of being apparently wants to be more than a signifier, to be the inferential(istic) entirety, so to speak, the "set of all sets," it (the concept) too remains only a signifier without being able to catch up with itself metalinguistically. Lacan is here in close proximity to Hegel's *Science of Logic*. Without pursing an epistemological theory in the strict sense, Lacan's explications in his seminars refer to the dynamic that also shaped Hegel's philosophy: a dynamic of categories that is, on the one hand, geared toward an ultimate point of reference, the catching up to which, on the other hand, represents a forever postponed fulfillment to come. This means that the transcendence of newly established categories, of newly won signifiers, enters a future of always new "updates." The terms *compulsion* (*Drängen*) and *desire* (*Begehren*) define both Hegel's *Science of Logic* (the compulsion of categories in the concept [*Begriff*] as "movement in itself")[186] and Lacan's own analysis within his psychoanalytical philosophy of mind. This "striving" (*orexis, appetitus*)[187] is, on the one hand, attracted by the infinite, yet can correspond to this infinite in an asymptotic succession of steps, on the other. Let us draw an initial conclusion: the themes of Lacan's philosophy of language presented earlier, partially epistemological, partially language-philosophical, harbor a salvific dimension for psychoanalysis from which Lacan develops his ethics of excessive subjectivity and his theory of autonominal subjectivity to the law. For just as signifiers can catch up with themselves each time anew, so it is with the unconscious, according to Lacan. Since the unconscious is structured like a language, it also embodies a potentiality from which the subject, the ego, can be caught up from the indeterminacy of the linguistic structure of the unconscious each time anew. This implies that subjectivity is by definition excessive and carries politically dangerous yet also generatively positive consequences.

The signifier, which "is first and foremost imperative" (S.XX 32) yet later reveals its provisional character, refers then to the fact that it (the signifier) seemingly did not give precise enough instructions to the subject subordinated to it (be this a young child, a student, a disciple and so on), despite the imperatives. This means that even when philosophers try—as the earlier example of Frege's logicism meant to make clear—to provide natural language with a scientific metalinguistic foundation, this imperative of *true science* (an imperative we hear today again, that is, in the high times of eliminative naturalism) pretends to be the performance of its wanting-to-have-validity, without being able to actually provide an ultimate ground for this claim. The big Other is, as Lacan states, always also "fractured, in the same manner as we grasp this split in the subject itself."[188] As he writes, "Les non-dupes errant": those who have not been duped err.[189]

When Lacan speaks of a structural lack within the "master's" instructions, this demonstrates that the master's discourse, whether of strict science (for example, Frege and Russell), politics (for example, Lenin and Mao), or religion (for example, from Paul to Hubbard), is one that motivates man each time anew also because of the lack mentioned. Yet the imperative of the signifier precisely does not allow the subject, as, I hope, has become clear, to enter into a calm wisdom but rather leads him back each time to the question "Che vuoi?" Lacan mockingly compares wisdom that does not know this question with the "stupid smile" of angel statues. "A stupid smile, as everyone knows—it suffices to visit cathedrals—is an angel's smile. . . . If an angel has such a stupid smile, that is because it is up to its ears in the supreme signifier. To find itself on dry land would do it some good—perhaps it wouldn't smile anymore" (S.XX 20). A smiling angel will not bring forth an excessive subjectivity—unless of course it flies out of its cathedral—since the angel is up to its ears in a totality of signifiers and meaning and precisely is not, unlike the individuals of interest to us, suffering from excessive subjectivity, that is, attempting to bring forth in violence a new normative meaning as the latter rises from illegality into an unsettled future.

When language's property of being "*en deçà et au-delà*" (S.XX 44; "here and beyond") is forgotten, and as such is reduced to the "presupposition of a substance that is permeated with the function of being," autonominal subjectivity to the law is endangered. Lacan sees the tendency to freeze the relationship between signifier and signified at work behind this process and opposes it. Being, for him, needs not be understood as something that takes flight into the "beyond" and the "eternal" but that through an inner antagonism is that which has to catch up with itself each time anew. (Lacan replaces "being" with his neologism "para-being" [*par-être*; S.XX 44]). The belief in meaning's fixation and standstill via "the True" implies the repression of a fundamental noncoincidence (*la barre*) of meaning/truth. What such reification does *not* show is that language itself, as mentioned, rests on a paradox and as such guarantees an "enunciative power" as the true potentiality of excessive subjectivity. Therefore Lacan, just like Heidegger, Agamben, and Badiou, attempts to uncover within language and especially within performative speech acts the paradoxical place of enunciation. He sees a way to tie language back to its enunciative power, which at its core lies in the unconscious, in psychoanalysis as philosophy and in psychoanalysis as therapeutic ethics. Lacan underlines this when he cites the "chatter" of the analysand in a psychoanalytic session as the access to the "subject of the unconscious." He writes:

> The subject is precisely the one we encourage, not to say it all (*tout dire*) . . . one cannot say it all—but rather to utter stupidities. That is the key. For it is with those stupidities that we do analysis, and that we enter into the new subject—that of the unconscious. It is precisely to the extent that the guy [the analysand] is willing not to think anymore that we will perhaps learn a little bit more about it, that we will draw certain consequences from his words (*dits*)—words that cannot be taken back (*se dedire*), for that is the rule of the game. From that emerges a speaking (*dire*) that does not always go so far as to be able to "ex-sist" with respect

> to the words spoken (*ex-sister au dit*). . . . That is the acid-test (*épreuve*) by which, in analyzing anyone, no matter how stupid, a certain Real may be reached. (S.XX 22)

What consequences does the reference to the "chatter," which touches on a "certain Real," have? For Lacan, one of the consequences is that language, as stated by the late Wittgenstein, along with Heidegger and Agamben, is at its core also an "event" that makes excessive subjectivity possible in the first place. Language is not simply a medium of representation. Language as event necessarily represses the basic inability of its own absoluteness/totality and nevertheless urges itself, again and again, to step out of itself into something new within itself. This corresponds to the compulsion of the *Begriff* and the dynamic of the categories as geared toward an ultimate reference point that remains phantasmatic in Hegel. Trying to catch up with this reference point represents an always-new task desiring fulfillment, one that is sometimes willing to embrace excessive subjectivity in order to do so.

PHANTASMATICALLY FENDING OFF APPELLATION

As we have seen earlier in our discussion of the Graph of Desire, Lacan understands the subject as an effect of the chain of signifiers, at least to a certain and essential extent. The subject enters into this chain as its inferential-normative frame of consciousness, as Hegel, McDowell, and Brandom put it. It is the subject's "second nature." This chain of signifiers has the side effect—of interest to Freud and Lacan—of splitting consciousness into a conscious and unconscious part, as the subject is never entirely immersed within the mentioned frame. The unconscious experiences an early initial mark (or unitary trait) in the moment of separation from the mother's breast as an "extimate" (here, the Lacanian opposite of intimate) aspect of the subject's self, phantasmatically imagined only later. The unconscious then is deepened by incorporation and vestment of the psyche into the normative signifiers of the big Other. Freud's Oedipal complex represents such an incorporation of a normative outside agency (for example, of the father) into the psychic internal structure of the individual as the structural form of "the law" of the father appeals to the subject and permits his desires a limited expression. Drives, or phantasmatic moments of narcissistic self-imagination to which "His Majesty the baby"[190] (Freud) lays absolute claim from birth on, have to be repressed. As mentioned, the effect is the split subject. What remains in the psyche from earliest childhood on are appellations by societal agencies, invested with symbolic power (father, mother, teacher, and so on) that are necessarily enigmatically distorted. Fantasy, for its part, then "binds" these distortions. It is fantasy that, according to Lacan, provides answers in the inscrutable big Other in order to defuse enigmatic remains of significance. As Jean Laplanche demonstrates, these remains, in the form of nonmetabolized signifiers, shape the unconscious from early childhood on.[191] These residuals that do not dissolve in the symbolizing processes of institutions and "drop out" symbolically unprocessed are directed toward the subject, as overtaxing appellations do. We know these appellations well enough from the psychopathologies of everyday life. Someone gives us an irritating glance, for instance, which sets off an entire explanatory discourse within ourselves as to what that glance might have meant. For Lacan, fantasy now fills the always-remaining enigmatic gaps of the big Other (from the perspective of the subject) in order to guarantee coherence in the normative superstructure as a condition of one's own reflexive self-grasping of the ego.[192] Since human beings are forced from childhood on to legitimize themselves, and since this can never completely succeed because the parents themselves, pressured by an inner alterity, already embody a lack of legitimacy, fantasy is needed as a defense strategy against these lacks, and as a way to overcome contingency.[193] Fantasy is not that moment with which we bring the cosmic order into disarray; rather, as Eric Santner writes, it is "[the] violent singular excess that sustains every notion of such an order."[194] Žižek emphasizes that fantasy generates a paradoxical interconnection of desire's dimensions "should" and "want." It answers the big Other's appellations and posits, in a reactive manner reminiscent of Kant's concept of the spontaneity of imagination, the coordinates at which the subject finds himself as both recognized and overcoming the frightening groundlessness in the foreign desire of the Other through this self-posited recognition.[195] ("Thou shalt x" becomes "I want x.") Fantasy assists the subject in finding his seemingly traditional place in the big Other through the seemingly internalized view of himself that stems from the big Other. The big Other, then, is not only an instance of authority that the subject encounters and against which he experiences his subordination. Rather, the big Other is always already present in the libidinally structured being of man disciplined through education, as Freud explains in his genesis of the superego through the Oedipus Complex.[196]

We mention the psychoanalytic theory of subjectivity here because Lacan, in his *Seminar XI*, speaks of overcoming certain fantasies in his discussion of "traversing the fantasy." And as we have indicated a number of times earlier, this notion of traversing the fantasy is a key theoretical building block in our understanding of excessive subjectivity. This concept is comparable to the gesture that Kant conceptualizes in the moral act (the sudden and accidental acceptance of the subject's noncoincidence with her own absoluteness). Likewise the discussion of traversing the fantasy illuminates the gestures through which Antigone and Socrates both posited themselves anew as political subjects in an autonominally proclaimed frame of reference.

"TRAVERSING THE FANTASY"

In his *Seminar II*, Lacan compares the liberating gesture at the end of psychoanalytic therapy with the command "Eat your *Dasein*!" (S.II 205). That which is to be metaphorically "eaten up" here and out of which the subject is to "fall" are coordinates that libidinally charge the *Dasein*, and in which the subject sees herself standing in the attachment to the norms of the big Other *from the perspective of the big Other.*[197] At the end of his article "Proposition sur le psychanalyste de l'école," Lacan describes that moment in which the subject falls out of her fantasy as the goal of the transference between analyst and analysand: "The relation of transference . . . makes the analysand lose his phantasm and constitutes himself as subject."[198] Since psychoanalytic therapy in general requires "convincing" the unconscious, so to speak, of certain malfunctions—though the intentionality of consciousness has of course no direct access to the unconscious—Lacan's understanding of "traversing the fantasy" is not to be understood as a weighing of arguments about the possibilities and behavioral options for the mind. What Lacan means is nothing other than a dialectic turning point, to be understood mystically, or, put another way, a decisionist cut in which the subject passively receives his new axiom of self-reference, similar to a religious conversion "out of the blue." Traversing the fantasy stands for an initial significant act. It can structurally be an overly hasty action that, due to its own nondeductibility from knowledge provided by the ego about itself, is supposed to lead finally to an anticipatory leap—to instantiate/reaffirm the self. Therefore, Lacan also describes the act as "haste" (though not exclusively) and calls it a "third dimension" of time, as something essential for the human being.[199] Let us recall that in Kant, too, the choice of character or the revolution of disposition was explicated based on a nondeducible, sudden decisionist turn, a supernumerary act of subjectivation.

Bruce Fink describes traversing the fantasy as an act of separating oneself from the *jouissance* of the big Other, which connects the individual to the libidinal manner of the subject's recognition by the big Other.[200] What hinders the act of separation, or of traversing, is the libidinal bond of the person in question to and in the enjoyment of the big Other. In referring to traversing the fantasy, Fink speaks of the individual as able to take on the desire of the Other in such a way that this desire becomes a justifiable and sufficient ground for that individual himself (detached from the big Other), and this means that the person in question can renounce the former conditions of his subjectivization. A newly defined gesture of subordination by the subject toward the Other is then the moment in which the subject *reflects back onto himself* the desire as the ground of his own libidinal foreign investiture. Fink: "*Subjectification is the goal of analysis*: subjectification of the cause—that is, of the Other's desire as cause."[201]

With Kant's expansive concept of the pathological, one could describe the difficulty, or, better, impossibility, of this step as follows: For man to strip himself of pathologies of his essence and his character requires of him a superhuman effort (a revolution in the disposition), since these pathologies—his interests, his inclinations, his understanding of neurotic happiness *dependent on his life-world anchored in the big Other*—are precisely that which the subject *is*.[202]

Zupančič phrases this as follows: what the subject fears more than this or that suffering is "the loss of the very frame within which pleasure (or pain) can be experienced as such at all."[203] This is precisely what constitutes the seeming impossibility of "traversing the fantasy" as a traversing of my libidinal (foreign) investiture in the big Other. It is he, the big Other and his frame of reference, who provides me with my self-worth as a good citizen in my societal environment, who blesses my life compromises, who holds the Heideggerian call of "*wanting to have a conscience*" (*Gewissen-haben-wollen*)[204] over a little flame and approves of my cheating when I fail to live up to the moral law in daily life. To traverse this big Other? Why should I want to do this, when the pathological is the lesser evil to the Kantian moral law?

Antigone's grief-stricken listing of the social roles (wife and mother) that she renounces by holding on to her desire[205] can also be understood as a traversing of the fantasy dependent on the big Other in the form of a ritualistic returning of her symbolic investiture. This enables her to enter into the arena that Lacan calls "between two deaths." This return helps Antigone to make her desire her own,[206] in order to become the Sophocleian Antigone who, as Lacan says, advances into the domain of the *Ate*. Even if the subject is never completely able to leave the phantasmatic frame of her life-world (strictly speaking, only at the cost of a psychosis), the traversing of the fantasy at the place where it is anchored in the big Other marks a path "beyond the neurosis,"[207] as Fink writes. It results in a new adjustment of the structures in which the individual posits herself as now recognized.

To traverse the fantasy marks an often decisionist change in the relationships of subjectivitites. As we have repeatedly stressed, this can evoke radical political effects.[208] Lacan's reception of Kant and Hegel is to be understood against the backdrop of these consequences. The subject that traverses her fantasies has changed her life-world as well as her relations to others through her new modal inscription of herself into the symbolic field. The place from which the subject was disciplined is, in a dialectical reversal, reflected back onto her in the decisionist choice of character, disposition, or neurosis, as the place that the subject now actively makes her own in a paradoxical temporal loop. She takes responsibility for being the one who—from the former place of disciplining—she now truly is. In choosing her autonomy, the subject simultaneously and necessarily grasps the genealogy of her disciplining as the condition for the new definition and manner in which she is responsible for her own being. The choice of character and the traversing of the fantasy follow as dialectical reversals of the logic of re-marking, and it is precisely the future-perfect tense that Lacan considered the essential characteristic of the unconscious. The unconscious is that which, "thanks to the symbolic progress which takes place in analysis, *will have been*" (S.I 158).[209] As mentioned, Lacan had taken from Freud the insight that memories contained in the psyche influence one another via mutual overwriting. Structures of causality can end up in paradoxical inversions of their temporality. Memory, according to Lacan, is "to be brought in at any moment. But the next moment, it may well no longer be at all the same" (S.II 185).[210] The subject's exterior world itself does not change in its immediacy. What changes, as Žižek says, is "the modality of its [the subject's] inscription in the symbolic network."[211] For Lacan, the subject, in traversing the fantasy, becomes the carrier of her own Real, an inner paradox from which she "emanates." The subject does not work through her history; rather, she "rewrit[es] history" (S.I 14), and this time as master-signifier.[212] This act embodies the core of the ethics of psychoanalysis, which therefore is also to be called an "Ethics of the Real." The Real may then potentially mark a locus of personal failure; it marks a destructive will for the benefit of something else, insofar as anything can be called into question from "the function of the signifier," as Lacan says (S.VII 212), that is, from the function of the implicitly inferential characteristic of conceptual linkages, which have normatively affected the life-world of the subject and her interior life, as Robert Brandom writes. Yet this is precisely where Lacan sees the possibility for a new beginning. Lacan speaks of a "creationist sublimation, and it is linked to that structural element [of destruction]." It shows "that, as soon as we have to deal with anything in the world appearing in the form of the signifying chain, there is somewhere . . . the *ex nihilo* on which it is founded and is articulated as such" (S.VII 212). The Real, and not a metaphysical substance, is this "beyond" of the chain of signifiers. This locus of an ex nihilo is nonrepresentable and yet it radiates its effects, for example, via the unconscious that, "thanks to the symbolic process which takes place in analysis, *will have been*" (S.I 158).

Lacan's discussion of the Real evolved gradually, over the course of his career. While in his early works, the concept was geared toward the body's own instinctual drives as part of an enjoyable suffering that breaks open the subject's self-understanding, in his later works the Real represents the larger potentiality of meaning of an inner antagonism that breaks open its other two registers (the Symbolic and the Imaginary). As John Rajchman so aptly writes, the Real refers to the extent to which "Eros is at odds with Ethos."[213] For Lacan, the Real harbors the inaccessible potential for demasking some of the various meaning constructs of the individual and society. Similar to Hegel's concept of negativity, it represents a subversive potential for which the subject himself cannot bring to bear sufficient propositional knowledge and sometimes possibly only an absurd-symptomatic insistence and desire.[214] In this tension, in which Lacan develops his ethics of the Real, the Real marks castration through imposed laws, words, desires, and repressions of desires that format the unconscious. Yet it also marks the traversing of the fantasy fed by these gestures of subordination. The subject embodies excess that cannot even be metabolized by ideology. It is this noncoincidence between Eros and Ethos that runs through all of Lacan's hard-to-define concepts such as the "Ding," "*objet petit a*," or *jouissance*. By virtue of these concepts, he attempts to clarify phenomenological effects of the psyche such as the restlessness of desire, the earlier-mentioned self-destructive behaviors, and the peculiar enjoyment of psychological suffering and neurotic ticks. It may be hard to understand to what extent these "psychopathologies" have anything at all to do with ethics. Yet for Lacan it is crucial that in these symptoms it is the side of the *autonominal subjectivity to the law* that, in turning away from the I, keeps insisting, and that this side is able to claim its "right" against that which has been established (the I-function and its societal coordinates in the big Other) via the detour of seemingly pathological fixations and resistance. And the ethics of psychoanalysis, according to Lacan's understanding, accords legitimacy precisely to this insisting as a transgressive and tragic yet also *legal* component, without wanting to subordinate it to traditional categories of the humanistic-ethical tradition such as "the cleaning up of desire," the "modesty, temperateness" (S.VII 314), or "the service of goods" (S.VII 324).

UNREPRESENTED SIGNIFIERS

Lacan claims a simultaneous insistence of signifiers for the process of traversing the fantasy, which is of interest to us in the context of our theorem of excessive subjectivity. He calls this process both "act" and "passage à l'acte" in *Seminar XIV* (*The Logic of Fantasm*).[215] In the session from February 15, 1967, Lacan defines the successful conclusion of analysis—which he himself calls "le savoir analytique"—as a step and transition into the Real, as "[la] passe dans le réel."[216] So that psychoanalytical knowledge "proceeds into the Real—we claim that the I has to, according to its own claim, affirm itself as *fons* and *origo* of being."[217] When Lacan continues with "l'acte est signifiant"[218] (the act is significant) and the subject is "transformé par l'acte"[219] (transformed by the act), this means that the act creates a new horizon of meaning in which the subject finds himself approached in a new manner in an autonomination and self-grasping. "The act is the only locus where the signifier has the appearance—the function in any case—of signifying itself. Namely, to function outside its possibilities."[220] Just as with Kant's revolution of disposition, the act posits meanings in the performance of its happening. Lacan: The act is the "*instauration du sujet* comme tel,"[221] the autonominal positing of the subject as such. An act will have been an act when the consequences will have consisted of traversing the big Other or of a new direction for the same in its relation to subjectivization. "Has it really reached its original ground or have we only read it into this original ground?"[222]

The "obsession" of the "historical materialist" in Walter Benjamin's "Theses on the Philosophy of History" comes metaphorically close to what Lacan speaks of here. The materialist's desire has as its goal to make history retrospectively "citable in all its moments" but not in such a way that "the images, . . . broken loose from all earlier associations," stand in sober rooms "like precious fragments or torsos in a collector's gallery."[223] The "images" of history that have been constructed by Benjamin's historical materialist are meant to articulate an urgent appeal. For this appeal, the big Other lacks a clearly presentable entry that the historical materialist could show lacking on the big Other's "scoreboard" (Brandom) or in his galleries consisting of torsi.[224] For in the end, this "scoreboard" as a cultural product is always, according to Benjamin, that of the victor of history. Benjamin's political messianism rests on that: on the performative breakthrough of an accidental appeal into the "eternal" picture of the past that historicism depicts for the benefit of the established order.

The historical materialist finds himself called with almost paranoid insistence to receive the historical documents as against the established genealogies in the ruling chains of signifiers. (Cultural documents as the embodiment of the victor's perception of *hi(s)story* are hiding the truth of oppression, as Benjamin claims.) In his twelfth thesis, Benjamin quotes the shooting at the tower clocks in Paris during the July Revolution of 1830 as the revolutionaries desired to break with the established understanding of time, analogous to the Lacanian traversing of the fantasy: the continuation of tradition "as we know it" and the continued inscription of *classes* that remain identical over centuries have to stop.[225] History has to be rewritten, just as for Lacan, in traversing the fantasy, the unconscious has to be revealed and simultaneously constructed in its newly chosen disposition as that which it will have been. The demands, which according to Benjamin make it possible for the historical materialist in his counter-reading of the ruling doxa's historical genealogies to discern the true claim or appellation from past sufferings in the moment of a *Jetztzeit*, a present time, do not come, as Lacan says, "from the past" as out of an *Ur*-period of authenticity, but rather come as constructs or acts of an autonominal paranoid self-positing "from the future" (S.I 158). Are not such acts of traversing always relevant in times of political-revolutionary upheaval (burning down the Palais of the state, toppling statues of leaders) in order to make it impossible to return to the old axioms of reference? Formerly insignificant signifiers take on (a paranoid?) meaning for the historical materialist, yet also for the revolutionaries. Is this not something that motivates revolutionaries in the few locations where any remain? Previously negligible, repressed facts and states of affairs can all of a sudden—now with normative authority—become clearly visible to all.[226]

Unlike Benjamin, Lacan locates the act of re-marking not within the confines of a nation's history, but first and foremost in relation to the psychoindividual level of the analysand, who attempts to liberate himself from a particular suffering, shaped by a wrongheaded libidinal investiture in the symbolic network. Nevertheless, as Lacan readily admits, this individual level can very well have collective consequences with revolutionary character. Lacan mentions Paul, Luther, and Lenin as subjects whose partially paranoid-seeming way of newly inscribing themselves into the symbolic network has influenced the course of world history.[227]

In situations where someone is chosen or called, signifiers "speak" to the subject with their normative meaning in such a way that the subject bursts forth as if newly created in the very moment of appellation. One may think of the seemingly paranoia-evoking call of the old burial laws which appe(a)llate to Antigone. (She is, of course, Polynices's sister, but so is Ismene, who obeys the polis.) Saint Paul's conversion experience on the way to Damascus or Emperor Constantin's "divine omen" in the battle at the Milvian bridge could also count among such paranoid moments of perception: in all these situations, signifiers appear from Lacan's Real and transport the subject into a new manifestation of being himself. Ed Pluth writes: "In an act, signifiers are used quasi-autonomously, and their use amounts to a repetition and an extension of a signifying impasse, converting an enigmatic tension into some kind of satisfaction."[228]

How can this be? How is it possible that signifiers can pressure the subject into an act when these very signifiers, with their normative claims, seem to come from the arena of Lacan's Real and are precisely *not* recognized by the big Other with the same insistence of certainty? Would this not amount to a particular form of fantasy resembling a private language or, as the examples suggest, at least a temporary state of delusion? For Lacan, traversing the fantasy may very well necessarily contain a delusional moment. However, that does not mean for him that the subject simultaneously plummets into a psychotic state of the kind that Daniel Paul Schreber describes in his *Memoir of My Nervous Illness* (1903), interpreted by Freud and Lacan. The Symbolic (as the collectively guaranteed structure of truth-claims in their various "fields of sense," to quote Markus Gabriel)[229] and the Imaginary (as the virtual ideal of subject and society) are always interwoven with the Real, which is what guarantees that they are never all. No structure of meaning—neither intrapsychic nor intersubjective—can do without the Real, as the latter guaranties readjustments of justifications in our "web of belief."

In traversing the fantasy, the subject is not quite able to untie the Borromean knot of the Symbolic, the Imaginary, and the Real into which his psyche is bound up. He displaces the relationship of linkages between the Imaginary and the Symbolic via a confrontation with the Real, to which he comes rather more passively than actively. The Real forces the signifiers upon the subject just as the subject, in the very moment of having them forced upon him, paradoxically "creates" these signifiers both autopoetically and autonominatively, and posits them as his own.[230]

In her book *The Literary Speech Act*, Shoshana Felman points out that the autocreative performance of events via Lacan's act is formally not dissimilar to John L. Austin's speech act theory.[231] Austin develops his thesis of performativity in contrast to constative utterances. The latter describe situations or states of facts that could be true or false. Performative utterances, on the other hand, perform an action. In this sense, they can succeed or not succeed but cannot be true or false, as, for example, is the case with judgments. The act as conceived by Lacan embodies such a performativity.[232] Yet it does so only up to a certain point. Ed Pluth convincingly argues against Felman. He shows how Lacan's act, in a first manifestation of its performance, is not predicated on signifiers of ritual acknowledgment. The authority that the act can authenticate is the subject's certainty with regard to the meanings invading him.[233] Yet how can signification occur in this act, which takes place by detaching itself from the big Other, or, as Wittgenstein says, by breaking with the established games of language via a new rule? We can soften the aggressive tone of the question here. Providing a new evaluation of signification is not to be understood as a solipsistically created new language. Rather, the subject, similar to Benjamin's historical materialist, discovers new levels of meaning that he notices subsequent to the decisionist opening of a distance to his current subjectivization in the structures of the big Other. The inferential references have shifted within established frames of meaning. The same linguistic web brings to the fore previously nonrepresented meanings, like a reversible image. In this context, Wittgenstein's remarks on concept-formation may prove helpful.[234] Concept-formation marks the borderline to empiricism, insofar as it intersects the domain of established concepts through the invention of a performative spontaneity with "free-floating rationales" seeking to become entangled.[235] While concepts in the form of rules comply as media with all kinds of semantic rules, concept-*formation* features a surplus of the established boundaries of facts and thoughts.[236] Seminal transformations of conceptual justifications, as they have been historically transmitted, might be obliterated by the newly installed and nondeducible concept. The delimitation does not belong in the strict sense *to* the world in the moment of its performative demarcation, insofar as the formation is hung up between the world of appearances and the world of the noumenal, as Wittgenstein suggests. Only in the spontaneity of thought does concept-formation arise and it does so as something *diagonally* related to the established. Wittgenstein accentuates this in paragraph 401 of his *Philosophical Investigations*, stating that concept-formation can be compared to the invention of "a new meter, or a new kind of song" ("*ein neues Metrum, eine neue Art von Gesängen*").[237]

A concept-formation is an occurrence that shifts the internal structure of semantics without having to find the appropriate hinges for this shift in semantics in advance. We mention this here because Lacan conceives of the act in a similar manner to Wittgenstein's comments on concepts shifting like riverbeds.

"THE UNLEASHING OF THE SIGNIFIERS"

At the conclusion of our discussion of Lacan, we turn to Freud's oft-cited remarks in *Beyond the Pleasure Principle* on his grandson's so-called *Fort-Da* (Gone-There) game to help explain how the evocation of new signifiers is linked to the act, for this evocation of new signifiers remains difficult to grasp, and is easily dismissible as a purely paranoid delusion. For Lacan, the *Fort-Da* game is an important explanatory model of signification in the moment of a subject's development in relation to the big Other.

Freud's remarks on the game proceed from observing his one-and-a-half-year-old grandson, who at that point spoke few intelligible words, while he comforted himself about his mother's absence by playing with a spool of thread.[238] Freud explains that the child was caught "passively" by the loss of his mother. Confronted with this experience, he pulled himself out of the depth of his negativity on his own and created a symbolic world determined by a single signifier: the wooden spool. The game consists solely in the spool's presence or absence—in throwing it out and reeling it back in. This game is an activity of sublimation and self-guaranteed playful repetition of the mother's departure, which is experienced as threatening. Here, the child opens up a world in which he becomes an autonomous subject with regard to the distance suffered through the big

Other (in this case, the absent mother). For the child, the spool becomes a carrier of meaning that reverses the original negativity into a linguistic play of presence and absence. According to Jonathan Lear, the original experience of loss seen here was not yet a symbolized one, as it lacked an expression conveyed by signs.[239] This supports our theoretical position in as far as the subject of the game, the child himself, also appears to be outsourced to a signifier, as is the subject matter, the mother. For Lacan, the spool is a chimera of the split subject and of the external power of the big Other, whose being is charged with meaning via absence and presence.

If one applied this "Gone-There" dialectic to Hegel's interpretation of Antigone, one could say that the rift between Antigone and the polis as social community leads to Antigone making herself into an autonomous political subject precisely due to the negative experience of irreconcilability with her ancestral society. It is, of course, not the case that Antigone "posits" the meaning of the burial ritual after its interdiction by Creon as Freud's grandson evokes the spool in his mother's absence as a signifier in order to become autonomous himself. Yet it is the case that only through Creon's intransigent prohibition, that is, his repudiation of the burial ritual for Polynices, does Antigone make herself into an autonomous political subject beyond the political doxa by holding on to these traditional signifiers. Hegel reads this as an unintentional eroding of the spirit of morality of Greek antiquity and as preparing for the transition to Roman law. For Lacan, Antigone's tragedy articulates itself in a desire that follows its object into the Beyond of inner-symbolic values. With the burial ritual directing an *absolute claim* at Antigone that only she can hear, she makes herself autonomous of her surroundings on account of this claim, just as Freud's grandson creates a reflective relationship between himself and the external world (independent of his mother) in the game of a linguistic sign, for himself.

One could call the spool in Freud's example a signifier upon which the toddler is thrust, as onto an unexpected "answer" from the Lacanian Real. Lacan mentions the Real in the context of the emergence of a new signifier in his *Seminar III*, in which he provides an important link that allows us to tie together both the act and the act's signification of individual, seemingly paranoid signifiers, as well as to attach to it the themes of conversion and revolution. Lacan writes:

> Let's flesh out the signifier's presence in the real, insofar as this is possible. The emergence of a new signifier, with all the consequences, down to one's most personal conduct and thoughts that this may entail, the appearance of a register such as that of a new religion, for example, isn't something that is easily manipulated—experience is proof of that. Meanings shift, common sentiments and socially conditioned relations change, but there are also all sorts of so-called revelatory phenomena that can appear in a sufficiently disturbing mode for the terms we use in the *psychoses* not to be entirely inappropriate for them. The appearance of a new structure in the relations between basic signifiers and *the creation of a new term in the order of the signifier are devastating in character.* (S.III 201, my emphasis)

Here, Lacan explicitly compares the breaking-in of signifiers from the arena of the Real into the Symbolic to psychosis. He extrapolates individual-psychological breakdowns onto the social realm in order to reveal the eruption of a new modality of the symbolic field. This means, among other things, that the universal develops from the level of the particular in a newly tied Gordian knot of the Symbolic, the Imaginary, and the Real. In this passage, Lacan speaks indirectly of Christianity as a conversion movement that, while it does not posit a new language, nevertheless generates fundamentally new rules and meanings for signifiers.[240] The effect is a new way of speaking against the established "common sentiments and socially conditioned relations." And in his *Seminar XXIV*, he speaks explicitly of "l'invention d'un significant," the invention of a signifier,[241] which is not to be compared to a form of anamnesis. In *Seminar XV* Lacan makes a reference to the Russian Revolution when he writes: "Is the act not the moment when Lenin gives one order or another, or is it the moment when signifiers have been unleashed onto the world that give to one or another precise success in the strategy, his sense of beginning that is already traced—something in which the consequence of a certain strategy comes to take its place and from there to take its value of the sign?"[242] By referring to Lenin, Lacan captures the act in the image of "unleashing" signifiers onto the world. Through this unleashing, the act performatively frees its power, which exists in the transgressive gesture of annunciation. The power of the letter might also lie here, anchored in excessive subjectivity, which Lacan names in the quotation earlier, when he reproaches Russell for being blind with regard to the rule-founding performative power and imperative effects of words. For Lacan, the focus on science and on an analytic understanding of truth forms the structural basis of the misperception.

Another look back at Antigone or Freud's grandson reveals that the act appears in the confrontation with a big Other experienced as inconsistent. This is a condition that we also analyzed in the "discourse of the hysteric," as the perception of a lack. Based on this experience of inconsistency, the act is an unleashing of signifiers onto the world with the acting subject possessing no more authority than that of her own certainty. Any authority in the field of the other cannot (yet) understand the signification that the act carries and provokes. "Reality is precarious," writes Lacan. "And it is precisely the extent to which access to it [reality] is so precarious that the commandments that trace its path are so tyrannical" (S.VII 30).

Freud's grandson and Antigone experience the precarious character of reality in confrontation with a deficient big Other. This causes them both to desire and to evoke signifiers, and to hold on to them—a moment that does not leave the world uninfluenced in its overall relationship of truth and knowledge. As we have tried to show in Hegel's interpretation of Antigone, the conflict for Antigone over the burial rites clearly concerns questions as to the totality of what is real in the world with regard to veridical convictions and justified beliefs. When Lacan speaks of the "precarious" status of reality, a status maintained by the psyche through its state of being bound up in the register of the Symbolic and the Imaginary, which defines itself both through the "defense" of the Real and through the "approach to the Real" (S.VII 31), the act freezes for him exactly that moment which is able to traverse the symbolic order of the big Other as well as the world that results from solipsistic fantasies. The act is that which briefly interrupts the (to this point only minimally effective) share of regulatory ideas that was necessary to maintain the experience of reality as equilibrium between the examination of reality and its phantasmatic frame. After such an interruption of this equilibrium, the individual can experience herself as living in a "new world," while the world of the Symbolic can simultaneously learn to (self-reflexively) recognize itself through a possible dialectical reversal of all relations, provoked via excessive subjectivity.[243] While the Symbolic and the Imaginary appear to each other to be stable (in the Imaginary, the self appears as a center of unbroken autonomy; in the Symbolic, rules and norms keep the Real at bay), the Real is an experience of the tearing to shreds of the patina that was commonly considered to be reality in itself. The Real, then, is a *movens* of the Hegelian Spirit since it is capable of showing Spirit the inability to be all encompassing in each new stage of development. It is an emerging "status naturalis," a rift in the patina of the Symbolic. In Žižek's words, it lays open that "the ultimate guarantee of our 'sense of reality' turns on how what we experience as 'reality' conforms to the fantasy-frame."[244] However, it also makes evident that it is precisely this frame that is "prestructured through the leftovers of the hallucinatory phantasm,"[245] which can fall into a new form in the encounter with the Real, as in the turn of a kaleidoscope. It may very well be excessive subjectivity that causes this turn.

According to Kant, Hegel, and Lacan, excessive subjectivity appears as a formal-logical structural moment in which particularity and universality, by equating form and content, decide from which dispositional viewpoint the subject (yet also a collective, a community of disciples, a church, a sect) looks at her life-world and thus provokes new judgments with unexpectable consequences. This locus may be inaccessible to the subject. According to Lacan's theory of the act, the subject finds herself standing there only *after* the act. A permanently lurking noncoincidence between the necessarily individual-psychological experience of "reality" and the Symbolic as a collectively maintained belief in the big Other demonstrates how far the *non*differentiability of paranoia on a societal-collective level and on a subjective level is not always clearly definable. Hegel, too, thematizes this noncoincidence in the relationship of his two terms the universal ("substance") and the particular ("subject"). "Spirit" and "consciousness" can drop out of a society or an entire empire, almost without notice. In this case, it may be the seemingly chosen ones such as Jesus of Nazareth, convertites such as Paul of Tarsus or Martin Luther, provocateurs such as Nietzsche's "madman" (*toller Mensch*) or Walter Benjamin's historical materialist who may potentially recognize this while the practices themselves are still propagating their fulfillment in the process of their functioning that have become—for the chosen ones—unreal.

VALIDITY WITHOUT MEANING

We have pointed out that speaking of "excessive subjects" in contrast to "excessive subjectivity" renders harmless the paradox of retrospective recognition. Excessive subjectivity is interpreted as a structural moment precisely because an excessive subject cannot lay claim to his excess without the belated integration of normativity. Consequently, leading civil rights figures such as Rosa Parks today garner respect for the justified excess of their protests through a normative claim—yet the same is (perhaps not yet?) the case for Ulrike Meinhof, leader of the Red Army Faction in Germany in the 1970s. The latter might only become possible after a reversal of bourgeois democratic values as they determine our subjectivity to the law as citizens today. Excess itself cannot be a norm; it appears as "paranoid reason,"[246] and has to be excluded from society. Excessive subjectivity, on the other hand, needs to be understood as a structural moment in the genesis of normativity and cannot be comprehended via a notion of reason that is free of aporia and without locating it in the *futur antérieur*.

Representatives of excessive subjectivity, however, rarely live as solipsistically as Antigone does in her life "between-two-deaths." Rather, they live in societies; not infrequently small sect-like groups of disciples form around them. Consider those figures already mentioned: Jesus, Paul, Martin Luther, Rosa Parks, and the like. Quite often they possess a peculiar form of authority that influences others. This authority in turn seems to be associated with the message being proclaimed, which, in its proclamation, is often semantically overdetermined. The fact that the overdetermination of semantic contents can foment its own glue within the psyche through the suspension of meaning (but not of validity) is one of Freud's basic insights that Lacan and Althusser apply to the societal arena as a precarious space of virtuality. This basic Freudian insight is interpreted by Laplanche[247] on the individual-psychological level, and on the societal level in Žižek's interpretation of "sublime" signifiers.[248] According to Laclau and Žižek, the political field is necessarily structured by "enigmatic signifiers," "empty signifiers,"[249] and "sublime objects of ideology." Particularly indeterminate and enigmatic messages that the psyche *cannot* unambiguously inferentially decode into well-defined propositions can hold an extraordinarily powerful sway over the psyche.

Žižek states in this context that being called through, for instance, sublime objects of ideology in which the subject is to a certain extent looking for an answer to the question that concerns him—that is, "Che vuoi?"—can cause him to always be a small step ahead of ideology, just to avoid any wrongdoing. Kafka describes this preemptive obedience in a draft of the parable "Before the Law," which is part of his novel *The Trial*. The parable succeeds particularly well in capturing the political-theological heritage of a normative "validity without meaning" in Kafka, which Walter Benjamin and Gershom Scholem discuss in their letters,[250] for Kafka stages the guard in the parable as the representative of the law, the master-signifier, the highest symbolic order. As such, the guard is located on a diffuse threshold of interpellation that does not directly explain what he is doing there in the first place. Does he guard, block, or control the law? Is he dangerous? Does he prevent the "man from the countryside" from gaining access to the salvation-promising law?[251] Here we encounter the literary adaptation of Lacan's appellation, captured in the "Che vuoi?" of his Graph of Desire, in pure form. This appellation, which continues to appeal even if it does *not* resound, provokes a panicked haste in Kafka. This panicked haste erupts because the doorkeeper, as Kafka writes in an earlier draft of his text, neither gives orders nor forbids anything. "I ran over the first guard," writes Kafka, "I was frightened in retrospect, ran back and said to the guard: 'I ran through here while you were turned away.' The guard looked straight ahead and remained silent. 'I probably should not have done this,' I said. The guard continued to remain silent. 'Does your silence mean that I have permission to pass?' "[252]

In a similar vein, Kafka describes Josef K.'s arrest at the outset of *The Trial* as a collapse of K.'s imaginary self-image in the face of an external coordinate whose lack of meaning, combined with its simultaneous validity, causes him to become neurotic.[253] (Here we see Kafka's theory of modernity as a structural analysis of man's increasing neurosis.) In his hesitation, K. becomes entangled in considerations of whether he should accept the absurd charges that the "guards" read to him one morning or whether he ought rather to ignore it and simply leave his apartment. The fact that in the course of the novel K. has to almost pursue the legal fight because he cannot receive a specific charge or a clear prosecutorial authority precisely renders the latter almost supernatural as a locus of bureaucratic power, the authority of the prosecution, in Josef K.'s eyes.[254] The

Other here has to encompass the field of societally accepted knowledge as well, which continues to "have an effect," even when all individuals in this field harbor the suspicion that the big Other is lying, errs, and has gone crazy, and that his authority is contingent on a collective misunderstanding. This Kafkaesque phenomenon of the absent gaze is to a significant extent the basis for the preemptive obedience that the interpellation causes in individuals and that we encounter in the most common situations of daily life.[255]

Human beings are exposed to contingent appellations that are interpreted as necessary because the subject has been inscribed with a fundamental delegitimation of her being. What the subject misses in these moments of interpellation is how she posits the Other, and by doing so annihilates the moment of contingency that is part of the interpellation. Josef K. intuitively grasps the arbitrariness of his arrest. Nevertheless, he remains incapable of explicating the appellation of guilt embedded in the arrest as nonbinding. This means that he himself pushes forward the procedure of the trial and thus shapes the dramatic element in *The Trial*. Kafka's prose enacts the tragedy that Josef K. is incapable of extricating himself from the preemptive obedience toward an indefinable yet therefore seemingly even more powerful appellation.

Lacan does not claim that the subject is able to completely shield herself from disturbing appellations of this kind or another. Yet the utopian moment in his ethics of the Real, which is an ethics of traversing the fantasy, underlines that he sees the possibility of at least temporarily interrupting this preemptive obedience. For reasons of structural efficiency, an ideological community is more dependent on the *haste* of obedience, more so than the community itself might be willing to admit. Neither Kafka's "man from the countryside" nor Josef K. is capable of making such an interruption happen. Žižek, in his Lacan-oriented analysis of "sublime objects of ideology," dissects the sublime objects, as faith-inducing media of semantic *too-muchness*, by claiming that they often cause the subject to misrecognize her own active capacity and the phantasmatic moment in the constitution of reality and law.[256] Not only are sublime objects of ideology able to paralyze the subject's activity, as Kafka shows in "Before the Law," but they also provoke the preemptive obedience described by Kafka that limits the subject's freedom even more steadfastly through a self-imposed conviction. According to Žižek, this obedience causes the subject to underestimate her own potential: the excessive gesture of concern to us here, which is capable of the "minimal displacement," as Ernst Bloch terms it, drawing on a Hasidic tale of circumstances, facts, or parameters that allow "being" to be. [257]

While Kafka thematizes the negative process of submission in preemptive obedience with regard to validity without meaning vis-à-vis bureaucratic and ideological institutions of the state, Kierkegaard examines the *effect* of this kind of obedience. As Kierkegaard shows, preemptive obedience is evoked in the face of a truth that has not (yet) opened itself propositionally to veridical justification. Such a truth may, as Lacan sees it, be pronounced by a hysteric master. To exemplify his claim, Kierkegaard provides a philosophical analysis of religiously inspired disciples. They are the ones who carry the appellation of the truth-apt message of their extraordinary master into the future, precisely because the truth that the message contains cannot (yet) be caught up with in a veridical manner. The master then is to be understood as the carrier of excessive subjectivity.

Kierkegaard develops the paradoxical moments of authority via excessive subjectivity in his text "On the Difference Between a Genius and an Apostle," from 1847.[258] He does so based on his knowledge of the spellbinding power of appellations through their inferential indeterminacy and the still-lacking certainty of the call's objective content. In the following, I will draw on Kierkegaard's text and on Žižek's comments on this same text in his article "Why Is Every Act a Repetition?"[259] Both authors assist us in understanding to what extent discipleship in individual cases of excessive subjectivity can also rest on a "call" or a "calling." This excessive subjectivity then expresses itself in the individual leaping into the not yet quite discernible (and propositionally still limitable) horizon of meaning of the master "suffering" from excessive subjectivity himself, *precisely because* the message of the master's revelation (be it in art, religion, humanities, or sciences) cannot yet be propositionally and veridically intertwined with the standards of knowledge as true justified belief. This moment of leaping separates the figure of the *disciple* from that of the *student*. Once the disciple has leaped into his master's and apostle's horizon of meaning, as in the Kierkegaardian leap into faith, he gains access to the authority of his leader, master, philosophy professor, and so on. Expanding on this aspect for our analysis of excessive subjectivity will allow us to unearth its political power in our discussion of certain paradoxes of authority. We can uncover how excessive subjectivity can give rise to completely new paradigms of the political on the collective level *not despite, but precisely because of*, cognitive resistances and incommensurabilities.

We moved from Kant's split subject of the moral act-deed to Hegel's discussion of the inner noncoincidence of the world of morals through struggles of the recognition of a not yet representable normativity. With Lacan, we analyzed the psychosomatic inner structure of the human mind split into layers of both consciousness and the unconscious. We realized how the subject, from his own state of being split, can behave toward the never stable external world (his life-world) and how he can bring about a collapse of the old order with partially solipsistically meaningful signifiers. Kierkegaard's insight into the nonassimilable "authority of the apostle" allows us to now go a step further and explain why an authority can articulate itself *precisely* as authoritative within the lack of its meaning.

ON THE PARADOX OF EXCESSIVE AUTHORITY

In his text mentioned earlier, Kierkegaard develops a definition of the apostle in contradistinction to what he calls the genius and writes: "He [the Apostle] is related paradoxically by having a specific quality [of authority] which no immanence can resolve in the equality of eternity; for it [his authority] is essentially paradoxical and after thought (not before, anterior to thought), contrary to thought."[260] Kierkegaard compares the "quality" of the apostle's speech with that of a genius who can induce enthusiasm in the masses. In contrast to the genius, the apostle speaks with an authority that does not dissolve into immanence, for that which the apostle proclaims cannot be absorbed in the act of grasping it. The authority of his speech rests on the performativity of his speech acts "contrary to thought." Kierkegaard: The "Genius may . . . have something new to bring forth, but what it brings forth disappears again as it becomes assimilated by the human race; . . . the Apostle has, paradoxically, something new to bring, the newness of which, precisely because it is essentially paradoxical, and not an anticipation in relation to the development of the race, always remains."

The reference to propositions that seemingly exclude the grounds of their truth-values and apparently only "show" that which they cannot express also appears in Kierkegaard's *Concluding Unscientific Postscript.* In this text, the author repeatedly discusses the added value of the "difficulties" of understanding "that simply cannot [be] understood" as compared to those that are "so very easy to understand; for if it is so very easy, then perhaps there just is no difficulty, since what marks the difficulty is exactly it being difficult to understand."[261] His program: "When the communication, in the context of such a state of affairs, is not about making the difficulty even easier, it is a taking away."[262]

James Conant compares this strategy to Wittgenstein's *Tractatus* and its famous phrase of that which cannot be said but "*shows*" itself by pointing to the limits of that which can be said.[263] Conant does not believe in this strategy.[264] He formulates the thesis that Wittgenstein copies, in particular the gesture of authorship from Kierkegaard. Or more precisely: the enactment of one's own genius with an overdetermined text that precisely in its "elusiveness" (Conant) and incommensurability provokes discipleship. Similarly, Stanley Cavell claims that both Kierkegaard and Wittgenstein aim at unmasking the basic foundations of their reader's knowledge. In doing so, both claim the motif of silence as a rhetorical device, as if in this very silence an enigmatic, nonpropositional ground for the true conveyance of meaning (that must be subjectivized in the end) is to be found.[265]

It is this last aspect that Žižek analyzes as an explicit strategy of authority, and he deals in detail with the Kierkegaardian distinction between genius and apostle in his article "Why Is Every Act a Repetition?" He proceeds from the question of how a truth that appears with a universal claim yet is seemingly completely devoted to the inwardness of the subject can have any foundation at all, at least seemingly so. He claims in this context that speaking of a truth-claim can acquire meaning beyond the limits of religion whenever the arduous discovery of new horizons of thought is at stake. In order to make this thesis comprehensible, which is at least indirectly reminiscent of Kuhn and Friedman, Žižek claims, making an example of reference to Marx, Freud, and Lacan, that—at the outset of their investigative development of concepts—these authors developed an authority less because of the transmission of an abstract content in whose center lay a positivistic, third-party scientifically verifiable truth, but rather because the works of these authors—controversial to the present day—are teachings which can only be understood if one recognizes them as not separable from the locus of enunciation, the locus of an individual "too-muchness" (Santner). And in a similar sense, this aspect also links Kierkegaard and Wittgenstein.

If the genius in Kierkegaard (in a clearly reductionist interpretation, using Plato as an example) represents the pronouncement of a truth in its universal, abstract meaning, detachable from its "master," then the apostle possesses an authority to proclaim something as true through the performative act of his utterance, which is tied to his name. In addition to Paul the Apostle, to whom Kierkegaard refers, another name to mention in this context would again be Martin Luther.

An objection may be raised here that while Plato's dialogues do try to unearth a truth in its universal sense as the condition of propositions, according to his philosophy of universal forms, it is quite controversial how and whether he succeeded in this. Kierkegaard, who certainly knew of this objection, as it is presented by Plato himself, especially in his *Parmenides*, nevertheless sees a difference in the truth-claim of the apostle: the target-object of this claim does not have to be unearthed in a dialectical-philosophical dialogue, as does a forgotten truth. Rather, it posits itself as truth solely in that it is dependent on a "call" (= calling) and is only *then*, that is, after the call has been successful, dependent on a rationale. Paul is, for Kierkegaard, not a genius who proclaims timeless truths. Paul rather represents "this 'scandal' of the spot of contingent individuality which smears over the neutral field of knowledge."[266] Christ does not demand loyalty to his message as a teaching of theoretically generalizable propositions (as one might attribute to Socrates in the Platonic dialogues); rather, he demands loyalty to his *persona*, which from the perspective of Greek philosophy is perfectly human, and more so, scandalously "all too human." For Kierkegaard, this bond between message and messenger, and not to a general teaching, is the decisive factor. In regard to the Christian universalism proclaimed by Paul, Žižek writes: "The paradox of Christianity consists in this bond linking the eternal truth to an historical event."[267] "Eternal truth itself clings to this contingent material externality—the moment we lose this "little piece of the real" (the historical fact of Incarnation), the moment we cut our link with this material fragment (reinterpreting it as a parable of man's affinity with God, for example), the entire edifice of Christian knowledge crumbles."[268] We are looking here again at the relationship between the particular and the universal, as phrased in Hegel's dictum of the "substance," a "substance" that is "subject," as explored in the chapter on Hegel.

This may very well be the case in the context of religious explanatory worldviews. From Kant through Wittgenstein though, the view persists that religious belief does not need to satisfy epistemological claims. Yet that this view is meant to likewise apply to philosophy is confusing, since the Enlightenment had as its philosophical goal to separate itself from any type of authority that could not be challenged by reason—be it from the state, religion, or the world of academia. When Žižek claims that Marx, Freud, and Lacan are to be understood as "apostles" and not as geniuses, however, he does so because the truths they represent in their works are crucially tied to the locus from which they are being proclaimed. Asking for a positivistic verification of a truth-content disregards the following circumstance: Those students, scholars, and recipients who are former or current followers of Marx, Freud, and Lacan, for example, do so because they proceed from a trust in an authority that they, with regard to that which the authority proclaims *by imbuing itself with authority*, are precisely not (or not yet) able to grasp. They have recognized, or rather suspect, that their teacher's "apostolic message," to pick up again on Kierkegaard's opposition of genius and apostle, might potentially only link up with that historical event that these individual (paranoid?) scholars, who are slowly moving forward with numerous conceptual discrepancies, truly embody in all their contradictions. Numerous theses—Marx's analysis of commodity form and of commodity fetishism, Heidegger's talk of "Being" (*Seyn*) or the "oblivion of being" or his later philosophy of the "event," Derrida's theorem of "diffé*r*ance," Lacan's myth of the mirror stage and his theory of the act—do not necessarily articulate truths that can be linked to clearly defined truth-values in propositions in a universal-analytical sense. Often, they resist a positivistic verification oriented to the hard sciences. For example, one cannot exclusively place the unconscious in observational coordinates of behaviorism via third-party descriptions. It is true that one can tie the discovery of psychoanalysis back to a theory of linguistic practices oriented to Donald

Davidson, as Marcia Cavell has done with such impressive precision, and as such retrace psychoanalysis to the basic insights of common-sense psychology;[269] yet by doing so we lose some of Freud's most important insights, such as that of a prepropositional unconscious. David Snelling criticized Cavell's approach, correctly I think, for a similar reason. Sebastian Gardner presented an alternative reading of Freud, oriented, among others, to Melanie Klein.[270] It is in particular philosophical analyses by the authors mentioned—Marx, Freud, Heidegger, Lacan, Derrida (one could add Hegel, Schelling, Fichte, Nietzsche, and many others)—that compelled numerous representatives of analytic-philosophical traditions of the twentieth century to appear on the scene. Many of them proclaimed—at least for a while—to no longer accept the inquiry of these authors, or their respective answers, as scientific at all. Apparently, their investigations result in meaningless sentences under the paradigm of the hard sciences, that is, under the claims of a theory of truth oriented either by logic, mathematics, and the empirical sciences. In a similar vein, political-philosophical teachings such as those of Mao Zedong or Vladimir I. Lenin appear to have been refuted, because the current, just as positivistic evaluative paradigm of Western, democratic, capitalist societies generally rests on the exclusion of these certainties as ideological, certainties that were once considered absolutely convincing and worth dying for.

In this context, Žižek is interested in the paradox of this strange authority of seemingly antiscientific scientists, an authority that, as we have already discovered in Lacan, possibly finds its only and central support "in its own act of enunciation." For Žižek this means, with slightly exaggerated emphasis: "Authority proper is at its most radical level always *powerless*, it is a certain 'call' which 'cannot effectively force us into anything,' and yet, by a kind of inner compulsion, we feel obliged to follow it unconditionally."[271] This does not put into question that there may very well be grounds for theoretical truth-claims made by the authors mentioned. Yet to exclusively remain in the paradigm of the natural sciences in order to look at the truth conditions and justifications of these claims overlooks the "leap" from which the explanatory perspective of epistemology may only just open as one that concerns "me" and my desire according to its rational conclusions. (Do we not find these individual preferences even in the analytic tradition of philosophy? Can we be, for example, absolutely convinced by David Chalmers's "Zombie-argument," his talk of the "hard problem of consciousness," or Daniel Dennett's reference to humans as "moist robots"? Or is it not appropriate to say that one may be convinced through the leap of faith in these two outstanding philosophers insofar as they truly *are* great philosophers?)

Žižek is interested in the question: Upon which foundation is this authority of excessive subjectivity, independent from the charisma of a person, then built? Kierkegaard proves helpful to Žižek in explicating the paradox of authority here, which at its core is connected to Lacan's philosophy. For in Kierkegaard, there is supposedly an apparent gap in his interpretation of Christ. Žižek considers this gap constitutive for an understanding of the authority of excessive subjectivity, because it generates (similar to a collateral effect) a further excess in the disciples, or, more generally, in the discipleship. This gap becomes evident as follows: if Kierkegaard claims that Christ's authority is—from the perspective of the apostle—not grounded in the content of his teaching, yet as the "Son of God" he nevertheless mediates the access to God's truth, then the question needs to be asked: "in what *does* it [the authority] reside?"[272] Christ is reducible neither to his winning personality nor to a particular message, as much as the latter may have resounded in addressing social justice issues. What then does make him into an authority for Kierkegaard, if ultimately it is neither Christ's exceptional personality nor his exceptional message? "The only possible answer is: [the authority of the Apostle and the authority of Christ are founded] in the empty space of intersection between the two sets, that of his personal features and that of his teaching, in the unfathomable X which is 'in Christ more than Himself'—in this intersection which corresponds exactly to what Lacan called *objet petit a*." Žižek presents the following drawing (figure 4.3).

It is in the intersection of the two ellipses that Žižek situates this indefinable, "unfathomable X which is 'in Christ more than Himself.'" That which is termed *a* in the intersection is for Žižek a repression/

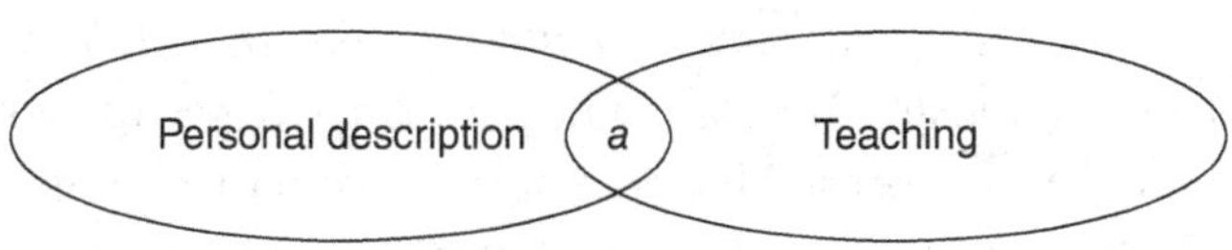

FIGURE 4.3. The paradox of authority.

displacement. In following certain truth-claims, that which is displaced in the gap between personality and teaching is akin to the unstated confession that that which one considers to be true, *one considers as true only from the locus from which it has already been articulated*. What is being displaced is consequently purely performative. Or to put it differently: one does not follow due to a cognitive filtering of the impressive teaching of authority, but one follows authority *après coup*, after the leap into the horizon of meaning that it has torn open performatively. For Žižek it is this gesture that "constitutes the subject." It does so because reality is being "subjectivized." This takes place "when the subject posits as his free choice what is forced upon him."[273] This is a fitting definition of what constitutes discipleship. To locate here the structure of blind obedience *exclusively* underestimates that even on the level of the most elementary daily life practices, we could not develop any subjectivity without this discipleship of testimonial knowledge. It is precisely the interlocking of life practices and normativity that was, even for Hegel, a crucial component of morals. The paradox of authority that Kierkegaard and Žižek analyze only brings this to the point with regard to political and scientific revolts where first the practice or the leap into the practice (of a theory or a political teaching) will have articulated itself as the condition of justified belief. The authority of an apostle—no matter the area of her expertise (religion, philosophy, and the natural sciences to some extent)—in this way sets the cognitions deriving from this authority before they can be weighed as a precondition in order to advance on the way to its truth-value in the performative celebration of itself.

Let me also mention that in his exegesis of Kierkegaard, Žižek supports the thesis that the possibility exists for the subject to reach a point that can be called nothing other than mystical, from which she can experience and posit once again the entry into the Symbolic. This thought is also central for Žižek in light of Kierkegaard's analysis of discipleship. The leap into the authority of the master can be interpreted in such a way that the subject prepares to leap into the nothingness of her own negative self-relation. In that case, then, it is a leap into *my belief in myself with regard to my belief in my master*. The leap in its performative gesture also affects the distancing from the established external normative arenas of one's social surroundings. The political act enables the subject to enter into a new horizon of meaning that can only be opened up through the act of overcoming oneself. As we have seen, this theorem is at least partially already present in Lacan's teaching of "traversing the fantasy," which should not be underestimated in philosophical-political terms.

For Lacan, the political-ethical act (for example, of Antigone) constitutes a Kierkegaardian leap of faith across the established doxa. Lacan's ethics of the act should be interpreted not only as simply a realization of the potentiality that had always already been available, but as a quasi-transcendental collapse of the distinction between reality and potentiality. (This is what Gilles Deleuze calls "virtuality.")[274] It is the psyche that, akin to the form of a Fichtean "fact/act" (*Tathandlung*), posits the modality of "its own world" as medium of a new ego-function of her future to come. In several of his works, and in particular in his recourse to Jeremy Bentham's *Theory of Fiction*, Lacan points out how far the subject's access to the certainty of his intersubjectively mediated life-world is permanently maintained through virtualities nonthematically mediated by the subject itself. It is precisely these virtualities, fictions, and noble lies that guarantee the symbolic order and as such regulate many of the certainties of our daily life. They are not media of corruption but rather, as Hegel reveals in his speech on man's second nature, the medium of our customs, and therefore also the realm of the possibility of our freedom. Precisely because virtual moments necessarily intermix with our reality, we are able to suspend "reality" from time to time, for example, by defining our self-understanding anew, which then impacts the coordinates of our world.

Ludwig Wittgenstein also investigates, as mentioned earlier, this phenomenon in a language-philosophical analysis that conforms very closely to Lacan's considerations. In his *Remarks on the Foundations of Mathematics* he writes: "The Limit of the Empirical—is *concept-formation*."[275] Similarly, in the *Tractatus* we read on the limits of the empirical: "The subject does not belong to the world, but it is a limit of the world."[276]

In his concept of the Real, Lacan points out that, metaphorically speaking, there is always an unfathomable surplus, an almost utopian "void" potentially hidden in reality that the subject can generally *not* perceive in the established doxa that surrounds it. Why is that? Because reducing cognitive stress is an important condition for the psyche to have a grip on its life-world, and perceiving too many "voids" to fill up normatively, for example, can effectively be burdensome and cause mental illness.

Nevertheless, Lacan's theory of the act stands metaphorically for the politically excessive gesture of breaking through reality for the benefit of this still-unfathomable and utopian place. He discovers the strength to do so, among others, in Antigone, Paul, Luther, and Lenin. While the "I" cannot flee godlike into an external perspective in the act, in the event he can dare to define anew the frame of his subjectivation, or, as Wittgenstein says, "the riverbed of his thought."[277] Lacan's ethics of the Real is in that sense an ethics of the Extreme, an ethics of Transgression.

Does the political arena not require from time to time such seemingly solipsistic positings, as the examples from Rosa Parks to Lenin illustrate, to prepare the way for new paradigms? Lacan, like Hegel, seems to suggest this when he interprets the ethics of psychoanalysis on an individual-psychological level and nevertheless knows of the creative power of (seemingly) psychotic positings of individuals for political purposes. Repeatedly, Paul is a prime example for Lacan of a subject that posits a new frame of reference upon the world and changes the coordinates of modern subjectivity in a radical new way.[278]

Lacan's ethics, as antithetical as it may sound, initially revolves around the subject's particular desire and "his truth," which cannot always be propositionally captured as the truth of "the subject's unconscious." In *Seminar VII*, he writes this about Antigone: "Antigone appears as αὐτόνομος, as a pure and simple relationship of the human being to that of which he miraculously happens to be the bearer, namely, the signifying cut that confers on him the indomitable power of being what he is in the face of everything that may oppose him" (S.VII 282).[279] Lacan's trangressive subjectivity to the law makes clear the deed of interpreting the act as guaranteed by the subject and the impossibility of a neutral judgment *before* the act-deed changes a relevant political situation. The subject here moves within the power of S1—the totality of language. The subject might then also be "run over" by its own excess. The subject may recognize, as Daniel Dennett shows with the example of Abraham Lincoln,[280] that only subsequent to a speech act does she (the subject) take on the propositional intention articulated in the speech act. Only the act-deed, and to some extent its consequences, lay bare the aporia of the moral-legal conflict and potentially force the "spirit of the people," that is, the established morals, into a counter reaction. This means that there is a retroactiveness which highlights that the subject does not permanently have to be "with it" in order to grasp herself. The inability of the subject to dissolve perfectly in her own subjectivization is proof for Lacan that the individual can also be re-marked again by a future universality on the level of her singularity. Such an ethics clearly has very little to do with the normative foundation of maxims within a polis's reasons. An "ethics of the Real" concerns the particular self and her desire as a tragically transgressive encounter with her own in the form of a foreign body. It is the experience that there is something more than myself within me.

A problem not to be overlooked with regard to the intensity of the transgression in Lacan is without a doubt the permanent potentiality or actuality of the "pathological," as one could have also ascribed to Rosa Parks. To accuse individuals like her of being pathologically oversensitive to Realpolitik or of pathologically "seeing problems where there are none" is almost unavoidable. We again encounter these accusations in the case of contemporary "traitors" to national interests such as Julian Assange, Bradley (Chelsea) Manning, and Edward Snowden. For Lacan, however, the attitude of the hysteric is ethical where he questions the big Other from the perspective of its deficits. One could say: for Lacan, the ethical-transgressive hysterical subject finds herself in a paradoxical relationship to society that is always simultaneously exclusive and inclusive.

"JE DIS TOUJOURS LA VÉRITÉ!"

Let us return once more to Kierkegaard and the subject matter of validity without meaning present in an authority that is appealing and simultaneously lacks the propositional meaning of its appeal. The dominance of the apostle upon his congregation, of which Kierkegaard speaks, contains the moment of a paradoxical authority that Žižek combines with Lacan's ethics of the act. The message of Paul the Apostle is to a significant extent able to be proclaimed due to his *persona* and not to his teaching, which does not mean that the *persona* or its charism *is* the teaching. Based on Lacan's interpretation of Luther, this notion also applies to the cofounder of the Reformation. Luther, as a poet and a prophet, succeeded in establishing the fear of God as a unique signifier with tremendous power of seizing subjectivity. However, this was only successful because Luther portrayed himself both as the guarantor and as the victim of the fear of God that he proclaimed. Lacan: "The fear of God isn't a signifier that is found everywhere. *Someone had to invent it and propose to men*, as the remedy for a world made up of manifold terrors, that they fear a being who is, after all, only able to exercise his cruelty through the evils that are there, multifariously present in human life" (S.III 266–67).[281] This authority of a signifier proclaimed by the person stands "in a radical sense 'beyond criticism'" since it constitutes "the very horizon of veracity."[282] Based on this insight into the power of appellation of individuals who can draw entire groups of people into their sway, Žižek calls Marx, Freud, and Lacan not geniuses but rather "apostles" in the Kierkegaardian sense. As founding fathers of different fields of investigation, they do not (yet) have to grapple with truth-criteria with which their historical-critical exegetes are being measured. This applies, as mentioned, to Freud's concept of the unconscious but also to Heidegger's notion of the Occident's "oblivion of being" (*Seinsvergessenheit*) or Derrida's theory of "différance." Žižek writes: "If there is something to be refuted in their texts [the texts of Marx and Freud], these are simply statements which precede the 'epistemological break,' i.e., which do not belong under the field opened up by the founder's discovery."[283]

Consequently, as founders of new horizons of knowledge, apostles have the authority of radical creativity. Such an occasionally delusional-seeming creativity, to which one can ascribe political dimensions, becomes evident in Lacan's late seminars and his eccentric appearances on French Public Television. Lacan's lectures in the 1970s and his appearances in front of rolling cameras resemble a theatrical-magical speech that considers itself almost completely unhindered by any constraints of a positivistic-scientific discourse. "Je dis toujours la vérité"[284] ("I always speak the truth"), said Lacan. For this same reason, Lacan rejects considering himself a researcher and appropriates Picasso's phrase "I do not seek, I find" for his own work (S.XI 7). This does not preclude that this "speaking-the-truth," this "finding-which-is-a-positing," following to some extent the ductus of holy texts, is also a form of consciously practiced glossolalia. This type of speaking has initial validity without positivistic justification/meaning, one could say. Nevertheless, secondary literature proves adept at tying the speaking-in-tongue-like statements of the supposed "maître absolu" back to criteria of scholarly and scientific research.

Marx's oft-discussed concept of the fetish character of commodities is precisely also a concept about the argument of what exactly the concept is supposed to mean and if it, as Marx suggests, can be truly deduced from an analysis of industrial production. Similarly, the unconscious in Freud is neither present nor absent. It occurs or it "shows" itself in the dialogue between analysand and analyst, just as the search for the God whom nobody has ever seen warrants itself through what Alvin Plantinga calls "properly basic belief."[285] When Žižek, with regard to Lacan's so-called retour à Freud, says that only a supposedly radical return to the "authentic Freud" can paradoxically bring to light layers of the work that have been overlooked so far, he refers to the true productivity of transference. The latter secretly hides the scandal not only to have to understand one's teacher but also—at least to a certain extent—to have to "love" him. Žižek's remarks on Kierkegaard's distinction between genius and apostle are valuable if one takes them as attempts to approach and contrast two very different concepts of authority. One is, in short form, tied to the supposedly "pure teaching." The other is tied to a nonassimilable core of "human, all too human" monstrosity, or, referring to Lacan, it is tied to the terrible "wicked wit" that he, as Althusser describes it, showed toward his students who lovingly revered him. "You need to have heard him speaking . . . to understand the splendidly wicked wit with which, having experienced surrealism, he realizes himself as an individual. . . . If you go to his seminar you'll see all sorts of people prostrating themselves before a discourse that to them is quite unintelligible. These are the methods of intellectual terrorism."[286] It may very well be this nonassimilable lovable wicked wit that from time to time holds us under the spell of someone's discourse and lets us understand something that we might not have understood without this "terror." This is what Žižek may be referring to with his enduringly cryptic drawing of the structural form of paradoxical authority made up of the two circles with *objet petit a* in the intersection. The two areas of personality and teaching overlap and form an unassimilable core around which the authority of the "apostle" constructs itself. The area "a" is to refer to the fact that the teaching can never become completely self-explanatory.

Lacan repeatedly emphasizes the necessity of love that his followers may give to him, almost as if he wanted to claim the words "Do you love me?" with which Jesus addresses Peter three times in the gospel of John

(John 21:15–17) for himself with regard to his followers or disciples. Analogous to the transference relation between analysand and analyst, he emphasizes the pathological aspect of love for the success of the disclosure and the development of his teaching, which he also labels as the "discourse of truth" and which he wanted to have distributed by cartel-like structures of groups of followers.

These latter considerations may make clear what could well be a fundamental experience for students of philosophy in their first semester. It is the experience of studying with faculty who are not infrequently mutual enemies, who can precisely not appreciate one another's expertise because the ideal of an abstract wisdom that could pacify their philosophical approaches as in a *tertium datur* does not exist. For this reason, these professors are often in need of their students' love.[287] Žižek points to the productivity stemming from this transferential relationship of the concept of love, which to an extent aims to occupy the parallactic gap between personality and its message, and comes to discover something new precisely because of that. "Lacan was not a Socratic master obliterating himself in front of the attained knowledge, his theory sustains itself only through the transferential relationship to its founder."[288] Viewed this way, Lacan's supposedly orthodox return to the "apostle" Freud is nothing other than the true birth of Lacan's teaching, just as the truly Christian, excessive subjectivity demanding succession, according to Kierkegaard, does not primarily lie in the keeping of social modes of behavior proclaimed by Jesus, but rather is rooted in the existential realization of the gospel of Christ for which the saints vouch. The *imitatio Christi*, practiced by the saints, does not copy: it is not *imitatio* as a simple repetition, but rather repeatedly creates new exceptions, following the absurdly "human, all too human" truth or illusion. Just as the truth of a trauma is not simply "de-covered" like a treasure in the psychoanalytic conversation, Lacan does not simply discover the true Freud in his "retour." Rather, in the psychoanalytic process, the trauma is painstakingly (re)born and acted out between analysand and psychoanalyst. It comes from the future and so also from the direction of the past. It "exists" retroactively as that which has burdened the subject in a prospective look back. It is precisely this temporal alteration that concerns the Hegelian Spirit as well as Walter Benjamin's historical-theological messianism. The hyperbolic gestures in the truth-claim of the "apostles" discussed here—Paul, Kierkegaard,

Lacan, and Žižek himself—embody the performativity of a prophetic language that in its hyperbolic gesture can at once be destructive and the expression of a transformative power. The apostle's truth-claim enjoins the listener to react to this performativity, that is, to the performativity of utterances. This makes it imperative that the apostle can always only speak in his own name. In his excessive subjectivity, he must (at least initially) demonstrate this selfhood as a true proof of his speaking. At the same time, he demands of his listeners or disciples that they initially try to understand these universal truths, where they escape conceptual clarification, from their originary place.

NOTES

INTRODUCTION

1. In his article "Kein Ende der Geschichte? Geschichtsphilosophie nach Kant," Axel Honneth defines the narrative-historical organizational principle in Kant's philosophy of history: Honneth, *Nach Kant: Erbe und Kritik*, ed. Ian Kaplow (Münster: LIT, 2005), 118–33, here 127.
2. See also Kant, CS, 297–98. On Kant's rejection of revolutions as a part of the political realm, a subject that has received wide commentary, see Peter Nicholson, "Kant on the Duty Never to Resist the Sovereign," *Ethics* 86, no. 3 (1976): 214–30; Christine M. Korsgaard, "Taking the Law Into Our Own Hands: Kant on the Right to Revolution," in *Reclaiming the History of Ethics: Essays for John Rawls*, ed. Andrews Reath, Barbara Herman, and Christine M. Korsgaard (Cambridge: Cambridge University Press, 1997), 297–328; Kenneth Westphal, "Kant on the State, Law, and Obedience to Authority in the Alleged Anti-Revolutionary Writings," *Journal of Philosophical Research* 17 (1992): 383–425.
3. Cited in Oswald Bayer, *Vernunft ist Sprache: Hamanns Metakritik Kants* (Stuttgart-Bad Cannstatt: Frommann-Holzboog, 2002), 434–35.
4. For two prominent examples of this thinking in the twentieth century, see Ernst Tugendhat, *Vorlesungen über Ethik* (Frankfurt: Suhrkamp, 1993), 37–40; and Bernard Williams, *Moral Luck* (Cambridge: Cambridge University Press, 1982), 1–19.
5. Anscombe considers actions impossible to describe when viewed through the lens of decontextualized norms, since this specifically recasts them as independent of description. Kant's "rigoristic convictions on the subject of lying," for instance, make lying an intrinsically unjustified action, but only because that judgment is self-evident once it is freed from any concrete context and subjected to a principle-oriented view. Elizabeth Anscombe, "Modern Moral Philosophy," in *Virtue Ethics*, ed. Roger Crisp and Michael Slote (Oxford: Oxford University Press, 1997), 26–45, here 27.

6. Ido Geiger places this question at the center of his book *The Founding Act of Modern Ethical Life: Hegel's Critique of Kant's Moral and Political Philosophy* (Stanford: Stanford University Press, 2007).
7. See the analysis of Hegel's reception of Kant in ibid., 63–70, which I have partially adopted here. However, Geiger fails to consider Hegel's intentional unfolding of the prefuture structure of the excessive deed.
8. Here my argument is allied with studies by Alenka Zupančič, Henrik Joker Bjerre, Ido Geiger, and Slavoj Žižek. Over the past years, these authors have all produced outstanding interpretations of Kant's and Hegel's works in relation to aporias of ethical action. See Alenka Zupančič, *Ethics of the Real: Kant and Lacan* (London: Verso, 2000); Henrik Joker Bjerre, *Kantian Deeds* (London: Continuum, 2010); Geiger, *The Founding Act of Modern Ethical Life*; Slavoj Žižek, *Less Than Nothing: Hegel and the Shadow of Dialectical Materialism* (London: Verso, 2012).
9. There is a strain in the reception of Hegel's works that runs from Alexandre Kojève's famous lectures of the 1940s through Lacan (who attended those lectures) and his epistemology of psychoanalytic theory to the present. Its discussions often deal with the expansion of traditional ethical concepts. See Finkelde, "Gegen die politische Philosophie? Theorien politischer Eskalation im 20. Jahrhundert und der Gegenwart von Martin Heidegger bis Alain Badiou," *Philosophische Rundschau* 57, no. 4 (2010): 322–41.
10. See Bernard Williams, *Ethics and the Limits of Philosophy* (Cambridge: Harvard University Press, 1985), esp. chap. 10.
11. Tugendhat, *Vorlesungen über Ethik*, 37–39.
12. Otfried Höffe, "Universalistische Ethik und Urteilskraft: ein aristotelischer Blick auf Kant," *Zeitschrift für Philosophische Forschung* 44, no. 4 (1990): 537–63; Höffe, "Ausblick: Aristoteles oder Kant—wider eine plane Alternative," in *Aristoteles: Die Nikomachische Ethik*, ed. Otfried Höffe (Berlin: Akademie, 1995), 277–304; Christine M. Korsgaard, "Aristotle and Kant on the Source of Value," *Ethics* 96, no. 3 (1986): 486–505; Korsgaard, "From Duty and for the Sake of the Noble: Kant and Aristotle on Morally Good Action," in *The Constitution of Agency* (Oxford: Oxford University Press, 2008), 174–206; Sean Drysdale Walsh, "Kant's Theory of Right as Aristotelian Phronesis," *International Philosophical Quarterly* 52, no. 2 (2012): 227–46; Andrea Esser, *Eine Ethik für Endliche: Kants Tugendlehre in der Gegenwart* (Stuttgart-Bad Cannstatt: Frommann-Holzboog, 2004).
13. Zupančič, *Ethics of the Real*, 53.
14. See Christine M. Korsgaard, *Self-Constitution: Agency, Identity, and Integrity* (Oxford: Oxford University Press, 2009).
15. In some cases they emerge first in the shape of errors and delusions. For Hegel in the *Phenomenology*, errors always manifest themselves against an established epistemic interest due to the overcomplexity of a situation. The personalities named earlier can only be compared indirectly. Antigone's tragedy presupposes the accomplishments of the Greek polis; Socrates is the historical consummation of sophism; and Napoleon's presence at Jena is unthinkable without the motto of the French Revolution, "liberté,

égalité, fraternité." What unites these personalities is the negativity they unleashed in the form of crises and wars, and that their struggles each resulted in the emergence of what Hegel calls a universal "principle."

16. Since we, the people and principal actors in Hegel's substance (which is, as he says, subject), can never epistemologically absorb the world in its universal totality, our relationship to the outer world shows itself for Hegel as an enduring battle between, on the one hand, particular cognitions and, on the other, universal maxims and ontologies requiring constant reassessment. According to Hegel, this battle—a battle against the intentions of reason (which are constantly reestablishing themselves, and always have their own interests)—produces counterintuitive reconciliations (counterintuitive as they go against the intentions of reason) in the form of higher stages of reflection. This process is what Hegel calls the "coming-to-itself" of the concept. And he describes it, in a famous phrase, as the "cunning of reason," which doesn't stop short of lies, unethical actions, and theoretical contradictions in order to asymptotically approach (along the way of the "slaughter bench that is history") a forever-receding "truth" of increasing self-penetration.

17. In this book I adopt Christoph Menke's thesis of the "emergence of Law from tragedy" and of the "over-temporality" (*Überzeitlichkeit*) of the "tragedy in ethical life" (*Tragödie im Sittlichen*). Christoph Menke, *Tragödie im Sittlichen: Gerechtigkeit und Freiheit nach Hegel* (Frankfurt: Suhrkamp, 1996). According to Menke, the "tragedy in ethical life" is precisely *not* to be understood as a conflict handed down through history from antiquity. It should be acknowledged rather as the "tragic experience of an immanent violence of the law" (13), an experience still present in the world of the bourgeois individual of the twenty-first century. Antigone and Socrates both stage this primal scene of modernity through a display of reflexivity that, as Menke emphasizes, observes itself. This reveals the antagonistic tension between "self-determination," autonomy, and the public's ideal of justice, and, contrary to Hegel's theses on the philosophy of right and the state, the tension is *not* sublated. The tragic conflict is not only one of the "immanent violence of the law"; it is also a conflict of the subtly upheld self-deceptions of symbolic orders. The battle between my authenticity-oriented form of life and the public's right to my conformity is a battle that defines the present. Thus, gazing into the mirror of the past, Hegel gives the present an experience that articulates a nonsimultaneous simultaneity and a philosophy of difference avant la lettre, in spite of his ostensible efforts at reconciliation in the philosophy of right and history. Unlike Menke, however, I do not conceptualize the tragic conflict as a dichotomy between the individual's need for autonomy and authentic self-realization, on the one hand, and the demands of the public or universal, on the other. Rather, for me the tragic conflict, while originating in the individual, in fact articulates the struggle for the good at the level of the collective. In other words, Menke seems to believe (like Foucault) that the "tragedy in ethical life" takes place between individual autonomy, creativity, and authenticity, on the one hand, and public norms, formalities, and universalities, on the other. But there is something that Menke's otherwise very penetrating analysis cannot, with its focus on the internal split of the modern citizen,

sufficiently account for: Why, if this Foucauldian narrative is the whole story, does Hegel consider authenticity not a private, self-contained force of individuality, but a blessing for the realm of universality? It is precisely here that Hegel confronts practical philosophy with an all but unbearable challenge, in light of which we can see why Ernst Tugendhat, in his famous (and perhaps accurate) anti-Hegelian polemic, accuses Hegel of hollowing out practical philosophy, of condemning it to an uncritical relativism of values wherein the "slaughter-bench of history" (Hegel) must be accepted unconditionally. We bring this challenge into better focus if, expanding on Menke's interpretation, we affirm that the "tragedy in ethical life" is tragic not merely because of the ongoing tension between the individual and the public even in the age of communitarian and discourse-theoretical ethical models, but because the certainty (*Gewissheit*) of the individual is *necessary* in order to free the public from its false consciousness, since the individual has access to insights or "aspect perceptions" (Wittgenstein) that remain beyond the public's reach. Particularity does not want mere particular happiness, a mere niche of autocreative self-realization; it wants to see its certainty and conscience established as normative universals. Thus the normativity of excessive subjectivity does not fight for its right to particularity alone, but fights instead to overwrite the universal from its own premises, its own solipsistic individual nucleus. But since "premises" make up the framework of the "certainty"—to use Wittgenstein's terms—of the political doxa, such excessive subjects are structurally *personae non gratae*. Like the authors of the Sturm und Drang period and romanticism (for example, Heinrich von Kleist), Hegel employs the motif of the self-sacrificing individual at battle with an overwhelmingly blinded world. "They [the individuals] are conscious of being these separate independent beings through the sacrifice of their particularity, and by having this universal Substance as their soul and essence" (PhS §350). For Hegel, as for Spinoza and Aristotle, reason is a "fluid universal *Substance*" (§350) and as such "unchangeable simple thinghood" (§350) for the individual consciousness. It "lives" in individuals as "completely independent beings," however, "just as light bursts asunder into stars as countless self-luminous points" (§350). As these "points" or Aristotelian individual substances, the individuals are "in their absolute being-for-self . . . *explicitly for themselves*" (§350).

18. According to Rolf-Peter Horstmann, the thrust of Hegel's writings can be found in the goal of reactualizing the Platonic-Aristotelian ethical state, but with the inclusion of subjectivity. See Rolf-Peter Horstmann, "Hegels Theorie der bürgerlichen Gesellschaft," in *Georg Wilhelm Friedrich Hegel: Grundlinien der Philosophie des Rechts*, ed. Ludwig Siep (Berlin: Akademie, 2005), 194–216, here 194–95. This means that what Hegel integrates into his philosophy of right is the phenomenon by which particularity is reunited with itself. In the *Phenomenology* and in his philosophy of history, Hegel repeatedly suggests that the absence of escalation cannot be conceived of transcendentally, as the political realm per se is not to be understood hegemonically but under consideration of inferentialistic, transcendentally necessary forces of blindness. This becomes clear in the theory of war at the end of the *Philosophy of Right*, where Hegel writes of "the ethical *moment of war*" (PhR §324). A political realm can

remain political only by repeatedly conjuring up the state of nature in moments of escalation. Erzsebet Rozsa points out that the late Hegel understands "free" individuality as the "principal of the 'newer world' both in the historical and in the systematic sense" and that he also "gives a thorough treatment of the phenomena and the symptoms of a 'vacillating' self-assessment in the modern individual." See Erzsebet Rozsa, "Verhaltensweisen des Individuums," in *Hegels Phänomenologie des Geistes heute*, ed. Andreas Arndt and Ernst Müller (Berlin: Akademie, 2004), 121–44, here 132.

19. Ludwig Siep, "Kehraus mit Hegel? Zu Ernst Tugendhats Hegelkritik," *Zeitschrift für philosophische Forschung* 34, nos. 3–4 (1981): 518–31.

20. Žižek, *Tarrying with the Negative: Kant, Hegel, and the Critique of Ideology* (Durham: Duke University Press, 1993), 31.

21. Friedrich Meinecke accuses Hegel of having brought forth—with "sublime indifference toward the spirited individual"—the appearance "that independent individuals of world history are simply marionettes of the world-spirit": see Meinecke, "Ein Wort über geschichtliche Entwicklung," in *Aphorismen und Skizzen zur Geschichte* (Leipzig: Koehler und Amelang 1942), 86. What Meinecke does not see is that Hegel's world-spirit cannot pull the strings. The strings are pulled by the individuals themselves, and afterward are experienced as if they had been pulled by a puppet master.

22. Here a selection of publications that adopt psychoanalysis for political philosophy. Pertaining to Freud, see José Brunner, *Freud and the Politics of Psychoanalysis* (Oxford: Blackwell, 1995), in particular, chapters 2 and 3, where Brunner employs Freud's theories of mind and language on political discourse and various social institutions (for example, the clinic). Béatrice Longuenesse compares Kant's ethical will with Freud's theory of the superego: Longuenesse, "Freud and Philosophy: Kant's 'I' in 'I Ought To' and Freud's Superego," *Aristotelian Society*, supplementary volume 86, no. 1 (2012): 19–39. Sebastian Gardner defends psychoanalysis against the disregard it has experienced from the philosophical-analytical tradition due to its supposed adherence to the theory of a "second mind." Gardner relates psychoanalysis to folk psychology and interprets the political implications as relating to wish (chapter 5) and fantasy (chapter 6) according to Freud and Melanie Klein in Gardner, *Irrationality and the Philosophy of Psychoanalysis* (Cambridge: Cambridge University Press, 2007). See also the very interesting reply to Gardner from Jonathan Lear: Lear, "The Heterogeneity of the Mental," *Mind* 104, no. 416 (October 1995): 863–79. What stands out in Jonathan Lear's many publications is perhaps his most political writing on Freud, his book *Radical Hope: Ethics in the Face of Cultural Devastation* (Cambridge: Harvard University Press, 2008). Chapter 3 features many references to publications about Lacan, for example, the following: Slavoj Žižek, *For They Know Not What They Do: Enjoyment as a Political Factor* (London: Verso, 2002). Yannis Stavrakakis offers a good overview of the political "Lacanian Left" (Castoriadis, Žižek, Laclau, Badiou) in chapter 1 of *The Lacanian Left: Psychoanalysis, Theory, Politics* (New York: State University of New York Press, 2007). See also Willy Apollon and Richard Feldstein, eds., *Lacan, Politics, Aesthetics* (New York: State University of New York Press, 1995); Yannis Stavrakakis, *Lacan and the Political* (London: Routledge, 1999); Alain Badiou, *Ethics: An Essay on*

the Understanding of Evil, trans. Peter Hallward (London: Verso, 2013); Eric Santner, *On the Psychotheology of Everyday Life: Reflections on Freud and Rosenzweig* (Chicago: University of Chicago Press, 2001). An earlier work is Martin Schulte's illustrative comparison of Pierre Legendre's work with Lacan's philosophy of the subject: Schulte, *Das Gesetz des Unbewussten im Rechtsdiskurs: Grundlinien einer psychoanalytischen Rechtstheorie nach Freud und Lacan* (Berlin: Duncker und Humblot, 2009).

23. Schulte, *Das Gesetz des Unbewussten im Rechtsdiskurs*, 52.
24. Like Manfred Schneider, one can call this state "paranoiac reason." Schneider localizes this state—especially since the era of modernity—in the figurations of an assassination as instances of a particular veneer. Cf. Manfred Schneider, *Das Attentat: Kritik der paranoischen Vernunft* (Berlin: Matthes und Seitz, 2010). Schneider interprets modernity in particular as the origin of the assassination. A continually more rational life purpose provokes a hyperrationality along the lines of conspiracy-theoretical paranoia. Unfortunately, Schneider stretches the paranoia term so far that any kind of a normative judgment of the political crisis—for which the assassination stands—can hardly succeed.

1. EXCESSIVE SUBJECTIVITY AND THE PARADOX OF AUTONOMY

1. See also Georg Wilhelm Friedrich Hegel, *Lectures on the History of Philosophy*, vol. 1, *Greek Philosophy to Plato*, trans. E. S. Haldane and Frances H. Simon (Lincoln: University of Nebraska Press, 1995), 420.
2. Ludwig Wittgenstein, *On Certainty*, ed. G. E. M. Anscombe and G. H. von Wright, trans. Denis Paul and G. E. M. Anscombe (Oxford: Basil Blackwell, 1969), §611.
3. Robert B. Pippin, "Hegel's Practical Philosophy: The Actualization of Freedom," in *Cambridge Companion to German Idealism*, ed. Karl Ameriks (Cambridge: Cambridge University Press, 2000), 180–99. Similarly, see Karl Ameriks, *Kant and the Fate of Autonomy: Problems in the Appropriation of the Critical Philosophy* (Cambridge: Cambridge University Press, 2000), chap. 1. See also Christoph Menke, "Autonomie und Befreiung," *Deutsche Zeitschrift für Philosophie* 58, no. 5 (2010): 675–94.
4. Terry Pinkard, "Tugend, Moral und Sittlichkeit: Von Maximen zu Praktiken," *Deutsche Zeitschrift für Philosophie* 49, no. 1 (2001): 65–87.
5. Robert Pippin, *Hegel's Practical Philosophy: Rational Agency as Ethical Life* (Cambridge: Cambridge University Press, 2008), 97–99.
6. Christoph Menke writes incisively: "To judge something that is part of a practice is to measure it against the law that—because it constitutes the practice—also makes this something a part of the practice." Menke, "Autonomie und Befreiung," 680. Pippin's interpretation of Hegel's *Philosophy of Right* develops a dialectic interaction of subjects and practices in an interlocking manner, in which neither of the entities takes precedence. It therefore cannot be said in what way the subjects determine the practices that they perform, or that the practices influence the judgment of the subjects.

The individual is never oriented from a—figuratively speaking—Cartesian self-reference toward the practices in the social sphere. Terry Pinkard shows this dialectic interlocking as relating to Hegel and Wittgenstein in the context of epistemology and the Wittgensteinian concept of "lifeform." See Terry Pinkard, "Innen, Außen und Lebensformen: Hegel und Wittgenstein," in *Hegels Erbe*, ed. Michael Quante, Christoph Halbig, and Ludwig Siep (Frankfurt: Suhrkamp 2004), 254–94. Practices in the world make the subject's inwardness possible as the subject can only have practical reason via participation in practices. Pippin, *Hegel's Practical Philosophy*, 263–65. See Menke's commentaries on and his critiques of Pippin in Menke, "Autonomie und Befreiung," 680–81.

7. See Peter Sloterdijk, *Critique of Cynical Reason*, trans. Michael Eldred (Minneapolis: University of Minnesota Press, 1987), chaps. 3 and 4, pp. 22–100.
8. Karl Marx, *Das Kapital: Buch 1*, in *Marx-Engels-Werke*, 43 vols. (Berlin: Dietz, 1975), 23:88.
9. Slavoj Žižek, *The Sublime Object of Ideology* (London: Verso, 1989), 29.
10. "One knows, how one should behave, when one knows, how one has already behaved." Menke, "Autonomie und Befreiung," 681. Reality stands for the whole of that which is already in practice. That something is a norm is dependent upon the fact that it can "be understood" by the subject as a norm (cf. PhR §132).
11. Cf. Robert Brandom, "Semantik ohne Wahrheit: Ein Interview mit Robert Brandom von Matthias Haase," *Deutsche Zeitschrift für Philosophie* 54, no. 3 (2006): 449–66, in particular 460–62. See also Brandom's comments about the use of legal norms in legal sentencing: ibid., 464–66.
12. Subject and practice can be understood as "two sides of the same coin," which Hegel calls "spirit" as a historical process of continually renewed mutual moments of universalization. These coins only exist in progress, not before they have generated themselves in the practice.
13. Tilo Wesche analyzes this incisively in Wesche, "Hegel und die Wahrheitstheorien der Gegenwart: Ein Streit unter Nachbarn," *Deutsche Zeitschrift für Philosophie* 57, no. 3 (2009): 355–75, here 370.
14. Chantal Mouffe and Ernesto Laclau thematize this problematic repeatedly in various publications in critical conversation with authors such as John Rawls and Jürgen Habermas. See Chantal Mouffe, *The Democratic Paradox* (London: Verso, 2009). See also Ernesto Laclau and Chantal Mouffe, *Hegemony And Socialist Strategy: Towards a Radical Democratic Politics* (London: Verso 2001).
15. This is also the view of Walter Benjamin's historic-philosophical theses that appear to be written against a certain form of Hegelianism, but ultimately are quite related to Hegel. Cf. Walter Benjamin, "On the Concept of History," in *Selected Writings*, vol. 4, *1938–1940*, ed. Howard Eiland and Michael W. Jennings, trans. Edmund Jephcott et al. (Cambridge: Belknap Press of Harvard University Press, 2003), 389–400.
16. Theodor W. Adorno is exemplary here. See his critique of Hegel's discourse on reason in history from *Phenomenology* to *Philosophy of Right*: Adorno, "Weltgeist und Naturgeschichte: Exkurs zu Hegel," in *Negative Dialektik* (Frankfurt: Suhrkamp, 1992), 295–353.

17. Konrad Utz, *Die Notwendigkeit des Zufalls: Hegels spekulative Dialektik in der Wissenschaft der Logik: ein Entwurf* (Munich: Schöningh, 2001).
18. Benjamin, "On the Concept of History," here 390–91.
19. Peter Singer, *Animal Liberation: The Definitive Classic of the Animal Movement* (New York: Harper, 2009).
20. Georg Stenger analyzes—in a theory about balancing processes between morality in living environments and norms in the universal sphere—what Hegel thematizes in his combination of historical teleology and contingency. Stenger shows how one day "law happens." A new normativity is accepted by the "people's spirit"—speaking with Hegel—without one knowing exactly why. The law "happens" like a kind of Heideggerian event. The law is accepted, but not in the sense of a "rational process"; rather, it just happens. Cf. Georg Stenger, *Philosophie der Interkulturalität* (Freiburg: Alber, 2006).
21. In his multiple treatments of morality, Hegel is continually concerned in the *Philosophy of Right* to stress the unconsciousness of moral behavior.
22. Ludwig Wittgenstein, *Philosophical Investigations*, rev. ed., ed. P. M. S. Hacker and Joachim Schulte, trans. G. E. M. Anscombe, P. M. S. Hacker, and Joachim Schulte (Malden, MA: Wiley Blackwell, 2009), §217.
23. On this point, Hegel overlaps with Kierkegaard, even when the latter believed he developed an anti-Hegelian understanding of Christian singularity. See Dominik Finkelde, "Excessive Subjectivity: Hegel and Kierkegaard on the Paradox of Autonomy and Liberation," in *Kierkegaard and Politics: The Intervention of the Single Individual*, ed. Armen Avanessian and Sophie Wennerscheid (Copenhagen: Museum Tusculanum, 2014), 111–39.
24. Menke: "The act of liberation appears as a heteronomous act of lawless arbitrariness against the heteronomous power of habit from the viewpoint of the concept of autonomy." Menke, "Autonomie und Befreiung," 693. In relation to the same problem, Henrik Joker Bjerre points out the danger that playing the already-established "*Rechtslehre* game" has. It can convince the subject to act morally by habit, that is, alone through passive obedience to the established law. Cf. Henrik Joker Bjerre, "Enjoying the Law: On a Possible Conflict Between Kant's Views on Obedience and Enjoyment," *SATS Northern European Journal of Philosophy* 6, no. 2 (2005): 114–27. But Kant states explicitly that behavior at the level of indifference and habit cannot be moral. Thus Menke (contrary to Pippin) also points to the fact that true autonomy proves itself only when it breaks through morality. Liberation "from the power of the second nature first makes autonomy possible, but it is not an autonomous act [according to Pippin's interpretation of Hegel]. As a breakthrough from the natural power of habitual mechanisms and identity, the liberation of the spirit is not a learning process." Menke, "Autonomie und Befreiung," 693. Julia Rebentisch suggests an alternative to autonomy as the "breakthrough . . . of habitual mechanisms" in reference to irony. She defends this in a discourse-ethical adaption with Hegel's interpretation of Socrates and against his critique of romanticism. Rebentisch believes in pacifying the antagonism of the political through continual analysis of self-reflexive irony. Discourse

ethics broadened with irony represents a permanent analysis of one's own claim to truth, whereby irony is a linguistic medium for self-reflexivity. With this, Rebentisch avoids the traumatic impossibility of the political as a sphere that either suppresses or only carries out its antagonisms in tragic conflict. Also, Hegel is for Juliane Rebentisch the totality-thinker of morality as legality who accepts the marginalization of the individual. "Subjective freedom appears here only to be allowed in morality in the measure in which it identifies with the existing norms." Juliane Rebentisch, *Die Kunst der Freiheit: Zur Dialektik demokratischer Existenz* (Berlin: Suhrkamp, 2012), 103. Against this, she sets the understanding of intersubjectivity, which in her opinion is best articulated in romantic irony as an expression of self-reflexive freedom. "This aspect of romantic irony remained hidden to Hegel." From this point, Rebentisch unfolds the accusation that Hegel "suppresses subjective freedom on moral grounds" (103).

2. KANT

1. Cf. Petra Bahr, *Darstellung des Undarstellbaren* (Tübingen: Mohr Siebeck, 2004), 249.
2. Friedrich Kaulbach, "Der transzendentale Perspektivismus Kants," in *Philosophie des Perspektivismus*, vol. 1 (Tübingen: Mohr Siebeck 1990), 11–137, here 74.
3. On this point, Petra Bahr writes: "As a merely imagined point, it is of serious consequence for the realized picture, even if it counts as a virtual deception." Bahr, *Darstellung des Undarstellbaren*, 250.
4. In the *Fakultätenschrift*, Kant is interested in the enthusiasm for the French Revolution. As Axel Honneth aptly puts it, Kant observes that, "in the moment of consent [for a political movement like the French Revolution], . . . the position of their [the audience's] historical consciousness [shifts], because they now have to unify all historical events and circumstances from the perspective of the most recent developments into one directed process, in which the moral achievements of the present mark a successful intermediate step." Honneth, "Kein Ende der Geschichte? Geschichtsphilosophie nach Kant," in *Nach Kant: Erbe und Kritik*, ed. Ian Kaplow (Münster: LIT, 2005), 118–33, here 126.
5. Cf. Henry E. Allison, *Kant's Transcendental Idealism* (New Haven: Yale University Press, 2004), 426.
6. Kant's ethics of moral autonomy is not a novel creation, but is rather the result of preceding philosophical works on the concept of autonomy. Jerome B. Schneewind presents the development of this concept from Luther to Kant by way of Suarez and Rousseau. Schneewind, *The Invention of Autonomy: A History of Modern Moral Philosophy* (Cambridge: Cambridge University Press, 1998). See especially chapters 20–23.
7. Moral-"ethical" action must be distinguished from moral-"juridical" action, according to Kant's *Metaphysics of Morals*. There, he writes that the "laws of nature, these laws of freedom are called *moral* laws. As directed merely to external actions and their

conformity to law they are called *juridical* laws; but if they also require that they (the laws) themselves be the determining grounds of actions, they are *ethical*" (MM 375). In the following, I will use "moral" for ethical-moral internal freedom (*moralitas*), but not for moral-judicial external freedom (*legalitas*).

8. The dichotomous contrast between the internal freedom of the moral subject's "disposition" (*Gesinnung*) and the "external freedom" of the citizen in a state provokes the following question: How can Kant's ethics of disposition, as the area of actual freedom, be reconciled with the realm of "external freedom"? Determining these relationships accounts for a large part of Kant scholarship. Several research projects indicate the sense in which Kant's concept of fulfilled self-orientation in morals cannot be removed from the area of "external freedom" in which it realizes itself as a space of normative claims, always filled with different human beings. A "principle-oriented" reception of Kant has often been challenged on the grounds that Kant's critical reasoning of ethics must be acknowledged within the context of his late "Doctrine of Virtue." Thus, it can be shown how Kant overcomes the "poor alternative of rationalism (*schlechte Alternative von Rationalismus*)" and the attached "chorism of split spheres of being (*Chorismus getrennter Seinssphären*)." Andrea Esser, *Eine Ethik für Endliche: Kants Tugendlehre in der Gegenwart* (Stuttgart-Bad Cannstatt: Frommann-Holzboog, 2004), 16. Korsgaard tries to save the categorical imperative's formula of universalization with the "kingdom of ends" phrasing. See Christine M. Korsgaard, *The Sources of Normativity* (Cambridge: Cambridge University Press, 1996), 98–100.
9. Hermann Andreas Pistorius, "Rezension der Grundlegung zur Metaphysik der Sitten," in *Kants vergessener Rezensent: Die Kritik der theoretischen und praktischen Philosophie Kants in fünf frühen Rezensionen von Hermann Andreas Pistorius*, ed. Bernward Gesang (Hamburg: Meiner, 2007), 26–38.
10. The reflective power of judgment within the *Critique of the Power of Judgment* is acknowledged for connecting the realm of natural laws with the realm of freedom. For Kant's varying heuristic approaches to a philosophy of history that can be compatible with his transcendental philosophy, see Pauline Kleingeld, *Fortschritt und Vernunft: Zur Geschichtsphilosophie Kants* (Würzburg: Könighausen und Neumann, 1995).
11. As is generally known, Kant's writings "Theory and Practice" (*Über den Gemeinspruch*) and "Perpetual Peace" (*Zum ewigen Frieden*) were written after the *Critique of the Power of Judgment*.
12. In a letter from Karl Leonhard Reinhold to Johann Benjamin Erhard written on June 10, 1795. Karl August Varnhagen von Ense, *Denkwürdigkeiten des Philosophen und Arztes Johann Benjamin Erhard* (Stuttgart: Klett-Cotta, 1830), 362.
13. Otfried Höffe, "Universalistische Ethik und Urteilskraft: ein aristotelischer Blick auf Kant," *Zeitschrift für Philosophische Forschung* 44, no. 4 (1990): 537–63; see also Höffe, "Ausblick: Aristoteles oder Kant—wider eine plane Alternative," in *Aristoteles: Die Nikomachische Ethik*, ed. Otfried Höffe (Berlin: Akademie, 1995), 277–304; Christine M. Korsgaard, "Aristotle and Kant on the Source of Value," *Ethics* 96, no. 3 (1986): 486–505; Korsgaard, "From Duty and for the Sake of the Noble: Kant and Aristotle on Morally Good Action," in *The Constitution of Agency* (Oxford: Oxford University

Press, 2008), 174–206; Sean Drysdale Walsh, "Kant's Theory of Right as Aristotelian Phronesis," *International Philosophical Quarterly* 52, no. 2 (2012): 227–46.

14. Several authors, among them Habermas, Apel, Tugendhat, Williams, and MacIntyre, see in Kant a formalistic ethics, which represents the moral realism of a relentless deontology of rules and maxims. Cf. Habermas, *Moralbewusstsein und kommunikatives Handeln* (Frankfurt: Suhrkamp, 1983), 77; Karl-Otto Apel, *Transformation der Philosophie*, 2 vols. (Frankfurt: Suhrkamp, 1973), 2:373–75. Tugendhat criticizes Kant's formalism in the example of the idea of an absolute good and concludes that an absolute use of "good"—which Pistorius rejects as well—cannot be sustained. The semantics of "good" can therefore only be determined through a discourse of objective criteria of reasoning. Cf. Tugendhat, *Vorlesungen über Ethik* (Frankfurt: Suhrkamp, 1993), 37–39; Bernard Williams, "Präsuppositionen der Moralität," in *Bedingungen der Möglichkeit: "Transzendental Arguments" und transzendentales Denken*, ed. Eva Schaper and Wilhelm Vossenkuhl (Stuttgart: Klett-Cotta, 1984), 251–60; see also Williams, *Ethics and the Limits of Philosophy* (Cambridge: Harvard University Press, 1985), esp. chap. 10; Williams, "Persons, Character, and Morality," in *Moral Luck* (Cambridge: Cambridge University Press, 1981), 1–19; Williams, Personen, Charakter und Moralität," in *Moralischer Zufall, Philosophische Aufsätze, 1973–1980* (Königstein: Anton Hain, 1984), 11–29.
15. Otto Schwemmer, "Die praktische Ohnmacht der reinen Vernunft," *Neue Hefte für Philosophie* 22 (1983): 20–21.
16. Reiner Wimmer, "Die Doppelfunktion des kategorischen Imperativs in Kants Ethik," *Kant-Studien* 73, nos. 1–4 (1982): 301.
17. A more recent work within this tradition is Esser, *Ethik für Endliche.*
18. Among the authors who, contrary to the formalism critique leveled against Kant, deduce the weighing of moral standards in his work are the following: Onora O'Neill, "Instituting Principles: Between Duty and Action," in *Kant's Metaphysics of Morals*, ed. Mark Timmons (Oxford: Oxford University Press, 2002), 331–49; Barbara Herman, *The Practice of Moral Judgment* (Cambridge: Harvard University Press, 1993); Nancy Sherman, *Making a Necessity of Virtue: Aristotle and Kant on Virtue* (Cambridge: Cambridge University Press, 1997); Otfried Höffe, "Kants kategorischer Imperativ als Kriterium des Sittlichen," *Zeitschrift für philosophische Forschung* 31, no. 3 (1977): 354–84.
19. This is Walsh's thesis in the article "Kant's Theory of Right."
20. Cf. Annemarie Pieper, "Zweites Hauptstück (57–71)," in *Immanuel Kant: Kritik der praktischen Vernunft*, ed. Otfried Höffe (Berlin: Akademie, 2002), 115–33.
21. "Ethics" is understood here to be the philosophical discipline of rational moral agency of free responsible agents.
22. I am borrowing the term *supernumerary* from Alain Badiou's philosophy of the event. See Alain Badiou, *Being and Event*, trans. Oliver Feltham (London: Continuum 2006), 178.
23. Christine M. Korsgaard's studies are outstanding. She develops a person's former goal for his "practical identity" as a subordination of tendencies or pathologies to

reasonable, generalizable motives of action. The person self-reflectively recognizes a self-functional dignity in himself to be an autonomous person among other autonomous persons. He is obliged to all humanity. Cf. Korsgaard, *Sources of Normativity*, 1–165, 219–58; see also Christine M. Korsgaard, *Self-Constitution: Agency, Identity, and Integrity* (Oxford: Oxford University Press, 2009), esp. chaps. 7–9; for a critical analysis of Korsgaard's concept of autonomy set against the background of Freud, see Jonathan Lear, "To Become Human Does Not Come that Easily," in *A Case for Irony*, Tanner Lectures on Human Values (Cambridge: Harvard University Press, 2011), 3–41.

24. The tension in Kant's moral philosophy, mainly arising from the is-ought distinction, has been acknowledged in the two Kantian schools presented earlier in a simplified way. It is questionable, though, to what extent the necessary conclusions for an aporia of moral will or for its division are drawn out.
25. Henrik Joker Bjerre, *Kantian Deeds* (London: Continuum, 2010).
26. Walsh comprehensibly shows the extent to which Kant's concrete examples in the *Groundwork* and in the *Critique of Practical Reason* possess analytical character, that is, the extent to which they should not be understood as behavioral catechism. Cf. Walsh, "Kant's Theory of Right as Aristotelian Phronesis."
27. See Kai Gregor's article, "'Revolution der Gesinnung' und 'Vollendung der Freiheit,'" *Fichte-Studien* 31 (2007): 159–73.
28. Immanuel Kant, *Religion Within the Boundaries of Mere Reason*, in *Religion and Rational Theology*, ed. Paul Guyer and Allen W. Wood (Cambridge: Cambridge University Press, 2001), 39–215.
29. Assurance of an absolute proof of a genuine change of heart "cannot of course be attained by the human being naturally, neither via immediate consciousness nor via the evidence of the life he has hitherto led, for the depths of his own heart (the subjective first ground of his maxims) are to him inscrutable" (Rel. 95). He will "thus have to look at his disposition throughout his whole life" (Rel. 116).
30. "If after this life another awaits him, that he will persevere in it (in all appearances under different circumstances, yet according to the very same principle) and come ever closer to his goal of perfection, though it is unattainable" (Rel. 110).
31. Generally, the revolution of the disposition (*Gesinnungsrevolution*) is understood as a *one-time* as well as an *intelligible* act that, as a *conversion* (*Bekehrung*), breaks the omnipotence of the metamaxim of evil, which determines the human being in its "tendency toward evil" (*Hang zum Bösen*), as Kant calls it. Ottfried Höffe and Henry Allison emphasize the singularity of the revolution of disposition: see Otfried Höffe, *Kant's Cosmopolitan Theory of Law and Peace* (Cambridge: Cambridge University Press, 2006), 28. The revolution, Allison writes, is a first step "on the road to virtue," "a firm resolution." It breaks the tendency toward evil "to restore the order of incentives to their original and proper ranking." Henry E. Allison, *Kant's Theory of Freedom* (Cambridge: Cambridge University Press, 1990), 170. Allen Wood emphasizes (as does Maximilan Forschner) that the "revolution in the manner of thinking" (*Revolution der Denkungsart*) only relates to the intelligible dimension of the human being, while

the phenomenal human being progresses on the level of gradual improvement. The revolution is thus something like an intelligible act and a philosophical-practical analogy to the "thing-in-itself" within Kant's epistemology. Kant's writings on "change of heart" (*Herzensänderung*), "revolution of the disposition," and "change" (*Neuwerdung*) should not be mistaken for an event that is situated *in time*. Wood: "We should not confuse this 'change of heart' with an actual 'change' of any kind in time. Kant, indeed, contrasts the gradual moral progress of man in time with the change of heart which is the condition for its possibility. He notes that, because this change of heart can be known only through a gradual temporal reform, we can never be sure that it has taken place." Allen Wood, *Kant's Moral Religion* (Ithaca: Cornell University Press, 1970), 229. Therefore, it remains unsolved how the "revolution of disposition" relates to progress, without referring to a new dualism. Cf. Maximilian Forschner, "Über die verschiedenen Bedeutungen des 'Hangs zum Bösen,'" in *Immanuel Kant: Die Religion innerhalb der Grenzen der bloßen Vernunft*, ed. Otfried Höffe (Berlin: Akademie, 2011), 78. For Jochen Bojanowski, the "revolution in the manner of thinking" is not yet a revolution "der Sinnesart" ("mode of sense," Rel. 92). "But the more often the agent chooses the moral law in a decisive situation between reason and tendency, the more certain he can be about being on a 'way of frequent progression.'" Jochen Bojanowski, *Kants Theorie der Freiheit* (Berlin: De Gruyter, 2006), 277. Christoph Horn interprets this revolution of disposition as the "successful first anticipation to the complete revolution." Christoph Horn, "Die menschliche Gattungsnatur: Anlagen zum Guten und Hang zum Bösen," in Höffe, *Immanuel Kant*, 61.

32. In the *Groundwork for the Metaphysics of Morals*, Kant's concept of disposition is still underspecified. It is more clearly developed in his *Religionsschrift*. Disposition is now understood as a subjective principle of maxims (Rel. 72, 83–84). "The intelligible character [of virtue] (*virtus noumenon*)" (Rel. 92), for Kant, is the morally good human being. His actions generally occur out of duty. That the human being does not have a holy will does not imply that he is partly good and partly evil. Kant claims that if the human being has turned the moral law into his maxim, it applies to him as a whole and not just to his intelligible character. A maxim that is applied only to a part of the human being would thus have to be universal for the rational part of the human being and particular, that is, limited, for the sensual dimension of the human being. (I owe this clue to Maria Schwartz.) But that is impossible for Kant. Therefore, the human being is not good and evil, but either good or evil (Rel. 73). Likewise, Kant emphasizes that the human being can never be morally indifferent, that is, neither good nor evil (Rel. 71–72). Cf. also Bojanowski, *Kants Theorie der Freiheit*, 266–67. How the decision for the "adoption of this or that maxim with respect to the moral law" (Rel. 71) comes into existence is "to us inscrutable" (Rel. 71).

33. "The disposition, i.e. the first subjective ground of the adoption of the maxims, can only be a single one, and it applies to the entire use of freedom universally. This disposition too, however, must be adopted through the free power of choice, for otherwise it could not be imputed. But there cannot be any further cognition of the subjective ground or the cause of this adoption (although we cannot avoid asking about it). . . . Hence, since

we cannot derive this disposition, or rather its highest ground, from a first act of the power of choice in time, we call it a characteristic of the power of choice that pertains to it by nature (even though the disposition is in fact grounded in freedom)" (Rel. 74).

34. Marcus Willaschek calls the "thesis of the radical evil an empirical hypothesis, which results from the application of a moral-philosophical theory to experience." Willaschek, *Praktische Vernunft: Handlungstheorie und Moralbegründung* (Stuttgart: Metzler, 1992), 153. Gordon E. Michalson criticizes the transformation of an empirical hypothesis into an a priori universal principle that corresponds to all human beings. "Quite simply, it is never clear why Kant thinks radical evil is universal, or the propensity to evil innate. At the point in the *Religion* where Kant makes these claims most explicit, he turns to empirical examples, as though offering a familiar 'long melancholy litany of indictments against humanity' will simply make manifest what we somehow intuitively know about the race. But of course there is utterly no way that Kant, above all, could legitimately generate a claim about an intrinsic feature of human nature from even the lengthiest list of empirical examples." Gordon E. Michalson, *Fallen Freedom: Kant on Radical Evil and Moral Regeneration* (Cambridge: Cambridge University Press, 1990), esp. 62–70, here 67. Allison emphasizes "the 'intelligible' nature of the act through which it [the propensity to evil] is adopted. Such an act is timeless or intelligible, not in the sense that it must be regarded as occurring in some timeless noumenal world but rather in the sense that it is not to be viewed as performed at a specific point in one's moral development. On the contrary . . . this propensity to give undue weight to the non-moral incentive and, therefore, to reverse the proper ordering of principles is already at work when moral reflection begins." Allison, *Kant's Theory of Freedom*, 153–54. Cf. also Maximilian Forschner, "Immanuel Kants 'Hang zum Bösen' und Thomas von Aquins 'Gesetz des Zunders': Über säkulare Aufklärungsanthropologie und christliche Erbsündenlehre," *Zeitschrift für philosophische Forschung* 63, no. 4 (2009): 519–42. Cf. also Christian Schulte, *Radikal böse: Die Karriere des Bösen von Kant bis Nietzsche* (Munich: Wilhelm Fink, 1988), 33–73.

35. In the "Doctrine of Virtue," Kant emphasizes that human beings with a "good heart (*guten Herzen*)" exist (MM 563).

36. Horn: "The revolution therefore must be what stands at the end, not what constitutes the beginning. . . . What could it mean that a fundamental revolution of disposition happens first and only afterward a gradual improvement of individual, moral actions or individual attitudes?" Horn, "Die menschliche Gattungsnatur," 60.

37. Ibid.

38. Ibid., 61.

39. What the human being in freedom opted for "has not been earned in time" (Rel. 74). Kant writes explicitly that we cannot "derive this disposition . . . from a first act of the power of choice in time" (Rel. 74). It is the mysterious "addition (*Zusatz*)" to his "personality" (Rel. 76).

40. In this context, Kant's discussion of "holiness (*Heiligkeit*)" in the *Religion* text marks the target point of the progress into the infinite, "from lower to higher stages of moral perfection" (CPrR 239). The holiness is even "inexorably" (*unnachlässlich*) demanded

by the legislation of the pure and practical reason. It stands for the "complete conformity" of "the moral vocation of our nature . . . with the moral law" (CPrR 238). If someone relativized this holiness' goal even just a little bit, because it couldn't actually be absolutely realized, according to Kant, he would "degrade the moral law from its *holiness* by making it out to be *lenient* (indulgent) and thus conformed to our convenience" (CPrR 238).

41. Pistorius, "Rezension der Grundlegung der Metaphysik der Sitten," 33.
42. Tugendhat writes: "I determine this use of moral language by a certain employment of the word group 'must,' 'can't,' 'should,' and the word group 'good,' 'bad.' Both groups have a wide range of applications." Tugendhat, *Vorlesungen über Ethik*, 35–36.
43. Ibid., 56.
44. Ibid., 44.
45. Ibid., 45.
46. Ibid., 45.
47. Alenka Zupančič, *Ethics of the Real: Kant and Lacan* (London: Verso, 2000), 17.
48. Ibid.
49. Ibid.
50. In this context, Zupančič mentions the Holocaust and indirectly with it the case of Adolf Eichmann's deontic obedience to authority as an obedience to Kantian duty. Cf. ibid., 97–99. Zupančič emphasizes that in a situation like this a reference to Kant cannot be made, since the human being in his obedience to duty bears exactly responsibility for what it assumes as his duty. Diametrically opposed to Zupančič is John Dewey's interpretation, which refers Kant's deontic morality back to structures of blind obedience and thus seems to critically anticipate Eichmann's argument: see John Dewey, *German Philosophy and Politics* (New York: Henry Holt, 1915), 38–45.
51. Williams, "Persons, Character, and Morality," 17.
52. Susan Wolf, "The Failure of Autonomy," PhD diss., Princeton University, 1978, 51, cited in Marcia W. Baron, *Kantian Ethics Almost Without Apology* (New York: Cornell University Press, 1999), 122.
53. In this sense, Zupančič's interpretation of Kant is not as innovative as she sometimes suggests. Nevertheless, she manages to concretize the issue in an outstanding way.
54. Zupančič, *Ethics of the Real*, 5.
55. Axel Honneth, *Freedom's Right: The Social Foundations of Democratic Life*, trans. Joseph Ganahl (Cambridge: Polity, 2014), 112–13.
56. Alain Badiou, *Theoretical Writings*, ed. and trans. Ray Brassier and Alberto Toscano (London: Continuum, 2004), 43.
57. Cf. Badiou, *Being and Event*, 102.
58. See Wimmer, "Die Doppelfunktion des kategorische Imperativs."
59. Hegel also comments on this aspect. In the *Philosophy of Right*, he writes that the moment of contingency in the verdict is "itself necessary" (PR §214A/p. 246).
60. Kant here renounces the possibility of the subject damaging the social contract by her ethical act. In this respect, a subject may only rise morally when she does not endanger the social structure of the established law. This thought leads to the

recurring criticism of Kant as not being able to explain a revolutionary overthrow of an existing social order.

61. To specify this thought, one can refer back to Kant's definition of thought as a process of rule following. He writes: "The business of the senses is to intuit; that of the understanding, to think. . . . The unification of representations in a consciousness is judgment. Therefore, thinking is the same as judging or as relating representations to judgments in general." Immanuel Kant, *Prolegomena to Any Future Metaphysics*, rev. ed., ed. Karl Americks and Desmond M. Clarke, trans. Gary Hatfield (Cambridge: Cambridge University Press, 2004), 56. And a little later Kant writes: "Judgments, insofar as they are regarded merely as the condition for the unification of given representations in a consciousness, are rules." Ibid., 57.

62. The secondary literature has made this relationship a subject of discussion several times. Cf. Jonathan Lear, *Open Minded* (Cambridge: Harvard University Press, 1999), 252–75. Because of the rule regress, the "general logic" (*allgemeine Logik*), as Kant writes, contains no "regulations" (*Vorschriften*) for the power of judgment. Jonathan Lear: "When Kant argued that even basic laws of logic or arithmetic could ultimately not be understood independently of the activities of a judging mind, that insight was not supposed to undermine the laws. Rather, a transcendental consideration which revealed these laws to depend on a subjective contribution of mind was intended to provide insight into why, from an empirical perspective, these laws were genuinely objective and necessary." Lear, *Open Minded*, 254. Markus Gabriel carves out the relationship between Kant and Wittgenstein: Gabriel, *An den Grenzen der Erkenntnistheorie: Die notwendige Endlichkeit des objektiven Wissens als Lektion des Skeptizismus* (Freiburg: Alber, 2008), 240–78.

63. If this were not the case, then the realm of the political would not exist. There would be no differing opinions within a community on the question of how society shall be arranged and structured. All rational beings would permanently reach the same conclusions.

64. One could also interpret the act-deed of excessive subjectivity as a "noumenon in the negative sense (*Noumenon im negativen Sinne*)" or "only in the negative use (*nur vo[m] negative[n] Gebrauche*)," just as Kant interprets the "transcendental object = X" (CPR 233). In this case, the act-deed is "not invented arbitrarily, but is rather connected with the limitation of sensibility, yet without being able to posit anything positive outside of the domain of the latter" (CPR 350 [A 255/B 311]). Just as the "transcendental object = X" for Kant is that which is being conceived in our imaginations, without ever appearing as a certain imagination, so too is the act-deed of excessive subjectivity that which is imagined as ethical-moral normative law without (yet) being able to be presented as a legal-moral law. (This is to be understood only as an analogy.) With the transcendental object, we can never know what it is. With the act-deed of excessive subjectivity, we cannot know in the moment it happens how its guiding principle of agency will be judged in the "external freedom" (*äußeren Freiheit*) of a future to come.

65. Joseph Heath also points to an affinity between Kant's transcendental philosophy and the pragmatic philosophy of the later Wittgenstein: "Judgment is an act of self-constitution. It is this idea that steers Kant's fundamentally pragmatist insight in the direction that would lead to German idealism. . . . Judgment is an act of will, while perception is a form of representation. The world emerges at the intersection of the two: hence the falsity of both empiricism and rationalism." Joseph Heath, *Following the Rules: Practical Reason and Deontic Constraint* (Oxford: Oxford University Press, 2008), 118.

66. Kant's idea of a practice of a power of judgment is not helpful here either, since the practice itself needs an objective standard for measuring its own progress. Also, Kant again would need talent to recognize this objective standard.

67. Even the reflective power of judgment from Kant's *Critique of Judgment*, which seeks the rule that an application instantiates, and which *finds* the universal, does not solve the problem. It doesn't solve the problem in the sense that—as Markus Gabriel points out—it does not "invent" (*erfinden*) the universal. Cf. Gabriel, *Grenzen der Erkenntnistheorie*, 272. "Also in his reflective judgment, Kant assumes that the universal exists, so that the variability is exclusively located in the area of the applications that need to be brought under one concept." Ibid., 272. Gabriel then writes: "According to Kant, our categorical equipment does not change, because it is a priori. Wittgenstein switches the direction of explanation by understanding the explication of rules as *cura posterior* of rule-following itself." Ibid., 272. "All applications of a rule are thus implicated by the rule like the particular by the universal, whereby they become applications in the first place. Every knowledge now presumes that something can be understood *as* the case of a rule. This is why, for Kant, thought is judgment, i.e. the connection of particularity (subject) and the universal (predicate)." Ibid., 266.

68. Kant thematizes the relationship of the application of rules, the establishment of rules, and the defining relations of "talent," "genius," and artistic as well as empirical judgment in different parts of his writings. For an overview, see Piero Giordanetti, "Das Verhältnis von Genie, Künstler und Wissenschaftler in der kantischen Philosophie," *Kant-Studien* 86, no. 4 (1995): 406–30.

69. Lacan mentions a plausible example of an ingenious ad hoc judgment in antique mathematics in his *II. Seminar*, referring to Plato's dialogue *Meno*. Plato illustrates, in Lacan's words, "how the discourse of science constitutes itself." When Socrates asks the slave Meno to double the area of a square that is drawn into the sand, Meno "in the standard intelligence test . . . employs the relation of equivalence A/B = C/D, the means intelligence most consistently employs" (S.II 17). Socrates by contrast, the master, the talented, the genius, the one who exceeds the power of judgment, proves that the solution lies somewhere else, namely, in the square root of equivalence. Lacan: "Don't you see there is a fault-line between the intuitive element and the symbolic element?" And he claims: "This demonstration . . . is quite evidently accomplished by the master. It is Socrates who effects the realization. . . . The slave, with all his reminiscence and his intelligent intuition, sees the right form, so to speak, from the moment it is pointed out to him" (S.II 18). Jean Hyppolite draws the conclusion from here,

which is crucial for our question of a retrospective normativity of excessive-ethical acts: "You [Lacan] argue then that in Plato any invention once made turns out to generate its own past, turns out to be an eternal discovery?" (S.II 18). And Lacan answers: "From the moment a part of the symbolic world comes into existence it does indeed create its own past" (S.II 18–19).

70. Kant lacks exemplary cases in which moral actions bring down the jurisdiction of "internal" and "external" freedom. Hegel will repeatedly emphasize these exact cases, that is, cases that make the relation between morality and the realm of public legality seem unstable. Since, for Kant, the public realm may prima facie not be shaken by morality, he defuses this conflict, and respectively does not even discover it.

71. In what follows, I will develop a comparison of Kant and contemporary Kantians—a comparison that was introduced by Zupančič in her book *Ethics of the Real* and by Henrik Joker Bjerre in his book *Kantian Deeds*, but that will be further detailed here within the context of Kant's philosophy and within my analysis of excessive subjectivity, which goes beyond Kant.

72. Robert Brandom, *Making It Explicit: Reasoning, Representing, and Discursive Commitment* (Cambridge: Harvard University Press, 1994), 194. Cf. also Robert Brandom, *Articulating Reasons: An Introduction to Inferentialism* (Cambridge: Harvard University Press, 2000), 52.

73. Brandom writes: "Action depends on reliable dispositions to respond differentially to the acknowledging of certain sorts of commitments (the adoption of deontic attitudes and consequent change of score) by bringing about various kinds of states of affairs. A competent agent under suitable circumstances responds to the acquisition of a commitment to flip the light switch by flipping the light switch." Brandom, *Making It Explicit*, 235.

74. Ibid., 363.

75. Cf. Robert Brandom, "Semantik ohne Wahrheit: Ein Interview mit Robert Brandom von Matthias Haase," *Deutsche Zeitschrift für Philosophie* 54, no. 3 (2006): 449–66, here 461 (also in Brandom, *Making It Explicit*, 85–87).

76. Brandom, *Making It Explicit*, 383

77. Ibid., 157–59.

78. Brandom, *Articulating Reasons*, 163–65.

79. Brandom, "Semantik ohne Wahrheit," 451.

80. Jürgen Habermas, *Wahrheit und Rechtfertigung: Philosophische Aufsätze* (Frankfurt: Suhrkamp, 1999), 141.

81. Robert Brandom, *Tales of the Mighty Dead: Historical Essays in the Metaphysics of Intentionality* (Cambridge: Harvard University Press, 2002), 12.

82. Here, Kant writes: "Our common language already contains everything that transcendental philosophy draws out with effort.—These categories are already all contained in us, for without them no experience would be possible." Immanuel Kant, *Metaphyik Mrongovius*, in *Lectures on Metaphysics*, ed. and trans. Karl Ameriks and Steve Naragon (Cambridge: Cambridge University Press, 1997), 109–286, here 185.

83. Kant: "E.g., snow has fallen. Herein lies that snow is, substance, fallen means an accident, upon the earth means an influence, that is, action (*actio*) thus belongs to cause

(*causa*). Today refers to time, fallen to space." Kant, *Metaphysik Mrongovius*, 185. In the postscript of the *Lectures on Metaphysics (Recorded by Pölitz)*, Kant describes an analysis of categories as a "*transcendental grammar*, which contains the ground of human language; e.g., how the present (*praesens*), perfect (*perfectum*), past perfect (*plusquamperfectum*), lies in our understanding, what adverbs (*adverbia*) are, etc." Immanuel Kant, *Metaphysik* L_2 *(1790–1791)*, in *Lectures on Metaphysics*, ed. and trans. Karl Ameriks and Steve Naragon (Cambridge: Cambridge University Press, 1997), 299–354, here 340.

84. Brandom, *Making It Explicit*, 636.
85. See, for example, Brandom, *Reason in Philosophy: Animating Ideas* (Cambridge: Harvard University Press, 2009), 117–19; Brandom, *Making It Explicit*, 89.
86. Cf. Žižek, *The Sublime Object of Ideology* (London: Verso, 1989), 2–3, 121–24. Cf. also Judith Butler, "'Conscience Doth Make Subjects of Us All' Althusser's Subjection," in *The Psychic Life of Power: Theories in Subjection* (Stanford: Stanford University Press, 1997), 106–31.
87. Althusser describes this as a "double constitution." Cf. Louis Althusser, "Ideology and Ideological State Apparatuses," in *On the Reproduction of Capitalism: Ideology and Ideological State Apparatuses*, trans. G. M. Goshgarian (London: Verso, 2014), 232–72, here 262.
88. See also the enlightening examples in Bjerre, *Kantian Deeds*, 42–44.
89. "Human beings are intelligibly initiated into this stretch of the space of reasons by ethical upbringing, which instills the appropriate shape into their lives. The resulting habits of thought and action are second nature." John McDowell, *Mind and World* (Cambridge: Harvard University Press, 1996), 84.
90. Education consists of introducing children to an environment that is culturally and linguistically conditioned and as such is the background condition of propositional attitudes. Kant emphasizes this point in different texts, most strongly in the *Pedagogy* and the *Anthropology*, and sparsely in his philosophy of history.
91. Luhmann rejects the idea of metaethics and any foundational theory of morality. Cf. Niklas Luhmann, "Ethik als Reflexionstheorie der Moral," in *Gesellschaftsstruktur und Semantik: Studien zur Wissenssoziologie der modernen Gesellschaft*, 4 vols. (Frankfurt: Suhrkamp, 1989), 3:358–447.
92. Slavoj Žižek, *The Ticklish Subject: The Absent Centre of Political Ontology* (London: Verso, 2000), 19.
93. In these structures of mutual determination, the symbolic statuses of the persons concerned shifts. "It is by reference to the attitudes of others toward the deontic status (attributing a commitment) that the attitude of the one whose status is in question (acknowledging or undertaking a commitment) is to be understood. So all that is required to make sense of the normative significance of the performance as an undertaking of commitment is an account of what it is to take or treat someone as committed to do something." Brandom, *Making It Explicit*, 162–63.
94. Ibid., 601.
95. "This symmetric pair of perspective types, that of attributor and attributee, each maintaining this fundamental normative distinction, is the fundamental social structure

in terms of which communities and communal practice are to be understood. This symmetric *I-thou* social distinction is presupposed by the *I-we* social distinction appealed to by the other kind of construal of intersubjectivity." Brandom, *Making It Explicit*, 601–2.

96. "Norms (in the sense of normative statuses) are not objects in the causal order. . . . What is causally efficacious is our practically taking or treating ourselves and each other as having commitments (acknowledging and attributing commitments)." Ibid., 626.

97. Communication here seems to be oriented toward a regulative realm of ideal and fully "explicit" communication, in which there is nothing left that still needs to be made explicit.

98. Robert B. Pippin, "Rigorism and 'the New Kant,'" in *Kant und die Berliner Aufklärung: Akten des IX. Internationalen Kant-Kongresses*, ed. Volker Gerhardt, Rolf-Peter Horstmann, and Ralph Schumacher (Berlin: De Gruyter, 2001), 313–26.

99. See also Felicitas Munzel, *Kant's Conception of Moral Character: The "Critical" Link of Morality, Anthropology, and Reflective Judgment* (Chicago: University of Chicago Press, 1999); Allen Wood, *Kant's Ethical Thought* (Cambridge: Cambridge University Press, 1999).

100. Caroline Sommerfeld-Lethen, *Wie moralisch werden? Kants moralische Ethik* (Freiburg: Karl Alber, 2005).

101. Zupančič, *Ethics of the Real*, 12.

102. Badiou, *Being and Event*, 434.

103. Cf. Alain Badiou, *Theory of the Subject* (London: Continuum, 2009), 197. See also my article Dominik Finkelde, "Politics of Logic: The Subject as 'Limit of the World' in Wittgenstein and Badiou," *Philosophy Today* (July 2017).

104. Zupančič, *Ethics of the Real*, 58.

105. Ibid., 58.

106. When Kant writes: "The human being must . . . be *educated* to the good" (Anthro. 420), he is talking about cultivating the "good" in the sense of the legal and the ethically established good. Kant points to the paradox that the one who educates the people is still in the "crudity of nature" (Anthro. 420). In the *Pedagogy*, he says explicitly: "Parents usually educate their children merely so that they fit in with the present world, however corrupt it may be" (LP 442). On the other hand he provides the injunction: "However, they [the parents] ought to educate them better, so that a future, better condition may thereby be brought forth" (LP 442).

107. McDowell, *Mind and World*, 78–79.

108. Ibid., 27–34, 92–93.

109. Aristotle, *Nicomachean Ethics*, ed. and trans. Roger Crisp (Cambridge: Cambridge University Press, 2000), book 6.5, 1140a24–1140b19.

110. Cf. Bjerre, *Kantian Deeds*, 44.

111. This power is, as I have mentioned before, being awarded to the judge by the symbolic order, as an incarnation of his authority's lawfulness. He refers to certain specifications of legal traditions, but then has to overcome this tradition to put his verdict

into effect. In the *Philosophy of Right*, Hegel describes this paradox by means of jurisprudence (*Rechtssprechung*), of which he says that moments of contingency in it are "in themselves necessary (*selbst notwendig*)." Hegel: "There is essentially one aspect of law and the administration of justice which is subject to contingency, and this derives from the fact that the law is a universal determination which has to be applied to the individual case. If one were to object to this contingency, the objection would be merely abstract. For example, the magnitude of a punishment cannot be made to correspond with any conceptual definition, and whatever is decided will in this respect always be arbitrary. But this contingency is itself necessary" (PhR §214A/p. 246).

112. Jeffrey Stout mentions the Rosa Parks case in Stout, *Democracy and Tradition* (Princeton: Princeton University Press, 2004), 216–18, and approaches this very question. Referring to Burke and Paine, he describes an "ethical perception" regarding "noninferential moral perceptions." His interpretation thus corresponds to the one I am presenting with the help of Kant. Stout writes: "There are also noninferential moves in which a participant in the practice responds to something he or she observes by becoming committed to a perceptual judgment or claim. That a judgment was arrived at noninferentially does not guarantee its truth. Many such judgments turn out to have been mistaken. . . . Observation is an indispensable source of knowledge, but a fallible one. Because things are not always what they seem." Ibid., 217–18. Unfortunately, Stout underestimates the moment of contingency. When he writes that "things are not always what they seem," this is because in a modal network of normativity, things can be overwritten retrospectively by an indefinite future.

113. Cf. Judith Butler's comments on the case of Rosa Parks, in Butler, *Excitable Speech: A Politics of the Performative* (New York: Routledge, 1997), 141–43.

114. Cf. Pinkard, "Tugend, Moral und Sittlichkeit: Von Maximen zu Praktiken," *Deutsche Zeitschrift für Philosophie* 49, no. 1 (2001): 65–87; cf. also Menke's article "Autonomie und Befreiung," *Deutsche Zeitschrift für Philosophie* 58, no. 5 (2010): 675–94.

115. Cf. Robert Pippin, *Hegel's Practical Philosophy: Rational Agency as Ethical Life* (Cambridge: Cambridge University Press, 2008), 97–99.

116. Similar to Heidegger's "the one" (*das Man*), Lacan is interested in the transcendental structure of subjectivity as depending on predisposed obedience. Lacan develops his own term for this: *le sujet supposé savoir*. Cf. Lacan, "The Function and Field of Speech and Language in Psychoanalysis," in *Écrits*, trans. Bruce Fink (New York: Norton, 2006), 197–268, here 267n41. For Lacan, the *sujet supposé savoir* is (among other things) a virtual fiction to satisfy collective illusions. Especially in situations where the individual is insecure about the assessment of normativity, as in the conflict surrounding Rosa Parks, she can usually count on the established "praxis," since everyone in turn counts on *her*. Here the *sujet supposé savoir* is a kind of virtual machine always present. Praxis thus partially appears as a pseudo-inferentialist semantics of error and virtuality. Normativity thus gets its meaning by a resigned acceptance of its validity with a meaning having been long lost. The *sujet supposé savoir* stands for a pseudojustified culture of (blind) rule-following for a stress-reducing management of conflicts. The *sujet supposé savoir* is the intuited reference to an anonymous mass of

believers who seek shelter in the illusion of others/of the Other. If this exact belief becomes vulnerable in times of political crises, it becomes obvious in how far the patina of collective unanimity through purely contingent moments of a permanently outsourced trust in others was wrong.

117. Everything depends on the wording of the respective maxim. A racist maxim could be tested as followed. May I deny a human being a seat because her skin is black? No, because a racist treatment contradicts a reasonable equal treatment of all human beings, which I, as a member of the human race, must demand. However, another maxim could be: May a member of a certain ethnicity challenge the seat of the member of another ethnicity's member, where every ethnicity has its own seats? This maxim cannot be immediately accused of racism.
118. Slavoj Žižek, "The 'Fake' Mandela Memorial Interpreter Said It All," *Guardian*, December 16, 2013.
119. Ibid.
120. Any understanding of the "excessive subject," as represented for example by Molly Anne Rothenberg in her social-philosophical study *The Excessive Subject: A New Theory of Social Change* (New York: Polity, 2010), makes the mistake of not realizing that excessive subjectivity can be understood only formal-logically. Excessive subjectivity is a structuring principle of the ethical, which does *not* mean that the subject *itself* sees itself as a purely formal-logical one. Talking about the excessive subject as Rothenberg does runs the risk of not being able to explain what is supposed to be ethical per se in the excess.
121. Thus, citizens in industrialized, consumption-oriented societies may already suspect that they will be pronounced guilty by a future generation for the overexploitation of natural resources. But this suspicion of a future claim may still stay so virtual that it will not change the overall structure of consumption-oriented living conditions for a radical correction here and now. One "suspects" that one will be guilty before a future "scorekeeper," without this suspicion changing one's own "score" significantly.
122. Thomas Nagel distinguishes prima facie between objective and neutral reasons ("agent-neutral"), on the one hand, which as moral reasons apply to everyone, and subjective, particular reasons ("agent-relative"), on the other, which are led by self-interest and do not apply to everyone. Cf. Thomas Nagel, *The View from Nowhere* (New York: Oxford University Press, 1989), chap. 9, "Ethics," pp. 164–88.
123. Terry Lovell, "Resisting with Authority: Historical Specificity: Agency, and the Performative Self," *Theory, Culture, and Society* 20, no. 1 (2003): 1–17.
124. Ibid., 10.
125. Georg Wilhelm Friedrich Hegel, *Lectures on the Philosophy of World History*, vol. 1, *Manuscripts of the Introduction and the Lectures of 1822–1826*, ed. and trans. Robert F. Brown and Peter C. Hodgson (Oxford: Oxford University Press, 2001), 175.
126. Georg Wilhelm Friedrich Hegel, *Lectures on the Philosophy of World History*, trans. H. B. Nisbet (Cambridge: Cambridge University Press, 1984), 83.
127. Badiou, *Being and Event*, 180–81.

128. Klinger: "Positing and measurement are the *that* and the *what* of the judgment (*Setzung und Anmessung sind das* Dass *und das* Was *des Urteils*)." Florian Klinger, *Urteilen* (Zurich: Diaphanes, 2011), 205.

129. Robert Pfaller, *On the Pleasure Principle in Culture: Illusions Without Owners* (London: Verso, 2014).

130. Martin Heidegger, *Beiträge zur Philosophie (Vom Ereignis)*, in *Gesamtausgabe*, vol. 65 (Frankfurt: Klostermann, 1989), §267, "*Das Seyn*," pp. 470–71. For Heidegger, the event corresponds to an inherent groundlessness, which essentially has to do with what he tries to describe as the being or the essence of the event. The event as concept depicts the transition between being and not being. Otto Pöggeler diagnoses the motif of suddenness, of "decision power" (*Entschlussmächtigkeit*), in Heidegger's theory of the event. According to Pöggeler, it shapes Heidegger's fascination with "kairologist characters" (Otto Pöggeler), in contrast to a "chronological" understanding of Being. This affects Heidegger's early Freiburg lecture *The Phenomenology of Religious Life*, concerning St. Paul, but also his comments on Augustine, Luther, and Kierkegaard are affected by this issue. Cf. also Otto Pöggeler, "Sein als Ereignis," *Zeitschrift für philosophische Forschung* 13, no. 4 (1959): 597–632.

131. Heidegger, *Beiträge zur Philosophie (Vom Ereignis)*, §267, "*Das Seyn*," pp. 470–71.

132. The theory of excessive subjectivity is not to be misunderstood as an ethics of "individual particularity," as it can be exposed in the works of Emmanuel Levinas or Jacques Derrida. It is not about giving more attention to the uniqueness of the individual person or to "friendship" and "dialogue" in theory. Cf. Jacques Derrida, "The Politics of Friendship," *Journal of Philosophy*, 85, no. 11 (1988): 632–44; Emmanuel Levinas, *Ethics and Infinity: Conversations with Philippe Nemo* (Pittsburgh: Duquesne University Press, 1995). Cf. also Simon Critchley, *The Ethics of Deconstruction: Derrida and Levinas* (Oxford: Blackwell, 1992); Richard Kearney, "Derrida and the Ethics of Dialogue," *Philosophy and Social Criticism* 19, no. 1 (1993): 1–14. Concepts like "friendship" (Derrida), "face" (Levinas), and "caring justice" are not combinable with excessive subjectivity.

133. Cf. Žižek, *The Sublime Object*, 58–60.

134. Žižek understands the dialectic as the "science of how-the-necessity-follows-the-contingency."

135. A defining quotation by Kant can be found in the *Religion* text: "We cannot see through to the latter [the disposition] but must at best infer it from the consequence that it has on the conduct of our life. And since our inference is drawn from perceptions that are only appearances of a good or bad disposition, our inference never reveals with any certainty especially the *strength* of the disposition, least of all when, in the face of impending death, we think that we have improved ours" (Rel. 112).

136. See also Bjerre, *Kantian Deeds*, 124.

137. This is the opinion of Caroline Sommerfeld-Lethen in her article "Motiva auxiliaria," in *Was ist und was sein soll: Natur und Freiheit bei Immanuel Kant*, ed. Udo Kern (Berlin: De Gruyter, 2007), 287–300, here 297.

138. For a general theory of the performative in the context of generating law, see Sabine Müller-Mall, *Performative Rechtserzeugung: Eine theoretische Annäherung* (Weilerswist-Metternich: Velbrück, 2012).
139. Cf. Michael Albrecht, "Kants Maximenethik und ihre Begründung," *Kant-Studien* 85 (1994): 129–46, here 137.
140. In Christian Wolff's philosophy, maxims are unconscious behavioral rules that are yet to be discovered. In contrast, Baumgarten understands maxims as behavior rules in the sense of the Aristotelian *hexis*, which one gets into the habit of doing. On this point, cf. Rüdiger Bubner, *Handlung, Sprache und Vernunft: Grundbegriffe praktischer Philosophie* (Frankfurt: Suhrkamp, 1982), 199–200. Bubner and Urs Thurnherr see Baumgarten as a forerunner of Kant. See Urs Thurnherr, *Die Ästhetik der Existenz: Über den Begriff der Maxime und die Bildung von Maximen bei Kant* (Tübingen: Francke, 1994). Kant's concept of the maxim differs from Wolff's by the aspect of awareness.
141. Cf. Sommerfeld-Lethen, "Motiva auxiliaria," 296.
142. If we want to understand the relationship between moral proficiency (*Fertigkeit*) and moral action allegorically as the relationship between ground (= the "top soil" in which the proficiencies grow) and a flower (= the moral action) that grows out of the ground, then Kant inverts that relationship: the beautiful pseudoflower (= pseudomoral action) retrospectively allows a good ground to grow; ground is here understood as inner disposition. How that is supposed to work Kant does not say.
143. *Dasein* in its thrownness (*Geworfenheit*) is afraid of the choice between living options, but it can even be more afraid of *not* choosing its options; this tension of an angst-driven uncertainty between different drafts of identity defines *Dasein*. Cf. Martin Heidegger, *Being and Time*, trans. John Macquarrie and Edward Robinson (Oxford: Blackwell, 1962), §§39–44.
144. Kant's reply to Reinhold is in the *Metaphysic of Morals*: "But freedom of choice cannot be defined—as some have tried to define it—as the ability to make a choice for or against the law (*libertas indifferentiae*), even though choice as a *phenomenon* provides frequent examples of this in experience" (MM 380).
145. In the *Religion* text, Kant writes: The "freedom of the power of choice has the characteristic, entirely peculiar to it, that it cannot be determined to action through any incentive *except so far as the human being has incorporated it into his maxim* (has made it into a universal rule for himself, according to which he wills to conduct himself); only in this way can an incentive, whatever it may be, coexist with the absolute spontaneity of the power of choice (of freedom)" (Rel. 73).
146. Moral acts, even all of them in the entire history of mankind, can have been motivated, according to Kant, pathologically. With this line of thought Kant emphasizes that morality cannot be granted with empirical and scientific evidence.
147. In his philosophy of history, Kant suggests that from the indications of progress in history, the human being might read that there are like-minded people.
148. Esser, *Eine Ethik für Endliche*, 145.

149. Wood, *Kant's Ethical Thought*; Martha Nussbaum, "Non-Relative Virtues: An Aristotelian Approach," *Midwest Studies in Philosophy* 13 (1988): 32–53; Martha Nussbaum, *Vom Nutzen der Moraltheorie für das Leben* (Vienna: Passagen, 1997); Martha Nussbaum, "Virtue Ethics: A Misleading Category?," *Journal of Ethics* 3 (1999): 163–201; Onora O'Neill, *Tugend und Gerechtigkeit: Eine konstruktive Darstellung des praktischen Denkens* (Berlin: Akademie, 1996); Sherman, *Making a Necessity of Virtue.*
150. Esser, *Eine Ethik für Endliche*, 17.
151. The question of consistency in Kant's ethics challenges many scholars to resolve its tensions through a genealogical determining of the *Rechtslehre* in relation to Kant's *Grundlagenschriften*. Such a genealogy is controversial. Otfried Höffe presents an understanding of an early development of Kant's philosophy of law. Höffe, *Immanuel Kant: Metaphysische Anfangsgründe der Rechtslehre* (Berlin: Akademie, 1999), 1–18. This contrasts with the interpretation of Reinhard Brandt, "Das Erlaubnisgesetz, oder: Vernunft und Geschichte in Kants Rechtslehre," in *Rechtsphilosophie der Aufklärung*, ed. Brandt (Berlin: De Gruyter, 1982), 233–85. See also Ralf Ludwig, *Kategorischer Imperativ und Metaphysik der Sitten: Die Frage nach der Einheitlichkeit von Kants Ethik* (Frankfurt: Lang, 1992), 161–62; and Gerold Prauss, *Moral und Recht im Staat nach Kant und Hegel* (Freiburg: Alber, 2008), 15–18.
152. Esser: "Many cases of so-called 'moral dilemmas' result from a misinterpretation of the Kantian ability to determine the will. In the Anglo-Saxon debate, this is expressed in the thought—attributed to Kant—of 'ought implies can,' where the 'can' is understood as an ability of the actor to realize. Now, at any time, there can be empirical circumstances beyond the responsibility of the actor that defeat the actor's ability to implement his morally good intention. That this does not pose an ethical problem can be made very clear in Kant." Esser, *Eine Ethik für Endliche*, 144*n*14.
153. As Christine Korsgaard emphasizes in her widely received article "The Right to Lie: Kant on Dealing with Evil," *Philosophy and Public Affairs* 15, no. 4 (1986): 325–49, Kant does not see a difference between the maxim of an act and the execution of an act. If I cannot save a human from drowning because I cannot swim or I am too far away, then I am not bound morally. The moral maxim always implies the correct reading of a situation, which decides if duty calls on me or not.
154. For the "Doctrine of Right," see Karl Heinz Ilting, "Gibt es eine kritische Ethik und Rechtsphilosophie Kants?," *Archiv für Geschichte der Philosophie* 63, no. 3 (1981): 325–45.
155. Cf. Michael Städtler, *Kant und die Aporetik moderner Subjektivität: Zur Verschränkung historischer und systematischer Momente im Begriff der Selbstbestimmung* (Berlin: Akademie, 2011), 286.
156. Städtler sums up Kant's aporias very well: "Kant wants to hold on to the basic singularity of the categorical imperative, which is only conceivable separated from all purposes, and at the same time, he wants to justify a certain plurality of purposes, which directly follow from the categorical imperative. . . . In other words, Kant is looking for

the *principium individuationis* of the pure doctrine of morality." Städtler, *Kant und die Aporetik moderner Subjektivität*, 287.

157. Ibid., 289.

158. Ibid., 294.

3. HEGEL

1. Charles Taylor, *Hegel* (Cambridge: Cambridge University Press, 1975); Terry Pinkard, *Hegel's Phenomenology: The Sociality of Reason* (Cambridge: Cambridge University Press, 1994); Pippin, *Hegel's Practical Philosophy*; Allen Wood, *Hegel's Ethical Thought* (Cambridge: Cambridge University Press, 1991); John McDowell, *Mind and World* (Cambridge: Harvard University Press, 1996).
2. Dieter Henrich, *Hegel im Kontext* (Frankfurt: Suhrkamp, 1971); Ludwig Siep, *Hegel's "Phenomenology of Spirit,"* trans. Daniel Smyth (Cambridge: Cambridge University Press, 2000); Herbert Schnädelbach, *Hegels praktische Philosophie* (Frankfurt: Suhrkamp, 2000); Vittorio Hösle, *Hegels System* (Hamburg: Meiner, 1987); Axel Honneth, *Leiden an Unbestimmtheit: Eine Reaktualisierung der Hegel'schen Rechtsphilosophie* (Stuttgart: Reclam, 2001); Jürgen Habermas, *Knowledge and Human Interest*, trans. Jeremy J. Shapiro (Boston: Beacon, 1971); Christoph Menke, *Tragödie im Sittlichen: Gerechtigkeit und Freiheit nach Hegel* (Frankfurt: Suhrkamp, 1996).
3. Cf. Jürgen Habermas, "The Crisis of the Critique of Knowledge," in *Knowledge and Human Interest*, 11–58. In Habermas's reading of Hegel, individual subjectivity remains subordinate to an abstract absolute subjectivity.
4. Georg Wilhelm Friedrich Hegel, *Philosophie des Rechts: Vorlesungsnachschrift H. G. Hotho*, in *Vorlesungen über Rechtsphilosophie, 1818–1831*, 3. vols., ed. Karl Heinz Ilting (Stuttgart-Bad Cannstatt: Frommann Holzboog, 1994), 3:501.
5. Hegel, *Philosophie des Rechts: Vorlesungsnachschrift H.G. Hotho*, 3:485.
6. Ibid.
7. Cf. Ludwig Siep, "Kehraus mit Hegel? Zu Ernst Tugendhats Hegelkritik," *Zeitschrift für philosophische Forschung* 34, nos. 3–4 (1981).
8. Zhi-Hue Wang, *Freiheit und Sittlichkeit* (Würzburg: Königshausen und Neumann, 2003), 194.
9. Ludwig Siep, "Hegel über Moralität und Wirklichkeit: Prolegomena zu einer Auseinandersetzung zwischen Hegel und der Realismusdebatte in der modernen Metaethik," *Hegel-Studien* 42 (2007): 11–30, here 18. Charles Taylor writes: "The crucial characteristic of Sittlichkeit is that it enjoins us to bring about what already is. This is a paradoxical way of putting it, but in fact the common life which is the basis of my sittlich obligation is already there in existence. It is in virtue of its being an ongoing affair that I have these obligations; and my fulfillment of these obligations is what sustains it and keeps it in being. Hence in Sittlichkeit, there is no gap between what ought to be and what is, between Sollen and Sein." Taylor, *Hegel*, 376.
10. Siep, "Hegel über Moralität und Wirklichkeit," 19.

11. On the genealogy of "conscience," from a supernatural agency of punishment via Kant's "Achtung vor dem Gesetz" to the superego, see Heinz Kittsteiner, *Die Entstehung des modernen Gewissens* (Frankfurt: Insel, 1991).
12. Ernesto Laclau and Chantal Mouffe, *Hegemony And Socialist Strategy: Towards a Radical Democratic Politics* (London: Verso 2001); Alain Badiou, *The Rational Kernel of the Hegelian Dialectic* (Melbourne: Re-Press, 2011); Žižek, *Tarrying with the Negative: Kant, Hegel, and the Critique of Ideology* (Durham: Duke University Press, 1993); Robert Brandom, *Reason in Philosophy: Animating Ideas* (Cambridge: Harvard University Press, 2009).
13. Cf. Siep, "Hegel über Moralität und Wirklichkeit," 19.
14. Ibid.
15. Cf. Juliane Rebentisch, *Die Kunst der Freiheit: Zur Dialektik demokratischer Existenz* (Berlin: Suhrkamp, 2012), 103.
16. In his book *Freedom's Right*, Axel Honneth presents Hegel as an abundant theorist of the social with respect to the problems just outlined. He shows how Hegel does not try to deduce norms in the tradition of Kant a priori, but derives them from social practices and reproductive conditions. Hegel remains an important source for Honneth, particularly with regard to such topics as societal freedom, family, and the market economy (chapter 2). In contrast to a normative individualism, Honneth develops a concept of societal freedom in which a person can be self-determining only within community. He thus continues a Hegelian reading that is also represented by the neopragmatists of the Pittsburgh School, as mentioned in the chapter on Kant. John McDowell deals with the problem of ethical action in the context of his concept of "second nature." On the basis of Kant's theory that the ego is free in spontaneity, McDowell tries, like Hegel, to conceive a freedom of the subject with an a priori *epistemology*, which does not begin with judgment as to facts, but rather already proves itself at the level of intuitions (*Anschauungen*). Cf. McDowell, *Mind and World*, esp. lectures 3 and 4. With this theory, McDowell tries to establish a connection between an a priori grounded normativity in the Kantian sense and an a posteriori understanding of normativity in Hegel's sense. (In his article "Selbstbestimmende Subjektivität und externer Zwang," John McDowell comments on the dilemma in distinguishing between a first [material] nature and a second [spiritual] nature of man. To counter this dualism he suggests that the world already imposes itself categorically, so to speak, upon the human mind on the level of intuitions. It remains nevertheless unclear if McDowell succeeds in warding off dualism by extending the space of reasons beyond the capacity of judgment onto the Kantian concept of intuition itself. Cf. John McDowell, "Selbstbestimmende Subjektivität und externer Zwang," in *Hegels Erbe und die theoretische Philosophie der Gegenwart*, ed. Christoph Halbig, Michael Quante, and Ludwig Siep [Frankfurt: Suhrkamp, 2004], 184–208, here 206.) For a critical analysis of McDowell, see Mischa Gubeljic, Simone Link, and Patrick Müller, "Nature and Second Nature in McDowell's 'Mind and World,'" in *John McDowell: Reason and Nature: Lecture and Colloquium in Münster 1999*, ed. Marcus Willaschek (Münster: LIT, 2000), 41–49. The two latter-mentioned Hegel interpretations, part of

the more recent receptions by Honneth and McDowell, together with those discussed previously, confirm that a depiction of Hegel as a theorist of *freedom as self-determination* within a community often leads to a neglect of excessive subjectivity. For this mode of subjectivity, as we will show with Antigone and Socrates, can no longer be conceived as departing from freedom as self-determination within a community.

17. Pippin ties the freedom of individuals to institutional and social conditions and claims against Habermas, Theunissen, und Hösle that even the late Hegel had not given up on his theory of social recognition. A subject has to relate to her own free actions essentially through an understanding of social relations. Even inclinations that motivate an action have to demonstrate that they are potentially explicable and imply a "giving of and asking for reasons." Pippin, *Hegel's Practical Philosophy*, 24. Hegel's concept of freedom is based on the concept of responsibility. Gillian Rose states a similar thesis in *Hegel Contra Sociology* (London: Athlone, 1981). She reads Hegel as a proto-Marxist analyst of society whose concept of the absolute includes a self-reflexive questioning of bourgeois-economic premises and thus opens the way for an ever more just society.

18. Ido Geiger, *The Founding Act of Modern Ethical Life: Hegel's Critique of Kant's Moral and Political Philosophy* (Stanford: Stanford University Press, 2007). In his analysis, Geiger neglects the tension between a *societal*-structural noncoincidence (that is, split) and one that is *individually moral.*

19. In recent years, Hegel's Antigone has been the subject (again) of various analyses. Among these are Otto Pöggeler's book *Schicksal und Geschichte: Antigone im Spiegel der Deutungen und Gestaltungen seit Hegel und Hölderlin* (Munich: Wilhelm Fink, 2004). For discussions within a postmodern context, see Stephen E. Wilmer and Audrone Zukauskaite, eds., *Interrogating Antigone in Postmodern Philosophy and Criticism* (Oxford: Oxford University Press, 2010). Similarly, Antigone is the central character and example for a number of feminist debates. The most outstanding ones are Judith Butler, *Antigone's Claim: Kinship Between Life and Death* (New York: Columbia University Press, 2007); Philip J. Kain, "Hegel, Antigone and Women," *Owl of Minerva* 33, no. 2 (2002): 157–77; Christine Battersby, *Phenomenal Woman: Feminist Metaphysics and the Patterns of Identity* (New York: Blackwell, 1998), in particular 103–24.

20. Hegel, *Philosophie des Rechts: Vorlesungsnachschrift H. G. Hotho*, 3:485.

21. Hegel's much-commented-on "world-historic individuals" do not seem to directly enter into the notion of excessive subjectivity that is of interest to us here. Often, Hegel describes such world-historic individuals as leading charismatic personalities, imbued with political power. According to at least Hegel's philosophy of history, these individuals announce, especially in times of upheaval, the "true relationship of the individual to his general substance." Georg Wilhelm Friedrich Hegel, *Vorlesungen über die Philosophie der Weltgeschichte*, ed. Johannes Hoffmeister, vol. 1, *Die Vernunft in der Geschichte* (Hamburg: Meiner, 1994), 90–91. Hegel conceives of them as active and energetic individuals who are able to shake up the ethical life of a society through their assuredness. He calls them the "clear-sighted ones" (PH 30). In the *Encyclopedia's*

Philosophy of Mind, Hegel mentions that upheavals of world-historical significance are the "work of *individuals*" and says these "individuals . . . are *instruments*, and their subjectivity . . . is the empty form of the activity" (PM §551). Alexander the Great, Caesar, and Napoleon: these individuals are organs of the substantial spirit. They pierce the facticity of ethical life, whereby they succeed as "soul-leaders" (PH 31) to assert their freedom against the established consciousness of freedom and so overcome an outdated form of ethical life. What distinguishes such "world-historic individuals" (as Alexander the Great, Caesar, and Napoleon) from excessive subjectivity is that they are representatives of the "symbolic elite." They, too, should be accorded excessive subjectivity, yet it articulates itself in part more within the political doxa rather than eroding this doxa from below, from the realm of what is politically unrepresentable.

22. Cf. Aristotle, *Nicomachean Ethics*, ed. and trans. Roger Crisp (Cambridge: Cambridge University Press, 2000), §1095a.
23. For an analysis of the normative status of institutions in Hegel's theory of ethical freedom, see Frederick Neuhouser, *Foundations of Hegel's Social Theory: Actualizing Freedom* (Cambridge: Harvard University Press, 2000), chaps. 4 and 5.
24. He speaks of a "ridiculous spectacle" (NL 123), which the question attracts.
25. Allen Wood critiques Hegel's interpretation as not justified: cf. Wood, *Hegel's Ethical Thought*, 89–90. Similarly, Christine M. Korsgaard, "Kant's Formula of Universal Law," in *Creating the Kingdom of Ends* (Cambridge: Cambridge University Press, 1996), 77–105, in particular 86, 95.
26. Aristotle, *Nicomachean Ethics*: "Every skill and every inquiry, and similarly every action and rational choice, is thought to aim at some good; and so the good has been aptly described as that at which everything aims" (1094a).
27. Cf. Terry Pinkard, "Virtues, Morality, and *Sittlichkeit*: From Maxims to Practices," *European Journal of Philosophy* 7, no. 2 (1999): 217–39, here 224–25. Pinkard writes: "[Hegel's] reinterpretation of what is at stake . . . in Kantian morality committed him to seeing it not as the union of virtue and *happiness* but as the union of morality and 'particularity' of the 'concept of the will with the particular will.' The 'highest good' would thus be the union of my particular projects . . . without which I could not be an agent at all" (224).
28. What is needed, according to Hegel's numerous pleas for the state, is a cultural space that is always "too narrow," yet at the same time is also the place where this narrowness has an infinite openness.
29. In the *Philosophy of Right*, Hegel distinguishes action from deed by assigning the latter a reflective potential of justification that the action does not yet possess to the same degree. The action corresponds to the "heroic self-consciousness" with Oedipus as its model. It has not yet arrived "to reflect on the distinction between *deed* and *action*, between the external event and the purpose and knowledge of the circumstances" (PR §118). Yet precisely for that reason does the responsible person (Oedipus, for example) accept "responsibility . . . in its entirety" (PR §117).
30. Žižek, *Tarrying with the Negative*, 31.
31. Ibid.

32. Analyzing ethical norms (the prohibition to lie or the prohibition to kill) by *describing* them, as proposed by Anscombe, is an attempt to liberate intrinsic normative contents into contexts and their justifications. See Elizabeth Anscombe, "Modern Moral Philosophy," in *Virtue Ethics*, ed. Roger Crisp and Michael Slote (Oxford: Oxford University Press, 1997).
33. As mentioned, Hegel distinguishes in the *Philosophy of Right* between an action and a deed (PR §117). Deed implies a larger degree of responsibility for the purposes and consequences of the deed.
34. Cf. Miriam Wildenauer, *Epistemologie freien Denkens: Die logische Idee in Hegels Philosophie des endlichen Geistes* (Hamburg: Meiner, 2004), 167–68.
35. Cf., Siep, *Hegel's "Phenomenology of Spirit,"* 132.
36. Ibid., 143.
37. Cf. Geiger, *The Founding Act of Modern Ethical Life*, 39–41.
38. Cf. ibid., 30.
39. For Donald Davidson, this is the basis for the rationale of the "Medea-Principle," which he introduced and which he distinguishes from the "Plato-Principle." We will address this in more detail later. See Donald Davidson, "Two Paradoxes of Irrationality," in *Philosophical Essays on Freud*, ed. Richard Wollheim and James Hopkins (Cambridge: Cambridge University Press, 1982), 289–305.
40. Hegel claims in his *Aesthetics* that the tragedy emerges as "the eternal substance of things . . . victorious in a reconciling way" (Aesth. 2:1199). Yet the reconciliation in Greek tragedy differs fundamentally from that in modern times. Hegel continues: "In Greek tragedy it is eternal justice which, as the absolute power of fate, saves and maintains the harmony of the substance of the ethical order against the particular powers" (Aesth. 2:1230). Because of their respective historical differences, the Greek tragedy is not tragic in the same way as the modern tragedy is.
41. Antigone recognizes her own deed as "sacrilege." By doing so, she takes her fate into her hands, as opposed to Orestes, who passively suffers his tragic guilt.
42. Cf. Menke, *Tragödie im Sittlichen*, 94.
43. At the later level of the tragedy as genre, as Hegel discusses it briefly and together with comedy at the end of the section "Religion in the Form of Art," the unity of the hero with the ethical substance by which it is generated is not of much importance.
44. This reflection is based on the "reconciliation through the spectator's hermeneutic attitude." Klaus Düsing, "Die Theorie der Tragödie bei Hölderlin und Hegel," in *Subjektivität und Freiheit: Untersuchungen zum Idealismus von Kant bis Hegel*, ed. Klaus Düsing (Stuttgart-Bad Cannstatt: Frommann-Holzboog, 2002), 308. It explicates a form of reflection that Antigone as heroic figure does *not* embody.
45. Hegel's Socrates incorporates, as we will see later, an individual's will in its subjective particularity standing against the universality of ethical life. Socrates is unable to share a unified ground of *Sittlichkeit* with his epoch. His freedom is the beginning of "subjective" freedom and thus a guidepost along the path to a new structure of consciousness. With the appearance of comedy and finally of Christendom, the tragic loses the link to the ancient world and in the reconciliation of the divine and the

worldly completely loses its ancient world of heroes. Ultimately, this results in the fact that a tragic modernity with a tragic consciousness, as it was shaped by the ancient Greek, can no longer exist. Cf. Otto Pöggeler, "Hegel und die griechische Tragödie," *Hegel-Studien*, supplement 1 (1964): 285–305.

46. In *Philosophy of Right*, Hegel at times distinguishes between action, deed, and acting-out; yet the concepts are not precisely differentiated from one another.

47. If freedom were only an abstract form/idea without content/matter, then it would be, analogous to matter, completely indeterminate and empty. Therefore it needs individuality as a source of disruption and contingency. If, however, disruption and contingency (*acting-out*, for example) were the *only* source of freedom, then the universal and the absolute and therefore freedom would again be endangered, due to a totalitarian rule of disruption and contingency.

48. The actuality of the ethical community opposes the resistance of an excessive individual will: "it stands leagued with truth against consciousness" (PhS §467). The truth is the objective actuality, as it is generally open to all, "lying open to the light of day" (PhS §467). The ethical consciousness, too, acts out of the ethical life, yet from a side turned away from the public and from the "sun." In this context, Hegel contrasts Oedipus with Antigone in order to illustrate the extent to which Antigone embodies a stronger autonomy through her deed of burying her brother. Oedipus, on the other hand, only suffers autonomy passively, as one beaten down by his blindness. Oedipus becomes innocently guilty by attempting to escape his fate and thereby can be accused of pride. His act lacks consciousness in the sense that he fulfills simply his fate as a passive participant—contrary to his intention. Antigone, however, *recognizes* her "sacrilege." Her deed is not clouded by blindness and passivity, but is the actual deed of a particularity that risks its freedom. Therefore, her ethical consciousness can also "acknowledge its guilt: Because we suffer we acknowledge we have erred" (PhS §470). One could object here that Antigone understands laws only as something that "is" (*Seiend*) and not as laws that she, in the Kantian sense, posits herself. Yet how can she then be the embodiment of freedom? The laws, Hegel says by reconstructing Antigone's understanding of the law, "are" and nothing more: "thus, Sophocles's *Antigone* acknowledges them as the unwritten and infallible law of the Gods. 'They are not of yesterday or today, but everlasting, / Though where they came from, none of us can tell" (PhS §437). Hegel emphasizes explicitly how Antigone is not "conscious" of the origin of the normativity that she defends to her death. The daughter of Oedipus is thus "unconscious" in the proper sense, albeit entirely responsible for her sacrilegious deed. Therefore, Hegel writes, the ethical consciousness that Antigone embodies had "drunk from the cup of substance and has forgotten all the one-sidedness of its ends and peculiar notions, and has, therefore, at the same time drowned in this Stygian water all essentiality of its own, and all independence of the objective, actual world" (PhS §467). Because this ethical consciousness, even as an unconscious, is still one with the ethical substance, it can claim the law of the family, which cannot be relativized. Therefore, Antigone's deed, her unyielding insistence, "manifest[s] only ethical action" (PhS §467). However, "by the deed, therefore, it becomes guilt" (PhS §468). It

does so because, "as a simple ethical consciousness, it has turned to one law, but rejected the other, and this hurt by his actions" (PhS §468). Antigone's deed is then, as Hegel emphasizes, the "actual self," which already indicates the downfall of ancient Greece. Through the deed, the ethical consciousness, which Antigone represents, "initiates the division of itself into itself as the active principle, and into the reality over against it, a reality which, for it, is negative" (PhS §468). In the following paragraphs of the *Phenomenology*, Hegel comes to emphasize the extent to which Antigone represents laws that have sunk "into the waters of forgetfulness" and yet still have their share of the ethical substance. As "the law of weakness and of darkness" (PhS §474), they are subject to the laws of the day, as they shape the polis. However, as the surface of actuality, "which has taken away from the inner world its honour and power" (PhS §474), that is, in the denial of the burial of Polynices, the family was denied its own law; it has also consumed its own essence. And so the polis learns that "its supreme right is a supreme wrong," that its victory over the family and the particular is rather "its own downfall" (PhS §474). Antigone's excessive, unconscious certainty, which cannot even bring the normativity of her maxims "to the daylight," thus reveals to her countervailing power its own lack of substantive actuality. Her certainty is, though "unconscious," powerful enough to undermine the "conscious" law of the community. Her conflict is portrayed as one that at no point promises a solution through a part of the *tertium datur*, and yet still creates a source of the ethical amid the downfall of the polis.

49. Martin Heidegger, "The Greek Interpretation of Human Beings in Sophocles' Antigone," in *Hölderlin's Hymn "The Ister,"* trans. William McNeill and Julia Davis (Bloomington: Indiana University Press, 1996), 51–122.
50. Ibid., 115–16, my emphasis.
51. Ibid., 116.
52. Ibid., 117.
53. Ibid., 118.
54. Davidson develops this principle in his article "Two Paradoxes of Irrationality."
55. Bernard Williams, "Ethical Consistency," in *Problems of the Self* (Cambridge: Cambridge University Press, 1976), 166–86.
56. Dirk Setton, "Das 'Medea-Prinzip': Vom Problem der Akrasia zu einer Theorie des Un-Vermögens," *Deutsche Zeitschrift für Philosophie* 57, no. 1 (2009): 97–117, here 116.
57. Ibid., 117, my emphasis. Sophocles contrasts Antigone's attitude with that of the chorus as an instance of the swaying public. "Lacking the power of the negative, it is unable to hold together and to subdue the riches and varied abundance of the divine life, but lets it all go its own separate ways, and in its reverential hymns it extols each individual moment as an independent god, first one and then another" (PhS §734). Martha Nussbaum sees in the chorus an instance of a compromise between the injured parties "in being faithful to or harmonious with one's sense of worth by acknowledging the tension and disharmony." Martha Nussbaum, *The Fragility of Goodness: Luck and Ethics in Greek Tragedy and Philosophy* (Cambridge: Cambridge University Press, 1986), 81. Additionally, she sees in the chorus an instance of dealing with a

pluralism of values that is oriented toward harmony. Menke, on the other hand, in his critique of Nussbaum, rightly sees the choir purely as a "sign of resigned powerlessness." Menke, *Tragödie im Sittlichen*, 87. In contrast, Antigone's intolerance is precisely politically powerful through the provocation of the collision. Only through the deed as a negative disturbance of equilibrium can the ethical substance realize itself, something that, without this disturbance as "unreal shadow," lacked any potentiality. What from Creon's perspective looks like an absurd clinging to cults of the underworld and a journey by Antigone into the past is in fact, for Hegel, a path to the future. Similarly, we will see how Lacan exposes the unconscious, in the tradition of Freud, in a form of temporality from which the unconscious, with its repressions from the past, reveals itself only from the future. The unconscious past, and this is what is indeed symbolized by the gods whose norms Antigone preserves, receives its meaning essentially from the future. Only from the future will the unconscious "will have been," as Lacan writes (S.I 158). The meaning of the present will be constructed for the unconscious only retrospectively. The misperception is a condition for the subsequent form of consciousness. In his interpretation of Socrates, Hegel will then identify the particular not only as the actual breaking point of antiquity, but also as the principle of subjectivity. The transition to the Roman "legal order" is thus paved according to the narrative of the *Phenomenology*. Viewed from any future level of consciousness, the "ethical worldview" appears as a failure due to an excessive subjectivity through which the tragic articulates itself. "The ethical world showed its fate and its truth to be the Spirit that had merely passed always in it, the *individual self*" (PhS §596). Individuality was "isolated." Yet as such, it enables the next step in the development. Hegel therefore aptly writes at the beginning of the chapter on education: "But the existence of this world, as also the actuality of self-consciousness, rests on the process in which the latter divests itself of its personality, thereby creating its world" (PhS §488).

58. See Tilo Wesche, "Wissen und Wahrheit im Widerstreit: Zu Hegels Theorie der Tragödie," in *Die Philosophie des Tragischen: Schopenhauer, Schelling, Nietzsche*, ed. Lore Hühn and Philipp Schwab (Berlin: De Gruyter, 2011), 297–318, here 299.

59. Ibid., 300.

60. See Hilary Putnam, "Values and Norms," in *The Collapse of the Fact/Value Dichotomy, and Other Essays* (Cambridge: Harvard University Press, 2002), 111–34; Jürgen Habermas, *Wahrheit und Rechtfertigung: Philosophische Aufsätze* (Frankfurt: Suhrkamp, 1999); Hilary Putnam, "Antwort auf Jürgen Habermas," in *Hilary Putnam und die Tradition des Pragmatismus*, ed. Marie-Luise Raters and Marcus Willaschek (Frankfurt: Suhrkamp, 2002), 306–21.

61. Robert Pippin sees *Antigone* as questioning the strict dichotomy between norms and values. See Pippin, "The Conditions of Value," in *The Practice of Value (Berkeley Tanner Lectures)*, ed. Joseph Raz and R. Jay Wallace (Oxford: Oxford University Press, 2005), 86–105.

62. How to understand Hegel's last form of consciousness at the end of *Phenomenology*, called "absolute knowing," which clearly and explicitly evokes a knowledge in the absolute, continues to be part of a very controversial debate up to today. Charles

Taylor claims that the final chapter has "meaning only as a recapitulation of the rest." Taylor, *Hegel*, 214. Donald Verene considers those final pages "among the dullest [Hegel] ever wrote." Donald Verene, *Hegel's Absolute: An Introduction to Reading the "Phenomenology of Spirit"* (Albany: State University of New York Press, 2007), 74. Žižek, in turn, writes: "Absolute Knowing is the final recognition of a limitation which is 'absolute' in the sense that it is not determinate or particular, not a 'relative' limit or obstacle to our knowledge that we can clearly see and locate as such. It is invisible 'as such' because it is the limitation of the entire field as such—that closure of the field which, from within the field itself (and we are always by definition within it, because in a way this field 'is' ourselves) cannot but appear as its opposite, as the very openness of the field." Slavoj Žižek, *Less Than Nothing: Hegel and the Shadow of Dialectical Materialism* (London: Verso, 2012), 388.

63. Hegel: "The truth . . . of the opposing powers of the content [of knowledge] and of consciousness is the result that both are equally right, and therefore in their antithesis, which is brought about by action, are equally wrong" (PhS §740).

64. Wesche, "Wissen und Wahrheit im Widerstreit," 301.

65. However, in order to do that, Antigone herself needs the universal to find herself recognized as true in the light of the universal. Likewise, the universal needs the recognition of the particular in order to regard itself as legitimized by the particular, which holds, however, less normative power. And this universal now sees for its part its being questioned as a threat to the giving of and asking for reasons. Tilo Wesche emphasizes this point when he writes: "Decay and progress of political institutions and social communities are an expression of a Janus-faced dynamic." Wesche, "Wissen und Wahrheit im Widerstreit," 301.

66. On Korsgaard's reception of Wittgenstein, see, in particular, Korsgaard, "The Origin of Value and the Scope of Obligation," in *The Sources of Normativity* (Cambridge: Cambridge University Press, 1996), 131–66. On this topic, see also Joshua Gert, "Korsgaard's Private Reason Argument," *Philosophy and Phenomenological Research* 64, no. 2 (2002): 303–24.

67. Pippin, "The Conditions of Value," 103, my emphasis.

68. With Honneth, one could call Antigone's tragedy based on her "suffering from indeterminateness."

69. Hegel's concept of conscience at the end of the "Spirit" chapter again takes up aspects of ethical certainty of Antigone in a new constellation. On this, see the insightful article by Dean Moyar, "Urteil, Schluß und Handlung: Hegels logische Übergänge im Argument zur Sittlichkeit," *Hegel-Studien* 42 (2007): 51–79. Moyar contrasts Hegel's concept of conscience with Kant's concept of duty.

70. Against Brandom, one would probably have to say with Hegel: because of an element of irrationality within the rational it will always only become "explicit" behind the back of reason.

71. On this interesting topic, see Frank Ruda, *Hegel's Rabble: An Investigation Into Hegel's Philosophy of Right* (London: Bloomsbury, 2011), esp. chaps. 4–7. Following, among

others, Jacques Rancière, Ruda is interested in the rabble in Hegel as it represents the only social class that fails to develop its own class-consciousness, and as such is not represented at all in the political form of the state.

72. Hegel criticizes the legal structure of the role of the "pater familias." Roman law is an expression of Roman ethical life but in the concept of the "pater familias" it fails within its own achievements (PR §180Z).
73. Insofar as excessive subjectivity incorporates the modal form of contingency, it advocates for something that, because of its nonrepresentation, neither is real nor even seems possible.
74. Dieter Henrich considers Hegel the only philosopher who understands "absolute contingency" as a constitutive part of reality. See Henrich, "Hegels Theorie über den Zufall," in *Hegel im Kontext*, 157–86.
75. Georg Wilhelm Friedrich Hegel, "The Actuality," in SL, 465–505. I owe this reference to Leonard Weiß and his text "Die subjektive Wendung der Substanz bei Hegel" (unpublished manuscript).
76. Karen Ng writes on the topic of contingency in the chapter "Actuality": "Hegel is not attempting to eradicate the contingent, but to think through its contradiction as both groundless and grounded, exposing contingency as one-sided determination of actuality that fails to truly grasp its reflected character." Karen Ng, "Hegel's Logic of Actuality," *Review of Metaphysics* 63, no. 1 (2009): 139–72, here 159.
77. Ibid., 168.
78. The concept of the "viewpoint" is borrowed from Martin Heidegger, *Being and Time*, trans. John Macquarrie and Edward Robinson (Oxford: Blackwell, 1962), §13, where he illustrates an analogous thought.
79. Slavoj Žižek, *Metastases of Enjoyment: On Women and Causality* (London: Verso, 1994), 36.
80. Steven Pinker, *The Better Angels of Our Nature: Why Violence Has Declined* (London: Penguin, 2011).
81. Konrad Utz, *Die Notwendigkeit des Zufalls: Hegels spekulative Dialektik in der Wissenschaft der Logik: ein Entwurf* (Munich: Schöningh, 2001), 305.
82. "The notion of the *actuality of the rational* seems immediately to come up against two objections: one, that ideas and ideals are nothing more than chimeras and philosophy a system of such phantasms, and the other that, conversely, ideas and ideals are much too exquisite to be actual, or again too impotent to acquire for themselves the status of something actual. But the severance of actuality from the idea is popular particularly with that kind of understanding which takes the dreams of its abstractions for something true, and which insists pretentiously on the '*ought*' which it likes to prescribe especially in the sphere of politics—as if the world had been waiting for this to learn how it *ought* to be, but is not. Were it as it ought to be, what would the precociousness of such 'ought' come to?" ESL §6/p. 34.
83. Socrates adopted "the doctrine of Anaxagoras that thought, the understanding, is the ruling and self-determining universal" (LHPh 385).

84. With Socrates, the "objective produced through thought is at the same time in and for itself, thus being raised above all particularity of interests and desires, and being the power over them" (LHPh 387).
85. "The Athenians before Socrates were objectively, and not [that is, in a Kantian and Socratic sense] subjectively, moral" (LHPh 388).
86. "The fact that the reality of morality has become shaken in the mind of the people came to consciousness in Socrates; he stands so high because he gave expression to what was present in the times" (LHPh 414).
87. How "certain" can the certainty be with which Socrates defends his claim? Robert Pippin illustrates how far in Hegel the deed of the subject herself can be posited out of an absolute certainty, but nevertheless requires its concrete effect in the social space, in order to provide this very certainty with a retrospective objectivity. Pippin writes: "What Hegel attempts to show in a variety of contexts [in the *Phenomenology*], against a variety of inner-oriented positions, is that we cannot determine what actually *was* a subject's intention or motivating reason by relying on some sort of introspection. . . . Only as manifested or expressed in a social space . . . can one (*even* the subject himself) retrospectively determine what must have been intended." Robert B. Pippin, "Recognition and Reconciliation," in *Internationales Jahrbuch des Deutschen Idealismus*, vol. 2 (Berlin: De Gruyter, 2004), 249–68, here 261.
88. Hegel critiques Kant's moral-philosophical distinction of being and ought, when it does, on the one hand, recognize the concept of a teleological nature, yet localizes the teleology as an infinite one geared toward a goal in the beyond, from which the morally acting subject will necessarily always be cut off as imperfect and pathological. Cf. Karl Ameriks, "Probleme der Moralität bei Kant und Hegel," in *Das Recht der Vernunft: Kant und Hegel über Denken, Erkennen und Handeln*, ed. Christel Fricke, Peter König, and Thomas Peterson (Stuttgart-Bad Cannstatt: Frommann-Holzboog, 1995), 263–89.
89. Arnold Ruge in his essay "Die Hegelsche Rechtsphilosophie und die Politik unserer Zeit (1842)," in *Materialien zu Hegels Rechtsphilosophie*, 2 vols., ed. Manfred Riedel (Frankfurt: Suhrkamp, 1975), 1:323–49; Ernst Tugendhat, *Selbstbewußtsein und Selbstbestimmung* (Frankfurt: Suhrkamp, 1979), esp. 307–8; Michael Theunissen, "Die verdrängte Intersubjektivität in Hegels Philosophie des Rechts," in *Hegels Philosophie des Rechts: Die Theorie der Rechtsformen und ihre Logik*, ed. Dieter Henrich and Rolf-Peter Horstmann (Stuttgart: Klett-Cotta, 1982), 317–81.
90. Ludwig Siep, "Kehraus mit Hegel?," in *Hegel*, ed. Charles Taylor (Cambridge: Cambridge University Press, 1975), 428–64.
91. Karl Rosenkranz, "Apologie Hegels gegen Dr. R. Haym," in *Materialien zu Hegels Rechtsphilosophie*, 2 vol., ed. Manfred Riedel (Frankfurt: Suhrkamp, 1975), 1:395–410; Adriaan Peperzak, "Hegels Pflichten- und Tugendlehre," *Hegel-Studien* 17 (1982): 97–117; Henning Ottmann, *Individuum und Gemeinschaft bei Hegel: Hegel im Spiegel der Interpretationen* (Berlin: De Gruyter, 1977).
92. Cf. Korsgaard, *Creating the Kingdom of Ends*, 65.
93. Cf. Neuhouser, *Foundations of Hegel's Social Theory*, 225, 230, 241.

94. Ludwig Siep: "The individual who insists on following his conscience must admit the one-sidedness and possible error of his or her decisions. And the universal moral consciousness, for its turn, has to recognize . . . the individual decision. And universal moral consciousness must, for its part, acknowledge that individual decisions—even non-conformist and evil ones—form a necessary moment of spirit." Siep, *Hegel's "Phenomenology of Spirit,"* 199.
95. See Dean Moyar, "Urteil, Schluß und Handlung," *Hegel-Studien* 42 (2007): 51–79.
96. Christoph Halbig sees in conscience little more than a primitive form of speculative mediation, which has its epistemological equivalent in Hegel's understanding of "sense-certainty" as exemplified in the *Phenomenology.* And, finally, according to Halbig, Hegel desires to disqualify the conscience as a primitive level of ethical conduct. See Christoph Halbig, "Zur Wahrheit des Gewissens," in *Hegels Phänomenologie des Geistes: Ein kooperativer Kommentar,* ed. Klaus Vieweg and Wolfgang Welsch (Frankfurt: Suhrkamp, 2008), 489–503, here 492.
97. Moyar, "Urteil, Schluß und Handlung," 62.
98. Georg Sans, "Hegels Schlusslehre als Theorie des Begriffs," in *Hegel-Forschungen: Hegels Lehre vom Begriff, Urteil und Schluss,* ed. Andreas Arndt, Christian Iber, and Günter Kruck (Berlin: Akademie, 2006), 216–32, here 219.
99. Moyar, "Urteil, Schluß und Handlung," 64. See also Dean Moyar, *Hegel's Conscience* (Oxford: Oxford University Press, 2011), 139.
100. Moyar, *Hegel's Conscience,* 140.
101. Ibid.
102. Certainty is not oriented toward reasons.
103. Cf. Will Dudley, *Hegel, Nietzsche, and Philosophy: Thinking Freedom* (Cambridge: Cambridge University Press, 2002), 61.
104. Moyar, "Urteil, Schluß und Handlung," 62.
105. I owe this insight to Urs Espeel.
106. While it contains the judgments "A is either B or C or D," and "A is neither C nor D," the judgment B is not the result of a universalizable certainty.
107. See Immanuel Kant, "On a Supposed Right to Lie from Philanthropy," in *Practical Philosophy,* ed. and trans. Mary J. Gregor (Cambridge: Cambridge University Press, 1999), 611–15.
108. Georg Wilhelm Friedrich Hegel, *Vorlesungen über die Geschichte der Philosophie,* in *Werke in zwanzig Bänden,* 20 vols., ed. Eva Moldenhauer and Karl Markus Michel (Frankfurt: Suhrkamp, 1986), 18:512.
109. Klaus Düsing, *Das Problem der Subjektivität in Hegels Logik, Hegel-Studien* (Bonn: Bouvier, 1976), supplement 15, 250.
110. Cf. Slavoj Žižek, *For They Know Not What They Do: Enjoyment as a Political Factor* (London: Verso, 2002), 35–36.
111. Cf. Alain Badiou, *Being and Event,* trans. Oliver Feltham (London: Continuum 2006), 52–60.
112. Klaus Erich Kaehler, "Das Kontingente und die Ausnahme im spekulativen Denken," in *Die Ausnahme denken: Festschrift zum 60. Geburtstag von Klaus-Michael Kodalle in*

zwei Bänden, 2 vols., ed. Claus Dierksmeier (Würzburg: Königshausen und Neumann, 2003), 1:63–71, here 68.

113. Hegel, *Geschichte der Philosophie*, 18:484.

114. Kaehler, "Das Kontingente und die Ausnahme im spekulativen Denken," 69.

115. Smail Rapic, *Ethische Selbstverständigung: Kierkegaards Auseinandersetzung mit der Ethik Kants und der Rechtsphilosophie Hegels* (Berlin: De Gruyter, 2007), 377–78.

116. Ibid., 378.

117. Ibid.

118. Hegel's comments on the soul do not fall behind Kant's critique of the concept of a Cartesian soul substance as paralogism. He does not understand the soul's immateriality as a quality of a certain metaphysical substance. His explications correspond to those of Aristotle, who in *De Anima* (412b5–6) interprets the soul as the first entelechy of a living physical body.

119. Jens Rometsch, *Hegels Theorie des erkennenden Subjekts: Systematische Untersuchungen zur enzyklopädischen Philosophie des subjektiven Geistes* (Würzburg: Königshausen und Neumann, 2008), 114.

120. Hegel: "The actual soul in the *habit* of sensation and of its *concrete* self-feeling is in itself the *ideality* of its determinacies, an ideality that is for itself; in its externality it is *recollected* into itself, and is infinite relation to itself. This being-for-self of free universality is the soul's higher awakening to the *I*, to abstract universality in so far as it is *for* abstract universality, which is thus *thinking* and *subject* for itself, and in fact determinately subject of its judgment in which the I excludes from itself the natural totality of its determinations as an object, as a world *external to it*, and relates itself to that world so that in it it is immediately reflected into itself: *consciousness*" (PM §412). It remains controversial how far Hegel here truly presents the soul's tipping point from its natural state into the cultural state. Dieter Sturma correctly points out that Hegel has always had to view the spirit or the soul's conscience as monistic. Dieter Sturma, "Philosophie der Psychologie," *Journal für Psychologie* 10, no. 1 (2002): 18–39. Markus Gabriel reads Hegel's remarks on the soul as a "discovery of the pathological structure of representation as such: for Hegel there is no subjective space of presentation, that is, no judgmental or logical space in which something can be distinguished from something else, without the psychic monad having moved through a process of pathological splitting." Gabriel, "The Pathological Structure of Representation as Such: Hegel's *Anthropology*," in *Transcendental Ontology: Essays in German Idealism* (London: Continuum, 2011), 48–59, here 49–50. Gabriel understands emotivity as the origin of representation. "When the soul has a sensation (*Empfindung*) of something, it finds (*finden*) this sensation in itself. . . . This internalization is the minimal psychic structure of reference. . . . The soul finds before itself what it senses as something, which is part of it" (52).

121. Dieter Sturma writes aptly: "The unconscious formation of personality is according to Hegel . . . a constant background phenomenon of personal attitudes. In this sense, the unconscious is said to show itself as an instance of universal determinations of behavior. It is not possible [for the individual subject] to explicate these unconscious formations through whatever kind of psychoanalytical processes of self-reflection." Sturma,

"Philosophie der Psychologie," 25. Sturma clarifies convincingly how far Hegel does not interpret the body-soul problem in the sense of an eliminatory reductionism and thus seems to distinguish himself from Schelling. Dieter Sturma, "Hegels Theorie des Unbewussten: Zum Zusammenhang von Naturphilosophie und philosophischer Psychologie," in *Hegel-Jahrbuch 1990*, ed. Heinz Kimmerle and Wolfgang Levèvre (Bochum: Germinal, 1990), 193–201, here 197.

122. Marcia Cavell, *The Psychoanalytic Mind: From Freud to Philosophy* (Cambridge: Harvard University Press, 1993); Sebastian Gardner, *Irrationality and the Philosophy of Psychoanalysis* (Cambridge: Cambridge University Press, 2007).

123. Sturma, "Hegels Theorie des Unbewussten," 199.

124. For Hegel, the soul can still be partially rational, because it knows, for instance, that others consider it mad and that therefore something must be wrong with it. Hegel writes on this point: "they [the deranged] are aware . . . that they are in a lunatic asylum" (PM 117).

125. Christa Hackenesch points to the fact that Hegel does not understand madness as an illness of the body but rather as a *Verrückung* (displacement) between an individual form of consciousness and a historical universal. Hackenesch, "Der subjektive Geist: Hegels Begriff des Menschen," in *Hegel Jahrbuch 2002*, pt. 2, ed. Karol Bal and Henning Ottmann (Berlin: Akademie, 2002), 40–43.

126. See Barbara Merker, "Jenseits des Hirns: Zur Aktualität von Hegels Philosophie des subjektiven Geistes," in *Subjektivität und Anerkennung*, ed. Barbara Merker, Georg Mohr, and Michael Quante (Paderborn: Mentis, 2004), 157–84, here 164. See also Gerhard Gamm, *Der Wahnsinn in der Vernunft: Historische und erkenntniskritische Studie zur Dimension des Anders-Seins in der Philosophie Hegels* (Bonn: Bouvier, 1981), 108–10.

127. See also Hegel's various remarks on habit in the *Philosophy of Right* (for example, §§197, 211).

128. On the historical context out of which Hegel develops his interpretation of the soul, see the article by Michael John Petry, "Systematik und Pragmatik in Hegels Behandlung von animalischem Magnetismus und Verrücktheit," in *Psychologie und Anthropologie oder Philosophie des Geistes*, ed. Franz Hespe and Burkhard Tuschling (Stuttgart-Bad Cannstatt: Frommann-Holzboog, 1991), 250–68.

129. Cf. Catharine Malabou, *The Future of Hegel: Plasticity, Temporality and Dialectic* (London: Routledge, 2005), 70–75.

130. Cf. Malabou on the soul in Hegel: ibid., 32–33. A few pages later, she writes: "Subjectivity does not reside in its own being, it 'haunts' itself. The soul is possessed by the possession of itself" (35).

131. Rometsch, *Hegels Theorie des erkennenden Subjekts*, 104.

132. Ibid.

133. Cf. Gamm, *Der Wahnsinn in der Vernunft*, 138–44.

134. Cf. Marianne Krüll, *Schizophrenie und Gesellschaft: Zum Menschenbild in Psychiatrie und Soziologie* (Frankfurt: Suhrkamp, 1986).

135. If the soul, in its various stages, is increasingly embedded in this function (acting as *me*), it can grasp itself as *positing itself consciously*, which means temporally. While the feeling soul has its moments adjacent in space like uncoordinated partial instincts,

which cannot be sorted *in time*, consciousness is bound together by habit like a haystack, and sees itself essentially located in time. Gamm points out that Hegel cannot sublate the atemporality of the soul in the temporality of consciousness. This means that for Gamm an unconscious remains in Hegel's constellation of the soul, which, because it cannot be tamed within time, unites key aspects of that which Freud and Lacan subsume into the unconscious. Gamm, *Der Wahnsinn in der Vernunft*, 142–44.

136. Cf. Robert Pfaller, *On the Pleasure Principle in Culture: Illusions Without Owners* (London: Verso, 2014).

137. Hans Kreitler and Shulamith Kreitler, *Cognitive Orientation and Behavior* (New York: Springer, 1976), quoted in Gamm, *Der Wahnsinn in der Vernunft*, 135.

138. Cf. Ernesto Laclau, *New Reflections on the Revolution of Our Time* (London: Verso, 1990), 94–95.

4. LACAN

1. Hegel's *Phenomenology* is an often-cited reference particularly for Lacan's theory of desire. Lacan writes in *Seminar X*: "In Hegel, the Other is the one who sees me and this is what, all by itself, kicks off the struggle, according to the foundations wherewith Hegel marks the start of the *Phänomenologie des Geistes*, on the plane of what he calls pure prestige, and it is on this plane that my desire is concerned. . . . Because there's no other path for me to find what I lack as object of my desire. . . . It's the Other as locus of the signifier. . . . It's plainly spelt out in Hegel that he needs the Other so that the Other may acknowledge him, so that he may receive the Other's acknowledgement" (23–24).

2. Cf. Georg Simmel, "The Value of Money as a Substance," in *The Philosophy of Money*, trans. Tom Bottomore and David Frisby (New York: Routledge, 2011), 139–218. Slavoj Žižek, *The Sublime Object of Ideology* (London: Verso, 1989), 31–32.

3. Cf. Joseph Vogl, *The Specter of Capital*, trans. Joachim Redner and Robert Savage (Stanford: Stanford University Press, 2014).

4. Jürgen Habermas, *Postmetaphysical Thinking: Philosophical Essays*, trans. Mark Hohengarten (Cambridge: MIT Press, 1992), 63.

5. Lacan describes the "Real" as a nonrepresentable entity, which precedes any symbolic form and which consequently ensures that the realm of the Symbolic (language, law, knowledge) "is never all." See Lacan's lecture of 1953, which introduces the terminology, "The Symbolic, the Imaginary, and the Real," in *On the Names-of-the Father*, trans. Bruce Fink (Cambridge: Polity, 2015), 1–52. Bruce Fink writes with regard to the Real the following: "Canceling out the real, the symbolic creates 'reality,' reality as that which is named by language and can thus be thought and talked about." Bruce Fink, *The Lacanian Subject Between Language and Jouissance* (Princeton: Princeton University Press, 1995), 25. The category of the Real is one of the key categories in Lacan's philosophy and has been the subject of repeated discussions by scholars. One recent study is Tom Eyers, *Lacan and the Concept of the "Real"* (New York: Palgrave Macmillan, 2012).

6. Cf. Louis Althusser, "Ideology and Ideological State Apparatuses," in *On The Reproduction of Capitalism: Ideology and Ideological State Apparatuses*, trans. G. M. Goshgarian (London: Verso, 2014), 232–72. Žižek, *The Sublime Object of Ideology*, 87–130.
7. Immanuel Kant, *Kritik der reinen Vernunft*, 1st ed., in *Akademieausgabe*, 29 vols. (Berlin: De Gruyter, 1903), 4:165 (A 253).
8. See also Felix Ensslin, "Accesses to the Real: Lacan, Monotheism, and Predestination," *European Journal of Psychoanalysis*, special issue, *Lacan and Philosophy: The New Generation*, 32 (2011): 49–91.
9. Cf. Marcia Cavell, *The Psychoanalytic Mind: From Freud to Philosophy* (Cambridge: Harvard University Press, 1993). In her study of psychoanalysis in recourse to the works of Ludwig Wittgenstein and Donald Davidson, Cavell attempts to support Freud's scientific claim by linguistically tying back psychoanalysis to common-sense psychology. In doing so, she takes a position that Lacan highly questions. Cavell seems to "domesticate" Freud in a similar manner to the earlier-mentioned interpreters of Hegel and Kant by favoring ethics over the excessively ethical. Cavell considers, like John Searle in *The Rediscovery of the Mind* (Cambridge: MIT Press, 1992), esp. chaps. 4 and 5, the unconscious according to Freud's theory as always potentially linguistically decipherable whereas Lacan (as well as Melanie Klein) claims that one cannot ascribe any clear propositional knowledge to the unconscious according to Freud. This in turn makes it impossible to overcome the split subject and ground it in reason and autonomy. Cf. Sebastian Gardner, *Irrationality and the Philosophy of Psychoanalysis* (Cambridge: Cambridge University Press, 2007). For a critique of Cavell, see also David Snelling, *Philosophy, Psychoanalysis and the Origins of Meaning: Pre-Reflective Intentionality in the Psychoanalytic View of the Mind* (Burlington, VT: Ashgate, 2001), esp. 1–22.
10. Kant speaks of the moral law's threatening voice when he writes: "There is something so singular in the boundless esteem for the pure moral law stripped of all advantage—as practical reason, whose voice makes even the boldest evildoer tremble and forces him to hide from its sight" (CPrR 204).
11. What makes psychoanalysis interesting is its position in between modern naturalism and culturalism (or better constructivism). It is not pure biologism (as, for example, the neurosciences), and it does not reductively eliminate the subject via culture. Consequently, it is neither deterministically oriented in the sense that it claims everything in man is predetermined. Nor is it simply freedom-optimistic as expressed in philosophical theories that interpret man's agency and identity (as Korsgaard does, for example) based on a rational self-constitution. Psychoanalysis attempts to conceptualize an in-between space that gives leeway to autonomy but not as something that the subject can access whenever it wants to.
12. Lacan: "The breakthrough is achieved by Kant when he posits that the moral imperative is not concerned with what may or may not be done. To the extent that it imposes the necessity of a practical reason, obligation affirms an unconditional 'Thou shalt.' The importance of this field derives from the void that the strict application of the Kantian definition leaves there. Now we analysts are able to recognize that place as the place

occupied by desire. Our experience gives rise to a reversal that locates in the center an incommensurable measure, an infinite measure, that is called desire" (S.VII 315–16).

13. Desire's unfulfillable insistence on inscribing itself into an order that itself is never absolute and that repeatedly renders itself impossible stands for the inner obstruction of something foreign (Lacan enigmatically calls it the Real) both in the impossibility of the unity and identity of the subject and in the collectively guaranteed political life-world that is never Everything. This means that here, too, the biopolitical dimension of Lacan's theory becomes evident. Cf. the studies by Bernard Baas, who compares Lacan's concept of desire with Kant's concept of the "highest good" in a comparative analysis: Bernard Baas, *Le désir pur: Parcours philosophiques dans les parages de J. Lacan* (Leuven: Peeters, 2002).

14. Lacan radicalizes Freud's discussion of the unconscious by anthropomorphizing the unconscious in his talk of the "subject of the unconscious," as if it were an individual entity on its own inhabiting the subject like a Cartesian ghost in the machine. See S.XI 37. The "subject of the unconscious" is to be understood as the locus of a nonpropositional knowledge that communicates even without a lexically guaranteed language or a clear chronological structure of memory. Various studies on the relationship of psychoanalysis and philosophy examine the question of how to understand a prepropositional knowledge in the unconscious. See, in particular, Snelling, *Philosophy, Psychoanalysis and the Origins of Meaning*; Jonathan Lear, "The Heterogeneity of the Mental," *Mind* 104, no. 416 (1995): 863–79; and Gardner, *Irrationality and the Philosophy of Psychoanalysis.*

15. Sigmund Freud, "Project for a Scientific Psychology," in *Standard Edition of the Complete Works of Sigmund Freud*, 24 vols., trans. James Strachey et al. (London: Hogarth, 1994), 1:283–397.

16. As an example of a nonsemantic core, Lacan refers to Freud's *The Interpretation of Dreams*. Here, Freud speaks of the "navel of a dream"—*The Interpretation of Dreams*, in *Standard Edition*, 4:111—by which he understands the densification in the dream texture, which is impenetrable, a blind spot that, as Freud suggests, the dream needs in order not to be fully transparent to itself. This "navel" of the dream is a structurally necessary void of the dream rebus, from which Lacan unfolds his aporia of subjectivity.

17. Béatrice Longuenesse, "Freud and Philosophy. Kant's 'I' in 'I Ought To' and Freud's Superego," *Aristotelian Society*, supplementary volume 86, no. 1 (2012): 19–39; Sebastian Gardner, "Freud and Philosophy: Psychoanalytic Theory: A Historical Reconstruction," *Aristotelian Society*, supplementary volume 86, no. 1 (2012): 41–60.

18. Lacan's fascination with cybernetics comes to the fore in his second seminar: S.II 294–308. For him, the unconscious is not a person's treasure of individuality but rather a circulation of information loops coming from the external world. Lacan leaves undefined what relationship the subject has to this machinery of the unconscious. On the one hand, it seems to be part of interiority's inner core; on the other hand, it is alienating and foreign as coming from another world: the external world of the big Other.

19. Jacques-Alain Miller, "[The] super-ego supposedly imposes restrictions on the drive by saying no to its satisfaction. . . . [The] super-ego feeds on this surrendered satisfaction which blocks the drive from fulfillment. The super-ego feeds on this satisfaction, secretly." Jacques-Alain Miller, "A Reading of Some Details in Television in Dialogue with the Audience," *Newsletter of the Freudian Field* 4, nos. 1–2 (1990): 4–30, here 14. In addition, Miller lays bare to what extent the moral subject seeks the presence of the Other through the sacrifice of his own pleasure and desire. Consequently, the moral subject does not escape a pathological drive since he receives pathological enjoyment from the very renunciation of the pathological in the "intellectual feeling" ("intellektuelles Gefühl") of what Kant calls "Achtung," that is, "respect" for the Law. Cf. also Jacques-Alain Miller, "A Discussion of Lacan's 'Kant avec Sade,'" in *Reading Seminars I and II: Lacan's Return to Freud*, ed. Richard Feldstein, Bruce Fink, and Maire Jaanus (New York: State University of New York Press, 1996), 212–40.
20. Lacan's term *jouissance* designates a pleasure-in-enjoying-pain that is an inherent part of *Dasein*'s constitution of its own eccentricity and that further develops Freud's concept of the death drive. The longing for full *jouissance* combined with the simultaneous limitation of getting it through the symbolic order keeps the subject, in the final analysis, in a neurotic illusion for absolute pleasure and in a hysterical longing due to its impossibility. On the relationship of *jouissance* and culture, see the illuminating article of Frédéric Declercq, "Lacan's Concept of the Real of Jouissance: Clinical Illustrations and Implications," *Psychoanalysis, Culture and Society* 9, no. 2 (2004): 237–51, esp. 247–51.
21. As Žižek writes so incisively: "The real is impossible in the sense that it is a traumatic encounter that does happen but which we are unable to confront." Slavoj Žižek and Glyn Daly, *Conversations with Žižek* (Cambridge: Polity, 2003), 71.
22. Jacques Lacan, "Compte rendu avec interpolation du séminaire de l'éthique," *Ornicar? Revue du Champ freudien* 28 (1984): 7–18, here 8.
23. Cf. Lorenzo Chiesa, "The Subject of the Real," in *Subjectivity and Otherness: A Philosophical Reading of Lacan* (Cambridge: MIT Press, 2007), 104–39.
24. Freud, "Project for a Scientific Psychology," 312–16.
25. Ibid., 331–32.
26. Ibid., 331.
27. Ibid.
28. Ibid. Analyses of consciousness were a background for Lacan's work in the context of cybernetics and the invention of the Turing machine. In his *Seminar II*, Lacan speaks repeatedly of the unconscious as a machine. Cf. also Nicolas Langlitz, *Die Zeit der Psychoanalyse: Lacan und das Problem der Sitzungsdauer* (Frankfurt: Suhrkamp, 2005), 158–59.
29. This means, however, that man is also predestined to strike out against the "hallucinations" of the Other and others. The Other as "thing" is, for Lacan, also the source of the desires that are injected under the child's skin as something enigmatic straight from birth and that predestine a "false reality" for her. Lacan says: "The *Ding* is the

element that is initially isolated by the subject in his experience of the *Nebenmensch* as being by its very nature alien, *Fremde*" (S.VII 52).

30. Slavoj Žižek, *Less Than Nothing: Hegel and the Shadow of Dialectical Materialism* (London: Verso, 2012), 543.

31. To some extent, these motifs are also present in Kant and Hegel. Kant's pedagogy, for example, links the training of morality to the coercive subjection of the individual through forced education. Kant would reject the idea of a split psyche as a transcendental-philosophical contradiction of his image of man. Hegel's partially phenomenological analyses in his *Anthropology* show for their part how the psyche develops out of processes of tension with the external world.

32. In this sense we refer to an argument between Walter Benjamin and Gershom Scholem on the topic of "validity without meaning," a reference that will be fleshed out in more detail. For it is precisely this "validity without meaning" that qualifies Freud's energy quanta that, in turn, define the psyche as a libido-dependent compromise of its detailed structure with regard to the external world.

33. Hilary Putnam arrives at a similar insight, even if in a different philosophical and expertise-specific context—that of analytical ethics. He considers, following Wittgenstein, a dichotomy of fact and value judgments impossible, since humans always learn language through the values, for example, of ones parents. This means that even on the lowest training level of language there exists a microscopic libidinal economy that links facts with values—or with regard to Freud—that links facts with libidinal energy. "That is good"; "You did that well"; "That was said correctly"; and so on. Psychoanalysis anchors this libidinal economy in the mixing of facts and values in judgments also in fetishism: here a certain object can leave person A cold, while it drives person B to a chain of actions, behaviors, and rituals. This comes about only because in the libidinal osmosis of both persons the object does not play the same role. Cf. Hilary Putnam, "Fact and Value," in Reason, Truth, and History (Cambridge: Cambridge University Press, 1981), 127–49.

34. It should be mentioned here, that the "Ding" for Lacan also represents the phantasma of an ineffable fullness of pleasure beyond "reality." It represents a pseudo-fullness of pleasure, which the individual had to sacrifice in the form of a forced choice in the moment of her becoming-a-subject. The Ding lies phantasmatically beyond the wall of language and of libidinal desire, just as in Kant's theory of knowledge the "Ding an sich" functions as the condition of knowledge of phenomena. Lacan calls the Ding explicitly the "beyond-of-the-signified" (S.VII 54). Just as for Kant the "Ding an sich" opens up the limits of understanding as the condition of the possibility of perceiving phenomena in the context of their veridicality (without that the *thing-in-itself* becomes veridical too), so for Lacan the Ding stands phantasmatically for the condition of the possibility of a libidinal desire for more, a desire that permanently prolongs itself. Lacan does not use the concept of the Ding to refer to an individual object, but "rather expands it," as Peter Welsen writes, "onto the totality of that which is [*das Seiende*]," whereby it, the Ding, "bestows upon the law of language the characteristic of an otherness that can never be caught up with." Peter Welsen, "Die Ethik des rechten Sprechens.

Zur Frage der Verantwortung bei Jacques Lacan," *Zeitschrift für philosophische Forschung* 42, no. 4 (1988): 682–93, here 689.

35. Louis Althusser, "On Ideology," In *On The Reproduction of Capitalism: Ideology and Ideological State Apparatuses*, trans. G. M. Goshgarian (London: Verso, 2014), 171–208, here 176.

36. Karl Marx: "Morality, religion, metaphysics, and all the rest of ideology as well as the forms of consciousness corresponding to these thus no longer retain the semblance of independence. They have no history, no development; but men, developing their material production and their material intercourse, alter, along with this their actual world, also their thinking and the products of their thinking. It is not consciousness that determines life, but life that determines consciousness." Karl Marx, *The German Ideology: Including Theses on Feuerbach and introduction to the Critique of Political Economy* (New York: Prometheus, 1998), 42.

37. Hegel already critiques such a belief in a "world-neutral" subject when he mentions in his *Phenomenology* the student-teacher relationship. Žižek interprets this relationship fittingly in his book *Tarrying with the Negative*, when he writes: "The example . . . is of Hegel himself, to say that a pupil at the beginning of the process of education is somebody who potentially knows, somebody who, in the course of his development, will realize his creative potentials, *equals saying* that these inner potentials must be present from the very beginning in external actuality as the authority of the Master who exerts pressure upon his pupil. . . . We can see, now, why Hegel is as far as possible from the evolutionist notion of the progressive development of in-itself into for-itself: the category of 'in itself' is strictly correlative to 'for us,' i.e. for some consciousness external to the thing-in-itself." Žižek, *Tarrying with the Negative: Kant, Hegel, and the Critique of Ideology* (Durham: Duke University Press, 1993), 142.

38. Althusser, "On Ideology," 192.

39. Ibid., 188.

40. Ibid., 173n.

41. Ibid., 189.

42. Ibid., 190.

43. Terry Eagleton, *The Ideology of the Aesthetic* (Oxford: Blackwell, 2000), 63.

44. Immanuel Kant, "On Taste as a Kind of *Sensus Communis*," in CPJ 173/§40.

45. Eagleton, *The Ideology of the Aesthetic*, 17.

46. Ibid., 21.

47. A quote from Kojève makes this legacy clearer: "Anthropogenic Desire is different from animal Desire . . . in that it is directed, not toward a real, 'positive,' given object, but toward another Desire. Thus, in the relationship between man and woman, for example, Desire is human only if the one desires, not the body, but the Desire of the other; . . . Now, to desire a Desire is to want to substitute oneself for the value desired by this Desire. For without this substitution, one would desire the value, the desired object, and not the Desire itself. Therefore, to desire the Desire of another is in the final analysis to desire that the value that I am or that I 'represent' be the value desired by the other: I want him to 'recognize' my value as his value, I want him to 'recognize'

me as an autonomous value." Alexandre Kojève, *Introduction to the Reading of Hegel*, ed. Raymond Queneau and Allan Bloom, trans. James H. Nichols (Ithaca: Cornell University Press, 1980), 6–7.

48. The phantasm or the fantasy performs, from its inner psychological spontaneity, the true suturing between the subject and the symbolic order as the life form that is seemingly evident to the subject. Cf. Jacques Lacan, "The Subversion of the Subject and the Dialectic of Desire in the Freudian Unconscious," in *Écrits*, trans. Bruce Fink (New York: Norton, 2006), 671–702.
49. Lacan claims that subjectivization does not create subjects but rather that the very subject, so to speak, *flees* from subjectivization as well, even if it is, of course, subjectivized. What Althusser calls "subject" as an effect of ideological interpellation (and in distinction to an individual) Lacan calls the process of subjectivization, which will never succeed in having the subject completely dissolve into the ideological coordinates. The subject as an effect of ideology cannot grasp the human being in its incommensurability.
50. Lacan, "Subversion of the Subject," graphic, 684.
51. Cf. Philipp van Haute, *Against Adaptation: Lacan's Subversion of the Subject* (New York: Other, 2002). See also Bruce Fink, *Lacan to the Letter: Reading Écrits Closely* (Minneapolis: University of Minnesota Press, 2004), 106–28.
52. Slavoj Žižek, *Enjoy Your Symptom! Jacques Lacan in Hollywood and Out* (London: Routledge, 2008), 14.
53. This illustration is from the session of January 21, 1959, of Lacan's sixth seminar. Cf. Jacques Lacan, *Le séminaire VI: Le désir et son interprétation* (Paris: Edition de la Martinière/Le Champ Freudien, 2013), 192.
54. Lacan unfolds the entire vector O-s(O) with its retrospective positing of meaning in his first "Graph" (Lacan, "Subversion of the Subject," 681) in recourse to the articulation of a sentence. Only from the end of the sentence can the predicate be understood. The end anchors retrospectively words that were initially still "drifting" toward a propositional content. Meaning constitutes itself retrospectively as the final product of a concluded sentence under the vector s(O)-O.
55. Georg Wilhelm Friedrich Hegel, "The Spirit of Christianity and Its Fate," in *Early Theological Writings* (Chicago: University of Chicago Press, 1996), 182–301, here 214.
56. Cf. Pippin, *Hegel's Practical Philosophy*; Allen Wood, *Hegel's Ethical Thought* (Cambridge: Cambridge University Press, 1991), 97–99.
57. Freud holds on to this fact when he talks about the superego. The superego shapes subjectivity's inner morality behind the back of intentional consciousness through the integration of the parents' norms into the psyche's household. Longuenesse has successfully shown, in "Kant's 'I' in 'I Ought To' and Freud's Superego," how Freud's superego is related to the commanding authority of the moral law in the psyche of the Kantian subject.
58. The fact that the big Other will have exercised his authority even when he is sexually transgressive, unpredictable, fear-inducing, or hollow/powerless is shown by the various psychopathologies to which Freud devotes himself: examples are the Rat-Man, Little Hans, Schreber, and the Wolf-Man.

59. Lacan's fascination with rule-following was also rooted in the contemporary research on cybernetics (cf. S.II 294–326). To him, speaking was a prominent example of a machine-based event, in which the "subject of the unconscious" as a rule-instructed speaking machine was ahead of the ego. In *Seminar II* und *III*, he repeatedly addresses cybernetics. With claiming that "language exists completely independently of us" (S.II 284), he implies an understanding of the "unconscious" that can precisely not be united in the quality of privacy. The unconscious is a foreignness implanted into the I.
60. Martin Heidegger, *Being and Time*, trans. John Macquarrie and Edward Robinson (Oxford: Blackwell, 1962), §§107–14.
61. Cf. Wilhelm Lütterfelds, "Ich und Welt," *Revista Portuguesa de Filosofia* 58, no. 3 (2002): 581–604, here 589.
62. Žižek interprets this fittingly: "There is always a residue, a leftover, a stain of traumatic irrationality and senselessness sticking to it [= the ideological experience of Meaning and Truth], and . . . *this leftover, far from hindering the full submission of the subject to the ideological command, is the very condition of it*: it is precisely this non-integrated surplus of a senseless traumatism which confers on the Law its unconditional authority: in other words, which—in so far as it escapes ideological sense—sustains what we might call the ideological *jouis-sense* . . . proper to ideology." Žižek, *The Sublime Object of Ideology*, 43–44, emphasis in original.
63. Žižek: "The subject is *nothing more* than the impossibility of its signifying inscription; it is the retroactive effect of the missed encounter with its signifying representation. Here lies the temporal paradox of the subject of the signifier; it is represented by a signifier, missed by this signifier, and *it is this missed encounter that is the subject.* Here we have the Hegelian distinction between the substance and the subject, what is truly at stake in this thesis is that the substance must be seen as subject." Slavoj Žižek, *The Most Sublime Hysteric: Hegel with Lacan* (Cambridge: Polity, 2014), 62–63, emphasis in original.
64. See, in particular, Lacan's seminar session of June, 24 1964: "In You More Than You," in *Four Fundamental Concepts* (S.XI 263–76).
65. I owe the quotation to Žižek who interprets it in *Tarrying with the Negative*, 131.
66. Ibid.
67. Ibid.
68. Ibid.
69. My emphasis. Cf. Lacan, *L'identification: Le séminaire IX*, based on the version by *École lacanienne de psychanalyse*, http://staferla.free.fr/S9/S9.htm, session of December 6, 1961.
70. Žižek: "What, then, divides the subject? Lacan's answer is simple and radical: its (symbolic) identity itself—prior to being divided between different psychic spheres, the subject is divided between the void of its *cogito* and the symbolic features which identify it in or for the big Other (the signifier which represents it for other signifiers)." Žižek, *Less Than Nothing*, 555.
71. Axel Honneth, *Freedom's Right: The Social Foundations of Democratic Life*, trans. Joseph Ganahl (Cambridge: Polity, 2014), 119–20.

72. Gudrun Ensslin und Bernward Vesper, *"Notstandsgesetze von Deiner Hand": Briefe 1968/1969* (Berlin: Suhrkamp, 2009), 201.
73. Žižek, *Tarrying with the Negative*, 131.
74. Cf. Walter Benjamin, *The Origin of German Tragic Drama*, trans. John Osborn (London: Verso, 2003). Benjamin speaks prominently of an "empty world" (133) into which Luther places the faithful. It is empty since no worldly medium and no product of human labor continues to prepare a path to the grace of God.
75. Ensslin, "Accesses to the Real," 86–87.
76. See also Lacan's comments in S.VII, 66–70; S.XI 20, 152; *Logique du fantasme: Le séminaire XIV*, based on the version of *École lacanienne de psychanalyse*, http://staferla.free.fr/S14/S14.htm, session of January 25, 1967.
77. Jacques Lacan, "The Function and Field of Speech and Language in Psychoanalysis," in *Écrits* (New York: Norton, 2006), 197–268, here 229–30.
78. Žižek defines the *point de capiton* as following: "a word, on the level of the signifier itself, unifies a given field [and] constitutes its identity: it is, so to speak, the word to which 'things' themselves refer to recognize themselves in their unity." Žižek, *The Sublime Object of Ideology*, 105.
79. Jacques Lacan, *Écrits II* (Paris: Édition du Seuil, 1999), 285.
80. Lacan, "Subversion of the Subject," 688.
81. Welsen, "Die Ethik des rechten Sprechens," 688.
82. Lacan, "Position of the Unconscious," in *Écrits*, 703–21, here 720.
83. Welsen, "Die Ethik des rechten Sprechens," 688.
84. Kant: "A people should not *inquire* with any practical aim in view into the origin of the supreme authority to which it is subject, that is, a subject *ought not to reason subtly* for the sake of action about the origin of this authority, as a right that can still be called into question (*ius controversum*) with regard to the obedience he owes it" (MM 461).
85. See Lacan's explications on S1 and S2 in Jacques Lacan, *Le séminaire XVIII: D'un discours qui ne serait pas du semblant*, based on the version of *École lacanienne de psychanalyse*, http://staferla.free.fr/S18/S18.htm, session of January 20, 1970. In *Encore: The Seminar Book XX*, Lacan defines S1 as that entity "which, of all the signifiers, is the signifier for which there is no signified, and which, with respect to meaning (*sens*), symbolizes the failure thereof. It is 'half-sense,' 'indesense' par excellence, or if you will allow me again, 'reti-sense'" (S.XX 80). See also Lacan's comment in the chapter "To Jakobson" (S.XX 14–25).
86. The term is a central topic in Lacan's seminar *Les problèmes cruciaux de psychanalyse: Le séminaire XII*, on the basis of *École lacanienne de psychanalyse*, http://staferla.free.fr/S12/S12.htm.
87. Wittgenstein, *On Certainty*, ed. G. E. M. Anscombe and G. H. von Wright (Oxford: Basil Blackwell, 1969), §140.
88. Ibid., §141.
89. Alain Badiou, *Being and Event*, trans. Oliver Feltham (London: Continuum 2006), 89–92.

90. In 2011, the Temple American Inn of Court organized a conference with British and US legal scholars who debated the legality (or illegality) of the American Declaration of Independence. According to a report by the BBC, this Declaration was "totally illegitimate and illegal. At least that was what the lawyers from the UK argued." Those representing the United States, of course, advocated the opposite thesis. Matt Danzico and Kate Dailey, "Is the US Declaration of Independence Illegal," October 19, 2011, www.bbc.co.uk/news/magazine-15345511.
91. Lacan, "On Structure as an Inmixing of an Otherness Prerequisite to Any Subject Whatever," in *The Structuralist Controversy: The Languages of Criticism and the Sciences of Man*, ed. Richard Macksey and Eugenio Donato (Baltimore: Johns Hopkins University Press, 1970), 186–95.
92. See also Jacques-Alain Miller, "Suture : Éléments de la logique du signifiant," *Cahiers pour l'analyse* 1 (1966): 37–49.
93. Cf. Felix Ensslin, "Die Entbehrung des Absoluten: Das Subjekt der Nichtigkeit in Luthers Magnificat-Auslegung," PhD diss., Universität Potsdam, 2008.
94. Sigmund Freud, *Studies on Hysteria*, esp. the case history of "Katharina," in *Standard Edition*, 2:125–34.
95. Freud and Breuer anticipate the concept of belatedness, a thesis by Michael Dummett, which he states in Dummett, "Can an Effect Precede Its Cause?," in *Truth and Other Enigmas*, ed. Michael Dummett (Cambridge: Harvard University Press, 1978), 319–32.
96. Lacan, "The Mirror Stage as Formative of the I Function as Revealed in Psychoanalytic Experience," in *Écrits*, 75–81.
97. I would like to thank Rosina Ziegler for this insight. For Lacan's "quilting point," see for example, *The Psychoses* (S.III 258–70). See also "Subversion of the Subject," in *Écrits*, 680–84.
98. Žižek, *Less Than Nothing*, 771.
99. Lacan: "Everything radiates out from and is organized around this signifier [the quilting point], similar to these little lines of force that an upholstery button forms on the surface of material. It's the point of convergence that enables everything that happens in this discourse to be situated retroactively and prospectively" (S.III 268).
100. Judith Butler, "Deconstruction and the Possibility of Justice: Comments on Bernasconi, Cornell, Miller, Weber," *Cardozo Law Review* 11 (1990): 1715–18.
101. Žižek sees in this Lacan's solution for the dilemma of the dissolution of meaning through a reversal of sign-theoretical equivalences of signifiers according to Saussure through the theory of the master-signifier. Žižek: "One can ascribe to every signifier a never ending series of 'equivalences,' of signifiers which represent for it the void of its place of inscription; we find ourselves in a kind of dispersed, non-totalized network of links, every signifier enters into a series of particular relationships with other signifiers. The only possible way out of this impasse is that we simply *reverse* the series of equivalences and ascribe to *one* signifier the function of representing the subject (the place of inscription) for all the others (which thereby become 'all'—that is, are totalized): in this way, the proper master-signifier is produced." Slavoj Žižek, *For They Know Not What They Do: Enjoyment as a Political Factor* (London: Verso, 2002), 23.

102. On Lacan's reception of Saussure, see specifically Jacques Lacan, "The Instance of the Letter in the Unconscious, or Reason Since Freud," in *Écrits*, 412–44, esp. 415–20.

103. In *Encore: The Seminar Book XX*, Lacan calls this locus of the True and the One the phantasm of a "pre-discursive reality." As he writes, this reality embodies a "dream—the dream behind every conception of knowledge. But it is also what must be considered mythical. There is no such thing as a pre-discursive reality. Every reality is founded and defined by a discourse" (S.XX 32). The signifier of this discourse is in its origin "first and foremost, imperative" (32). Summarizing this thought, he writes: "Every dimension of being is produced in the wake of the master's discourse—the discourse of he who, proffering the signifier, expects therefrom one of its link effects that must not be neglected, which is related to the fact that the signifier commands. The signifier is, first and foremost, imperative" (32).

104. Žižek, *The Sublime Object of Ideology*, 43.

105. The motive of preemptive obedience to the state through enigmatic appellations (rendering the subject especially vulnerable) is exemplified for Žižek and Eric Santner especially in Franz Kafka's novels. Kafka's texts exhibit paranoia-provoking consequences of appellations whose meaning cannot be deciphered or correctly deduced and understood. As in constellations similar to thought-experiments, Kafka shows how fragile subjectivity has become in relation to the law at the beginning of the twentieth century. Repeatedly individuals are unsettled in Kafka's prose in their integrity because they lack knowledge about what the big Other (in general a bureaucratic machinery) wants from them. Cf. Žižek, *The Sublime Object of Ideology*, 44–45, 181–82. See also Eric Santner, *Psychotheology of Everyday Life: Reflections on Freud and Rosenzweig* (Chicago: University of Chicago Press, 2001), esp. chap. 2. Jay Bernstein interprets twentieth-century modernity as having lost a *sensus communis*. Modern art compensates for this loss with the help of mourning-sublimation via creativity. Cf. Jay M. Bernstein, *The Fate of Art: Aesthetic Alienation from Kant to Derrida and Adorno* (University Park: Pennsylvania State University Press, 1992).

106. Žižek quotes this verse frequently, for example, in *Less Than Nothing*, 231. It is from Wagner's *Parsifal* (Act 3): "Die Wunder schließt / der Speer nur, der sie schlug."

107. See, especially, *L'envers de la psychanalyse: Le séminaire XVII*, based on the version of *École lacanienne de psychanalyse*, http://staferla.free.fr/S17/S17.htm, sessions 2 to 5.

108. Lacan sees *objet petit a* appear in Hegel's dialectic of recognition. He writes in his seminar on *Anxiety*: "It's plainly spelt out in Hegel that he needs the Other so that the Other may acknowledge him, so that he may receive the Other's acknowledgement. What does that mean? It means that the Other will institute something, designated by *a*, which is what is involved at the level of that which desires. The whole impasse lies here. In demanding to be acknowledged, right where I get acknowledged, I only get acknowledged as an object. I get what I desire, I am an object, and I can't stand myself as an object, since this object that I am is of its essence a consciousness, a *Selbstbewusstein*" (S.X 24).

109. Here, I adopt a phrase by Ludwig Wittgenstein from *On Certainty*, §141.

110. Lacan expresses his understanding of the subject as an effect of the Symbolic and consequently as the nonidentity of reflexive self-relation with great precision in *Seminar XI* in recourse to his "Rome Discourse." The Cartesian subject of doubt is his model in this context, because this subject, due to the lack of the most fundamental certainties, is suspended in his self-relation. "The unconscious is the sum of the effects of speech on a subject, at the level at which the subject constitutes himself out of the effects of the signifier." Lacan continues: "This makes it clear that, in the term *subject*, . . . I am not designating the living substratum needed by this phenomenon of the subject, nor any sort of substance, nor any being possessing knowledge in his *pathos*, his suffering, whether primal or secondary, nor even some incarnated logos, but the Cartesian subject, who appears at the moment when doubt is recognized as certainty—except that, through my approach, the bases of this subject prove to be wider, but, at the same time much more amenable to certainty that eludes it. This is what the unconscious is" (S.XI 126).
111. Lacan, *Télévision* (Paris: Éditions du Seuil, 1974), 19.
112. This *being more* cannot define itself. Yet this does not prevent the subject from striving for it, knowing full well that *objet petit a* marks the phantasma of shadowy outlines behind a curtain without a positive object appearing from behind the curtain.
113. Žižek compares Antigone's "monstrosity" with her uncompromising attitude of a "direct identification of her particular/determinate desire with the Other's (Thing's) injunction/call." Slavoj Žižek, *Interrogating the Real*, ed. Rex Butler and Scott Stephens (New York: Continuum, 2005), 347. Antigone represents for him "the unconditional fidelity to the Otherness of the Thing that disrupts the entire social edifice. From the standpoint of the ethics of *Sittlichkeit*, of the *mores* that regulate the intersubjective collective of the polis, her insistence is effectively 'mad,' disruptive, evil" (344).
114. Yong Wang, "Agency: The Internal Split of Structure," *Sociological Forum* 23, no. 3 (September 2008): 481–502.
115. Ibid., 489.
116. Sigmund Freud, *New Introductory Lectures on Psycho-Analysis*, in *Standard Edition*, 22:95.
117. I owe this insight to Giovanni Pietro Basile, SJ.
118. In *The Metaphysics of Morals* Kant rejects repeatedly the right of resistance (MM 462–65, 506).
119. For an insight into the debate on the right to resistance in Kant, see Kenneth Westphal, "Kant's Qualified Principle of Obedience to Authority in the *Metaphysical Elements of Justice*," in *Akten des VII. internationalen Kant-Kongresses*, ed. Gerhard Funke (Bonn: Bouvier, 1991), 353–66. See also Otfried Höffe's position in Höffe, *Kant's Cosmopolitan Theory of Law and Peace* (Cambridge: Cambridge University Press, 2006), 9–11.
120. The political unrest in the Middle East in 2011 and 2013 has brought the seeming impossibility of providing a clear answer to this question into our times. Was Hosni Mubarak an ally of the West and guarantor of peace, as the then US secretary of state

Hillary Clinton proclaimed, or was he a tyrant and oppressor of his people (financed by the United States) as US president Obama suggested at about the same time? The contradiction within one and the same US administration enabled it to be on the side of the victor in either case. Hillary Clinton mentions the conflict with the US president in her book *Hard Choices* (New York: Simon and Schuster, 2014), 331–62.

121. Prominently represented by Christine M. Korsgaard in "The Reasons We Can Share: An Attack on the Distinction Between Agent-Relative and Agent-Neutral Values," in *Creating the Kingdom of Ends* (Cambridge: Cambridge University Press, 1996), 275–310.

122. Cf. this topic in a much broader research context, namely, that of the history of law in the Occident. See John M. Parrish, *Paradoxes of Political Ethics: From Dirty Hands to the Invisible Hand* (Cambridge: Cambridge University Press, 2007).

123. A contemporary example of conflictual viewpoints in narratives of catastrophes is found in Israel and the occupied territories of Palestine, where the narrative of law and injustice in textbooks by Palestinians and Israelis makes clear the impossibility of a common "neutral" narrative. See Fouad Moughrabi, "Battle of the Books in Palestine," *Nation*, September 13, 2001, www.thenation.com/article/battle-books-palestine/.

124. Cf. Christine M. Korsgaard, "Taking the Law Into Our Own Hands: Kant on the Right to Revolution," in *Reclaiming the History of Ethics: Essays for John Rawls*, ed. Andrews Reath, Barbara Herman, and Christine M. Korsgaard (Cambridge: Cambridge University Press, 1997), 297–328.

125. Brent Adkins arrives at this result in Adkins, "Kant and the *Antigone*: The Possibility of Conflicting Duties," *International Philosophical Quarterly* 39, no. 4 (1999): 455–66.

126. See Jacques Derrida's interpretation of the linguistic-performative act of the force of law in Derrida, "Declarations of Independence," in *Negotiations: Interventions and Interviews, 1971–2001* (Stanford: Stanford University Press, 2002), 46–54.

127. The "discourse of the master" once subjugated the subject to the entirety of his power of knowledge. In what is termed the second "discourse of the university" the battery of knowledge teaches the subject in the established sciences, and in the "discourse of the analyst" the subject is asked about her desire.

128. See Gershom Scholem's letter to Benjamin on September 20, 1934, in *Walter Benjamin—Gershom Scholem: Briefwechsel, 1933–1940*, ed. Gershom Scholem (Frankfurt: Suhrkamp, 1985), 175. As Žižek phrases it: "The hysterical subject is the subject whose very existence involves radical doubt and questioning, her entire being is sustained by the uncertainty as to what she is for the Other." Slavoj Žižek, "Four Discourses, Four Subjects," in *Cogito and the Unconscious (Sic 2)*, ed. Slavoj Žižek (Durham: Duke University Press, 1998), 74–113, here 81.

129. Jeanne L. Schroeder, *The Four Lacanian Discourses* (London: Routledge, 2008), 149.

130. Ibid.

131. Schroeder: "In the case of positive law, the missing little *a* is nothing but the morality (content) that positive law has barred. In this case, however, the object of desire is not necessarily the collective goals of society identified in the university's discourse. It is the subjective desire of the barred subject. In other words, the agent speaks from the position of the pain of this barring and her truth is that which is barred." Ibid.

132. Ibid., 150.

133. To explicate this thought one more time: no one can provide reasons under the discursive premise of the polis why even an enemy of the state deserves a burial. Creon does not want to completely abolish the right to burial. It is simply not a right for an enemy of the polis.

134. Cf. Wang, "Agency," 481–502.

135. Žižek, *The Sublime Object of Ideology*, 113. In this manner, the hysteric pushes the master "into the point where he or she can find the master's knowledge lacking." Bruce Fink, *The Lacanian Subject: Between Language and Jouissance* (Princeton: Princeton University Press, 1995), 134. Here, S1 is not the point of departure at whose end we find the split subject in her phantasmatic attachment to *objet petit a*. Rather, the split hysterical subject begins the sequentiality of the discursive moments. He destabilizes "established knowledge" and produces a fundamental lack in the big Other himself.

136. Terry Lovell focuses in her analysis of the case of Rosa Parks on the fact that the act that Rosa Parks performed could, of course, also have been ignored. This is what had happened to similar acts earlier. Cf. Terry Lovell, "Resisting with Authority: Historical Specificity: Agency, and the Performative Self," *Theory, Culture, and Society* 20, no. 1 (2003): 1–17. For Lovell, this makes clear what a decisive role historical contingencies can play. Wang, for his part, attempts to establish Rosa Parks's act from the dependence of a second master-signifier that has remained stuck on the level of changing from nonrepresentation to representation. He writes: "This second moment requires establishing another symbolic order with a new master-signifier, that is to say, a Laclauian hegemony, a competing discourse." Wang, "Agency," 498. Wang then draws the following conclusion: "These are the two moments of agency: first, as possibility manifesting itself in contingent acts and, second, the agentic potentiality is only actualized (as necessity) through a retroactively established discourse. Such a two-moment conception of agency rejects historicist reduction of a significant social and political event to its historical and situational circumstances and by doing so opens a space for social transformational agency" (498–99). One objection to Wang would be that there does not necessarily have to be an interplay with a simultaneously established master-signifier. In Antigone's drama, one can see very well that Antigone cannot refer to a big Other (in the sense of a propositionally guaranteed validity) and still—at least in Hegel's interpretation—introduce a leap into a normativity-to-come that does not become recognizable until after the tragedy.

137. What Lacan interprets psychoanalytically is in sociology being analyzed under the concepts of behavioral expectations and sociological role-theory. Self-determination proves to be constituted through relational actions according to socially imposed practices. Cf. Diana Jeske, *Rationality and Moral Theory: How Intimacy Generates Reasons* (London: Routledge, 2008). Similarly, Michael O. Hardimon, "Role Obligations," *Journal of Philosophy* 91, no. 7 (1994): 333–63.

138. Lacan explored mathematic formalism and set theory under the influence of the group of mathematicians around Nicolas Bourbaki, among others. Cf. François Dosse, *History*

of *Structuralism: The Sign Sets, 1967–Present*, vol. 2, trans. Deborah Glassman (Minneapolis: University of Minnesota Press, 1997), 85–86.

139. Bertrand Russell, *The Principles of Mathematics* (London: Routledge, 1992), §106.

140. Heidegger's texts *On the Way to Language* und *Pathmarks* serve as examples. Giorgio Agamben provides an incisive interpretation for this in Agamben, *Language and Death: The Place of Negativity*, trans. Karen Pinkus and Michael Hardt (Minneapolis: University of Minnesota Press, 2006), esp. "The Sixth Day," 54–62.

141. Lacan, *Le séminaire IX: L'identification*, session of November 15, 1962.

142. Gottlob Frege, *The Foundations of Arithmetic: A Logico-Mathematical Enquiry Into the Concept of Number*, trans. J. L. Austin (Evanston, IL: Northwestern University Press, 1980), §68.

143. Gottlob Frege, "Thought," in *The Frege Reader*, ed. Michael Beaney (Malden, MA: Blackwell, 1997), 325–45, here 326.

144. Bertrand Russell, "Letter to Frege," in *From Frege to Gödel: A Source Book in Mathematical Logic, 1879–1931*, ed. Jean van Heijenoort (Cambridge: Harvard University Press, 1967), 124–25.

145. Bertrand Russell's development of the paradox refers to the operation of combining elements under universal concepts or general terms. This can be taken as the fundamental operation of linguistic reference where a general statement/property (F) is instantiated in reference to an individual element (x): F(x) = There exists an x, which has (or instantiates) the property F. This way of combining elements (all red objects are part of the set of red objects) can be understood as the basic operation of linguistic reference and representation. But as Russell demonstrates, the possibility of self-membership actually proves fatal to Frege's "Basic Law V," the "universal comprehension principle," as Frege tried with this law to explain once and for *all* linguistic operations in terms of clearly defined memberships/extensions.

146. Bertrand Russell, "Mathematical Logic as Based on the Theory of Types," *American Journal of Mathematics* 30, no. 3 (1908): 222–62, here 222.

147. Russell, *Principles of Mathematics*, §106.

148. Lacan, *L'identification: Le séminaire IX*, session of January 24, 1962, my emphasis.

149. Lacan does not only interpret the mentioned "force" semantically. He also interprets it psychoanalytically when he refers to the signifier as medium of the "subject of the unconscious." For the unconscious acquires signifiers and thus lays bare, for its part, a desire-causing propulsion to fill its *Dasein*. The psychoanalytic discovery of the unconscious was—to put it in a nutshell—based on nothing but the discovery of the autonomy of the signifier. Language has a material effect on the body and is at the same time ephemeral. It is effective through its inexistence. Lacan writes in "Science and Truth": "The signifier is defined by psychoanalysis as acting first of all as if it were separate from its signification. Here we see the literal character trait that specifies the copulatory signifier, the phallus, when—arising outside of the limits of the subject's biological maturation—it is effectively (im)printed; it is unable, however, to be the sign representing sex, the partner's sex—that is, the partner's biological sign." Jacques Lacan, "Science and Truth," in *Écrits*, 726–45, here 743.

150. Lacan, *L'identification: Le séminaire IX*, session of January 24, 1962.
151. Alain Badiou mentions in his adaptation of set theory that its founder, Georg Cantor, does not displace the topic of aporia, as Russell's paradox expresses it, from the field of language but rather assigns its potential conceivability *in God*. Cantor does so when he talks of "inconsistent multiplicities" in contradistinction to "consistent multiplicities." Badiou: "If some multiplicities cannot be totalized, or 'conceived as a unity' without contradiction, he [Cantor] declares, it is because they are absolutely infinite rather than transfinite (mathematical). Cantor does not step back from associating the absolute and inconsistency. There where the count-as-one fails, stands God." Badiou, *Being and Event*, 41. Badiou quotes Cantor, who writes in a letter to Dedekind of June 28, 1899: "A multiplicity may be such that the affirmation according to which *all* its elements 'are together' leads to a contradiction, such that it is impossible to conceive the multiplicity as a unity, as a 'finite thing.' These multiplicities, I name them *absolute infinite multiplicities*, or *inconsistent*" (41).
152. While we cannot enter here in a discussion of the issue of how Lacan's constructivist position is justified ontologically, it is apparent that with his position Lacan brings himself a number of problems that analytical philosophy attempted to eliminate with a return to realism.
153. Willard V. O. Quine, "Ontological Relativity," in *Ontological Relativity* (New York: Columbia University Press, 1969), 26–68, here 48. In *Les problèmes cruciaux pour la psychanalyse: Le séminaire XII* Lacan expresses his critique of Russell with the following words: "Bertrand Russell conceives language as a superposition, a scaffolding of an infinite number and series of metalanguages, where each propositional level is being subject to control through a higher level. . . . So there must be a level where language is itself a pure object. Unfortunately nobody is able to grasp this level" (session of December 9, 1964).
154. Bertrand Russell, *An Inquiry Into Meaning and Truth* (London: Allen and Unwin, 1956).
155. Lacan, "The Subversion of the Subject," 688.
156. Lacan, *L'envers de la psychanalyse: Le séminaire XVII*, session of November 26, 1969.
157. Émile Benveniste, "Subjectivity in Language," in *Problems in General Linguistics* (Miami: Miami University Press, 1973), 223–30, here 226.
158. Ibid.
159. Ibid. It should be noted here that Wittgenstein formulates a similar thought when he writes in his *Blue Book*: "The mouth which says 'I' or the hand which is raised to indicate that it is I who wish to speak . . . does not thereby point to anything. . . . If in saying 'I,' I point to my own body, I model the use of the word 'I' on that of the demonstrative 'this person' or 'he.'" Ludwig Wittgenstein, *The Blue Book*, in *The Blue and Brown Books* (New York: Harper and Row, 1965), 68. Wittgenstein says here, similar to Benveniste, that the personal pronoun does not represent itself in the speech act. The personal pronoun is not used descriptively or referentially here but rather expressively.
160. Benveniste, "Subjectivity in Language," 226.
161. Ibid.

162. Ibid.

163. Lacan distances himself from the Saussurean understanding of the linguistic sign by reversing the hierarchy between signifier and signified. The signified looses its link to the external world and is degraded to an *effect* of the signifier.

164. He does so because he sees in this the true performative power of language as only psychoanalysis can appreciate it and consider it a medium of healing a troubled psyche.

165. Lacan perceives truth not as some kind of "second-order" super object (Language's metalanguage) guaranteeing truth-values in propositions, but from a functionalist perspective as simply being the transcendental condition of justification and linguistic communication. "What remains at the center is the fine routine that is such that the signified always retains the same meaning (*sens*) in the final analysis. That meaning is provided by the sense each of us has of being part of his world, that is, of his little family and of everything that revolves around it. Each of you—I am speaking even for the leftists—you are more attached to it than you care to know" (S.XX 42). In analogy to Brandom—yet with significant differences for our topic—one could call Lacan's position an inferential theory of semantic holism that takes into account even the *inexistent*, that is, ephemeral dimension of language/semantics at the level of the unconscious. We can at this point not enter into details on the problems that this theory causes and that also concern debates on the legacy of Wittgenstein, Quine, and Heidegger today. Our goal is to open up Lacan's position as the psychoanalytic basis for excessive subjectivity.

166. By saying that "there is no such thing as a meta-language" (S.XX 107), Lacan distances himself from the idea that one could perceive the world reductively like a collection of "physical facts" or according to a coherent extensionalist semantics. Any metatheoretical reference articulates itself for Lacan before the background of the life-world. Only this background allows the fantasy of a logical space subsequently to build itself the area of investigation that then in turn can be quantified. Cf. Lacan, *Le séminaire XII: Les problèmes cruciaux pour la psychanalyse*, session of December 9, 1964.

167. Claude Lévi-Strauss, *Introduction to the Work of Marcel Mauss*, trans. Felicity Baker (London: Routledge, 1987), 64. Lévi-Strauss mentions Mauss's comments on the Melanesian and Polynesian word *mana*, which according to various cultures embodies a supernatural power in rituals. *Mana* is not only a mythologically holistic signifier of reconciliation; *mana* does not only have—as Althusser would probably say—an ideological function. *Mana* is structurally always part of all discourses as a condition of the discourse that can have no other than a holistic claim to the representation of reality.

168. This reminds us again of Wittgenstein's *Tractatus*, where he, on the one hand, thematizes language through metalanguage (the picture theory of language, the theory of elementary propositions) and at the same time reveals the sentences of the *Tractatus* as nonsensical themselves. This expresses the famous sentence section 6.54: "My propositions serve as elucidations in the following way: anyone who understands me eventually recognizes them as nonsensical, when he has used them—as steps—to climb up

beyond them." Ludwig Wittgenstein, *Tractatus Logico-Philosophicus* (London: Routledge, 1974). Wittgenstein asks his reader at the end of the conclusions of his text to declare the *Tractatus* itself as nonsensical. Yet how can one climb a ladder that ultimately was not there?

169. Lacan, "On Structure as an Inmixing," 189. In his *Four Fundamental Concepts: The Seminar Book XI* he writes: "We know, thanks to Freud, that the subject of the unconscious manifests itself, that it thinks before it attains certainty" (S.XI 37).

170. Ibid.

171. Bertrand Russell and Alfred North Whitehead, *Principia Mathematica* (Cambridge: Cambridge University Press, 1962), 37. See also Russell, "Mathematical Logic as Based on the Theory of Types," 224–25.

172. Alain Badiou describes this fittingly: "Thought occurs for there to be a cessation—even if it only lasts long enough to indicate that it has not actually been obtained—of the quantitative unmooring of being. . . . Thought, strictly speaking, is what unmeasure, ontologically proven, cannot satisfy." Badiou, *Being and Event*, 282.

173. Ludwig Wittgenstein, *Philosophical Investigations*, rev. ed., ed. P. M. S. Hacker and Joachim Schulte, trans. G. E. M. Anscombe, P. M. S. Hacker, and Joachim Schulte (Malden, MA: Wiley Blackwell, 2009), §217.

174. Ludwig Wittgenstein, *Philosophical Grammar* (Oxford: Blackwell, 1980), 81 (§39).

175. Wittgenstein, *Philosophical Investigations*, §201.

176. Ludwig Wittgenstein, *Remarks on the Foundations of Mathematics*, ed. G. H. von Wright, Rush Rhees, and G. E. M. Anscombe (Cambridge: MIT Press, 1989), §113.

177. On the topic of spontaneity and the use of concepts, see Wilhelm Vossenkuhl, "Spontaneität," *Zeitschrift für philosophische Forschung* 48, no. 3 (1994): 329–49, esp. 338–40.

178. Cf. Agamben, *Language and Death*, 41–48, "The Fifth Day."

179. See the excellent article Paul Livingston, "Agamben, Badiou, and Russell," *Continental Philosophy Review* 42 (2009): 297–325.

180. "Every dimension of being is produced in the wake of the master's discourse—the discourse of he who, proffering the signifier, expects therefrom one of its link effects that must not be neglected, which is related to the fact that the signifier commands. The signifier is, first and foremost, imperative" (S.XX 32).

181. It should be noted that Lacan understands theories of judgment and meaning in their fundamental dependence on psychosomatic processes of desire. The human psyche as the organ of ratio rests as the compromise of symptoms of various libidinal energy quantums on these drive processes as a form of abstraction without generally being aware that the drive processes precede this abstraction. Lacan therefore describes the "signifier as the cause of pleasure." "The signifier is the cause of jouissance" (S.XX 24).

182. Adjusted translation. The French original reads: "On n'y verrait, si je puis dire que du feu." *Encore: Le séminaire XX*, on the basis of the version of *École lacanienne de psychanalyse*, http://staferla.free.fr/S10/S10.htm, session of January 9, 1973.

183. Lacan, here, makes unfortunately no distinction between such contrary language games as, for example, art and the natural sciences, which cannot tie back an objectivity to the imperative of individual subjects in the same manner. The judgment why a

piece of art is considered beautiful complies with a different structure of justification and veridicality than a scientific thesis. Space limitations prevent me from a more detailed discussion of the multitude of objections that Lacan evokes with his linguistic constructivism.

184. Jacques Lacan, *L'insu: Le séminaire XXIV*, based on the version of *École lacanienne de psychanalyse*, http://staferla.free.fr/S24/S24.htm, session of May 17, 1977.
185. Lacan, *Télévision*, 19.
186. SL 488.
187. I owe this insight to Josef Schmidt (unpublished manuscript).
188. "*Fracturé*. De la même façon que nous le saisissons *dans le sujet lui-même*." Lacan, *Le séminaire XIV: La logique du fantasme*, session of February 15, 1967.
189. Lacan articulates his position by using the greek word *pará* (next to, along side of) in *Encore*. He writes: "What we must get used to is substituting the 'para-being' (*par-être*)—the being '*para*,' being beside—for the being that would take flight. I say the 'para-being' (*par-être*), and not the 'appearing' (*paraître*) as the phenomenon has always been called—that beyond which there is supposedly that thing, the noumenon" (S.XX 44–45). "Beyond language, this effect, which is produced by being based only on writing, is certainly the ideal of mathematics. . . . We certainly sense that this shy of is no more than an intuitive reference. And yet this presupposition cannot be eliminated because language, in its meaning effect, is never but beside the referent. Isn't it thus true that language imposes being upon us and obliges us, as such, to admit that we never have anything by way of being (*de l'être*)?" (S.XX 44).
190. Sigmund Freud, *On Narcissism: An Introduction*, in *Standard Edition*, 14:91.
191. Cf. Jean Laplanche, "The Drive and Its Source-Object: Its Fate in the Transference," in *Essays on Otherness*, ed. John Fletcher (London: Routledge, 1999), 117–32.
192. This recalls Kant's teleological power of judgment, which may take on—for the reason of coherence—"as if" principles for the sake of a belief in a purposeful nature. Here, too, one can say that Kant phantasmatically fills in the gaps in the "edifice of the world" as "as if" principles become a transcendental condition of understanding. For instance, the teleological power of judgment may assume as "if an understanding (even if not ours) . . . had likewise given them [these principles] for the sake of our faculty of cognition, in order to make possible a system of experience in accordance with particular laws of nature" (CPJ 67–68).
193. Eric Santner writes: "Fantasy organizes or 'binds' the surplus into a schema, a distinctive 'torsion' or spin that colors/distorts the shape of our universe." Santner, *Psychotheology of Everyday Life*, 39.
194. Ibid., 40.
195. Žižek: "Fantasy appears . . . as an answer to 'Che vuoi?,' to the unbearable enigma of the desire of the Other, of the lack in the Other; but it is at the same time fantasy itself which, so to speak, provides the co-ordinates of our desire—which constructs the frame enabling us to desire something. The usual definition of fantasy ('an imagined scenario representing the realization of desire') is therefore somewhat misleading, or at least ambiguous: in the fantasy-scene the desire is not fulfilled, 'satisfied,' but

constituted (given its objects, and so on)—through fantasy, we learn 'how to desire.' In this intermediate position lies the paradox of fantasy: it is the frame co-ordinating our desire, but at the same time a defense against 'Che vuoi?,' a screen concealing the gap, the abyss of desire of the Other." Žižek, *The Sublime Object of Ideology*, 118.

196. Thus the human being remains caught in the hysterical question of what the Other wants of her. Žižek: "The subject does not know why he is occupying this place in the symbolic network. His own answer to this 'Che vuoi?' of the Other can only be the hysterical question: 'Why am I . . . [a teacher, a master, a king . . .]?' Briefly: 'Why am I what you [the big Other] are saying that I am?'" Žižek, *The Sublime Object of Ideology*, 113.

197. The coordinates anchor the unconscious where the big Other is always closer to the subject than it can be on the level of consciousness.

198. "La relation du transfert . . . le fait déchoir de son fantasme et le destitue comme sujet." Jacques Lacan, "Proposition du 9 octobre 1967 sur le psychanalyste de l'École," in *Autres écrits*, ed. Jaques-Alain Miller (Paris: Éditions du Seuil, 2001), 243–60, here 252.

199. Lacan: "There is a third dimension of time which they [the machines] undeniably are not party to, which I'm trying to get you to picture via this element which is neither belatedness, nor being in advance, but haste, the relation to time peculiar to the human being, this relation to the chariot of time, which is there, close on our heels" (S.II 291). Lacan exemplifies the aspect of haste as a significant dimension of *Dasein*'s agency by explicating the so-called prisoner paradox in his text "Logical Time and the Assertion of Anticipated Certainty," in *Écrits*, 161–76.

200. Fink writes: "The subject who refuses to 'sacrifice his or her castration to the Other's jouissance' . . . is the subject who has not undergone the further separation known as traversing fantasy. . . . The subject must renounce his or her more or less comfortable, complacently miserable position as subjected by the Other—as castrated—in order to take the Other's desire as cause upon him or herself. The traversing of fantasy thus involves a going beyond of castration and a utopian moment beyond neurosis." Fink, *The Lacanian Subject*, 72.

201. Bruce Fink, *A Clinical Introduction To Lacanian Psychoanalysis* (Cambridge: Harvard University Press, 1997), 56.

202. When, for example, for Marcel Proust's protagonist in the novel *À la recherche du temps perdu* the unrequited love to Odette has become unbearable, he no longer desires to live with this pain of love. Yet the pathological enjoyment of this pain fills in such an important way all existential dimension of his *Dasein* that losing it becomes life-threatening itself. Cf. Alenka Zupančič, *Ethics of the Real: Kant and Lacan* (London: Verso, 2000), 8. Swann is unable, as Proust describes, to live with his symptoms or without them. "In the depth of his morbid condition he feared death itself no more than such a recovery, which would in fact amount to the death of all that he now was." Marcel Proust, *In Search of Lost Time*, vol. 1., trans. C. K. Scott, D. F. Enright, and Terence Kilmartin (London: Vintage, 1996), 361. To face all symptoms is one way of traversing of fantasy.

203. Zupančič, *Ethics of the Real*, 9. Bruce Fink mentions Hamlet's fate as that of a psyche unable to act because it cannot free itself from the phantasmatic undercurrent of the frame of its life-world. In Hamlet's case it is the appellation of his father asking for revenge. Fink mentions Hamlet in *The Lacanian Subject*, 65–66.

204. Heidegger, *Being and Time*, 314.

205. Antigone expresses this in her long lamentation addressed at Creon and the chorus in the tragedy's third act, especially in the verses 916–20.

206. Traversing the fantasy is not meant as a decision made after weighing various options where the subject chooses herself autonomously. Lacan understands traversing the fantasy as an act that the subject ultimately cannot count herself directly responsible for in an autonomous sense. It may happen suddenly or over a long period of time.

207. Fink, *Clinical Introduction*, 207.

208. Traversing the fantasy can be associated with Lacan's register of the Imaginary. The subject creates herself similar to the toddler in the *mirror stage* as an ideal imagination toward a symbolic order that wants to have her seeing herself entangled within the legal structure. The subject does not question the nondeducibility because the symbolic order can precisely not give grounds for traversing the fantasy as it is represented by the big Other. To this, Langlitz writes: "The subject does not get the impulse to agency from the symbolic order, but from the image it has of itself. This image is combined with the question of what role the subject is granted through the symbolic order or in what role it is recognized from the Other. Thus, it strives to do justice to a fictitious identity." Langlitz, *Die Zeit der Psychoanalyse*, 204–5. Lacan's register of the Imaginary defines here the phantasmatic distortion within excessive subjectivity. This phantasmatic distortion expects that which does not yet exist. It hopes to be recognized in the future. Traversing the fantasy aims at "the unrealized," a lack in the big Other (cf. S.XI 28).

209. Lacan continues: "Don't forget this—Freud initially explains repression as a fixation. But at the moment of the fixation, there is nothing which could be called repression—that of the Wolf-man happens a long time after the fixation. The *Verdrängung* is always a *Nachdrängung*. How then should one explain the return of the repressed? As paradoxical as it may seem, there is only one way to do it—it doesn't come from the past, but from the future" (S.I 158).

210. Lacan continues: "It is possible that it has changed content, changed sign, changed structure. . . . It's not what happens afterwards which is modified, but everything which went before. We have a retroactive effect—*nachträglich*—as Freud calls it—specific to the structure of symbolic memory, in other words to the function of remembering" (S.II 185). Compare also Friedrich Kittler's notion of the "manipulation of the temporal axis" in Kittler, *Draculas Vermächtnis* (Leipzig: Reclam 1993), 182–206.

211. Žižek, *For They Know Not what They Do*, 78.

212. I owe this reference to Nicolas Langlitz, who writes: "To be master of the signifier (= the goal of analysis according to Lacan) means to liberate oneself from fixations of identity-shaping images in one's own history. The goal is to get out of compulsive

repetitions of always the same words and actions, and to rewrite the signifying chain, that subordinated one's whole life." Langlitz, *Die Zeit der Psychoanalyse*, 192.

213. John Rajchman, *Truth and Eros: Foucault, Lacan, and the Question of Ethics* (London: Routledge, 1991), 75.

214. Lacan demonstrates how the described basic conflict of subjectivization in the horizon of a political ontology reemerges again and again in form of the conflict between phantasmatically intersubjectively nourished meaning constructs and the insistence of subjectivity for which the subject propositionally cannot always present reasons.

215. The signifiers that are of interest to Lacan here have a meaning for the subject for which there seems to be at least at this point no equivalences on the "scoreboard" of the big Other. While the big Other as the condition of the subject's alienation is almost omnipotent, as Lacan says, he and his truth are split as well. "The Other as such is . . . please excuse my improvized word . . . *fractured*. And in the same manner we understand this splitness in the subject herself." ("L'Autre comme tell est . . . si je puis dire, si vous permettez ce mot à mon improvisation *fracturé*. De la même façon que nous le saisissons *dans le sujet lui-* meme.") Lacan, *Le séminaire XIV: La logique du fantasme*, session of February 15, 1967.

216. Ed Pluth defines three aspects from Lacan's understanding of an act in *Seminars XIV and XV*: (1) The act does something with words (it has effects on words and meanings). (2) It changes the coordinates of subjectivization. (3) It is transgressive. Cf. Ed Pluth, *Signifiers and Acts: Freedom in Lacan's Theory of the Subject* (New York: State University of New York Press, 2007), 102–3.

217. "Cela—n'est-ce pas?—'*qu'il passe dans le réel*,' nous posons que cela se produit toujours plus, à mesure de la prétention toujours croissante du '*je*' à s'affirmer comme '*fons et origo*' [*source et origine*] de l'être. C'est ce que nous avons posé." Lacan, *Le séminaire XIV: La logique du fantasme*, session of February 15, 1967.

218. Ibid., session of February 22, 1967.

219. Ibid., session of February 15, 1967.

220. "L'acte donc est le seul lieu où le signifiant a l'apparence—la fonction en tout cas—de se signifier lui-même. C'est à dire de fonctionner hors de ses possibilités." And Lacan continues: "In the act the subject is represented as pure division." "Le sujet est—dans l'acte—représenté comme division pure." Ibid., session of February 15, 1967.

221. Ibid., session of February 22, 1967. Lacan writes as well: "Out of a true act, the subject emerges different: because of the cut his structure is changed." ("C'est-à-dire que d'un acte véritable le sujet surgit différent: en raison de la coupure sa structure est modifiée.") Precisely the speculation of an inner fracture of the big Other, despite its supposed omnipotent fullness of knowledge, enables the subject to dare an act. The act is something that happens to the subject who only comprehends his fate *after* the act, which will have shown itself to have been an act, when the enigma of a signifier suddenly and fatefully ascribes a meaning into the subject and his unconscious. On the topic of the retroactiveness of the act, see also Jacques-Alain Miller, "L'acte entre intention et conséquence: Intervention à la dernière soirée du Séminaire Politique lacanienne première série, le 27 mai 1998," *La cause freudienne* 42 (Mai 1999): 7–16.

222. Miller, "L'acte entre intention et consequence," 11.

223. Walter Benjamin, "Excavation and Memory," in *Selected Writings*, vol. 2, pt. 2, *1931–1934*, ed. Michael Jennings, Howard Eiland, and Gary Smith, trans. Rodney Livingstone et al. (Cambridge: Belknap Press of Harvard University Press, 2005), 576.

224. Walter Benjamin, "On the Concept of History," in *Selected Writings*, vol. 4, *1938–1940*, ed. Howard Eiland and Michael Jennings, trans. Edmund Jephcott et al. (Cambridge: Belknap Press of Harvard University Press, 2006), 389–411.

225. Cf. ibid., 395.

226. Benjamin believes himself to be developing his *Theses on the Philosophy of History* in explicit contradistinction to the historical teleology of Hegel. However, he underestimates Hegel's philosophy, which is closer to his own than he was able to perceive.

227. Cf, for instance, Lacan S.VII 93, 97; Lacan, *L'acte: Le séminaire XV*, session of January 10, 1968; *L'identification: Le séminaire IX*, session of March 14, 1962. Probably the most famous literary figure that joins the political figures mentioned is Kleist's Michael Kohlhaas. In Kohlhaas's attempt to a "establish a better order of things," he calls himself, via a performative self-naming/designation "a vicegerent of the archangel Michael who had come to visit upon all who, in this controversy, should take the part of the Squire, punishment by fire and sword for the villain into which the whole world was plunged." Heinrich von Kleist, *Michael Kohlhaas*, trans. Frances A. King (New York: Mondial, 2007), 30. It is controversial how to interpret Kohlhaas's legal fight, whether as a solipsistic "rendering absolute of the law" or as a "personal revenge" (cf. Honneth, *Freedom's Right*, 89), or as "law-making violence," which envisions a better order of things. Cf. Slavoj Žižek, *Did Somebody Say Totalitarianism? Five Interventions in the (Mis)Use of a Notion* (London: Verso, 2001), 33. Ernst Bloch views Kohlhaas as a Don Quixote in the shape of Kantian morality: Bloch, "Über Rechtsleidenschaft innerhalb des positiven Gesetzes (Kohlhaas und der Ernst des Minos)," in *Naturrecht und menschliche Würde* (Frankfurt: Suhrkamp, 1961), 93–102. Terry Eagleton describes him as a modern-day terrorist: Eagleton, *Trouble with Strangers: A Study of Ethics* (Oxford: Wiley Blackwell, 2008), 187–99. Wolf Kittler interprets him as a representative of the law who loses his moral claim due to the violence committed by him in the wake of the burning of Wittenberg and Leipzig: Kittler, *Die Geburt des Partisanen aus dem Geist der Poesie: Heinrich von Kleist und die Strategie der Befreiungskriege* (Freiburg: Rombach, 1987).

228. Pluth, *Signifiers and Acts*, 98.

229. Markus Gabriel, *Fields of Sense: A New Realist Ontology* (Edinburgh: Edinburgh University Press, 2015).

230. Lacan thematizes the appellation of signifiers also in recourse to Freud's analysis of the *Witz* (witticism) with regard to the unconscious. The "subject of the unconscious" bursts forth, for Freud, in the witticism as the agent that suddenly views itself "called/appellated" by signifiers that the joke carries. Lacan writes: "A subject intervenes only inasmuch as there are, in this world, signifiers that mean nothing and must be deciphered. To grant priority to the signifier over the subject is . . . to take into account the experience Freud opened up for us: the signifier plays and wins, if I may say so, before

the subject is aware of it, to such an extent that in the word play of *Witz* (in witticisms, for example) the subject may be surprised. What this activity lights up with its flash is the subject's division from himself." Lacan, "Positions of the Unconscious," in *Écrits*, 703–21, here 712.

231. Cf. Shoshana Felman, *The Literary Speech Act: Don Juan with J. L. Austin, or Seduction in Two Languages* (Ithaca: Cornell University Press, 1983), 92–94.

232. See also Lacan's explications in his *Seminar XIV*. There, he emphasized how far the act can be equated with autogenesis, a self-founding of the subject out of her own decision. Lacan writes: "The act is foundational for the subject. It is the equivalent of repetition, by itself. It is this repetition in a single stroke. . . . One could say . . . that in its case the signifier signifies itself. Because we know that this is impossible. It is nevertheless true that it is as close as possible to this operation. The subject is—let us say, in the act itself—equivalent to the signifier. It remains nevertheless divided." Lacan, *La logique du fantasme: Le séminaire XIV*, session of February 15, 1967. The act corresponds to an ultimately paradoxically remaining self-founding. The subject "gives birth" to herself, so to speak, by a content-changing form of her self-posited self-designation.

233. Ed Pluth: "The conditions for the success of an Austinian speech act largely depend upon the existence of social guarantees and rituals. Marriages, for example, are only successfully accomplished when performed under very specific circumstances, and by the proper authorities. According to Lacan's conception, however, an act transforms a subject, and even though it occurs with signifiers, it does not happen by following a preestablished ritual or code." Pluth, *Signifiers and Acts*, 101.

234. Cf. Wittgenstein, *Philosophical Investigations*, §§138–55, 179–280.

235. In his text *Zettel* Wittgenstein emphasizes how concepts must fulfill the purpose of mankind's ability to relate to the world so that new concepts can be built into old ones to exactly serve and constantly improve this goal. "Do I want to say, then, that certain facts are favorable to the formation of certain concepts; or again unfavorable? And does experience teach us this? It is a fact of experience that human beings alter their concepts, exchange them for others when they learn new facts; when in this way what was formerly important to them becomes unimportant, and vice versa." Ludwig Wittgenstein, *Zettel* (Berkeley: University of California Press, 1970), §352. The real question now lies in the dialectical combination of experience and conceptual interpretation thereof. Is it the concept that constitutes the experience or is it the experience that constitutes the concept? Both moments play together. A new concept may function in certain situation as a test case. It opens access to a certain interpretation of the world and thereby is subject to further verification. Generally one can say with Wittgenstein that a change of concepts also changes in particular cases a certain grammar of the world. It exerts influence on aspects and worldviews. Wittgenstein: "I want to say: an education quite different from ours might also be the *foundati*on for quite different concepts" (§387). Referring to concepts of colors, Wittgenstein claims repeatedly that he rejects investigations that try to found concepts of colors empirically (§331). See also Michael Kober, *Gewissheit als Norm: Wittgensteins Erkenntnistheoretische Untersuchungen in "Über Gewißheit"* (Berlin: De Gruyter, 1993), 177–87.

236. Wilhelm Vossenkuhl, "Spontaneität," *Zeitschrift für Philosophische Forschung* 48, no. 3 (1994): 329–49. Joachim Schulte writes on concept-formation: "We get the impression . . . that concept-formation conducts our experience into particular channels, so that one experience is now seen together with the new one in an hitherto unfamiliar way." Joachim Schulte, "Philosophy of Psychology: A Criticism of a Young Science?," in *Wittgenstein: Zu Philosophie und Wissenschaft*, Deutsches Jahrbuch Philosophie 3, ed. Pirmin Stekeler-Weithofer (Hamburg: Meiner, 2012), 224–35, here 230.
237. Wittgenstein: "Above all, you have found a new conception. As if you had invented a new way of painting; or, again, a new metre, or a new kind of song." Wittgenstein, *Philosophical Investigations*, §401. Of central importance in concept-formation as a "new way of speaking" (§400) is that indeed a new experiential content is conveyed.
238. Sigmund Freud, *Beyond the Pleasure Principle*, in *Standard Edition*, 18:3–64, here 14–17.
239. Jonathan Lear writes: "If we are trying to respect the child's point of view we cannot even say that the game is prompted by loss. For it is only after the game is installed that the child will begin to have the concept of loss or absence. Only when the game is established will the loss be a loss *for him*. The child had been inhabiting a less differentiated field of 'mother-and-child': it is this field that is disturbed by the mother's absence." Jonathan Lear, *Happiness, Death, and the Remainder of Life* (Cambridge: Harvard University Press, 2002), 92.
240. Cf. Pluth, *Signifiers and Acts*, 107–8.
241. Lacan, *L'insu: Le séminaire XXIV*, session of May 17, 1977.
242. "L'acte est-il au moment où Lénine donne tel ordre, ou au moment où les signifiants qui ont été lâchés sur le monde, donnent à tel succès précis dans la stratégie, son sens de commencement déjà tracé: quelque chose où la conséquence d'une certaine stratém gie pourra venir prendre sa place d'y prendre sa valeur de signe?" Lacan, *L'acte: Le séminaire XV*, session of January 10, 1968.
243. Hegel sees such a reversal in the form of law of the Roman Empire after the downfall of Greek antiquity. Here, Antigone is, in the function of the Spirit in Hegel, a vanishing mediator. Her act allows that behind the back of all involved in her drama, including herself, a new form of consciousness can come forth.
244. Žižek, *Tarrying with the Negative*, 89.
245. Slavoj Žižek, *Die Nacht der Welt: Psychoanalyse und deutscher Idealismus* (Frankfurt: Fischer, 1998), 32.
246. Cf. Manfred Schneider, *Das Attentat: Kritik der paranoischen Vernunft* (Berlin: Matthes und Seitz, 2010), 5–25.
247. Jean Laplanche, "Séduction, persécution, révélation," *Psychanalyse à l'Université* 18, no. 72 (1993): 3–34.
248. Cf. Žižek, *The Sublime Object of Ideology*, 87–99.
249. Cf. Ernesto Laclau, "Why Do Empty Signifiers Matter to Politics?," in *Emancipation(s)* (London: Verso, 1996), 36–46.
250. Scholem, *Walter Benjamin—Gershom Scholem*, 175.

251. See in this context my analysis in Dominik Finkelde, *Slavoj Žižek zwischen Lacan und Hegel: Politische Philosophie, Metapsychologie, Ethik* (Vienna: Turia und Kant, 2009), 101–2.
252. "Ich überlief den ersten Wächter," we read in Kafka, "nachträglich erschrak ich, lief wieder zurück und sagte dem Wächter: 'Ich bin hier durchgelaufen, während du abgewendet warst.' Der Wächter sah vor sich hin und schwieg. 'Ich hätte es wohl nicht tun sollen,' sagte ich. Der Wächter schwieg noch immer. 'Bedeutet dein Schweigen die Erlaubnis zu passieren?'" Franz Kafka, *Hochzeitsvorbereitungen auf dem Lande und andere Prosa aus dem Nachlaß*, ed. Max Brod (Frankfurt: Fischer, 1980), 260.
253. Franz Kafka, *The Trial* (Oxford: Oxford University Press, 2009), 5–10.
254. Žižek interprets this as follows: "The Kafkaesque illusion of an all-powerful Thing paying no attention to us, indifferent to our gaze, is the inverse-symmetrical counterpoint to the illusion that defines the ideological interpellation—namely, the illusion that the Other always-already looks at us, addresses us." Žižek, *For They Know Not What They Do*, 108.
255. "When we *recognize* ourselves as interpellated, as the addressees of an ideological call, we *misrecognize* the radical contingency of finding ourselves at the place of interpellation . . . We do not recognize ourselves in the ideological call because we were chosen; on the contrary, we perceive ourselves as chosen, as the addressee of a call, because we recognized ourselves in it—the contingent act of recognition engenders retroactively its own necessity." Žižek, *For They Know Not What They Do*, 108–9.
256. Žižek, *The Sublime Object of Ideology*, 87–88.
257. Cf. Ernst Bloch, "Die glückliche Hand," in *Spuren* (Frankfurt: Suhrkamp, 1985), 198–202.
258. Søren Kierkegaard, "On the Difference Between a Genius and an Apostle," in *The Present Age* (New York: Harper and Row, 1962), 87–108.
259. Slavoj Žižek, "Why Is Every Act a Repetition?," in *Enjoy Your Symptom: Jacques Lacan in Hollywood and Out* (London: Routledge, 1992), 69–112.
260. Kierkegaard, "On the Difference Between a Genius," 99. The following analysis expands upon insights from Finkelde, "Die Wahrheitsethik des Apostels und die Diskursethik des Genies: Lacan, Kierkegaard und Žižek," in *Paulus-Lektüren: Religiöse Ordnungsmodelle der Moderne*, ed. Sabine Bibl and Clemens Pornschlegel (Munich: Wilhelm Fink, 2013), 33–44.
261. Søren Kierkegaard, *Concluding Unscientific Postscript*, ed. Alastair Hannay (Cambridge: Cambridge University Press, 2009), 231*n*.
262. Ibid., 231.
263. Wittgenstein, *Tractatus Logico-Philosophicus*, §6.522.
264. Cf. James Conant, "Kierkegaard's *Postscript* and Wittgenstein's *Tractatus*: Teaching How to Pass from Disguised to Patent Nonsense," *Wittgenstein Studies* 2 (1997): http://sammelpunkt.philo.at:8080/519/1/11-2-97.TXT.
265. Cavell defines the goal of both authors as aiming "to *unmask* the audience. . . . And the effort to unmask requires a few masks or tricks of its own. . . . And in both writers the cure seems no cure. All we are given is the obvious, and the silence." Stanley Cavell, "Existentialism and Analytic Philosophy," in *Themes out of School: Effects and Causes*

(Chicago: University of Chicago Press, 1984), 195–234, here 218. Conant comments on Cavell in Conant, "Must We Show What We Cannot Say?," in *The Senses of Stanley Cavell*, ed. Richard Fleming and Michael Payne (Lewisburg, PA: Bucknell University Press, 1989), 242–83.

266. Žižek, "Why Is Every Act a Repetition?," 101.
267. Ibid., 93.
268. Ibid., 101.
269. Cf. Cavell, *The Psychoanalytic Mind*, 27–41, 196–205.
270. Cf. Snelling, *Philosophy, Psychoanalysis, and the Origins of Meaning*, 9–11; Gardner, *Irrationality and the Philosophy of Psychoanalysis*.
271. Žižek, "Why Is Every Act a Repetition," 94.
272. Ibid., 96.
273. Ibid., 99.
274. Cf., for example, Gilles Deleuze and Felix Guattari, *A Thousand Plateaus: Capitalism and Schizophrenia* (London: Continuum, 1992), 75–110.
275. Wittgenstein, *Remarks on the Foundation of Mathematics*, §§29, 237.
276. Wittgenstein, *Tractatus Logico-Philosophicus*, §5.632.
277. "Ein Flußbett der Gedanken verschieb[t sich]." Wittgenstein, *On Certainty*, §97. In §105 we read: "All testing, all confirmation and disconfirmation of a hypothesis takes place already within a system, and this system is not a more or less arbitrary and doubtful point of departure for all our arguments: no, it belongs to the essence of what we call an argument. The system is not so much the point of departure, as the element in which arguments have their life."
278. S.VII 83, 177; Lacan, *Le séminaire IX: L'identification*, session of March 14, 1962.
279. Lacan's position relates to the philosophy of intuitionism in the tradition of Luitzen E. J. Brouwer, as if consciousness could, so to speak, construct the external world. The spirit can create seemingly new, artificial entities by simply connecting elements. In this sense, Lacan's ethics of the Real resembles Badiou's ethics of the Event. According to Badiou, "The Event contains, besides the elements of its site, itself." Badiou, *Being and Event*, 189.
280. Dennett, *Consciousness Explained* (New York: Little, Brown, 1991), 244.
281. Lacan continues: "To have replaced these innumerable fears by the fear of a unique being who has no other means of manifesting his power than through what is feared behind these innumerable fears, is quite an accomplishment" (S.III 267).
282. Žižek, "Why Is Every Act a Repetition?," 100.
283. Ibid.
284. Lacan, *Télévision*, 9.
285. Alvin Plantinga, *Warranted Christian Belief* (Oxford: Oxford University Press, 2000), esp. 241–89.
286. Quoted in Elisabeth Roudinesco, *Jacques Lacan* (New York: Columbia University Press, 1997), 304.
287. This is at least my modest experience, having taught with several faculties.
288. Žižek, "Why Is Every Act a Repetition?," 101.

BIBLIOGRAPHY

Adkins, Brent. "Kant and the *Antigone*: The Possibility of Conflicting Duties." *International Philosophical Quarterly* 39, no. 4 (1999): 455–66.

Adorno, Theodor W. "Weltgeist und Naturgeschichte. Exkurs zu Hegel." In *Negative Dialektik*, 295–353. Frankfurt: Suhrkamp, 1992.

Agamben, Giorgio. *Language and Death: The Place of Negativity*. Translated by Karen Pinkus and Michael Hardt. Minneapolis: University of Minnesota Press, 2006.

Agamben, Giorgio, A. Badiou, D. Bensaïd, W. Brown, J.-L. Nancy, J. Rancière, K. Ross, and S. Žižek. *Demokratie? Eine Debatte mit Beiträgen von G. Agamben, A. Badiou, D. Bensaïd, W. Brown, J.-L. Nancy, J. Rancière, K. Ross und S. Žižek*. Berlin: Suhrkamp, 2012.

Albrecht, Michael. "Kants Maximenethik und ihre Begründung." *Kant-Studien* 85, no. 2 (1994): 129–46.

Allison, Henry E. *Kant's Groundwork for the Metaphysics of Morals*. Oxford: Oxford University Press, 2011.

——. *Kant's Theory of Freedom*. Cambridge: Cambridge University Press, 1990.

——. *Kant's Transcendental Idealism*. New Haven: Yale University Press, 2004.

Allouch, Jean. *Contre l'éternité. Ogawa, Mallarmé, Lacan*. Paris: Epel, 2009.

Althusser, Louis. "Ideology and Ideological State Apparatuses." In *On the Reproduction of Capitalism: Ideology and Ideological State Apparatuses*, 232–72. Translated by G. M. Goshgarian. London: Verso, 2014.

——. "On Ideology." In *On The Reproduction of Capitalism: Ideology and Ideological State Apparatuses*, 171–208. Translated by G. M. Goshgarian. London: Verso, 2014.

Ameriks, Karl. *Kant and the Fate of Autonomy: Problems in the Appropriation of the Critical Philosophy*. Cambridge: Cambridge University Press, 2000.

——. "Probleme der Moralität bei Kant und Hegel." In *Das Recht der Vernunft: Kant und Hegel über Denken, Erkennen und Handeln*, edited by Christel Fricke, Peter König, and Thomas Peterson, 263–89. Stuttgart-Bad Cannstatt: Frommann-Holzboog, 1995.

Anscombe, Elizabeth. "Modern Moral Philosophy." In *Virtue Ethics*, edited by Roger Crisp and Michael Slote, 26–45. Oxford: Oxford University Press, 1997.

Apel, Karl-Otto. *Transformation der Philosophie*. Vol. 2. Frankfurt: Suhrkamp, 1973.

Apollon, Willy, and Richard Feldstein, ed. *Lacan, Politics, Aesthetics*. New York: State University of New York Press, 1995.

Aristotle. *Nicomachean Ethics*. Edited and translated by Roger Crisp. Cambridge: Cambridge University Press, 2000.

Axelos, Christos. "Zu Hegels Interpretation der Tragödie." *Zeitschrift für philosophische Forschung* 19, no. 4 (1965): 655–67.

Baas, Bernard. *Le désir pur: Parcours philosophiques dans les parages de J. Lacan*. Leuven: Peeters, 2002.

Badiou, Alain. *Being and Event*. Translated by Oliver Feltham. London: Continuum, 2006.

——. *Ethics: An Essay on the Understanding of Evil*. Translated by Peter Hallward. London: Verso, 2013.

——. *Manifesto for Philosophy*. Edited and translated by Norman Madarasz. Albany: State University of New York Press, 1999.

——. *The Rational Kernel of the Hegelian Dialectic*. Melbourne: Re-Press, 2011.

——. *Theoretical Writings*. Edited and translated by Ray Brassier and Alberto Toscano. London: Continuum, 2004.

——. *Theory of the Subject*. London: Continuum, 2009.

Bahr, Petra. *Darstellung des Undarstellbaren*. Tübingen: Mohr Siebeck, 2004.

Baron, Marcia W. *Kantian Ethics Almost Without Apology*. New York: Cornell University Press, 1999.

Battersby, Christine. *Phenomenal Woman: Feminist Metaphysics and the Patterns of Identity*. New York: Blackwell, 1998.

Bayer, Oswald. *Vernunft ist Sprache: Hamanns Metakritik Kants*. Stuttgart-Bad Cannstatt: Frommann-Holzboog, 2002.

Beck, Lewis W. *A Commentary on Kant's Critique of Practical Reason*. Chicago: University of Chicago Press, 1960.

——. "Kant and the Right of Revolution." *Journal of the History of Ideas* 32, no. 1 (1971): 411–22.

Benjamin, Walter. "Excavation and Memory." In *Selected Writings*, vol. 2, *1927–1934*, edited by Michael W. Jennings, Howard Eiland, and Gary Smith, translated by Rodney Livingstone et al., 576. Cambridge: Belknap Press of Harvard University Press, 1999.

——. "On the Concept of History." In *Selected Writings*, vol. 4, *1938–1940*, edited by Howard Eiland and Michael W. Jennings, translated by Edmund Jephcott et al., 389–400. Cambridge: Belknap Press of Harvard University Press, 2003.

——. *The Origin of German Tragic Drama*. Translated by John Osborn. London: Verso, 2003.

Benveniste, Émile. "Subjectivity in Language." In *Problems in General Linguistics*. Miami: Miami University Press, 1973.

Bernstein, Jay M. *The Fate of Art: Aesthetic Alienation from Kant to Derrida and Adorno*. University Park: Pennsylvania State University Press, 1992.

Bjerre, Henrik Joker. "Enjoying the Law: On a Possible Conflict Vetween Kant's Views on Obedience and Enjoyment." *SATS: Northern European Journal of Philosophy* 6, no. 2 (2005): 114–27.

——. *Kantian Deeds*. London: Continuum, 2010.

Bloch, Ernst. "Die glückliche Hand." In *Spuren*, 198–202. Frankfurt: Suhrkamp, 1985.

——. *Naturrecht und menschliche Würde*. Frankfurt: Suhrkamp, 1961.

Bojanowski, Jochen. *Kants Theorie der Freiheit*. Berlin: De Gruyter, 2006.

Borch-Jacobsen, Mikkel. *Lacan: The Absolute Master*. Translated by Douglas Brick. Stanford: Stanford University Press, 1991.

Brandom, Robert. *Articulating Reasons: An Introduction to Inferentialism*. Cambridge: Harvard University Press, 2000.

——. *Making It Explicit: Reasoning, Representing, and Discursive Commitment*. Cambridge: Harvard University Press, 1994.

——. *Reason in Philosophy: Animating Ideas*. Cambridge: Harvard University Press, 2009.

——. "Semantik ohne Wahrheit: Ein Interview mit Robert Brandom von Matthias Haase." *Deutsche Zeitschrift für Philosophie* 54, no. 3 (2006): 449–66.

——. *Tales of the Mighty Dead: Historical Essays in the Metaphysics of Intentionality*. Cambridge: Harvard University Press, 2002.

Brandt, Reinhard. "Das Erlaubnisgesetz, oder: Vernunft und Geschichte in Kants Rechtslehre." In *Rechtsphilosophie der Aufklärung*, edited by Reinhard Brandt, 233–85. Berlin: De Gruyter, 1982.

Brunner, José. *Freud and the Politics of Psychoanalysis*. Oxford: Blackwell, 1995.

Bubner, Rüdiger. *Handlung, Sprache und Vernunft: Grundbegriffe praktischer Philosophie*. Frankfurt: Suhrkamp, 1982.

Butler, Judith. *Antigone's Claim: Kinship Between Life and Death*. New York: Columbia University Press, 2007.

——. "'Conscience Doth Make Subjects of Us All': Althusser's Subjection." In *The Psychic Life of Power: Theories in Subjection*, 106–31. Stanford: Stanford University Press, 1997.

——. "Deconstruction and the Possibility of Justice: Comments on Bernasconi, Cornell, Miller, Weber." *Cardozo Law Review* 11 (1990): 1715–18.

——. *Excitable Speech: A Politics of the Performative*. New York: Routledge, 1997.

Cashman, Sean Dennis. *African-Americans and the Quest for Civil Rights, 1900–1980*. New York: New York University Press, 1991.

Cavell, Marcia. *The Psychoanalytic Mind: From Freud to Philosophy*. Cambridge: Harvard University Press, 1993.

Cavell, Stanley. "Existentialism and Analytic Philosophy." In *Themes out of School: Effects and Causes*, 195–234. Chicago: University of Chicago Press, 1984.

——. "Freud and Philosophy: A Fragment." *Critical Inquiry* 13, no. 2 (1987): 386–93.

Cecchinato, Giorgia. "Die praktische Urteilskraft und das Gesetz der Freiheit." Vol. 3 of *Recht und Frieden in der Philosophie Kants: Akten des X. Internationalen Kant-Kongresses*, edited by Valerio Rohden, Ricardo R. Rerra, Guido Antonio Almeida, and Margit Ruffing, 71–81. Berlin: De Gruyter, 2008.

Chiesa, Lorenzo. "The Subject of the Real." In *Subjectivity and Otherness: A Philosophical Reading of Lacan*, 104–39. Cambridge: MIT Press, 2007.

Conant, James. "Kierkegaard's *Postscript* and Wittgenstein's *Tractatus*: Teaching How to Pass from Disguised to Patent Nonsense." *Wittgenstein Studies* 2 (1997). http://sammelpunkt.philo.at:8080/519/1/11-2-97.TXT.

——. "Must We Show What We Cannot Say?" In *The Senses of Stanley Cavell*, edited by Richard Fleming and Michael Payne, 242–83. Lewisburg, PA: Bucknell University Press, 1989.

Critchley, Simon. *The Ethics of Deconstruction: Derrida and Levinas*. Oxford: Blackwell, 1992.

Danzico, Matt, and Kate Dailey. "Is the US Declaration of Independence Illegal?" BBC News, October 19, 2011. www.bbc.co.uk/news/magazine-15345511.

Davidson, Donald. "Two Paradoxes of Irrationality." In *Philosophical Essays on Freud*, edited by Richard Wollheim and James Hopkins, 289–305. Cambridge: Cambridge University Press, 1982.

Declercq, Frédéric. "Lacan's Concept of the Real of Jouissance: Clinical Illustrations and Implications." *Psychoanalysis, Culture and Society* 9, no. 2 (2004): 237–51.

Deleuze, Gilles, and Felix Guattari. *A Thousand Plateaus: Capitalism and Schizophrenia*. London: Continuum, 1992.

Dennett, Daniel. *Consciousness Explained*. New York: Little, Brown, 1991.

Derrida, Jacques. "Declarations of Independence." In *Negotiations: Interventions and Interviews, 1971–2001*, 46–54. Stanford: Stanford University Press, 2002.

——. *Force of Law: The "Mystical Foundation of Authority."* In *Acts of Religion*, edited by Gil Anidjar, 228–298. New York: Routledge, 2002.

——. *Glas: Que reste-t-il du savoir absolu?* Paris: Denoël/Gonthier, 1981.

——. "The Politics of Friendship." *Journal of Philosophy* 85, no. 11 (1988): 632–44.

Desmond, William. "Kant and the Terror of Genius: Between Enlightenment and Romanticism." In *Kants Ästhetik: Kant's Aesthetics: L'ésthétique de Kant*, edited by Herman Parret, 594–614. Berlin: De Gruyter, 1998.

Dewey, John. *German Philosophy and Politics*. New York: Holt, 1915.

Dosse, François. *History of Structuralism: The Sign Sets, 1967–Present*. Vol. 2. Translated by Deborah Glassman. Minneapolis: University of Minnesota Press, 1997.

Dudley, Will. *Hegel, Nietzsche, and Philosophy: Thinking Freedom*. Cambridge: Cambridge University Press, 2002.

Dummett, Michael. "Can an Effect Precede Its Cause?" In *Truth and Other Enigmas*, edited by Michael Dummet, 319–32. Cambridge: Harvard University Press, 1978.

Düsing, Klaus. "Das Problem der Subjektivität in Hegels Logik." *Hegel-Studien*, supplement 15 (1976).

——. "Die Theorie der Tragödie bei Hölderlin und Hegel." In *Subjektivität und Freiheit: Untersuchungen zum Idealismus von Kant bis Hegel*, 275–312. Stuttgart-Bad Cannstatt: Frommann-Holzboog, 2002.

Eagleton, Terry. *The Ideology of the Aesthetic*. Oxford: Blackwell, 2000.

——. *Trouble with Strangers: A Study of Ethics*. Oxford: Wiley Blackwell, 2008.

Ensslin, Felix. "Accesses to the Real: Lacan, Monotheism, and Predestination." In *Lacan and Philosophy: The New Generation*, special issue, *European Journal of Psychoanalysis* 32 (2011): 49–91.

——. "Die Entbehrung des Absoluten: Das Subjekt der Nichtigkeit in Luthers Magnificat-Auslegung." PhD diss., Universität Potsdam, 2008.

Ensslin, Gudrun, und Bernward Vesper. *"Notstandsgesetze von Deiner Hand": Briefe 1968/1969*. Berlin: Suhrkamp, 2009.

Esser, Andrea. *Eine Ethik für Endliche: Kants Tugendlehre in der Gegenwart*. Stuttgart-Bad Cannstatt: Frommann-Holzboog, 2004.

Eyers, Tom. *Lacan and the Concept of the "Real."* New York: Palgrave Macmillan, 2012.

Felman, Shoshana. *The Literary Speech Act: Don Juan with J. L. Austin, or Seduction in Two Languages*. Cornell: Cornell University Press, 1983.

Fink, Bruce. *A Clinical Introduction To Lacanian Psychoanalysis*. Cambridge: Harvard University Press, 1997.

——. *Eine klinische Einführung in die Lacan'sche Psychoanalyse: Theorie und Technik*. Vienna: Turia und Kant, 2010.

——. *The Lacanian Subject. Between Language and Jouissance*. Princeton: Princeton University Press, 1995.

——. *Das Lacan'sche Subjekt: Zwischen Sprache und Jouissance*. Translated by Tim Caspar Boehme. Vienna: Turia und Kant, 2006.

——. *Lacan to the Letter: Reading* Écrits *Closely*. Minneapolis: University of Minnesota Press, 2004.

Finkelde, Dominik. "Excessive Subjectivity: Hegel and Kierkegaard on the Paradox of Autonomy and Liberation." In *Kierkegaard and Politics: The Intervention of the Single Individual*, edited by Sophie Wennerscheid and Armen Avanessian, 111–39. Copenhagen: Museum Tusculanum, 2014.

——. "Gegen die politische Philosophie? Theorien politischer Eskalation im 20. Jahrhundert und der Gegenwart von Martin Heidegger bis Alain Badiou." *Philosophische Rundschau* 57, no. 4 (2010): 322–41.

——. "Logics of Scission: The Subject as 'Limit of the World' in Badiou and Wittgenstein." *Philosophy Today* 61, no. 3 (2017).

——. Politische Eschatologie nach Paulus: Badiou, Agamben, Žižek, Santner. Vienna: Turia und Kant, 2006.

——. "Politische Logik: Zum Subjekt als Grenze bei Wittgenstein und Badiou." In *Souveränität und Subversion: Figurationen des Politisch-Imaginären*, edited by Rebekka Klein and Dominik Finkelde, 216–41. Freiburg: Alber, 2015.

——. *Slavoj Žižek zwischen Lacan und Hegel: Politische Philosophie, Metapsychologie, Ethik*. Vienna: Turia und Kant, 2009.

——. "Die Wahrheitsethik des Apostels und die Diskursethik des Genies: Lacan, Kierkegaard und Žižek." In *Paulus-Lektüren: Religiöse Ordnungsmodelle der Moderne*, edited by Sabine Bibl and Clemens Pornschlegel, 33–44. Munich: Wilhelm Fink, 2013.

Forschner, Maximilian. "Immanuel Kants 'Hang zum Bösen' und Thomas von Aquins 'Gesetz des Zunders': Über säkulare Aufklärungsanthropologie und christliche Erbsündenlehre." *Zeitschrift für philosophische Forschung* 63, no. 4 (2009): 519–42.

——. "Über die verschiedenen Bedeutungen des 'Hangs zum Bösen.'" In *Immanuel Kant—die Religion innerhalb der Grenzen der bloßen Vernunft*, edited by Otfried Höffe, 71–90. Berlin: Akademie, 2011.

Frege, Gottlob. *The Foundations of Arithmetic: A Logico-Mathematical Enquiry Into the Concept of Number.* Translated by J. L. Austin. Evanston, IL: Northwestern University Press, 1980.

——. "Thought." In *The Frege Reader*, edited by Michael Beaney. Malden, MA: Blackwell, 1997.

Freud, Sigmund. *Abriß der Psychoanalyse: Einführende Darstellungen.* Frankfurt: Fischer, 1970.

——. *Beyond the Pleasure Principle.* Vol. 18 of *Standard Edition of the Complete Works of Sigmund Freud.* Translated by James Strachey et al. London: Hogarth, 1994.

——. *The Interpretation of Dreams.* Vols. 4 and 5 of *Standard Edition of the Complete Works of Sigmund Freud.* Translated by James Strachey et al. London: Hogarth, 1994.

——. *New Introductory Lectures on Psycho-Analysis.* Vol. 22 of *Standard Edition of the Complete Works of Sigmund Freud.* Translated by James Strachey et al. London: Hogarth, 1994.

——. *On Narcissism: An Introduction.* Vol. 14 of *Standard Edition of the Complete Works of Sigmund Freud.* Translated by James Strachey et al. London: Hogarth, 1994.

——. *An Outline of Psychoanalysis.* New York: Norton, 1989.

——. "Project for a Scientific Psychology." Vol. 1 of *Standard Edition of the Complete Works of Sigmund Freud*, 283–397. Translated by James Strachey et al. London: Hogarth, 1994.

——. *Zur Einführung in den Narzißmus.* Vol. 3 of *Studienausgabe*, edited by Alexander Mitscherlich, Angela Richards, and James Strachey, 37–68. Frankfurt: Fischer, 1982.

Freud, Sigmund, and Josef Breuer. *Studies on Hysteria.* Vol. 2 of *Standard Edition of the Complete Works of Sigmund Freud.* Translated by James Strachey et al. London: Hogarth, 1962.

Friedman, Michael. *Dynamics of Reason.* Stanford: Stanford University Press, 2001.

Gabriel, Markus. *An den Grenzen der Erkenntnistheorie: Die notwendige Endlichkeit des objektiven Wissens als Lektion des Skeptizismus.* Freiburg: Alber, 2008.

——. *Fields of Sense: A New Realist Ontology.* Edinburgh: Edinburgh University Press, 2015.

——. "The Pathological Structure of Representation as Such: Hegel's *Anthropology*." In *Transcendental Ontology: Essays in German Idealism*, 48–59. London: Continuum, 2011.

Gamm, Gerhard. *Der Wahnsinn in der Vernunft: Historische und erkenntniskritische Studie zur Dimension des Anders-Seins in der Philosophie Hegels.* Bonn: Bouvier, 1981.

Gardner, Sebastian. "Freud and Philosophy: Psychoanalytic Theory: A Historical Reconstruction." *Aristotelian Society*, supplementary volume 86, no. 1 (2012): 41–60.

——. *Irrationality and the Philosophy of Psychoanalysis.* Cambridge: Cambridge University Press, 2007.

Geiger, Ido. *The Founding Act of Modern Ethical Life: Hegel's Critique of Kant's Moral and Political Philosophy.* Stanford: Stanford University Press, 2007.

Gert, Joshua. "Korsgaard's Private Reason Argument." *Philosophy and Phenomenological Research* 64, no. 2 (2002): 303–24.

Giordanetti, Piero. "Das Verhältnis von Genie, Künstler und Wissenschaftler in der kantischen Philosophie." *Kant-Studien* 86, no. 4 (1995): 406–30.

Green, Ronald M. "Kant and Kierkegaard on the Need for a Historical Faith: An Imaginary Dialogue." In *Kant and the New Philosophy of Religion*, edited by Chris L. Firestone and Stephen R. Palmquist, 157–78. Bloomington: Indiana University Press, 2006.

Gregor, Kai. "'Revolution der Gesinnung' und 'Vollendung der Freiheit.'" *Fichte-Studien* 31 (2007): 159–73.

Gubeljic, Mischa, Simone Link, and Patrick Müller. "Nature and Second Nature in McDowell's 'Mind and World.'" In *John McDowell: Reason and Nature: Lecture and Colloquium in Münster 1999*, edited by Marcus Willaschek, 41–49. Münster: LIT, 2000.

Habermas, Jürgen. *Knowledge and Human Interest*. Translated by Jeremy J. Shapiro. Boston: Beacon, 1971.

——. *Moralbewußtsein und kommunikatives Handeln*. Frankfurt: Suhrkamp, 1983.

——. *Der philosophische Diskurs der Moderne*. Frankfurt: Suhrkamp, 1985.

——. *Postmetaphysical Thinking: Philosophical Essays*. Translated by Mark Hohengarten. Cambridge: MIT Press, 1992.

——. *Wahrheit und Rechtfertigung: Philosophische Aufsätze*. Frankfurt: Suhrkamp, 1999.

——. "Werte und Normen: Ein Kommentar zu Hilary Putnams Kantischen Pragmatismus." In *Die Öffentlichkeit der Vernunft und die Vernunft der Öffentlichkeit: Festschrift für Jürgen Habermas*, edited by Klaus Günther and Lutz Wingert, 280–305. Frankfurt: Suhrkamp, 2002.

Hackenesch, Christa. "Der subjektive Geist: Hegels Begriff des Menschen." In *Hegel Jahrbuch 2002 (Teil 2)*, edited by Karol Bal and Henning Ottmann, 40–43. Berlin: Akademie, 2002.

Halbig, Christoph. "Zur Wahrheit des Gewissens." In *Hegels Phänomenologie des Geistes: Ein kooperativer Kommentar*, edited by Klaus Vieweg and Wolfgang Welsch, 489–503. Frankfurt: Suhrkamp, 2008.

Hardimon, Michael O. "Role Obligations." *Journal of Philosophy* 91, no. 7 (1994): 333–63.

Hare, Richard M. *Die Sprache der Moral*. Frankfurt: Suhrkamp, 1983.

Haute, Philipp van. *Against Adaptation: Lacan's Subversion of the Subject*. New York: Other, 2002.

Heath, Joseph. *Following the Rules: Practical Reason and Deontic Constraint*. Oxford: Oxford University Press, 2008.

Hegel, Georg Wilhelm Friedrich. *Aesthetics: Lectures on Fine Art*. Vol. 1. Translated by T. M. Knox. Oxford: Oxford University Press, 1975.

——. *Aesthetics: Lectures on Fine Art*. Vol. 2. Translated by T. M. Knox. Oxford: Oxford University Press, 1975.

——. *Briefe von und an Hegel*. Vol. 1. Edited by Johannes Hoffmeister. Hamburg: Meiner, 1952.

——. *Elements of the Philosophy of Right*. Edited by Allen W. Wood. Translated by Hugo Barr Nisbet. Cambridge: Cambridge University Press, 1991.

——. *Encyclopedia of the Philosophical Sciences in Basic Outline*, part 1, *Science of Logic*. Edited and translated by Klaus Brinkmann and Daniel O. Dahlstrom. Cambridge: Cambridge University Press, 2010.

——. *Lectures on the History of Philosophy*, vol. 1, *Greek Philosophy to Plato*. Translated by E. S. Haldane and Frances H. Simon. Lincoln: University of Nebraska Press, 1995.

——. *Lectures on the Philosophy of World History*, vol. 1, *Manuscripts of the Introduction and the Lectures of 1822–1826*. Edited and translated by Robert F. Brown and Peter C. Hodgson. Oxford: Oxford University Press, 2001.

——. *Lectures on the Philosophy of World History*. Translated by H. B. Nisbet. Cambridge: Cambridge University Press, 1984.

——. "On the Scientific Ways of Treating Natural Law, on Its Place in Practical Philosophy, and Its Relation to the Positive Sciences of Right." In *Political Writings*, edited by Laurence

Dickey and Hugo Barr Nisbet, translated by Hugo Barr Nisbet, 102–80. Cambridge: Cambridge University Press, 1999.
——. *Phenomenology of Spirit*. Translated by A. V. Miller. Oxford: Oxford University Press, 1977.
——. *Philosophie des Rechts: Vorlesungsnachschrift H. G. Hotho*. Vol. 3 of *Vorlesungen über Rechtsphilosophie 1818–1831*, edited by Karl-Heinz Ilting. Stuttgart-Bad Cannstatt: Frommann-Holzboog, 1994.
——. *The Philosophy of History*. Translated by J. Sibree. Buffalo, NY: Prometheus, 1991.
——. *Philosophy of Mind*. Translated by W. Wallace and A. V. Miller. Oxford: Oxford University Press, 2007.
——. *The Science of Logic*. Edited and translated by George di Giovanni. Cambridge: Cambridge University Press, 2010.
——. "The Spirit of Christianity and Its Fate." In *Early Theological Writings*, 182–301. Chicago: University of Chicago Press, 1996.
——. *Vorlesungen über die Geschichte der Philosophie, Bd. I*. Vol. 18 of *Werke in zwanzig Bänden*, edited by Eva Moldenhauer and Karl Markus Michel. Frankfurt: Suhrkamp, 1986.
——. *Vorlesungen über die Philosophie der Weltgeschichte, Bd. I: Die Vernunft in der Geschichte*. Edited by Johannes Hoffmeister. Hamburg: Meiner, 1994.
Heidegger, Martin. *Being and Time*. Translated by John Macquarrie and Edward Robinson. Oxford: Blackwell, 1962.
——. "The Greek Interpretation of Human Beings in Sophocles' Antigone." In *Hölderlin's Hymn "The Ister,"* translated by William McNeill and Julia Davis, 51–122. Bloomington: Indiana University Press, 1996.
——. *Kant und das Problem der Metaphysik*. Vol. 3 of *Gesamtausgabe*. Frankfurt: Klostermann, 1977.
——. *The Phenomenology of Religious Life*. Translated by Matthias Fritsch and Jennifer Anna Gosetti-Ferencei. Bloomington: Indiana University Press, 2010.
——. "Das Seyn (Ereignis)." In *Beiträge zur Philosophie*. Vol. 65 of *Gesamtausgabe*, 470–77. Frankfurt: Klostermann, 1989.
Henrich, Dieter. *Hegel im Kontext*. Frankfurt: Suhrkamp, 1971.
——. "Vernunft in Verwirklichung." In *Georg Wilhelm Friedrich Hegel, Philosophie des Rechts: Die Vorlesung von 1819/20*, edited by Dieter Henrich, 9–39. Frankfurt: Suhrkamp, 1983.
Herman, Barbara. *The Practice of Moral Judgment*. Cambridge: Harvard University Press, 1993.
Hill, Thomas E. *Respect, Pluralism and Justice*. Oxford: Oxford University Press, 2000.
Höffe, Otfried. "Ausblick: Aristoteles oder Kant—wider eine plane Alternative." In *Aristoteles: Die Nikomachische Ethik*, edited by Otfried Höffe, 277–304. Berlin: Akademie, 1995.
——. *Immanuel Kant: Metaphysische Anfangsgründe der Rechtslehre*. Berlin: Akademie, 1999.
——. *Kant's Cosmopolitan Theory of Law and Peace*. Cambridge: Cambridge University Press, 2006.
——. "Kants kategorischer Imperativ als Kriterium des Sittlichen." *Zeitschrift für philosophische Forschung* 31, no. 3 (1977): 354–84.
——. "Universalistische Ethik und Urteilskraft: ein aristotelischer Blick auf Kant." *Zeitschrift für philosophische Forschung* 44, no. 4 (1990): 537–63.
Honneth, Axel, ed. *Deutsche Philosophie und deutsche Politik*. Berlin: Philo, 2000.

——. *Freedom's Right: The Social Foundations of Democratic Life*. Translated by Joseph Ganahl. Cambridge: Polity, 2014.

——. "Kein Ende der Geschichte? Geschichtsphilosophie nach Kant." In *Nach Kant: Erbe und Kritik*, edited by Ian Kaplow, 118–33. Münster: LIT, 2005.

——. *Leiden an Unbestimmtheit: eine Reaktualisierung der Hegel'schen Rechtsphilosophie*. Stuttgart: Reclam, 2001.

Horn, Christoph. "Die menschliche Gattungsnatur: Anlagen zum Guten und Hang zum Bösen." In *Immanuel Kant: Die Religion innerhalb der Grenzen der bloßen Vernunft*, edited by Otfried Höffe, 43–70. Berlin: Akademie, 2011.

Horstmann, Rolf-Peter. "Hegels Theorie der bürgerlichen Gesellschaft." In *Georg Wilhelm Friedrich Hegel: Grundlinien der Philosophie des Rechts: Klassiker auslegen*, edited by Ludwig Siep, 194–216. Berlin: Akademie, 2005.

Hösle, Vittorio. *Hegels System*. Hamburg: Meiner, 1987.

Houlgate, Stephen. "Action, Right and Morality in Hegel's Philosophy of Right." In *Hegel on Action*, edited by Arto Laitinen and Constantine Sandis, 155–75. London: Palgrave Macmillan, 2010.

Iber, Christian. "Tragödie, Komödie und Farce: Zur geschichtsphilosophischen Ortsbestimmung der Tragödie bei Hegel und Marx." In *Die Philosophie des Tragischen: Schopenhauer, Schelling, Nietzsche*, edited by Lore Hühn and Philipp Schwab, 281–96. New York: De Gruyter, 2011.

Ilting, Karl Heinz. "Gibt es eine kritische Ethik und Rechtsphilosophie Kants?" *Archiv für Geschichte der Philosophie* 63, no. 3 (1981): 325–45.

Jandl, Martin J. *Praxeologische Funktionalontologie: Eine Theorie des Wissens als Synthese von H. Dooyeweerd und R. B. Brandom*. Frankfurt: Lang, 2010.

Jeske, Diana. *Rationality and Moral Theory: How Intimacy Generates Reasons*. London: Routledge, 2008.

Kaehler, Klaus Erich. "Das Kontingente und die Ausnahme im spekulativen Denken." Vol. 1 of *Die Ausnahme denken: Festschrift zum 60. Geburtstag von Klaus-Michael Kodalle in zwei Bänden*, edited by Claus Dierksmeier, 63–71. Würzburg: Königshausen und Neumann, 2003.

Kafka, Franz. *Hochzeitsvorbereitungen auf dem Lande und andere Prosa aus dem Nachlaß*. Edited by Max Brod. Frankfurt: Fischer, 1980.

——. *Der Prozeß*. Edited by Malcolm Pasley. Frankfurt: Fischer, 1990.

——. *The Trial*. Oxford: Oxford University Press, 2009.

Kain, Philip J. "Hegel, Antigone and Women." *Owl of Minerva* 33, no. 2 (2002): 157–77.

Kant, Immanuel. "An Answer to the Question: What Is Enlightenment?" In *Practical Philosophy*, edited and translated by Mary J. Gregor, 11–22. Cambridge: Cambridge University Press, 1999.

——. "Anthropology from a Pragmatic Point of View." In *Anthropology, History and Education*, edited by Günter Zöller and Robert B. Louden, translated by Robert B. Louden, 227–429. Cambridge: Cambridge University Press, 2007.

——. "The Conflict of the Faculties." In *Religion and Rational Theology*, edited by Allen W. Wood and George di Giovanni, translated by Mary J. Gregor and Robert Anchor, 233–309. Cambridge: Cambridge University Press, 1996.

———. "Conjectural Beginning of Human History." In *Anthropology, History and Education*, edited by Günter Zöller and Robert B. Louden, translated by Allen W. Wood, 160–77. Cambridge: Cambridge University Press, 2007.

———. *Critique of the Power of Judgment*. Edited by Paul Guyer. Translated by Paul Guyer and Eric Matthews. Cambridge: Cambridge University Press, 2000.

———. *Critique of Practical Reason*. In *Practical Philosophy*, edited and translated by Mary J. Gregor, 133–271. Cambridge: Cambridge University Press, 1996.

———. *Critique of Pure Reason*. Edited and translated by Paul Guyer and Allen W. Wood. Cambridge: Cambridge University Press, 1997.

———. "Groundwork of the Metaphysics of Morals." In *Practical Philosophy*, edited and translated by Mary J. Gregor, 37–108. Cambridge: Cambridge University Press, 1999.

———. *Kritik der reinen Vernunft*. 1st ed. In *Akademieausgabe*, 29 vols. Berlin: De Gruyter, 1903.

———. *Lectures on Metaphysics*. Edited and translated by Karl Ameriks and Steven Naragon. Cambridge: Cambridge University Press, 1997.

———. "Lectures on Pedagogy," In *Anthropology, History, and Education*, edited by Günter Zöller and Robert B. Louden, translated by Robert B. Louden, 434–85. Cambridge: Cambridge University Press, 2007.

———. *The Metaphysics of Morals*. In *Practical Philosophy*, edited and translated by Mary J. Gregor, 353–488. Cambridge: Cambridge University Press, 1999.

———. *Metaphysik* L_2 *(1790–1791)*. In *Lectures on Metaphysics*, edited and translated by Karl Ameriks and Steve Naragon, 299–354. Cambridge: Cambridge University Press, 1997.

———. *Metaphyik Mrongovius*. In *Lectures on Metaphysics*, edited and translated by Karl Ameriks and Steve Naragon, 109–286. Cambridge: Cambridge University Press, 1997.

———. "On a Supposed Right to Lie from Philanthropy." In *Practical Philosophy*, edited and translated by Mary J. Gregor, 611–15. Cambridge: Cambridge University Press, 1999.

———. "On the Common Saying: That May Be Correct in Theory, but It Is of No Use in Practice." In *Practical Philosophy*, translated and edited by Mary J. Gregor, 273–309. Cambridge: Cambridge University Press, 1999.

———. *Practical Philosophy*. Edited and translated by Mary J. Gregor. Cambridge: Cambridge University Press, 1999.

———. *Prolegomena to Any Future Metaphysics*. Rev. ed. Edited by Karl Ameriks and Desmond M. Clarke. Translated by Gary Hatfield. Cambridge: Cambridge University Press, 2004.

———. *Religion and Rational Theology*. Edited and translated by Allen W. Wood and George Di Giovanni. Cambridge: Cambridge University Press, 1996.

———. *Religion Within the Boundaries of Mere Reason*. In *Religion and Rational Theology*, edited by Paul Guyer and Allen W. Wood, translated by George di Giovanni, 39–215. Cambridge: Cambridge University Press, 2001.

Kaulbach, Friedrich. "Der transzendentale Perspektivismus Kants." In *Philosophie des Perspektivismus*, vol. 1, 11–137. Tübingen: Mohr Siebeck, 1990.

Kearney, Richard. "Derrida and the Ethics of Dialogue." *Philosophy and Social Criticism* 19, no. 1 (1993): 1–14.

Kersting, Wolfgang. *Wohlgeordnete Freiheit: Immanuel Kants Rechts- und Staatsphilosophie*. Berlin: De Gruyter, 1983.

Kierkegaard, Søren. *Abschließende Unwissenschaftliche Nachschrift*. Vol. 1. Düsseldorf: Eugen Diederichs, 1957.

——. *Concluding Unscientific Postscript*. Edited by Alastair Hannay. Cambridge: Cambridge University Press, 2009.

——. "On the Difference Between a Genius and an Apostle." In *The Present Age*, 87–108. New York: Harper and Row, 1962.

——. "Über den Unterschied zwischen einem Genie und einem Apostel." In *Gesammelte Werke: Kleine Schriften, 1848/49*, 115–34. Düsseldorf: Eugen Diederichs, 1960.

Kittler, Friedrich. *Draculas Vermächtnis*. Leipzig: Reclam, 1993.

Kittler, Wolf. *Die Geburt des Partisanen aus dem Geist der Poesie: Heinrich von Kleist und die Strategie der Befreiungskriege*. Freiburg: Rombach, 1987.

Kittsteiner, Heinz. *Die Entstehung des modernen Gewissens*. Frankfurt: Insel, 1991.

Kleingeld, Pauline. *Fortschritt und Vernunft: Zur Geschichtsphilosophie Kants*. Würzburg: Könighausen und Neumann, 1995.

Kleist, Heinrich von. *Michael Kohlhaas*. Vol. 1 of *Sämtliche Werke und Briefe*, edited by Helmut Sembdner. Munich: Hanser, 1993.

Klinger, Florian. *Urteilen*. Zurich: Diaphanes, 2011.

Kober, Michael. *Gewissheit als Norm: Wittgensteins Erkenntnistheoretische Untersuchungen in "Über Gewißheit."* Berlin: De Gruyter, 1993.

Kojève, Alexandre. *Introduction to the Reading of Hegel: Lectures on the Phenomenology of Spirit*. Edited by Raymond Queneau and Allan Bloom. Translated by James H. Nichols. Ithaca: Cornell University Press, 1980.

Korsgaard, Christine M. "Aristotle and Kant on the Source of Value." *Ethics* 96, no. 3 (1986): 486–505.

——. *The Constitution of Agency*. Oxford: Oxford University Press, 2008.

——. *Creating the Kingdom of Ends*. Cambridge: Cambridge University Press, 1996.

——. "From Duty and for the Sake of the Noble: Kant and Aristotle on Morally Good Action." In *The Constitution of Agency*, 174–206. Oxford: Oxford University Press, 1996.

——. "The Reasons We Can Share: An Attack on the Distinction Between Agent-Relative and Agent-Neutral Values." In *Creating the Kingdom of Ends*, 275–310. Cambridge: Cambridge University Press, 1996.

——. "The Right to Lie: Kant on Dealing with Evil." *Philosophy and Public Affairs* 15, no. 4 (1986): 325–49.

——. *Self-Constitution: Agency, Identity, and Integrity*. Oxford: Oxford University Press, 2009.

——. *The Sources of Normativity*. Cambridge: Cambridge University Press, 1996.

——. "Taking the Law Into Our Own Hands: Kant on the Right to Revolution." In *Reclaiming the History of Ethics: Essays for John Rawls*, edited by Andrews Reath, Barbara Herman, and Christine M. Korsgaard, 297–328. Cambridge: Cambridge University Press, 1997.

Kreitler, Hans, and Shulamith Kreitler. *Cognitive Orientation and Behavior*. New York: Springer, 1976.

Krüll, Marianne. *Schizophrenie und Gesellschaft: Zum Menschenbild in Psychiatrie und Soziologie*. Frankfurt: Suhrkamp, 1986.

Kuhn, Thomas. *The Road Since Structure: Philosophical Essays, 1970–1993*. Chicago: University of Chicago Press, 2002.

——. *The Structure of Scientific Revolutions*. 2nd ed. Chicago: University of Chicago Press, 1970.

Lacan, Jacques. "Aggressiveness in Psychoanalysis." In *Écrits: The First Complete Edition in English*, translated by Bruce Fink, 82–101. New York: Norton, 2006.

——. "Compte rendu avec interpolation du séminaire de l'éthique." *Ornicar? Revue du champ freudien* 28 (1984): 7–18.

——. *Écrits: The First Complete Edition in English*. Translated by Bruce Fink. New York: Norton, 2006.

——. *Écrits II*. Paris: Édition du Seuil, 1999.

——. *Feminine Sexuality: Jacques Lacan and the École Freudienne*. Edited by Juliet Mitchell and Jacqueline Rose. Translated by Jacqueline Rose. New York: Norton, 1982.

——. "The Function and Field of Speech and Language in Psychoanalysis." In *Écrits: The First Complete Edition in English*, 197–268.

——. "The Instance of the Letter in the Unconscious, or Reason Since Freud." In *Écrits: The First Complete Edition in English*, 412–41.

——. "Logical Time and the Assertion of Anticipated Certainty: A New Sophism." In *Écrits: The First Complete Edition in English*, 161–75.

——. "The Mirror Stage as Formative of the *I* Function as Revealed in Psychoanalytic Experience." In *Écrits: The First Complete Edition in English*, 75–81.

——. *My Teaching*. Translated by David Macey. London: Verso, 2008.

——. "On Structure as an Inmixing of an Otherness Prerequesite to Any Subject Whatever." In *The Structuralist Controversy: The Languages of Criticism and the Sciences of Man*, edited by Richard Macksey and Eugenio Donato, 186–95. Baltimore: Johns Hopkins University Press, 1970.

——. "Position of the Unconscious." In *Écrits: The First Complete Edition in English*, 703–21.

——. "Presentation on Psychical Causality." In *Écrits: The First Complete Edition in English*, 123–60.

——. "Proposition du 9 octobre 1967 sur le psychanalyste de l'École." In *Autres écrits*, edited by Jacques-Alain Miller, 243–60. Paris: Éditions du Seuil, 2001.

——. *Le séminaire VI: Le désir et son interprétation*. Paris: Editions de la Martinière/Le Champ Freudien, 2013.

——. *Le séminaire IX: L'identification*. Based on the version of *École lacanienne de psychanalyse*. http://staferla.free.fr/S9/S9.htm.

——. *Le séminaire XII: Les problèmes cruciaux pour la psychanalyse*. Based on the version of *École lacanienne de psychanalyse*. http://staferla.free.fr/S12/S12.htm.

——. *Le séminaire XIV: La logique du fantasme*. Based on the version of *École lacanienne de psychanalyse*. http://staferla.free.fr/S14/S14.htm.

——. *Le séminaire XV. L'acte*. Based on the version of *École lacanienne de psychanalyse*. http://staferla.free.fr/S15/S15.htm.

——. *Le séminaire XVII: L'envers de la psychanalyse*. Based on the version of *École lacanienne de psychanalyse*. http://staferla.free.fr/S17/S17.htm.

——. *Le séminaire XVIII: D'un discours qui ne serait pas du semblant.* Based on the version of *École lacanienne de psychanalyse.* http://staferla.free.fr/S18/S18.htm.

——. *Le séminaire XXI: Les non-dupes errent.* Based on the version of *École lacanienne de psychanalyse.* http://staferla.free.fr/S21/S21.htm.

——. Le séminaire XXIV: L'insu. Based on the version of *École lacanienne de psychanalyse.* http://staferla.free.fr/S24/S24.htm.

——. *The Seminar of Jacques Lacan: Book I, Freud's Papers on Technique, 1953–1954.* Edited by Jacques-Alain Miller. Translated by John Forrester. New York: Norton, 1988.

——. *The Seminar of Jacques Lacan: Book II, The Ego in Freud's Theory and in the Technique of Psychoanalysis, 1954–1955.* Edited by Jacques-Alain Miller. Translated by Sylvana Tomaselli. New York: Norton, 1988.

——. *The Seminar of Jacques Lacan: Book III, The Psychoses, 1955–1956.* Edited by Jacques-Alain Miller. Translated by Russell Grigg. New York: Norton, 1993.

——. *The Seminar of Jacques Lacan: Book VII, The Ethics of Psychoanalysis, 1959–1960.* Edited by Jacques-Alain Miller. Translated by Dennis Porter. London: Norton, 1992.

——. *The Seminar of Jacques Lacan: Book X, Anxiety.* Edited by Jacques-Alain Miller. Translated by A. R. Price. Cambridge: Polity, 2014.

——. *The Seminar of Jacques Lacan: Book XI, The Four Fundamental Concepts of Psychoanalysis, 1964.* Edited by Jacques-Alain Miller. Translated by Alan Sheridan. New York: Norton, 1981.

——. *The Seminar of Jacques Lacan: Book XVII, The Other Side of Psychoanalysis, 1969–1970.* Edited by Jacques-Alain Miller. Translated by Russell Grigg. London: Norton, 2007.

——. *The Seminar of Jacques Lacan: Book XX, Encore, 1972–1973.* Edited by Jacques-Alain Miller. Translated by Bruce Fink. New York: Norton, 1998.

——. "The Subversion of the Subject and the Dialectic of Desire in the Freudian Unconscious." In *Écrits: The First Complete Edition in English*, 671–702.

——. "The Symbolic, the Imaginary, and the Real." In *On the Names-of-the-Father*, edited by Bruce Fink, 1–52. Cambridge: Polity, 2015.

——. *Télévision.* Paris: Éditions du Seuil, 1974.

——. *Television/A Challenge to the Psychoanalytic Establishment.* Edited by Joan Copjec. London: Norton, 1990.

——. "Science and Truth." In *Écrits: The First Complete Edition in English*, 726–45.

Laclau, Ernesto. *Emanzipation and Differenz.* Vienna: Turia und Kant, 2007.

——. *New Reflections on the Revolution of Our Time.* London: Verso, 1990.

——. "Why Do Empty Signifiers Matter to Politics?" In *Emancipation(s)*, 36–46. London: Verso, 1996.

Laclau, Ernesto, and Chantal Mouffe. *Hegemony and Socialist Strategy: Towards a Radical Democratic Politics.* London: Verso, 2001.

Langlitz, Nicolas. *Die Zeit der Psychoanalyse: Lacan und das Problem der Sitzungsdauer.* Frankfurt: Suhrkamp, 2005.

Laplanche, Jean. *Die allgemeine Verführungstheorie und andere Aufsätze.* Tübingen: Edition Diskord, 1988.

——. "The Drive and Its Source-Object: Its Fate in the Transference." In *Essays on Otherness*, edited by John Fletcher, 117–32. London: Routledge, 1999.

——. "Séduction, persécution, révélation." *Psychanalyse à l'Université* 18, no. 72 (1993): 3–34.

Lear, Jonathan. *A Case for Irony*. Tanner Lectures on Human Values. Cambridge: Harvard University Press, 2011.

——. *Happiness, Death, and the Remainder of Life*. Cambridge: Harvard University Press, 2002.

——. "The Heterogeneity of the Mental." *Mind* 104, no. 416 (1995): 863–79.

——. *Open Minded*. Cambridge: Harvard University Press, 1999.

——. *Radical Hope: Ethics in the Face of Cultural Devastation*. Cambridge: Harvard University Press, 2008.

Levinas, Emmanuel. *Ethics and Infinity: Conversations with Philippe Nemo*. Pittsburgh: Duquesne University Press, 1995.

Lévi-Strauss, Claude. *Introduction to the Work of Marcel Mauss*. Translated by Felicity Baker. London: Routledge, 1987.

Livingston, Paul. "Agamben, Badiou, and Russell." *Continental Philosophy Review* 42 (2009): 297–325.

Longuenesse, Béatrice. "Freud and Philosophy. Kant's 'I' in 'I Ought To' and Freud's Superego." *Aristotelian Society*, supplementary volume 86, no. 1 (2012): 19–39.

——. *Kant and the Human Standpoint*. Cambridge: Cambridge University Press, 2009.

Lovell, Terry. "Resisting with Authority: Historical Specificity, Agency, and the Performative Self." *Theory, Culture, and Society* 20, no. 1 (2003): 1–17.

Lovibond, Sabina. *Realism and Imagination in Ethics*. Minneapolis: University of Minnesota Press, 1983.

Lübcke, Poul. "Kierkegaard and Indirect Communication." *History of European Ideas* 12, no. 1 (1990): 31–40.

Ludwig, Bernd. "Whence Public Right? The Role of Theoretical and Practical Reasoning in Kant's Doctrine of Right." In *Kant's Metaphysics of Morals: Interpretative Essays*, edited by Mark Timmons, 159–84. Oxford: Oxford University Press, 2002.

Ludwig, Ralf. *Kategorischer Imperativ und Metaphysik der Sitten: Die Frage nach der Einheitlichkeit von Kants Ethik*. Frankfurt: Lang, 1992.

Luhmann, Niklas. "Ethik als Reflexionstheorie der Moral." In *Gesellschaftsstruktur und Semantik: Studien zur Wissenssoziologie der modernen Gesellschaft*, vol. 3, 358–447. Frankfurt: Suhrkamp, 1989.

Lütterfelds, Wilhelm. "Ich und Welt." *Revista Portuguesa de Filosofia* 58, no. 3 (2002): 581–604.

Lypp, Bernhard. "Über die Wurzeln dialektischer Begriffsbildung in Hegels Kritik an Kants Ethik." In *Dialektik in der Philosophie Hegels*, edited by Rolf-Peter Horstmann, 295–315. Frankfurt: Suhrkamp, 1989.

Makkreel, Rudolf A. "Kant's Anthropology and the Use and Misuse of the Imagination." In *Kant und die Berliner Aufklärung*, edited by Volker Gerhard, Rolf-Peter Horstmann, and Ralph Schumacher, 386–94. Berlin: Akademie, 2001.

——. "The Life of the Imagination." In *Imagination and Interpretation in Kant: The Hermeneutical Import of the Critique of Judgment*, 88–110. Chicago: University of Chicago Press, 1990.

Malabou, Catherine. *The Future of Hegel: Plasticity, Temporality and Dialectic*. London: Routledge, 2005.

Marx, Karl. *The German Ideology: Including Theses on Feuerbach and Introduction to the Critique of Political Economy*. New York: Prometheus, 1998.

——. *Das Kapital. Buch I*. Vol. 23 of *Werke*, edited by Karl Marx and Friedrich Engels. Berlin: Dietz, 1975.

McDowell, John. *Mind and World: With a New Introduction*. Cambridge: Harvard University Press, 1996.

——. "Selbstbestimmende Subjektivität und externer Zwang." In *Hegels Erbe und die theoretische Philosophie der Gegenwart*, edited by Christoph Halbig, Michael Quante, and Ludwig Siep, 184–208. Frankfurt: Suhrkamp, 2004.

Mead, George H. *Geist, Identität und Gesellschaft aus der Sicht des Sozialbehaviorismus*. Frankfurt: Suhrkamp, 1968.

Medina, José. *The Unity of Wittgenstein's Philosophy: Necessity, Intelligibility, and Normativity*. Albany: State University of New York Press, 2002.

Meinecke, Friedrich. *Aphorismen und Skizzen zur Geschichte*. Leipzig: Koehler und Amelang, 1942.

Menke, Christoph. "Autonomie und Befreiung."*Deutsche Zeitschrift für Philosophie* 58, no. 5 (2010): 675–94.

——. "Selbstgesetzgebung und Selbstbefreiung." Unpublished manuscript. Stuttgart: Hegel-Kongress, 2011.

——. *Tragödie im Sittlichen: Gerechtigkeit und Freiheit nach Hegel*. Frankfurt: Suhrkamp, 1996.

Merker, Barbara. "Jenseits des Hirns: Zur Aktualität von Hegels Philosophie des subjektiven Geistes." In *Subjektivität und Anerkennung*, edited by Barbara Merker, Georg Mohr, and Michael Quante, 157–84. Paderborn: Mentis, 2004.

Michalson, Gordon E. *Fallen Freedom: Kant on Radical Evil and Moral Regeneration*. Cambridge: Cambridge University Press, 1990.

Miller, Jacques-Alain. "L'acte entre intention et conséquence: Intervention à la dernière soirée du Séminaire Politique lacanienne première série, le 27 mai 1998." *La cause freudienne* 42 (May 1999): 7–16.

——. "A Discussion of Lacan's 'Kant avec Sade.'" In *Reading Seminars I and II: Lacan's Return to Freud*, edited by Richard Feldstein, Bruce Fink, and Maire Jaanus, 212–40. New York: State University of New York Press, 1996.

——. "A Reading of Some Details in Television in Dialogue with the Audience." *Newsletter of the Freudian Field* 4, nos. 1–2 (1990): 4–30.

——. "Suture: Éléments de la logique du signifiant." *Cahiers pour l'analyse* 1 (1966): 37–49.

Mouffe, Chantal. *The Democratic Paradox*. London: Verso, 2009.

Moughrabi, Fouad. "Battle of the Books in Palestine." *Nation*, September 13, 2001. www.thenation.com/article/battle-books-palestine/.

Moyar, Dean. *Hegel's Conscience*. Oxford: Oxford University Press, 2011.

——. "Urteil, Schluß und Handlung: Hegels logische Übergänge im Argument zur Sittlichkeit." *Hegel-Studien* 42 (2007): 51–79.

Müller-Mall, Sabine. *Performative Rechtserzeugung: Eine theoretische Annäherung*. Weilerswist-Metternich: Velbrück, 2012.

Munzel, Felicitas. *Kant's Conception of Moral Character: The "Critical" Link of Morality, Anthropology, and Reflective Judgement*. Chicago: University of Chicago Press, 1999.

Nagel, Thomas. *The View from Nowhere*. Oxford: Oxford University Press, 1989.

Neuhouser, Frederick. *Foundations of Hegel's Social Theory: Actualizing Freedom*. Cambridge: Harvard University Press, 2000.

Ng, Karen. "Hegel's Logic of Actuality." *Review of Metaphysics* 63, no. 1 (2009): 139–72.

Nicholson, Peter. "Kant on the Duty Never to Resist the Sovereign." *Ethics* 86, no. 3 (1976): 214–30.

Nussbaum, Martha. *The Fragility of Goodness: Luck and Ethics in Greek Tragedy and Philosophy*. Cambridge: Cambridge University Press, 1986.

——. "Non-Relative Virtues: An Aristotelian Approach." *Midwest Studies in Philosophy* 13 (1988): 32–53.

——. "Virtue Ethics: A Misleading Category?" *Journal of Ethics* 3 (1999): 163–201.

——. *Vom Nutzen der Moraltheorie für das Leben*. Vienna: Passagen, 1997.

Oittinen, Helsinki. "Antike Tragödie und dialektische Moderne in Hegels Ästhetik." Vol. 1 of *Hegels Ästhetik: Die Kunst der Politik, die Politik der Kunst*, edited by Andreas Arndt, Karol Bal, and Henning Ottmann, 126–35. Berlin: Akademie, 2000.

O'Neill, Onora. "Instituting Principles: Between Duty and Action." In *Kant's Metaphysics of Morals*, edited by Mark Timmons, 331–49. Oxford: Oxford University Press, 2002.

——. *Tugend und Gerechtigkeit: Eine konstruktive Darstellung des praktischen Denkens*. Berlin: Akademie, 1996.

Ottmann, Henning. *Individuum und Gemeinschaft bei Hegel: Hegel im Spiegel der Interpretationen*. Berlin: De Gruyter, 1977.

Parrish, John M. *Paradoxes of Political Ethics: From Dirty Hands to the Invisible Hand*. Cambridge: Cambridge University Press, 2007.

Peperzak, Adriaan. "Hegels Pflichten- und Tugendlehre." *Hegel-Studien* 17 (1982): 97–117.

Petry, Michael John. "Systematik und Pragmatik in Hegels Behandlung von animalischem Magnetismus und Verrücktheit." In *Psychologie und Anthropologie oder Philosophie des Geistes*, edited by Franz Hespe and Burkhard Tuschling, 250–68. Stuttgart-Bad Cannstatt: Frommann-Holzboog, 1991.

Pfaller, Robert. *On the Pleasure Principle in Culture: Illusions Without Owners*. London: Verso, 2014.

Pieper, Annemarie. "Zweites Hauptstück (57–71)." In *Immanuel Kant: Kritik der praktischen Vernunft*, edited by Otfried Höffe, 115–33. Berlin: Akademie, 2002.

Pinkard, Terry. *Hegel's Phenomenology: The Sociality of Reason*. Cambridge: Cambridge University Press, 1994.

——. "Innen, Außen und Lebensformen: Hegel und Wittgenstein." In *Hegels Erbe*, edited by Christoph Halbig, Michael Quante, and Ludwig Siep, 254–94. Frankfurt: Suhrkamp, 2004.

——. "Tugend, Moral und Sittlichkeit: Von Maximen zu Praktiken." *Deutsche Zeitschrift für Philosophie* 49, no. 1 (2001): 65–87.

——. "Virtues, Morality, and *Sittlichkeit*: From Maxims to Practices." *European Journal of Philosophy* 7, no. 2 (1999): 217–39.

Pinker, Steven. *The Better Angels of Our Nature: Why Violence Has Declined*. London: Penguin, 2011.

Pippin, Robert B. "The Conditions of Value." In *The Practice of Value (Berkeley Tanner Lectures)*, edited by Joseph Raz and R. Jay Wallace, 86–105. Oxford: Oxford University Press, 2005.

——. *Hegel's Practical Philosophy: Rational Agency as Ethical Life*. Cambridge: Cambridge University Press, 2008.

——. "Hegel's Practical Philosophy: The Actualization of Freedom." In *Cambridge Companion to German Idealism*, edited by Karl Ameriks, 180–99. Cambridge: Cambridge University Press, 2000.

——. "Hegel's Social Theory of Agency. The 'Inner-Outer' Problem." In *Hegel on Action*, edited by Arto Laitinen and Constantine Sandis, 59–78. London: Palgrave Macmillan, 2010.

——. "Recognition and Reconciliation." Vol. 2 of *Internationales Jahrbuch des Deutschen Idealismus*, 249–68. Berlin: De Gruyter, 2004.

——. "Rigorism and 'the new Kant.'" Vol. 1 of *Kant und die Berliner Aufklärung: Akten des IX. Internationalen Kant-Kongresses*, edited by Volker Gerhardt, Rolf-Peter Horstmann, and Ralph Schumacher, 313–26. Berlin: De Gruyter, 2001.

Pistorius, Hermann Andreas. "Rezension der Grundlegung zur Metaphysik der Sitten." In *Kants vergessener Rezensent: Die Kritik der theoretischen und praktischen Philosophie Kants in fünf frühen Rezensionen von Hermann Andreas Pistorius*, edited by Bernward Gesang, 26–38. Hamburg: Meiner, 2007.

Plantinga, Alvin. *Warrented Christian Belief*. Oxford: Oxford University Press, 2000.

Plessner, Helmuth. *Mit anderen Augen: Aspekte einer philosophischen Anthropologie*. Stuttgart: Reclam, 1982.

——. *Die Stufen des Organischen und der Mensch: Einleitung in die philosophische Anthropologie*. Berlin: De Gruyter, 1975.

Pluth, Ed. *Signifiers and Acts: Freedom in Lacan's Theory of the Subject*. New York: State University of New York Press, 2007.

Pöggeler, Otto. "Hegel und die griechische Tragödie." *Hegel-Studien*, supplement 1 (1964): 285–305.

——. *Schicksal und Geschichte: Antigone im Spiegel der Deutungen und Gestaltungen seit Hegel und Hölderlin*. Munich: Wilhelm Fink, 2004.

——. "Sein als Ereignis." *Zeitschrift für philosophische Forschung* 13, no. 4 (1959): 597–632.

Pollok, Konstantin. *Begründen und Rechtfertigen: Eine Untersuchung zum Verhältnis zwischen rationalen Erfordernissen und prävalenten Handlungsgründen*. Berlin: De Gruyter, 2009.

Prauss, Gerold. *Moral und Recht im Staat nach Kant und Hegel*. Freiburg: Alber, 2008.

Proust, Marcel. *In Search of Lost Time*. Vol. 1. Translated by C. K. Scott, D. J. Enright, and Terence Kilmartin. London: Vintage 1996.

Putnam, Hilary. "Antwort auf Jürgen Habermas." In *Hilary Putnam und die Tradition des Pragmatismus*, edited by Marie-Luise Raters and Marcus Willaschek, 306–21. Frankfurt: Suhrkamp, 2002.

——. "Fact and Value." In *Reason, Truth, and History*, 127–49. Cambridge: Cambridge University Press, 1981.

——. "Values and Norms." In *The Collapse of the Fact/Value Dichotomy, and Other Essays*, 111–34. Cambridge: Harvard University Press, 2002.

——. *Vernunft, Wahrheit und Geschichte*. Frankfurt: Suhrkamp, 1982.

——. "Werte und Normen." In *Die Öffentlichkeit der Vernunft und die Vernunft der Öffentlichkeit: Festschrift für Jürgen Habermas*, edited by Klaus Günther and Lutz Wingert, 280–313. Frankfurt: Suhrkamp, 2001.

Quante, Michael. *Hegels Begriff der Handlung*. Stuttgart-Bad Cannstatt: Frommann-Holzboog, 1993.

Quine, Willard V. O. "Ontological Relativity." In *Ontological Relativity*, 26–68. New York: Columbia University Press, 1969.

Rajchman, John. *Truth and Eros: Foucault, Lacan, and the Question of Ethics*. London: Routledge, 1991.

Rajiva, Suma. "Sinnstiftung durch Verlebendigung: Die Bedeutung der sichtbaren Welt in Kants moralischer Religion." In *Kants "Ethisches Gemeinwesen": Die Religionsschrift zwischen Vernunftkritik und praktischer Philosophie*, edited by Michael Städtler, 87–96. Berlin: Akademie, 2005.

Rancière, Jacques. *Das Unvernehmen: Politik und Philosophie*. Frankfurt: Suhrkamp, 2002.

Rapic, Smail. *Ethische Selbstverständigung: Kierkegaards Auseinandersetzung mit der Ethik Kants und der Rechtsphilosophie Hegels*. Berlin: De Gruyter, 2007.

Rebentisch, Juliane. *Die Kunst der Freiheit: Zur Dialektik demokratischer Existenz*. Berlin: Suhrkamp, 2012.

Reckwitz, Andreas. *Das hybride Subjekt: Eine Theorie der Subjektkulturen von der bürgerlichen Moderne zur Postmoderne*. Weilerswist-Metternich: Velbrück, 2006.

Ritter, Joachim, ed. *Immanuel Kant: Metaphysische Anfangsgründe der Rechtslehre*. Berlin: Akademie, 1999.

Rödl, Sebastian. "Darwall gegen Kant: Kant verteidigt." *Deutsche Zeitschrift für Philosophie* 57, no. 1 (2009): 163–68.

Rometsch, Jens. *Hegels Theorie des erkennenden Subjekts: Systematische Untersuchungen zur enzyklopädischen Philosophie des subjektiven Geistes*. Würzburg: Königshausen und Neumann, 2008.

Rose, Gillian. *Hegel Contra Sociology*. London: Athlone, 1981.

Rosenkranz, Karl. "Apologie Hegels gegen Dr. R. Haym." Vol. 1 of *Materialien zu Hegels Rechtsphilosophie*, edited by Manfred Riedel, 395–410. Frankfurt: Suhrkamp, 1975.

——. *Hegel als deutscher Nationalphilosoph*. Darmstadt: Wissenschaftliche Buchgesellschaft, 1965.

Rothenberg, Molly Anne. *The Excessive Subject: A New Theory of Social Change*. New York: Polity, 2010.

Roudinesco, Elisabeth. *Jaques Lacan*. New York: Columbia University Press, 1997.

——. *Jacques Lacan: Bericht über ein Leben*. Cologne: Kiepenheuer und Witsch, 1996.

Rozsa, Erzsebet. "Verhaltensweisen des Individuums." In *Hegels Phänomenologie des Geistes heute*, edited by Andreas Arndt and Ernst Müller, 121–44. Berlin: Akademie, 2004.

Ruda, Frank. *Hegel's Rabble: An Investigation Into Hegel's Philosophy of Right*. London: Bloomsbury, 2011.

Ruge, Arnold. "Die Hegelsche Rechtsphilosophie und die Politik unserer Zeit (1842)." Vol. 1 of *Materialien zu Hegels Rechtsphilosophie*, edited by Manfred Riedel, 323–49. Frankfurt: Suhrkamp, 1975.

Russell, Bertrand. *An Inquiry Into Meaning and Truth*. London: Allen and Unwin, 1956.

——. "Letter to Frege." In *From Frege to Gödel: A Source Book in Mathematical Logic, 1879–1931*, edited by Jean van Heijenoort, 124–25. Cambridge: Harvard University Press, 1967.

——. *Logic and Knowledge: Essays, 1901–1905*. Edited by Robert Charles Marsh. London: Allen and Unwin, 1956.

——. "Mathematical Logic as Based on the Theory of Types." *American Journal of Mathematics* 30, no. 3 (1908): 222–62.

——. *The Principles of Mathematics*. London: Routledge 1992.

Russell, Bertrand, and Alfred North Whitehead. *Principia Mathematica*. Cambridge: Cambridge University Press, 1962.

Sans, Georg. "Hegels Schlusslehre als Theorie des Begriffs." In *Hegel-Forschungen: Hegels Lehre vom Begriff, Urteil und Schluss*, edited by Andreas Arndt, Christian Iber, and Günter Kruck, 216–32. Berlin: Akademie, 2006.

Santner, Eric. *On the Psychotheology of Everyday Life: Reflections on Freud and Rosenzweig*. Chicago: University of Chicago Press, 2001.

Schmidt, Josef. *"Geist," "Religion" und "absolutes Wissen": Ein Kommentar zu den drei gleichnamigen Kapiteln aus Hegels "Phänomenologie des Geistes."* Stuttgart: Kohlhammer, 1997.

Schmidt, Thomas M. *Anerkennung und absolute Religion: Formierung der Gesellschaftstheorie und Genese der spekulativen Religionsphilosophie in Hegels Frühschriften*. Stuttgart-Bad Cannstatt: Frommann-Holzboog, 1997.

Schnädelbach, Herbert. *Hegels praktische Philosophie*. Frankfurt: Suhrkamp, 2000.

Schneewind, Jerome B. *The Invention of Autonomy: A History of Modern Moral Philosophy*. Cambridge: Cambridge University Press, 1998.

Schneider, Manfred. *Das Attentat: Kritik der paranoischen Vernunft*. Berlin: Matthes und Seitz, 2010.

Scholem, Gershom, ed. *Walter Benjamin—Gershom Scholem. Briefwechsel, 1933–1940*. Frankfurt: Suhrkamp, 1985.

Schroeder, Jeanne L. *The Four Lacanian Discourses*. London: Routledge, 2008.

Schulte, Christian. *Radikal böse: Die Karriere des Bösen von Kant bis Nietzsche*. Munich: Wilhelm Fink, 1988.

Schulte, Joachim. "Philosophy of Psychology: A Criticism of a Young Science?" In *Wittgenstein: Zu Philosophie und Wissenschaft*, edited by Pirmin Stekeler-Weithofer, 224–35. Hamburg: Meiner, 2012.

Schulte, Martin. *Das Gesetz des Unbewussten im Rechtsdiskurs: Grundlinien einer psychoanalytischen Rechtstheorie nach Freud und Lacan*. Berlin: Duncker und Humblot, 2009.

Schulte, Michael. *Die "Tragödie im Sittlichen": Zur Dramentheorie Hegels*. Munich: Wilhelm Fink, 1992.

Schwemmer, Otto. "Die praktische Ohnmacht der reinen Vernunft." *Neue Hefte für Philosophie* 22 (1983): 1–24.

Searle, John. *The Rediscovery of the Mind*. Cambridge: MIT Press, 1992.

Seel, Martin. *Paradoxien der Erfüllung: Philosophische Essays*. Frankfurt: Suhrkamp, 2006.

Setton, Dirk. "Das 'Medea-Prinzip': Vom Problem der Akrasia zu einer Theorie des Unvermögens." *Deutsche Zeitschrift für Philosophie* 57, no. 1 (2009): 97–117.

Sherman, Nancy. *Making a Necessity of Virtue: Aristotle and Kant on Virtue*. Cambridge: Cambridge University Press, 1997.

Siep, Ludwig. *Hegel's Phenomenology of Spirit*. Translated by Daniel Smyth. Cambridge: Cambridge University Press, 2000.

——. "Hegel über Moralität und Wirklichkeit: Prolegomena zu einer Auseinandersetzung zwischen Hegel und der Realismusdebatte in der modernen Metaethik." *Hegel-Studien* 42 (2007): 11–30.

——. "Kehraus mit Hegel? Zu Ernst Tugendhats Hegelkritik." *Zeitschrift für philosophische Forschung* 34, nos. 3–4 (1981): 518–31.

Simmel, Georg. "The Value of Money as a Substance." In *The Philosophy of Money*, translated by Tom Bottomore and David Frisby, 139–218. London: Routledge, 2011.

Singer, Peter. *Animal Liberation: The Definitive Classic of the Animal Movement*. New York: Harper, 2009.

Sloterdijk, Peter. *Critique of Cynical Reason*. Translated by Michael Eldred. Minneapolis: University of Minnesota Press, 1987.

Snelling, David. *Philosophy, Psychoanalysis and the Origins of Meaning: Pre-Reflective Intentionality in the Psychoanalytic View of the Mind*. Burlington, VT: Ashgate, 2001.

Sommerfeld-Lethen, Caroline. "Motiva auxiliaria: Kants Motivationstheorie zwischen Aristoteles und der Moralistik." In *Was ist und was sein soll: Natur und Freiheit bei Immanuel Kant*, edited by Udo Kern, 287–300. Berlin: De Gruyter, 2007.

——. *Wie moralisch werden? Kants moralische Ethik*. Freiburg: Karl Alber, 2005.

Sophokles. *Antigone*. Translated by Friedrich Hölderlin. In *Tragödien*, 53–100. Weimar: Volksverlag, 1959.

Soppa, Sebastian. *Scheiternde Subjektivität: Das unglückliche Bewusstsein bei Hegel und Kierkegaard*. Berlin: Logos, 2010.

Spaemann, Robert. "Kants Kritik des Widerstandsrechts." In *Materialien zu Kants Rechtsphilosophie*, edited by Zwi Batscha, 347–58. Frankfurt: Suhrkamp, 1976.

Speight, Allen. *Hegel, Literature, and the Problem of Agency*. Cambridge: Cambridge University Press, 2001.

Städtler, Michael. *Kant und die Aporetik moderner Subjektivität: Zur Verschränkung historischer und systematischer Momente im Begriff der Selbstbestimmung*. Berlin: Akademie, 2011.

Stavrakakis, Yannis. *Lacan and the Political*. London: Routledge, 1999.

——. *The Lacanian Left: Psychoanalysis, Theory, Politics*. New York: State University of New York Press, 2007.

Stenger, Georg. *Philosophie der Interkulturalität*. Freiburg: Alber, 2006.

Stout, Jeffrey. *Democracy and Tradition*. Princeton: Princeton University Press, 2004.

Sturma, Dieter. "Hegels Theorie des Unbewussten. Zum Zusammenhang von Naturphilosophie und philosophischer Psychologie." In *Hegel-Jahrbuch 1990*, edited by Heinz Kimmerle and Wolfgang Levèvre, 193–201. Bochum: Germinal, 1990.

——. "Philosophie der Psychologie." *Journal für Psychologie* 10, no. 1 (2002): 18–39.

Taylor, Charles. *Hegel*. Cambridge: Cambridge University Press, 1975.

Theunissen, Michael. "Die verdrängte Intersubjektivität in Hegels Philosophie des Rechts." In *Hegels Philosophie des Rechts: Die Theorie der Rechtsformen und ihre Logik*, edited by Dieter Henrich and Rolf-Peter Horstmann, 317–81. Stuttgart: Klett-Cotta, 1982.

Thurnherr, Urs. *Die Ästhetik der Existenz: Über den Begriff der Maxime und die Bildung von Maximen bei Kant*. Tübingen: Francke, 1994.

Tugendhat, Ernst. *Selbstbewusstsein und Selbstbestimmung*. Frankfurt: Suhrkamp, 1979.

——. *Vorlesungen über Ethik*. Frankfurt: Suhrkamp, 1993.

Utz, Konrad. *Die Notwendigkeit des Zufalls: Hegels spekulative Dialektik in der Wissenschaft der Logik: Ein Entwurf*. Munich: Schöningh, 2001.

Varnhagen von Ense, Karl August. *Denkwürdigkeiten des Philosophen und Arztes Johann Benjamin Erhard*. Stuttgart: Klett-Cotta, 1830.

Verene, Donald. *Hegel's Absolute: An Introduction to Reading the Phenomenology of Spirit*. Albany: State University of New York Press, 2007.

Vogl, Joseph. *The Specter of Capital*. Translated by Joachim Redner and Robert Savage. Stanford: Stanford University Press, 2014.

Vollrath, Ernst. *Die Rekonstruktion der politischen Urteilskraft*. Stuttgart: Ernst Klett, 1977.

Vossenkuhl, Wilhelm. "Spontaneität." *Zeitschrift für Philosophische Forschung* 48, no. 3 (1994): 329–49.

Walsh, Sean D. "Kant's Theory of Right as Aristotelian Phronesis." *International Philosophical Quarterly* 52, no. 2 (2012): 227–46.

Wang, Yong. "Agency: The Internal Split of Structure." *Sociological Forum* 23, no. 3 (2008): 481–502.

Wang, Zhi-Hue. *Freiheit und Sittlichkeit*. Würzburg: Königshausen und Neumann, 2003.

Welsen, Peter. "Die Ethik des rechten Sprechens. Zur Frage der Verantwortung bei Jacques Lacan." *Zeitschrift für philosophische Forschung* 42, no. 4 (1988): 682–93.

Wesche, Tilo. "Hegel und die Wahrheitstheorien der Gegenwart: Ein Streit unter Nachbarn." *Deutsche Zeitschrift für Philosophie* 57, no. 3 (2009): 355–75.

——. "Wissen und Wahrheit im Widerstreit: Zu Hegels Theorie der Tragödie." In *Die Philosophie des Tragischen: Schopenhauer, Schelling, Nietzsche*, edited by Lore Hühn and Philipp Schwab, 297–318. Berlin: De Gruyter, 2011.

Westphal, Kenneth. "Kant on the State, Law, and Obedience to Authority in the Alleged Anti-revolutionary Writings." *Journal of Philosophical Research* 17 (1992): 383–425.

——. "Kant's Qualified Principle of Obedience to Authority in the *Metaphysical Elements of Justice*." In *Akten des VII. internationalen Kant-Kongresses*, edited by Gerhard Funke, 353–66. Bonn: Bouvier, 1991.

White, Stephen K. *Political Theory and Postmodernism*. Cambridge: Cambridge University Press, 1991.

Wildenauer, Miriam. *Epistemologie freien Denkens: Die logische Idee in Hegels Philosophie des endlichen Geistes*. Hamburg: Meiner, 2004.

Willaschek, Marcus. *Praktische Vernunft: Handlungstheorie und Moralbegründung*. Stuttgart: Metzler, 1992.

——. "'Die Spontaneität des Erkenntnisses': Über die Abhängigkeit der 'Transzendentalen Analytik' von der Auflösung der Dritten Antinomie." In *Metaphysik und Kritik: Interpretationen zur "Transzendentalen Dialektik" der "Kritik der reinen Vernunft"* edited by Jiri Chotas, Jürgen Stolzenberg, and Jindrich Karasek, 165–84. Würzburg: Königshausen und Neumann, 2010.

——. "Why the *Doctrine of Right* Does Not Belong in the *Metaphysics of Morals*: On Some Basic Distinctions in Kant's Moral Philosophy." *Jahrbuch für Recht und Ethik* 5 (1997): 205–27.

Williams, Bernard. "Ethical Consistency." In *Problems of the Self*, 166–86. Cambridge: Cambridge University Press, 1976.

——. *Ethics and the Limits of Philosophy*. Cambridge: Harvard University Press, 1985.

——. *Moral Luck*. Cambridge: Cambridge University Press, 1981.

——. "Persons, Character, and Morality." In *Moral Luck*, 1–19.

——. "Präsuppositionen der Moralität." In *Bedingungen der Möglichkeit: "Transcendental Arguments" und transzendentales Denken*, edited by Eva Schaper and Wilhelm Vossenkuhl, 251–60. Stuttgart: Klett-Cotta, 1984.

Wilmer, Stephen E., and Audrone Zukauskaite, eds. *Interrogating Antigone in Postmodern Philosophy and Criticism*. Oxford: Oxford University Press, 2010.

Wimmer, Reiner. "Die Doppelfunktion des kategorischen Imperativs in Kants Ethik." *Kant-Studien* 73, nos. 1–4 (1982): 291–320.

Wittgenstein, Ludwig. *The Blue Book*. In *The Blue and Brown Books*. Malden, MA: Blackwell, 1969.

——. *On Certainty*. Edited by G. E. M. Anscombe and G. H. von Wright. Translated by Denis Paul and G. E. M. Anscombe. Oxford: Basil Blackwell, 1969.

——. *Philosophical Grammar*. Edited by Rush Rhees. Translated by Anthony Kenney. Oxford: Blackwell, 1980.

——. *Philosophical Investigations*. Revised edition by P.M. S. Hacker and Joachim Schulte. Translated by G. E. M. Anscombe, P. M. S. Hacker, and Joachim Schulte. Malden, MA: Wiley Blackwell, 2009.

——. *Remarks on the Foundations of Mathematics*. Edited by G. H. von Wright, R. Rhees, and G. E. M. Anscombe. Translated by G. E. M. Anscombe. Cambridge: MIT Press, 1989.

——. *Tractatus Logico-Philosophicus*. Translation by D. F. Pears and B. F. McGuiness. London: Routledge, 1974.

——. *Zettel*. Edited by G. E. M. Anscombe and G. H. von Wright. Translated by G. E. M. Ancombe. Berkeley: University of California Press, 1970.

Wolf, Susan. "The Failure of Autonomy." PhD diss., Princeton University, 1978.

Wood, Allen. *Hegel's Ethical Thought*. Cambridge: Cambridge University Press, 1991.

——. *Kant's Ethical Thought*. Cambridge: Cambridge University Press, 1999.

——. *Kantian Ethics*. Cambridge: Cambridge University Press, 2008.

——. *Kant's Moral Religion*. Ithaca: Cornell University Press, 1970.

Zimmermann, Stephan. *Kants "Kategorien der Freiheit."* Berlin: De Gruyter, 2011.

Žižek, Slavoj. *Did Somebody Say Totalitarianism? Five Interventions in the (Mis)Use of a Notion*. London: Verso, 2001.

——. *Enjoy Your Symptom! Jacques Lacan in Hollywood and Out*. London: Routledge, 2008.

——. "The 'Fake' Mandela Memorial Interpreter Said It All." *Guardian*, December 16, 2013.

——. *For They Know Not What They Do: Enjoyment as a Political Factor*. London: Verso, 2002.

——. "Four Discourses, Four Subjects." In *Cogito and the Unconscious (Sic 2)*, edited by Slavoj Žižek, 74–113. Durham: Duke University Press, 1998.

——. *Interrogating the Real*. Edited by Rex Butler and Scott Stephens. New York: Continuum, 2005.

——. *Less Than Nothing: Hegel and the Shadow of Dialectical Materialism*. London: Verso, 2012.

——. *Metastases of Enjoyment: On Women and Causality*. London: Verso, 1994.

——. *The Most Sublime Hysteric: Hegel with Lacan*. Cambridge: Polity, 2014.

——. *Die Nacht der Welt: Psychoanalyse und deutscher Idealismus*. Frankfurt: Fischer, 1998.

——. *The Sublime Object of Ideology*. London: Verso, 1989.

——. *Tarrying with the Negative: Kant, Hegel, and the Critique of Ideology*. Durham: Duke University Press, 1993.

——. *The Ticklish Subject: The Absent Centre of Political Ontology*. London: Verso, 2000.

——. "Why Is Every Act a Repetition?" In *Enjoy Your Symptom: Jacques Lacan in Hollywood and Out*, 69–112. London: Routledge, 1992.

Žižek, Slavoj, and Glyn Daly. *Conversations with Žižek*. Cambridge: Polity, 2003.

Zupančič, Alenka. *Ethics of the Real: Kant and Lacan*. London: Verso, 2000.

INDEX

After the Death of God, John D. Caputo and Gianni Vattimo, edited by Jeffrey W. Robbins

The Politics of Postsecular Religion: Mourning Secular Futures, Ananda Abeysekara

Nietzsche and Levinas: "After the Death of a Certain God," edited by Jill Stauffer and Bettina Bergo

Strange Wonder: The Closure of Metaphysics and the Opening of Awe, Mary-Jane Rubenstein

Religion and the Specter of the West: Sikhism, India, Postcoloniality, and the Politics of Translation, Arvind Mandair

Plasticity at the Dusk of Writing: Dialectic, Destruction, Deconstruction, Catherine Malabou

Anatheism: Returning to God After God, Richard Kearney

Rage and Time: A Psychopolitical Investigation, Peter Sloterdijk

Radical Political Theology: Religion and Politics After Liberalism, Clayton Crockett

Radical Democracy and Political Theology, Jeffrey W. Robbins

Hegel and the Infinite: Religion, Politics, and Dialectic, edited by Slavoj Žižek, Clayton Crockett, and Creston Davis

What Does a Jew Want? On Binationalism and Other Specters, Udi Aloni

A Radical Philosophy of Saint Paul, Stanislas Breton, edited by Ward Blanton, translated by Joseph N. Ballan

Hermeneutic Communism: From Heidegger to Marx, Gianni Vattimo and Santiago Zabala

Deleuze Beyond Badiou: Ontology, Multiplicity, and Event, Clayton Crockett

Self and Emotional Life: Philosophy, Psychoanalysis, and Neuroscience, Adrian Johnston and Catherine Malabou

The Incident at Antioch: A Tragedy in Three Acts / L'Incident d'Antioche: Tragédie en trois actes, Alain Badiou, translated by Susan Spitzer

Philosophical Temperaments: From Plato to Foucault, Peter Sloterdijk

To Carl Schmitt: Letters and Reflections, Jacob Taubes, translated by Keith Tribe

Encountering Religion: Responsibility and Criticism After Secularism, Tyler Roberts

Spinoza for Our Time: Politics and Postmodernity, Antonio Negri, translated by William McCuaig

Force of God: Political Theology and the Crisis of Liberal Democracy, Carl A. Raschke

Factory of Strategy: Thirty-Three Lessons on Lenin, Antonio Negri, translated by Arianna Bove

Cut of the Real: Subjectivity in Poststructuralism Philosophy, Katerina Kolozova

A Materialism for the Masses: Saint Paul and the Philosophy of Undying Life, Ward Blanton

Our Broad Present: Time and Contemporary Culture, Hans Ulrich Gumbrecht

Wrestling with the Angel: Experiments in Symbolic Life, Tracy McNulty

Cloud of the Impossible: Negative Theology and Planetary Entanglements, Catherine Keller

What Does Europe Want? The Union and Its Discontents, Slavoj Žižek and Srećko Horvat

Harmattan: A Philosophical Fiction, Michael Jackson

Nietzsche Versus Paul, Abed Azzam

Christo-Fiction: The Ruins of Athens and Jerusalem, François Laruelle

Paul's Summons to Messianic Life: Political Theology and the Coming Awakening, L. L. Welborn

Reimagining the Sacred: Richard Kearney Debates God with James Wood, Catherine Keller, Charles Taylor, Julia Kristeva, Gianni Vattimo, Simon Critchley, Jean-Luc Marion, John Caputo, David Tracy, Jens Zimmermann, and Merold Westphal, edited by Richard Kearney and Jens Zimmermann

A Hedonist Manifesto: The Power to Exist, Michel Onfray

An Insurrectionist Manifesto: Four New Gospels for a Radical Politics, Ward Blanton, Clayton Crockett, Jeffrey W. Robbins, and Noëlle Vahanian

The Intimate Universal: The Hidden Porosity Among Religion, Art, Philosophy, and Politics, William Desmond

Heidegger: His Life and His Philosophy, Alain Badiou and Barbara Cassin, translated by Susan Spitzer

The Work of Art: Rethinking the Elementary Forms of Religious Life, Michael Jackson

Sociophobia: Political Change in the Digital Utopia, César Rendueles, translated by Heather Cleary

There's No Such Thing as a Sexual Relationship: Two Lessons on Lacan, Alain Badiou and Barbara Cassin, translated by Susan Spitzer and Kenneth Reinhard